Red Man's America

Red Man's America

A History
of Indians in the United States

Revised Edition

Ruth Murray Underhill

Illustrations by Marianne Stoller

THE UNIVERSITY OF CHICAGO PRESS

CHICAGO AND LONDON

THE UNIVERSITY OF CHICAGO PRESS, CHICAGO 60637
The University of Chicago Press, Ltd., London

© 1953, 1971 by The University of Chicago. All rights reserved
Published 1953. Revised Edition 1971
Printed in the United States of America

ISBN: 0–226–84164–2 (clothbound); 0–226–84165–0 (paperbound)
Library of Congress Catalog Card Number: 79–171345

86 85   8 7 6

Foreword

A HISTORY of Indians in the United States seems a project so vast as to be almost comic. It is true that for every tribe there should be a volume describing its prehistory as far as that can be deduced, its material resources and the use made of them, and its social customs, religion, and mythology, with the changes these underwent under stimulation from other Indians and finally from whites. Some such volumes have been written, and others appear as our store of facts grows larger. However, they cannot often show the movement of peoples and ideas over the whole country or the relations of one area to another. Nor does the nonspecialist often read them.

It is time, however, that the average citizen should have some picture of the red man, not as a figure of myth or children's games, but as a fellow-citizen, with problems important to us all. The following pages have space only for the highlights of Indian history, but they can, at least, arrange these in a connected pattern. They can make plain the Indian's varied origins, backgrounds, and customs and point out reasons why one group may have failed, so far, in adjustment to new ways while another has succeeded. Moreover, they can turn the familiar facts of American history so that they are seen from the Indian's point of view rather than that of the white.

Apology is made, with all humility, to those specialists who may be offended by the omission of details and of subdivisions which bulk large in their fields. Important lapses have doubtless occurred, in spite of careful combing and expert criticism, and publications issued after September, 1951, were not included. We can but explain that to survey such a field in one volume entails an almost lethal cutting. At least this sketch of the Indian's past may break a trail for more complete volumes to come.

Most cordial thanks are due to W. W. Beatty, Education Branch, United States Indian Service, for advice and opportunities for investigation; to F. H. Douglas and Willena D. Cartwright, Denver Art Museum, for the use of books and illustrative material; to the University of Denver for a grant which allowed some time for writing; and to H. M. Wormington, Denver Museum of Natural History, and

J. Nixon Hadley, United States Indian Service, for information and documents.

The following specialists gave most generously of their time in reading and criticizing chapters on particular areas: John Cotter, National Park Service, Tupelo, Mississippi; Herbert Dick, The Museum, University of Colorado; E. B. Danson, University of Arizona; James B. Griffin, University Museum, Ann Arbor; Wesley Hurt, Museum of Anthropology, University of Michigan; Frederick Johnson, R. S. Peabody Foundation, Andover; Alex D. Krieger, Department of Anthropology, University of Texas; Paul S. Martin, George I. Quimby, and Alexander Spoehr, Chicago Natural History Museum; Erik Reed, National Park Service, Santa Fe; John H. Rowe, Peabody Museum, Harvard University, Cambridge; and Professor Arnold M. Withers, Department of Anthropology, University of Denver.

Thanks are also due to Dorothy Field for her help in preparing the material culture lists and the tables, in doing many of the footnotes and descriptions of the various plates, and in checking copy and making the Index; to Marcy Murphy for assistance in many ways; to Malcolm Russell for help with drawings; to Arminta Neal for maps; to Marianne Stoller for the illustrations and for help on the footnotes, plate descriptions, and maps; to Jean Owens and Frank Ellis for typing; and to Dorothy N. Ellis for typing and reading proof.

Ruth Murray Underhill

FOREWORD 1971

Since this book was first published in 1953, many dates in pre-Columbian history have been radically changed, known facts have been reinterpreted, and new facts have appeared. It has not been possible to bring the book up to date at every point, but it is hoped that its major errors have been corrected. For help in this work the author is grateful to Lee Earley of Arapahoe Junior College and Mary Coen of Denver. Mr. Honda of the Department of Health, Education, and Welfare and Mr. Nelson of Housing and Urban Development have given information on modern conditions; and Dr. Omer Stewart, University of Colorado, on the Court of Claims.

R. M. U.

Table of Contents

List of Illustrations

PLATES

MAPS

CHAPTER I

The Red Man Discovers America

Aᴍᴇʀɪᴄᴀ has been "discovered" at least three times. The last and most publicized arrival was that of Columbus, less than five hundred years ago. Before that, about A.D. 1004, Leif Erikson, the Icelander, had landèd on the Canadian coast. He reported a land with good pasturage and mild climate, where grapes and grain grew wild. He called it Vinland, or Vine Land.

Climate in the North Atlantic was warmer in those days than it is now. Refugees from Iceland had been able to found a colony in Greenland, across Davis Strait from Canada. Their two settlements, with stone houses, churches, and pastureland, survived in the increasing cold until the fourteen hundreds. Old sagas indicate that during those four hundred years the colonists explored the American coast from Baffinland to Nova Scotia and further south.

These ancient poems, so often changed and rewritten, can hardly be taken as coherent history; yet their details have a ring of truth. They tell of several camps made along the newly discovered coast, which they divided from north to south into Barren Land, Forest Land, and Vine Land. One expedition must have come to stay, for it brought 160 men, in two ships, with their cattle and some womenfolk. During its second winter, this party was driven away by "Skraelings," or natives, who came to trade and ended by fighting.[1]

The scene was probably Newfoundland, where archaeologists have found signs of a Norse camp dated by the radio carbon method as between A.D. 900 and 1,000. The Skraelings, with their arrows, canoes, and dried meat, may have been Beothuk Indians, the original inhabitants of that area. After this misadventure, there are no further accounts of settlement in the New World. Within the next few hundred years, the Greenland colony dwindled and disappeared, leaving the American continent to the Indians.

"Indians" they will be called in this narrative and even "red men," though both terms are misnomers. The people of India rightfully wonder why our first Americans must hold to the mistaken name given them by Columbus, instead of having one of their own. As for the idea of red skin, we now know that Indian complexions vary from dark brown to yellow and even white. An explorer over the two Americas would meet Indians who were tall and rangy or short and plump, with all varieties between. Their hair might be brown or black, straight or wavy, and their noses anywhere from the Roman type, seen on the Indian penny, to a small snub nose or even a flat one. To communicate with them, he would need more languages than are spoken on the continent of Europe. Indians are, in fact, a mixed race, as are white Americans.

The "Indian" (quotes after this are to be understood) has usually received small place in American history. Most often he appears like a scene-shifter just before the curtain goes up and departs before the real drama begins. Actually, he should be the star of the performance. It was he who first discovered and populated the two continents. He made the trails which are now our highways. He found the useful plants, trees, and animals. His ways of hunting, cooking, and housebuilding were taught to the first white men and often saved their lives.

Yet our historic acquaintance with Indians covers only a few centuries. Before Columbus and even before Leif Erikson, there were thousands of years when Indians moved about the two continents, traveling, mixing, learning, inventing. That period in Indian history is like the submerged seven-eighths of an iceberg, the part which supports the one-eighth above water but which can be known and measured only by scientific calculation. Such calculations can be made, however, with reasonably accurate results.

Now something similar is being done for Indian history with a whole team of scientists engaged. Archaeologists are excavating in most major areas of North and South America, looking for a bone, a stone tool, even a bit of charcoal which might evidence the presence of man. Paleontologists have provided the data on extinct animals which man hunted. Geologists have calculated dates—within a few hundred years or so—by the evidences of climate and glacial movements, even by the layers of silt at the bottom of extinct lakes. Palynologists have identified the pollen of long-dead plants and compared living species by counting their chromosomes. Dendrochronologists have counted the rings of annual growth in ancient logs. Chemists, metallurgists, and mineralogists have studied the sand and clay in

Indian pots and have worked out the derivation of ancient metals.

Recently, physicists and chemists have entered the arena with an apparatus which gets closer to actual dates. The radio-carbon method is built on the fact that every living thing absorbs from the atmosphere a percentage of the isotope carbon 14. When the organism dies, this isotope begins to disintegrate at a known rate. Therefore, to arrive at the age of such materials as bone, shell, wood, cloth, or charcoal, the researcher must ascertain the amount of carbon 14 remaining to it. The amount gone will tell the number of years since the organism died.

Even though a date may sometimes have to be reported as plus or minus some hundreds of years, this is a light in obscurity for the archaeologists. They now look eagerly for the patch of black which may mean the charcoal of an old campfire. Even if no bones or pots are found, this charcoal may indicate the presence of man. The margin of error is being greatly reduced as samples are more carefully chosen and treated. For best results, several technicians work on the same problem and compare findings. Then the results are correlated with the facts from geologic and stratigraphic dating and with comparative materials. By this method an atlas of dates for the prehistory of man is being achieved.

Radio-carbon dates cover, at the most, some seventy thousand years. For earlier dates, scientists depend on the slow change of potassium into argon. This can date rocks existing at the time of the earliest men and even before. Finds new and old are being dated by these methods so that the drama of Indian history is moving from myth into daylight.

The first act, archaeologists are agreed, did not take place in the New World. In the two Americas, there are no signs of man's long development from primitive ape-like forms through the "half men" with projecting jaws, huge brow ridges, and small brain cases. There are no signs, either, of the great apes, man's relatives in the primate stock, who branched off with him from some monkey-like form over twelve million years ago. Yet such signs of the human past are being found increasingly in Africa, Asia, and Europe. Man's infancy and first learning period has left traces in the Old World, where he slowly taught himself to make fire and to shape some stone tools. He arrived in the New World developed and equipped for settling a new continent.

How did he come and when? The answer to the second question must come first, since the time when man came has a great deal to do with the route he followed and the country he left. The time, geologists say, was the Pleistocene, the geologic period which preceded our present. That period, of a million years duration, covers one of the ice ages of which the earth has had several. All occurred before there were men on earth except this latest, whose name Pleistocene is Greek for the Full Dawn, which was the Age of Man. Four times during the Pleistocene, ice welled out from northern centers and covered the northern thirds of Europe and America with long, irregular streamers, different for each advance. The ice began to retreat for the last time about ten to twelve thousand years ago.[2] Rather, we hope it was the last time. The period which has elapsed since then is far shorter than some other intervals. We have no proof that the whole drama of movement and change will not be performed again, making what we call "world history" merely an episode in an interim.

The infinitely slow grind of the spreading ice meant death or change for all life that came in its way. Forests were crushed; lake basins were dug out; rivers were deflected. At the edge of the ice, where once there had been lush vegetation, there were bogs and tundra, then tall dank forest. Beyond the freezing area the moisture turned to rain, so that more southern countries had periods called Pluvial or Rainy. This was a time of drastic change, when whole races of animals died out and others moved. As for man, that slowly developing animal without claws or fur, he came into his own during the fourth advance, known as the Würm in Europe, the Wisconsin in America. For some two million years he had been limping along, his brain case growing larger, his stance more upright, his hands more able. Then, some thirty-five thousand years ago, in mid-Pleistocene, he stands out clearly as Homo sapiens, thinking or modern man.

Archaeologists have dated his arrival in America during the latter part of the Pleistocene glaciations, perhaps some ten to fifteen thousand years ago.[3] By that time the human race had been plodding along its upward path for several hundred thousand years, yet it still was not raising crops, taming animals, or even using such a complicated tool as the bow and arrow. Certainly there were no boats fit to cross hundreds of miles of ocean. How, then, could primitive people, traveling on foot, have come from the Old World to the New, as their relics indicate they did? The only possible place is where Siberia and Alaska stretch out toward each other as though straining to make contact. Bering Strait, which separates the two, is only fifty-six miles wide, with two islands to break the water trip. The widest expanse of unbroken sea is twenty-five miles, with land in sight on clear days.

Siberia and Alaska actually have been connected at different times in the remote past. The strait is so shallow that, if even 120 feet of its water were drawn off, some of this ancient land bridge would reappear and perhaps all of it. In the glacial age more than 600 feet of water was drawn from the sea[4] to fall on the land as snow and to remain there, without melting. At the height of the Wisconsin glaciation, between 35,000 and 11,000 years ago, Siberia and Alaska were connected by a stretch of tundra almost a thousand miles long. If early travelers passed and camped here, their traces must now be under water. No bones of these earliest men have been found. Perhaps, like some later groups of foodgatherers, they feared the dead and buried them separately far from camp. Nevertheless, all across the country, quantities of stone tools have been found and dated, by the methods mentioned, around 12,000 to 15,000 years ago. This would fit well with crossings toward the end of the ice age. But did none come earlier? Now and then a find turns up indicating an earlier date, but further research generally proves it wrong.

What about the Lost Atlantis? Or the wonderful island of Mu? Geographers and oceanographers say they never existed. It is true that continents have moved and split, that islands have risen and fallen, but that was long before man came on earth. If anyone reached America from some now-vanished land, it was a dinosaur.

Let us return to the possibilities. Twenty thousand years ago or even fifteen thousand, there was no civilized country in the Old World which could send a colony to America. Men of the Old World were still living as hunters or seed-gatherers, scattered in little groups throughout Europe to Asia and Africa where the Sahara of the Pluvial was a green expanse. We know little about Siberia, whence our first immigrants would have had to come, but some geologists think there may have been ice-free valleys there; and, if so, there were probably men moving about in search of the best hunting.

Who were they? Since none of their bones has been found, we cannot tell to what "race" they belonged. The fact that they were in Asia does not mean that they resembled today's Chinese or Koreans, for those specialized groups had not yet developed. Perhaps they were ancestors of today's yellow people or even of some blacks and whites. There has been a great deal of mixing since man was first on earth, and a pure race, as the scientists long ago admitted, is a figment of the imagination.

Some day the bones of these particular wanderers may be discovered.

So far, even their tools are a matter of question, Siberia having been occupied with projects other than archaeology. Yet there are facts we can use in imagining what may have happened. In scattered valleys, amid the mountain glaciers, the prey of hunters would have been the mastodon and mammoth, that woolly elephant which once spread over northern countries all around the world. The mammoth was an Old World animal, but it had migrated to America at some time when there really was a land bridge and vegetation for it to eat. The herds of mammoth must have been roving, as such animals do, followed by human hunters. Perhaps it was they who led the huntsmen along well-worn trails, from valley to valley, until a new land was in sight.

Here there must be a hiatus, since we cannot tell when or how the fifty-six-mile crossing was made. We know that the interior of Alaska, a green bowl protected by mountain walls, was not glaciated during the last phase of the Pleistocene, nor was the northern low-level coast line of Alaska to the Mackenzie River and down that valley. It even had a more temperate climate than at present, for large trees associated with mammoth bones have been found in the "bowl" where now there is only barren tundra. This ice-free country became a haven of refuge for birds and animals driven from other areas by lack of food. Many of them had come from Asia. This includes not only the mammoth but several other forms of elephant, the musk ox, moose, caribou, mountain sheep, and a huge ancient form of bison.

This was big game on a kingly scale. If men made their way over from Asia, in the wake of this flood of wildlife, they would be gloriously wealthy in the primitive sense—which means plenty to eat. We can picture them slaughtering the mammoth they found trapped in bogs or by that most simple of methods, stampeding them over a cliff. Cape Prince of Wales, in Alaska, which now rises almost from the sea, was once an inland cliff. At its base is such a quantity of mammoth bones that the Eskimo for years have made a living by carving the ivory tusks. Quite possibly this was an ancient hunting ground. There are, in fact, some chipped-stone points scattered throughout Alaska which may well have come from ancient spears.

In the same way, points have been found along a trail leading south. We can imagine that, if the gorgeous hunting country of Alaska became crowded, little groups might have ventured in this direction.[5] They would have found the Rockies at their right still topped with glaciers and a hard country for travel. To the east, the Keewatin Ice Sheet covered the land from Hudson Bay and the Great Lakes to the Atlantic Coast. Ice-free country, some think, was in what we now call the Great Plains, that stretch of grassland between the Mississippi and the Rockies. That is, it is grassland at present. If man came during these glaciated times, it may have been tundra and forest. There are scattered points here, too, coming from sites that have been dated at an early age, one about nine thousand years ago.[6] However, the best known and most studied finds come from the Southwest.

That country today contains some of the driest sections in the United States, and only a half-century ago it appeared on maps as the Great American Desert. Its gaunt red and gray rocks, rising from sagebrush plains and sandy gullies, are weirdly picturesque. The green patches where Indians today can raise corn are few and far between. The wild game now is mostly rabbits and, in the wastes of southern Utah, even lizards, although deer and antelope were not uncommon long ago.

Far different was its appearance during the last glaciation. The cool temperatures of the north had here relaxed so that moisture fell not in the form of snow but of rain. The higher mountaintops might be iced, but the lower slopes were clothed with trees. On the flat land there was lush tall grass, threaded with streams and dotted with lakes, where herds of animals came to drink. This was big-game country scarcely equaled by Africa today. The mammals of the Pleistocene had reached their peak in size and soon would be giving way to smaller modern forms. However, there were still several kinds of elephant (the Columbian mammoth and perhaps the northern mammoth and mastodon) trumpeting on the plains. The ground sloth, a large, hairy, awkward creature, ambled through the forest, knocking down saplings in order to eat their leaves. It had arrived from South America as soon as the connecting isthmus rose from the water. The bison had arrived from Asia. There were also herds of smaller, swifter animals which were native to America—the horse and camel.

It is true that, when Columbus came, there were no horses in America and that camels were reduced to their small varieties, the llama and alpaca, of South America. Still, many paleontologists believe that both the horse and the camel originated in the New World. Evolving from a little five-toed animal, no bigger than a dog, the horse had, by the end of the Pleistocene, developed ten varieties, one as large as a cart horse. Already it had spread to Eurasia, where it grew and multiplied. We now speak of the Mongolian or Arabian horse, just as we do of the "Irish" potato or the "Spanish" pepper, without realizing that all these are American products.

Why did the horse disappear at the end of the Ice Age, while the bison, another grass-eater, was able to survive and spread? One guess is an epidemic. Or a pest. There are rocks of Miocene date showing the tsetse fly, the same that today kills off the cattle in Africa.[7] Did this scourge exist among the big game of New Mexico? Was it the reason why our later Indians were deprived of horses and therefore of one means to more advanced civilization? A more likely theory is concerned with climatic changes, for with the retreat of the glaciers the climate became much warmer and dryer. This postglacial climatic optimum reached its height about six thousand years ago when arid conditions prevailed in the Plains and the Southwest.

America's first immigrants probably were in New Mexico before the Pleistocene had ended. Deep under the floor of a cave in the Sandia ("watermelon") Mountains lie nineteen stone points and a few other tools which one geologist has been willing to date not only in the Pleistocene but before the peak of its last substage, the Mankato.[8] True, the points are not of the best workmanship. Yet they could never be ascribed to unskilled Dawn Man, for they show the kind of stone craft attained in the Old World only in the Upper Old Stone Age. They have, in fact, been likened to one of its stages—the Solutrean.[9] This, of course, does not mean that men came all the way from Europe bearing Solutrean points. What it does show is that these first dated immigrants were no beginners at the art of stoneworking. They also had tools of bone and probably of wood, though the last have disintegrated with time. They were equipped for big-game hunting.

It was hunting on an Old Stone Age scale, which means that the weapons were crude and inaccurate. Men had scarcely gone beyond the stage where it was a miracle that they had weapons at all. The stone points they made, some two to four inches long, must have been used on spears (for the bow was not invented until around 5000 B.C. in Europe),[10] which had to be thrown in the open, either by hand or from a throwing board, such as the Eskimo still use. Without hoofs, claws, or tusks and with their skins unprotected by fur, they must have felt themselves anything but lords of creation when faced with a herd of mammoths or mastodons.

Man could at least pick off the old and sick. A mammoth at the Denver Museum of Natural History has bones which show an advanced case of arthritis, and as such it would have been fair prey. Perhaps a spear, thrown at the rear of the herd, could stampede them into a bog or over a cliff, as we guess happened at Clovis, New Mexico. The motorist near Clovis today sees only a vista of barren sand dunes, but in lush Pluvial times there was a string of lakes, or bogs, with deep clay bottoms. In the deposits left by these are mammoth bones and, among them, beautifully fluted points. Was stonecraft improving or are the Clovis points simply the work of another group? Questions of that sort will soon be cleared up as the archaeologists continue work. What is important to the average reader is that these same Clovis fluted points, or something rather like them, turn up also in Colorado, in Texas, in some of the southern states, and in Alaska. (The cores and flakes of this stone complex have been compared favorably to similar ones found in Mongolia.) [11] They are the trade-mark of the mammoth-hunters, the proof that man was in America in the Ice Age and that he was moving and spreading.

What signs of him do we have besides his stone manufactures? There are precious few. Yet, in Gypsum Cave in Nevada, high on a bluff which was once a lake shore, there are sloth bones scraped and cut as though to make tools. In among sloth dung and sloth hair are wooden dart shafts and dart points, the remains of a torch, and the charcoal of campfires extinguished ten thousand years ago, or about 8504 B.C. [12]

Slowly the scene changed. Moisture lessened, and grasslands decreased. Mammoth, horse, and camel, which should have been pasturing upon them, were disappearing. The chief ruminant now was one of the latest immigrants from Asia, a large bison. This was not the buffalo we know today (*Bison bison*) but an enormous brute (*B. antiquus*) with a much wider spread between its horntips. Even a herd of these monsters could be stampeded by a spear artfully thrown. Perhaps this happened near Folsom, New Mexico, where twenty-three of them were found slaughtered and skinned. Skinned we feel sure, for not one of the twenty-three had a tail bone, and tail bones normally come off with the hide. Folsom Man—or his mate—may have been making skin clothing, containers, or even tents.

The Folsom points are among the most beautifully chipped of all, a refinement, perhaps, by people who were specialists in bison-hunting and the weapons for it. It seems plain by this time that there were a number of different groups gaining a livelihood in the New World, each with its particular technique of stoneworking, to which it clung as tenaciously as Indians clung to pottery and arrow types later. Meticulous and brilliant work is being done in the comparison of points found at different sites and in working out their possible descent from Sandia, Clovis, or Folsom. It is an intricate task to deduce the lifeway of a whole people from a few points, some skin-working tools, or—exciting find!—a gouge, a bone needle, or perhaps a grinding stone for wild seeds. This last is an epoch-making discovery, for it means that one little group was turning from the approved practice of big-game hunting to that acqaintance with plants which would, one day, lead to agriculture. One group in Cochise County, Arizona, seems to have taken this step even in the Ice Age.[13] Had they a seed-gathering tradition? Or was their part of Arizona rich in seed grasses? The new carbon technique dates this little group over seven thousand years ago, or about 5400 B.C.[14]

By this time the ice was well in retreat, going toward Greenland and the tops of the Rockies. A warmer and drier period was setting in. The horse and camel must have become almost extinct, for few of their bones are found, but the bison multiplied and spread. With it spread the hunters. Their stone points are now found over the Plains, from Nebraska to Texas.

This must have been a time of dispersal. Groups which had lived for centuries as lords of a hunting paradise now had to content themselves with deer and even rabbits. Some, willing to put up with this small game, even as Indians did later, eked out their diet with seeds. Some gatherers also pushed east, west, and south, finding new kinds of seeds and, finally, shellfish. Their heaps of clam, mussel, and other shells are piled along ocean coasts and riverbanks with dates as late as A.D. 1318[15]—to the white man, the Middle Ages. Those who felt that a meat diet was the only right way of life, as many later Indians did, must have followed the animals. In the Plains they found bison of a modern variety; to the southeast there were deer and, farther north, larger animals—possibly the last of the mammoths.[16]

Some groups must have gone south. There was a fairly clear migration route along the plateau of Mexico, across the Isthmus of Panama, and down along the Andes. An expert on Chile and the Andean area believes that the mountains would offer no great difficulties to foot travelers once they had got used to the altitude.[17] There was enough game and wild food to keep them going, to the tip of South America, which some did reach. Caves in the extreme southern part of Patagonia, near the Straits of Magellan, show spear points and scrapers along with the bones of horse and ground sloth, and the guanaco, a woolly little member of the camel tribe. The carbon dating is over eight thousand years ago, or about 6688 B.C.[18] That is some two thousand years later than the ground-sloth hunters of Gypsum Cave, Nevada—ample time for a group, or its descendants, to traverse South America, even on foot. We can imagine that some determined big-game hunters followed the ground sloth as it retreated from the dying Southwest and at last found themselves stopped at this isolated and chilly tip of the New World. Other hunters may have gone north, following the big animals and the retreating ice.

And new people arrived. Some groups may have made the trip in boats via Bering Strait and some via the Aleutians, though the last is a stormy and hazardous journey. It is likely that some of these later groups brought the dog. The "friend of man" was, apparently, the first animal domesticated in the Old World, or, rather, it domesticated itself by following men at their hunting camps and eating the remains of their food. Even this step toward civilization must have occured after the first migrants left for the New World, for no dog bones are found among their relics. However, when Columbus touched shore, there were dogs over much of the two Americas and in many varieties.

Another importation was the bow and arrow. This complicated weapon, made of wood, stone, sinew, and feathers, was as great an improvement over the spear as the spear over a stone thrown from the hand. We do not know when the new weapon arrived. The guess would have to be made from stone points, and it is hard to tell wheather these were meant for arrows or small darts.

It is apparent, then, that by one route or another new contingents were arriving. As the northern part of the country was freed from ice, they could take many routes, probably spreading out fanwise. Perhaps they followed paths along the Pacific coast, for some sandals in a cave in Oregon are dated over nine thousand years ago.[19] The routes east, as the glaciers melted, would appeal to cold-country people with a knowledge of warm clothing and winter hunting. Some surely went this way, for the peoples around the Arctic Circle in Europe, Asia, and America show an impressive likeness of techniques and customs.

The possibilities of such migrations, as of others farther south, belong in later chapters. This narrative must turn to changes which went on within the borders of the United States as the Ice Age gave way to the warmer and drier period and this in turn to a slightly cooler one. By this time the country looked almost as it does at present except for some lakes in desert areas which have since gone dry. Travel was possible in all directions, and the groups who were to become our present Indians were settling to their habitats and their different ways of life. It is interesting to see that some of those with the most primitive customs, both in North and in South America, seem to have been pushed to the marginal lands, the deserts and mountains. Among these simpler people there is often a surprising similarity of customs and of myths. We are beginning slowly to form opinions as to which Indian groups may have been early comers to the New World and which came later, armed with better techniques. Soon we may have facts enough to decide.

What we do know is that, when the whites arrived to stay, in the 1500's, there were Indians all over the two Americas. In the area of the United States, our special subject, there were hundreds of named tribes, of varied appearance and speaking languages incomprehensible to one another. Some linguists have arbitrarily gathered these into six enormous families, each as different from the others as English from Chinese. Had these developed from one basic tongue since the period of the first migrations? It seems more reasonable to suppose that the early comers who seem to have borne such different physical characters had also different languages. These, as the people dispersed, might have flowered into numberless dialects. A map and a list of North American Indian languages will be found on the front endpaper.

The first question to ask about any tribe concerns its language, for those with similar speech are likely to have a stock of basic customs in common. However, the kind of country where they have elected to live is equally important, since it dictates their possibilities for a livelihood, it sets the stage for contacts, which mean learning, mixture, or conquest. Above all, when we consider the period of white arrival, it was the area occupied by each Indian tribe which decided whether that tribe should be exterminated, used as an ally, or moved.

Therefore, in this history, the tribes will be grouped in geographic areas. The fate of each is the subject of a chapter. Brief notice, indeed, for some of the most dramatic events of American history! Still, even this quick succession of highlights may be useful for a little further understanding of the past and present of the red man's America.

CHAPTER II

America Blooms

THE time is five thousand years ago, always allowing that wide margin of error which such ancient dates demand. The ice has receded to that northern position, where we hope it will remain. Bering Strait has attained its width of fifty-six miles, and no land animals now cross between Siberia and America. If men make that particular journey—and we do not deny the possibility—they will be northern hunters from the margins of the Old World, not from its inland centers. Yet in those inland centers the first strides toward civilization have been taken. While the first Americans are still gathering seeds and hunting animals, dressing in skins or bark fiber, and cooking, perhaps, by placing hot stones in a container of basketry, bark, or skin, the Old World has undergone what V. Gordon Childe calls the "First Revolution."[1] That is, men have begun to breed plants and animals. They had ceased merely to take what nature provided and had begun to make her produce. This step was taken in the Old World almost at the same time as in the New.

It was not due to the brilliance of any one "race." Of the peoples concerned in it, the Sumerians of Mesopotamia are still an enigma; the inhabitants of the Indus Valley in northern India were dark-skinned, while the Egyptians were a branch of the white race known as Hamites and Semites.

Nature set the stage for these varied groups, so that they were tempted and even pushed into agriculture. The scene was an east-west strip of warm and fertile country including the river valleys of the Nile, the Tigris-Euphrates, and the Indus. Here, or near by, grew wild grains similar to modern wheat, barley, and millet. Available in one region or another were the apple, fig, olive, and grape and other such edible plants as lettuce, melons, vegetable marrow, chick-peas, and garlic. Even these opportunities might not have tempted man—or, rather, woman, for she was the plant-gatherer—into cultivation with no planting tool but a sharpened stick. The deciding factor was, perhaps, the river bottom or the mountain slope, clean of sod and underbrush and flooded every year. Here was a smooth expanse of fertile mud where seeds could be thrown, perhaps by accident at first. With scarcely any care, they would produce a dependable crop.

This permanent food supply must have meant a change in human life as great as did the discovery of fire. Hunters and plant-gatherers can never settle down in large groups, since that would scare the game animals and exhaust the wild plants. However, when planting began, real villages were possible even though they were only built of sticks and mud. There is one in western Asia dating over six thousand years ago, or 4756 B.C.[2] Dwellings could be furnished with heavy and permanent household goods, such as clay pots. The ceramic craft, carried on by women and without a wheel, was to grow and proliferate until it became the chief artistic expression of its time. Cloth is almost as old. Flax was grown and woven by the early Egyptians, as was cotton, in the Indus Valley. Mesopotamia domesticated sheep in order to weave their wool. Women were the planters, potters, and weavers, but men tamed the animals. Rather, it looks as though the animals tamed themselves, and men accepted them. It was the good fortune of Mediterranean peoples that the wild ox and ass, the sheep, goat, and swine, lived in the hills or the plains around them. As the country grew drier and as men began to irrigate, perhaps the beasts gathered around green fields and irrigation ditches. Men may have begun to protect and even feed them. Then step by step the animals may have been used for sacrifice, wool, milk, burden-bearing, and food. Mankind need not now spend all its time in merely keeping alive. The way was open for civilization, and inventions pyramided. Metal tools—first of copper, then of bronze, then of iron! Great buildings in stone and brick! Scales, money, the calendar, ships, writing!

Keeping pace with these practical improvements were changes in human organization such as the rise of a warrior class who now had no duties except to fend off enemies and reduce them to tributaries. Then came the emergence of a king, far more powerful than the old chieftains, who were followed only while they were useful. Religion shared in the change. Instead of the nature-spirits who came close to every hunter and received part of the kill and harvest, there grew up a galaxy of deities, demanding as the king himself and propitiated with costly gifts. Of these, the most costly of all was human life. Never think that human sacrifice is a sign of the most primitive and barbaric peoples! Such groups cannot spare their members, even to please the gods. It is usually when slaves and war captives are available that the supernaturals can be honored with killings and burnings. In Babylon, at least, such sacrifices took place, and the custom sent ripples through Palestine, Crete, and even Greece.

Every country in the Old World could hear of the new lifeways, sooner or later, without having to invent them. The huge continent of Eurasia was all one land mass, with Africa hanging from it by the Isthmus of Suez. In early days, too, there was a land bridge via Sicily. People could walk all over this area, even before the days of horses and ships. There is ample proof that inventions did pass in this way, and some of them may never have been made but once.

The wheel, for instance! It rolls into history under a Sumerian war chariot, and who knows how many accidents and little changes were necessary before that came to pass! Once the first crude wheel had been made, chariots and carts began to appear all over Eurasia. Today, our civilization is based on the wheel. We use it for everything, from automobiles and dynamos to cigarette lighters and egg-beaters. Yet we cannot tell when and if our machine age would have got its start if the materials, the need, and the idea had not happened to come together, long ago, in the Near East.

While the new techniques were passing to and fro in the Old World, receiving constant revisions and changes, America remained remote. Whether stray boatloads crossed the Pacific, bringing odd-ments of news, remains under discussion. Even without them there seems no reason why America's inhabitants should not have dis-covered agriculture, just as Old World people did, if given the right conditions.

Such conditions existed, particularly in South America. For long periods in the past the southern continent had been separated from the northern and forced to lead a life of its own. In fact, if man had needed a Panama Canal a few million years ago, he would not have had to dig it, for it was there. At other times there was water across the Isthmus of Tehuantepec, farther north. The lands thus cut off by water included all America's share of the equator with its hothouse warmth and plentiful rain. It was a fit birthplace for our warmth-loving plants like squash, beans, tomatoes, peppers, and perhaps tobacco. These, every gardener realizes, have a different heritage from Europe's peas, which can be "planted in the snow," or her cabbages ripening in the mists of autumn. The garden spot also had cool, moist uplands which gave birth to potatoes, and hot jungles, the habitat of peanuts and pineapples. Moreover, there were river bottoms inviting to irrigation. Before 7000 B.C. these conditions had tempted the local food-gatherers to begin weeding around their favorite plants or scattering some seeds at harvest time.

The news of their achievement spread, just as such news spread in the Old World. There the heartland, the cradle of civilization, was the eastern Mediterranean, from which the ripples of civilization spread even to the barbarians of western Europe, ancestors of today's white Americans. In the New World the favored land was what might be called the waist and hips of the Americas, including some of Mexico, the fertile parts of Central America, and a stretch at the east of South America. To students of Indian history this is Nuclear America, scene of the highest cultures in the New World. Agriculture began here almost as early as in the Old World. A possible date for maize on the central coast of Peru is 1900–1700 B.C.[3] Indian corn or maize was being grown in the valley of Mexico about 7000 B.C., squash about 6000 B.C., and beans about 5000 B.C.[4] The botanists think that probably each area began to foster its own native plants, the starchy roots and the cereals being the favorites. The accompanying list of the principal ones may be interesting.

PLANTS NATIVE TO NUCLEAR AMERICA[5]

ROOTS

Arracacha (*Arracacia xanthorrhiza* or *esculenta*)
Arrowroot (*Maranta arundinacea*)
Jerusalem artichoke (*Helianthus tuberosus*)
Manioc (*Manihot utilissima*, and others)
Oca (*Oxalis crenta* and *O. tuberosa*)
Potato (*Solanum spp.*; there are at least five known "primitive" species)
Sweet potato (*Ipomoea batatas*)

FRUITS AND VEGETABLES

Beans (kidney: *Phaseolus vulgaris*; lima: *P. lunatus*; scarlet runner: *P. multiflorus*; tepary: *P. acutifolius var. latitelius*)—in fact, all beans but the European broad bean
Chili pepper (*Capsicum annuum*)
Chirimoya (*Annona cherimola*)
Corn (Indian) or maize (*Zea mays*)—the varieties include flint, flour, dent, pop, and pod corn
Guava (*Psidium guayava*)
Papaw (*Carica papaya*)

Pineapple (*Ananas sativus*)
Prickly pear (*Opuntia ficus-india*)
Pumpkin (*Cucurbita pepo*)
Squash (*Cucurbita spp.; four species*)
Star apple (*Chrysophyllum cainito*)
Tomato (*Lycopersicum esculentum*)

SEEDS AND NUTS

Cacao (*Theobroma cacao*)
Cashew nut (*Anacardium occidentale*)
Quinoa (*Chenopodium quinoa*)

MEDICINAL

Quinine (*Chinchona spp.*, esp. *C. pubescens*)
Ipecac (*Cephaelis ipecacuanha*)

DRINKING, SMOKING, AND CHEWING

Chicle—milky juice from the zapote tree (*Achras zapota*) which was chewed as gum; also various other gummy substances
Coca (*Erythroxylum cocoa*)—source of our cocaine; the leaves especially were chewed by mountain people in Peru to give them strength for long journeys
Maguey (*Agave spp.*)—the sap in the flower bud was fermented to make a beer known as *pulque*; a great many other plant juices were fermented, including those of maize, prickly pear, palm hearts, and manioc; although few areas in Nuclear America were without a fermented drink, apparently no distilling was done
Peyote (*Anhalonium williamsii*)—this and other cacti and succulent plants with narcotic effect were used ceremonially in Mexico
Tobacco (*Nicotiana tabacum* and *N. rustica*)—in different areas tobacco was chewed, taken as snuff, and smoked in pipes, cigars, and cigarettes
Yerba mate, or Paraguay tea (*Ilex paraguariensis* and *I. conocarpo*)

MANUFACTURING

Maguey (*Agave spp.*)
Rubber (*Sapium jenmani, S. cladegyne, S. eglan dulosum, Castilla elastica, Hevea brasiliensis,* and several others)

Some of these plants, like the medicines and fruits, such as star apple, were not cultivated but were picked wild. Others were cultivated in the areas suited to them, such as the potato in the chilly uplands and manioc in hot, swampy country.

This list* shows how immensely the diet of the world has profited from America's contributions. The "Irish" potato, "Hungarian" paprika, and "Spanish" sauce (made of tomatoes and peppers) are all American products so intensively cultivated in the Old World that their source has been forgotten. Above all, however, it was tobacco which made the round-the-world record. Brought to Europe by the

---

* Recent botanical studies show that some of the foregoing domesticated plants may have had a remote Old World origin.

Spaniards in 1558, it spread during the 1600's through most of that continent and Asia. The Eskimo, in the 1700's, were found getting their tobacco by trade from Siberia.

The principal character in the whole piece is corn, or *Zea mays*. Its very name is a misnomer, like that of the Indians themselves, for the English who applied it meant by corn any kind of grain, even black peppers. Only to Americans does the word "corn" stand always for the fat, yellow, or white ears oozing milk and as luscious as any food the earth produces. Purists call it "maize."

The origin of maize was long a problem, since no wild plant that looked like an ancestor could be found either in the Old World or in the New. Finally a corps of anthropologists and botanists found a seed-bearing grass which was hybridized with another grass,[6] then hybridized again, until small cobs about the size of a child's finger were developed. Much of this seems to have occurred in the valley of Mexico. The hybridizers were early food-gathering people who passed the seeds about from group to group and planted them by chance near other grasses. The use of the new food spread very slowly.[7] It was A.D. 1 before some villages in New Mexico were raising corn for subsistence. Much of the United States area had a climate or rainfall unsuitable for corn growing under primitive conditions. Still, maize culture spread and improved. By the time the whites arrived, almost all our present varieties had been developed, including flint, flour, dent, pop, pod, and sweet corn. Ears were produced in at least six colors. Plant forms varied from the tall corn of the eastern United States to the bushlike form of the western desert, adapted to wind and drought. The white man added no new varieties until hybrid corn appeared in the twentieth century.

Cotton is another staple whose origin has not been determined. It grew wild, was found and cultivated both in the Old World and the New; but the chromosome count in the two areas was different. Present theories suggest a very early hybridization, though the means are unknown.

With agriculture well begun, pottery and weaving developed, with techniques which spread through Nuclear America and into the southern portion of the United States.[8]

So two steps of Old World civilization were duplicated in the New. But what of the domestication of animals, what of iron tools, and, above all, what of the wheel? One of these took place only partially; the others not at all and for good reason. The opportunities were not at hand. In view of prehistory in America and in other areas gradually becoming known, students have given up the old dogma that all civilization passes first through a given set of stages and that a people can be identified as in the Stone Age, the Bronze Age, or the Iron Age. This was true of Europe, whose prehistory was once the only one known. Now that new facts are cropping up all over the world, we realize that the techniques a people develop depend on the area and resources and that civilization cannot be gauged by the use of any particular material.

In South America the domestication of animals did indeed begin in classical fashion. However, the convenient cow, ass, and horse were all absent. The only animal fit to bear burdens of any size was the little camel known as the llama. These beasts were pastured in herds and used as pack animals. They could not have dragged a cart of any size, even had the mountain paths of Peru been suited to it. This may be one reason why no wheel was invented in Peru. The llama was sheared for its wool, and so were its wilder relatives, the alpaca and vicuna, but none of them was milked. When we remember that milking came late in the Old World and that the idea never reached China at all, this is not surprising.

Farther north, in Yucatán and the valley of Mexico, there were no beasts of burden whatever. How very different might have been the history of those populous agricultural areas had the American horse not been extinct. Or had they known about the bison and the mountain goat, far away in northern wildernesses. No one has ever tamed a bison, but no one has ever had the circumstances or the centuries of time which domesticated the wild cattle of Europe. As it was, the Indians did domesticate such animals as they had use for: the llama, guinea pig, and guinea hen in South America, bees in Yucatán, and turkeys in the valley of Mexico. None of these tempted them to use a wheel. Yet the principle was known, for wheeled toys have been found in various parts of Mexico. The idea remained undeveloped since there was no use for it.

Metal for tools was another New World lack. In the Old World the Near East early found usable copper and imported tin so that stone tools could be replaced with more efficient ones made of bronze. In Nuclear America neither copper nor tin was easily obtained. (The tin of Bolivia, which now supplies the United States, requires very difficult and expensive extraction.) The Peruvians did manage a few bronze tools, from metal washed down in the streams, but the rest of Nuclear America was, when the whites came, "still in the Stone Age." That is, it was a Stone Age as far as tools were concerned. In other respects, both the Andean area and several other parts of Nuclear America had an Age of Gold. The yellow metal, "excrement of the gods," was washed down by mountain streams and panned as white prospectors later panned it. The wealth of delicate ornament made from it, by almost every technique known to modern man, is no part of the present narrative, except to prove that, when a people is technologically in the Stone Age, they need not be what is thought of as a "Stone Age people."

Although Nuclear America had no wheel and no iron tools, it did proceed with some of the steps usually thought of as following these inventions. Irrigation was highly developed in the Andean area, as were the building of roads and bridges and the organization of a socialized state, with an army, a welfare system, and a census and accounting arrangements to keep track of them. The Andes were too far from the wilds of North America, and the Inca Empire developed too late, for some of these refinements to touch the Indians of our narrative. Still, some of the Andean technology spread far through the Americas. It would be a mistake not to have this history in mind when we find among northern Indians not only agriculture but such arts as painted pottery, weaving, and featherwork.

The Andean area, Central America, Yucatán, and the valley of Mexico must, of course, be considered as one interacting area, just as Sumeria, Egypt, and their environs are considered in the Old World. Still, as we reach the more northern part of Nuclear America, the means of communication with United States Indians are more evident, and we can identify more traits which stand out prominently in the coming narrative. Yucatán and the valley of Mexico were not terrains for irrigation. They relied upon rain, and rain had, in some places, produced such thick forests as to make agriculture difficult. The people had resorted to a device usual in forest areas all over the world and known as slash-and-burn agriculture. The Maya called it "milpa," a word which has become standardized.

The milpa system means that trees are girdled so that they die and fall, then they are burned, leaving the ground moderately clear and strewn with wood ash. Here planting may be done, and the crops will prosper for one year, maybe three or four. Then new fields must be cleared, and, if the farmer's dwelling remains in the same place, he will have to walk farther and farther to his work. Ultimately he and all his neighbors will have to move. This occurred several times with the Mayan cities, but before that was necessary they had built an interesting arrangement of farms and farmers' dwellings, surrounding a civic center.

The centers which have been unearthed are magnificent stone structures, including plazas, temples, chiefs' houses, and highways, all decorated with carved and painted stone. One feature of particular interest is the tall, truncated pyramids on which the important buildings stand. (Some were as high as 229 feet,[9] with as many as sixty-two tall, narrow steps.)[10] Whether these lofty pedestals were first devised for practical purposes, we do not know. Certainly they became the style in the valley of Mexico[11] and far into the forest country along the Caribbean, where they were merely banks of earth. Temple mounds will form one of the interesting features in our picture of North American Indians.

The whole civic center was built, rebuilt, and repaired by the farmers in their slack time. They owned the land in common, after the usual Indian method, instead of working it for a landlord like European peasants. Still, the status and rights of the chiefs had grown so great and those of the farmers were left so small that the situation looked much like that of a feudal establishment. Says the Spanish Bishop Landa: "The common people at their own expense made the houses of the lords. . . . Beyond the house all the people did their sowing for the lord, cared for his fields and harvested what was necessary for him and his household; and when there was hunting or fishing or when it was time to get their salt, they always gave the lord his share."[12]

As in Europe and in the ancient world, the community also supported a hierarchy of priests who were not only its religious officiants but its scholars. They worked out a system of counting which would allow the writing of figures up to 1,280,000,000. They used a sign for zero five hundred years before the Hindus invented it.[13] They were astronomers enough to have worked out a year of 365 days and the cycle of the planet Venus taking fifty-two years. They could even calculate eclipses. And they wrote it all down! The Maya had writing which was partly picture-writing, partly symbols that stood for sounds, as do our letters of the alphabet.

Among them were theologians who had developed a whole hierarchy of gods, including a god of the heavens and gods of the upper world, the lower world, and the calendar. Among the most important were the gods of rain, for in this riverless country (the chalk plain of Yucatán has not a single running stream) the farmer no longer felt secure about his water supply. Here we meet the rain-gods of the four directions, each with his sacred color, and often to be heard of later. There is also a special god of corn, as well as deities for weaving and human sacrifice. The Maya considered, as the ancient Babylonians had, a human life the most valuable thing on earth and therefore the most pleasing gift to the gods. Sometimes they dressed and treated the victim as a god and felt that his death took him straight to the supernaturals with their message of fealty. Sometimes this service to the gods was combined with the more ancient custom of which we shall hear again—the eating of the victim's body in order to obtain his virtues. The Maya did this particularly if the victim had been a valiant and brave soldier, for thus they also might become valiant and brave. Cutting the heart from a victim's breast and holding it up toward the image of a god, their priest would pray: "All powerful god, these sacrifices we make to thee and we offer thee these hearts, so that thou mayest give us health and temporal goods."[14]

Streams of influence from the Maya went north into the valley of Mexico, and others, in time, came back to them. Most people identify Mexico with the Aztec, but these conquerors, like the Inca in Peru, were late-comers, even barbarians, who had little enough time to absorb the culture of the southern people before they in turn were snuffed out by the Spaniards in 1520. The Aztec were northerners with a language related to that of the Ute, Paiute, Hopi, Pima, and Papago of our Southwest (Uto-Aztecan). They arrived perhaps in about A.D. 1200 and, made energetic by their very limitations, built up an organized, militaristic empire. With our eyes on the north, we are interested to note their slash-and-burn agriculture and their raingods of the four directions, each with his appropriate color. Some of their equipment shared by the United States Indians includes wooden stools, platform beds, litters, feather mantles, and, finally, temple mounds, with their priests and idols.

Aztec temples have become famous as the scene of human sacrifices which continued in a bloody round throughout the year in order, the Aztec averred, to feed Sun and keep him on his course. Here, again, is a wealthy and developed people turning to human sacrifice, as the poorer tribes of Mexico never did. Some anthropsychiatrist should make a thorough study of Aztec sadism and of the milder forms of it which can be found even among United States Indians. Meanwhile, we should not forget the more aesthetic side of Aztec ceremonies: the magnificent processions in honor of the gods; the masked dancers representing supernatural beings; the eternal fire burning in the temple.

The eternal fire is of particular interest. Every fifty-two years, the period of the Venus cycle, it was extinguished. Priests then sacrificed a victim, tore out his heart, and made a new fire in the cavity. While this was going on, every fire in the city was put out, and people waited in trepidation to see if the blaze would be lighted successfully. If not, the world would come to an end. Throughout a wide area in Mexico and the southern United States, Indians had a belief something like this, an evidence of age-old connections.

Did this elaborate culture grow up in isolation, without any Old World contacts? Scholars once felt sure that it must have. Then the Norwegian, Thor Heyerdahl, after study of winds and currents, sailed from South America to the Pacific Islands in a craft made exactly like those of the ancient Incas.[15] Later he crossed the Atlantic in a papyrus boat like those of Egypt. So contact was not impossible. There is no sign that it occurred on a large scale and at a definite time. But unusual customs found here and there in South America and in the Pacific give food for thought. Such are the chewing of tasty leaves in New Guinea; coca in the Andes; pan pipes in Peru and the Pacific tuned to the same scale; pottery which looks identical in Ecuador and the Japanese island of Kyushu.[16] Serious study of this subject is only beginning.

More interesting for our purposes is the spread of customs from Nuclear America around the Caribbean, into the United States, and, by slow seepage, into its far corners. We understand, by now, that no group of people invents its customs in isolation. Ideas percolate to them, now from one direction, now from another, and are arranged in new combinations which go to form a particular lifeway. So the Indians of the United States area did not invent agriculture, pottery, war methods, mythology, or any other element of their various lifeways. Nor did anyone else invent them. These traits grew up by tiny accretions of behavior until something worth while appeared at one point and was copied or adapted by all peoples who found it useful. Often, therefore, this narrative will point out that an element in technology, organization, or religion seems to have relationships in this direction or that.

This does not mean that its Indian users were copyists, any more than white Americans are copyists because they make use of dynamite and printing and porcelain, invented in China, or iron-smelting, first known somewhere in the Old World. The lines of influence are interesting to follow, but more interesting still is the use made of each one by a particular group with regard to its particular interests.

In considering the Indians of the United States, we cannot look at the country as a whole. Its Indians belong to five enormous language families, each differing from the others in sounds and grammar as much as English from Chinese. This may mean at least five immigrations of people with different backgrounds and different origins. More important still, those immigrants, when arriving in America, settled in areas with different possibilities. Some had the right climate for agriculture. Some had such lack of rain or warmth that farming would have been impossible no matter what knowledge their inhabitants had possessed. Some had easy communication with Nuclear America, whose achievements could be learned and fitted to their own needs. Some were remote or in contact rather with Asia than with Mexico.

For complete accuracy, each tribe and section of a tribe should be considered separately, and much work of that sort has been done. Here we follow six large divisions, mostly on the geographic lines so competently worked out by Dr. Kroeber.[17] Occasionally, however, people in the same geographic environment have, because of history and contacts, worked out very different systems of living. Moreover, the whites, for various reasons, have treated them differently, and so they need separate consideration here.

Would that the whites, on first meeting an Indian group, had considered not whether their domain was desirable plowland or undesired forest but had taken note of the activities of the Indians themselves! Some were agriculturists living in organized confederacies and needing little change of attitude in order to step into modern life. Others moved in small food-gathering groups, unacquainted with farming and finding a remote, impersonal government almost incomprehensible. Others were fighters, whose interest in life depended on adventure and renown. Yet all could learn and change. These pages are a record of the ways in which one group after another came into contact with new ideas and adapted them to its own way of life.

Events, after the white arrival, moved too quickly for such adaptation. Also the whites, two centuries ago, had not the knowledge of psychology and educational methods which is now coming into common use. The Indian cultures were extinguished without regard to what they might give the new nation. Yet they were not quite extinguished. It is amazing to see how much manual expertness, what deeply imbedded tendencies to co-operation, have been kept alive in Indian groups. There are generations to come in which these tendencies may be developed to the advantage of the American nation.

CHAPTER III

Civilized Tribes

Along the streams in Mississippi, Alabama, and all the way up to Ohio, white pioneers used to plow up fine, thin pottery often in human and animal shapes which reminded students of wares from Nuclear America. There were copper plates and shell ornaments depicting warriors in feather mantles; there was cloth with painted designs. As these sites were excavated, it turned out that they were groups of pyramids, crude, perhaps, and made of earth rather than of decorated stone but nevertheless a form of civic center.[1]

Were the "Mound-builders" who left them a vanished race, even a white race? So went the first fantastic explanations, but it is now plain that the Indians in the Lower and Middle Mississippi area were the ancestors of Indians seen there in historic times and some of whom remain there today.

Their connection with Nuclear America is obvious and possible. The Caribbean Sea and its extension, the Gulf of Mexico, are practically encircled by a ring of warm, forested countries. It would be natural for slash-and-burn farmers in all this area to have worked out the same general arrangement of temples and public buildings in one spot, with the fields and dwelling huts in a wide circle around them. Perhaps the public buildings were placed on pyramids because of swampy land, but, the impressiveness of this style having once been established, many people might copy it.

So much for the civic center, a natural development where the fields cannot be close to town as they are in irrigated countries. There must, however, have been migration of people or ideas from Nuclear America north and at different dates. Why not? Trekking through the forests around the Caribbean would be difficult work, but coasting along its shores in a canoe or even crossing it would not be difficult, granted the canoe.

Indians of that region did have canoes. They were seaworthy enough so that the Arawak could cross from South America[2] to

26

settle the West Indies and part of Florida. The Carib, who followed them across the Caribbean, had dugouts with two or three masts and sails of palm-leaf matting. The Maya, met by Bartholomew Columbus in 1502,[3] were on a trading trip from Yucatán to Spanish Honduras. Other Indians of Mexico and Central America—the Mosquito, Sumo, Paya, Jicaque, Cuna, Bribri, Guaymi, and Cabecar—had seagoing canoes and even sails. Did canoe fleets make their way along the coasts of the twin seas, the Caribbean and the Gulf of Mexico, to trade, conquer, or settle? And, if so, when? Details are lost in the shadows of Indian myth, yet we have archaeological facts which speak for themselves.

Scattered through the countries on the map, which may be called the circum-Caribbean area, we find such specialized equipment as feather mantles, litters, wooden stools, platform beds, weaving, tatooing, fish-poisoning, blowguns, and even the thatched house, with its walls of poles, smeared with clay, all of which can be duplicated in Nuclear America. So can the war system, with its insignia and names for warriors and its torture of captives and occasional eating of their flesh. So, too, can the religious system, with its temple mounds, its appointed priesthood, its god-images and undying fire. All these were to be found in our southeastern states, among such Indians as the Creek, Chickasaw, Choctaw, Cherokee, Caddo, Natchez, and Quapaw (see Map I). The first four, which were later bought out and moved to Oklahoma, so impressed their white fellow-citizens that they, in company with the Seminole, an offshoot of the Creek, were put down in government records as the Five Civilized Tribes.

They were not the first occupants of the Southeast. Indian history in any area usually shows a succession of peoples who passed through or who remained to form a mixture, for let it be understood that no Indian group is a "pure race" any more than a white group is. The Southeast perhaps formed a refuge for food-gatherers seeking a better home than the drying Southwest. Acres of shells from fresh-water clams show, at least, that someone made a living there. The someone, whose bones were often left in the shell heaps, was of the slender, longheaded type frequent among America's early inhabitants, and his earliest remains date to 4200 B.C.[4]

Thousands of years later—in fact, about A.D. 600 or 700[5]—we can identify a new immigration. These were broadheaded people coming from the north or perhaps direct from Asia. With them, or at least at the same time, came some new ideas which have given cause for much theorizing. One was the custom of collecting bones of the recent dead and burying them under mounds. "Barrows" is the Old World term. The other was the making of pottery. This was not the fine modeled or painted ware that we have noted as connected with Nuclear America. It was rough, unpainted, and marked as though with a cord. Such pottery was made in Eurasia about 2000 b.c., and it would be interesting, indeed, had it been brought across by a new set of immigrants.

That fascinating problem must be left to the archaeologists while we follow our mixed group of southeastern Indians in their first steps toward civilization. Did they hear a rumor that wild plants could be cultivated, or did they work out the idea for themselves? At least they began to plant primrose and sunflower, especially that starchy rooted variety known as Jerusalem artichoke (*Helianthus tuberosus*). They moved out of their temporary camps into dwellings thatched with grass and smeared with mud. Grinding stones show that they were making some kind of flour.

Then must have come the first migration or stimulus from the south. Perhaps it was a new migration or perhaps merely dissemination of ideas. Certainly, it could not have been mere chance which reproduced, with crude materials, the civic center of Nuclear America, with its plaza, its mounds topped with important buildings, its effigy pots and ornaments. We have shown that in slash-and-burn country, as this was, the arrangement of a civic center is normal. Yet it would be hard to explain the plazas and pyramids of Coles Creek, Louisiana,[6] or the Emerald Mound in Mississippi as original inspirations. Coles Creek, as reconstructed, looks grotesquely like a copy of a Mayan temple, though the pyramid is of debris and the "temple" of poles and thatch. Emerald Mound is more imposing, with a mound thirty-five feet high, covering seven acres and topped with six smaller mounds. There are other such centers throughout Mississippi, Georgia, Alabama, and far to the north and west. Within them is pottery and engraving which gives every proof of a close connection with Mexico or South America.

That connection may have been very recent, perhaps even after white arrival. Certainly mounds were being built into the sixteenth century, for De Soto saw them among Creek and Cherokee and probably by-passed others without knowing it. So the Civilized Tribes were, at one time, actually mound-builders, and so were a number of now-vanishing groups in Louisiana, such as the Atakapa, Avoyel, and Chitimacha.[7]

It would be interesting to know whether the life lived around these civic centers had anything in common with the organized government described in Yucatán,[8] where the common people were practically serfs, the ruler holy, and human sacrifice a virtue. Certainly there are few signs of such a system among historic Indians, but we can point to one group, visited by the French from 1698 to 1732,[9] who had a system decidedly different from the usual democracy of American Indians.

This group was the Natchez, living in Mississippi, near the site of the great Emerald Mound mentioned above. Their seven villages of thatched huts were ruled by an absolute monarch, known as Sun, who held such state that no one addressed him except from a distance with shouts and genuflections. When he went out, arrayed in feather mantle and feather crown, he was carried in a litter so that his feet did not touch the ground. He maintained a household of volunteer henchmen who hunted and worked for him and who were killed at his death along with his wife and any others who sought to be with him in the afterlife. When the French were in need of hunters or boatmen, they could always apply to Sun, who would call up as many men as he chose, allowing them no recompense. This may provide a hint as to how the heavy work of mound-building might have been done.

Sun had under him a number of officials, including a war chief and ceremonial officers. Four of these were the guardians of the temple, a wattle-and-daub building mounted on an eight-foot mound. Here a perpetual fire was kept burning, and in an inner room were spirit images and also the bones of former Suns, packed in cane baskets.[10] Many a temple throughout the mound area may have had the same general plan.

The Natchez had a social system with well-defined classes, known as Suns, Nobles, Honored Men, and common people, whom the French called Puants or Stinkards.[11] We cannot be sure that the Natchez class divisions, with their peculiar revolving system of marriages to commoners, were practiced by other southeastern tribes. What we can suppose is that the Southeast was familiar with class titles and class privileges, a condition not usual except among organized people with enough surplus to incite rivalry. Other Natchez customs, echoed over and over again around the Caribbean, are the elevated temple, with its priests, its god-image, and its undying fire, and the war system, including special costumes and names for the warriors, torture of captives, and eating their flesh. More obvious still are items of material equipment—the litter, the bed, the feather cloak, and, of course, the temple mound.

The tribes of this chapter, although they show some traces of an elaborate equipment and organization, may have been late-comers to the area who did not share the full mound-builder culture. The Creek, or Muskogi, largest member of the group, state that they came in from the north when the country was already occupied. So, perhaps, did their relatives, the Chickasaw and Choctaw, all speaking a language known as Muskogean; the Cherokee, their neighbors, both in early southeastern days and after removal, spoke a related language, Iroquoian. They had perhaps separated from the famous Iroquois of New York State during some early migration. These four show many differences, owing to resources and history, but we shall concentrate on the Creek, the only ones really well known.[12]

The land occupied by these tribes was part of the almost unbroken forest which once stretched from the Mississippi to the Atlantic, threaded with rivers and providing a magnificent food supply. There were nuts, berries, roots, birds, fish, and beasts in such plenty that perhaps it was natural for the Indians not to spend too much time on agriculture. Fields around a Creek civic center usually constituted only 1 per cent of the arable land in the area.[13]

Such work as was done, however, was thoroughly organized. In spring an appointed overseer went through the town blowing on a conchshell to summon all families to the fields. Each family had its own plot, and while the men worked, singing from one to the next, the women cooked the meal, and the day ended with games. Then came summer, when women did the hoeing, while children scared away birds and marauding animals. For harvest, the whole town was called out again, except that now each family reaped its own plot. Produce from the town plot went to the chief by way of both salary and taxes. A more democratic system than that described by Landa for the Maya but with a like flavor of planned organization!

The family plots, with their clusters of bark-covered dwellings, stretched along the creeks of Georgia and Alabama, whence the Indians got their English name. In some central open place was the "town," with its open plaza, the chief's house at one end, and the "great" or council house at the other. One of these, seen in the 1870's, would accommodate several hundred people. Near it was the summer gathering place, where seats were ranged in ranks around a quadrangle. There were a pole for torturing prisoners and a yard for playing the tribal game of chunky, or throwing poles after a rolling stone disk. Some such arrangement was kept long after the Creek moved across the Mississippi, and even the booths for a Baptist camp meeting still show the quadrangular arrangement.

Wood, bark, and stalks supplied the materials for houses and equipment, just as they did throughout the eastern Woodland. Wood, however, was hard to work with stone tools, and the Creek and Chickasaw used the tall cane which waved in their swamps for thatching, house partitions, litters, cradleboards, and even the wall spaces between posts of a barricade. The fibers of nettle, silk grass, and mulberry bark they spun into thread which the Spaniards judged "as good as the best thread from Portugal."[14] It was woven on a loom, but not the well-known and intricate apparatus of the Southwest, which duplicates looms of Peru. This horizontal frame, staked out a few inches above the ground, was the Arawak loom, used by many of the simpler South American peoples[15]—another circum-Caribbean trait.

To picture the southeastern Indian, one must get rid of the popular image of a tall, blanketed figure, with long black braids and a sweeping feather headdress. The southeastern man went barefoot, in a breechclout of skin or cloth, and had nothing to decorate except his own body. On this he did elaborate work or had it done by an expert tattooer, with a garfish jaw and soot from the campfire. Each design was an official insigne, beginning with those allowed a youth when he first attained warrior age and then indicating further exploits. A full-fledged warrior, at a distance, might look as though he were wearing a figured skintight garment. His long black hair was pulled out with clamshell tweezers in all sorts of patterns, leaving the head bald on one side, or in front, or everywhere except for the topknot called a scalp lock and left as a challenge to the enemy to "come and get it." Nose and ears were decorated with huge pendants of shell, which were so popular that, in later days, whites made medals of silver and presented them to chiefs for this purpose. This elaborate decoration was for men. Women, having no war honors, were not tattooed. They wore a wrap-around skirt of cloth and, perhaps, some shell necklaces.[16]

The Creek and, in fact, most all southeasterners, counted descent

PLATE I

A Tattooed Man

This elaborately decorated chief is Saturiba of the Timucua. The drawing shows him exciting a war party to action; he has taken a bowl of water, which he flung into the air while saying, "As I have done with this water, so I pray that you may do with the blood of your enemies." The tattooing was done by pricking the skin with a bone needle until the blood started, and then rubbing in various colored tints, usually indigo. Tattooing was commonly a mark of honor awarded to warriors and chiefs and often to their women. (From Swanton, 1946; Lorant, 1946.)

through the mother. This is a common arrangement with agricultural peoples over the world and was once thought to be the rule for all of them. However, the factors controlling human behavior are too varied for any fixed line of development. All the expert can say is that, since women were the first plant-gatherers and therefore the first planters, an agricultural tribe quite often allows its women to own the fields and perhaps the houses, taking in husbands to live with them. Women are not, however, the heads of families. Since the husbands are, quite often, transitory visitors, the position of family head is taken by the woman's brother. He comes away from his own family to discipline that of his sister, just as her husband goes to attend to his sister's family. It may sound complicated, but to those brought up to expect such an arrangement it works.

The mother-right families of the Southeast were usually organized in clans, groups which were, supposedly, descended from the same woman and who all thought of themselves as relatives, forbidden to intermarry. Each clan was named after some local animal, such as bear, deer, or beaver. Perhaps those "totems" were once treated with profound respect, but in the days we know of the relation had become shadowy. So had the tribal division into halves, or moieties, an arrangement which had more to do with government and public games than with family life.

Members of a number of clans might live in any town, and each had its local clan elder who took special responsibility for training the clan boys and guarding the clan morals. Creek training was stricter than that of many Indians, who rarely whip or punish their children and are shocked at the whites who do so. The clan elder saw that boys went out every morning to bathe in the creek which ran by every Creek village. Indeed, the whole population bathed, even breaking the ice in winter. As punishment for misdeeds, children had their arms and legs scratched with the sharp teeth of ever ready garfish. Boys were often scratched for their own good to make them manly and to accustom them to the sight of blood. In such a case, the skin was first bathed with warm water. "Dry scratching," however, was a punishment meant to hurt. For really bad behavior unbecoming a future warrior, a boy might be beaten with canes—another use for that omnipresent material.

The regular road to success for a young man was war. For the gentle, for the poetic, for the would-be administrator or inventor, there was still no route to public respect but this. A youth before he had been on a war party was called by a "baby name." He sat in a special arbor at ceremonies and performed the most menial tasks. No wonder that the desire to be a great warrior seemed to every boy like a basic human instinct. What a joy and relief it was, at the age of fifteen or so, to follow the men of his first war party! Even if he achieved no killing, he could now have a new name. At the annual New Fire ceremony his clan elder would scratch him ceremonially, lecturing him well on his new status, and then the name would be called out before the assembled villagers. Now he might move to the arbor of the Little Warriors, but even here comrades would look askance upon him until he had brought home scalps or even limbs of enemies. This meant a new name and perhaps more tattooing and the right to wear certain paint and feathers. Occasionally, some youth of gentle nature found himself unable to face this strenuous life. Then he was permitted to don women's clothes and work with the women. No one reproached him, but, like a woman, he could not gain fame.

If he attained a war name in the normal way, a marriage would be arranged for him with some industrious girl of another clan. The affair was conducted by the maternal relatives on both sides, and the young people were not consulted. Even the fathers had little to say, since this was a clan matter and the children belonged to their mother's clan, not to his. The person in charge was usually the maternal uncle, who would insist that the girl be well trained in pottery, weaving, and matmaking. Also she must be careful to keep away from men at the regular times when a supernatural power came upon her. The miracle which made a female capable of bearing children was, to most Indians, something to be feared as well as honored. They considered that a man who approached a woman at such times, ate what she cooked, or touched her belongings would lose his male strength. Therefore, southeastern women were secluded, both at menstruation and at pregnancy, a custom observed to the present day by some Cherokee and Choctaw.

The couple set up housekeeping in the wife's town, sometimes after a simple ceremony such as breaking a corn ear in two or planting two reeds. The Creek, like most Indians, considered marriage a secular and economic event, not under the domain of the spirits, as were the physical crises of birth, puberty, and death. They did allow a trial period, when the couple lived together until the next busk, or green-corn ceremony. At that time, when all debts were forgiven and the new year started, the trial marriage might be dissolved and different mates found.

This entry of the boy into a new family gave plenty of opportunities for friction, and the Creek, along with most southeasterners, used the remedy provided by other mother-right peoples in such a case—the mother-in-law taboo. This custom demands that the young man shall not speak to his mother-in-law and, in some tribes, not even see her. Thus quarrels about supremacy are avoided, and the two, sending ceremonious gifts to each other, regard their relationship as one of respect. With the Creek, the daughter-in-law is said also to have avoided her father-in-law, though, of course, she saw him less often. The whole custom was given up in later days. A man might have several wives if he could support them, but bringing a new woman into his wife's village was a ticklish matter, and her consent was required. If she needed a household helper, she might give it, but otherwise the new wife was visited in her own home, and her children belonged there. There were some elopements and infringements of the marriage rules, but the two clans who had made the alliance were severe on their young people. An unfaithful wife might have the tips of her nose and ears cut off, and her lover might be killed. Divorce, however, was possible with family consent.

Neither divorce nor death freed husband or wife from the marriage tie. The clan of the dead or abandoned spouse took care of the remaining one and saw that proper mourning was observed (one year for a man, four for a woman), and even talking with a person of the opposite sex during that time was adultery. Finally, the clan members provided a new mate from among their numbers, so that the alliance should not lapse. If this was impossible, they provided the widow or widower with new clothes and "set him free."

Southeasterners were elaborate in their mourning, the Creek even paying people to wail, long after the corpse had been interred with elaborate offerings, the house purified, and a new fire lighted there. The Choctaw and Natchez had a custom which suggests ancient burial mounds. They exposed a corpse until the flesh could be picked off by a Buzzard Man or Bone-picker and then placed in, with other skeletons, an earthen mound.

Souls of the dead traveled along the Milky Way, encountering numerous perils until the brave, who had faithfully followed Indian customs, reached the happy hunting ground. This primitive paradise, which had such appeal for whites, did not exist in the beliefs of all

Indians, but the southeasterners seem really to have pictured it. Some even talked of its opposite, a sterile place which was the abode of cowards and lawbreakers.

The government of the Creek may seem informal to a modern white, but, compared with that of many Indian groups, it was well advanced in organization. Among historic Indians, only the Iroquois had gone further. Creek towns, when the whites first knew them in the early 1700's, were scattered over a huge expanse in the plateau country of present Alabama and Georgia. They did not all have the same traditions and ancestry or speak the same dialect. The small, compact group which called itself Muskogi told of arriving first in the country and settling down, with most of their towns in the northern part of the area. They became loosely known as the Upper Creeks. Other peoples, like the Hitchiti and the Alabama, drifted in, with the same general traditions but speaking slightly different languages. These got the name of Lower Creeks. The geographic division was not accurate, and the Creek themselves made another on the basis of descent. The old Muskogi group, no matter where located, called themselves the White People, while the others were the People of Alien Speech. All together they formed a loose alliance, recognizing each other as friends, sometimes sharing ceremonies, and looking to each other for help against enemies—not that they always got it.

A further division along administrative lines was growing up, though it never was thoroughly worked out. By this, the White People called themselves the People of Peace. Their towns were sanctuary for murderers and fleeing enemies. They never took the initiative in war, though they helped their allies when necessary. The People of Alien Speech, the Lower Creeks, were the War, or Red, towns who started wars and furnished no sanctuary. It sounds like a clear and interesting arrangement, but it was never completely workable, clans often gravitating somehow to the wrong side. One would like to know how efficient such an arrangement would have been if it had matured.

As it was, the static conditions of old Indian days did not enforce a tight organization. Each town was a little city-state, which joined the activities of either side only if convenient. Each had a *mico* whom the whites later called a king, and indeed, like the Natchez king, he was carried in a litter and wore a feather cloak. However, the Creek had no such reigning family as the Natchez. The king might be any suitable man chosen from some particular White clan. Other clans furnished his official entourage, consisting of a herald or public orator, an agricultural overseer, a feast manager, and perhaps several assistants. At public ceremonies these all had their places ranged according to rank in one of the four arbors, booths, or "beds." A special bed was usually reserved for the Beloved Men, whose very name is reminiscent of the Natchez castes. However, they were not a hereditary body but retired warriors with fine records who deliberated with the king before action was taken. Indians throughout the Southeast and, indeed, all over the country had councils something like this. However, we do not know of other southeasterners having so many officials as the Creek or making so much of rank.

In tranquil times the Creek council met with the king every day in the public square to talk over village affairs to see that everyone "walked the White path." The occasion was almost as much a religious as a civil one, and before it the whole company often purified themselves with an emetic. This "black drink," ceremonially mixed and handed around, was an infusion of *Ilex vomitoria* esteemed by all the tribes around the Gulf and known to the Cherokee as the "beloved tree."

Over against this civilian organization were the self-made men, the warriors, who had attained rank and title by their prowess. They usually had two "beds," one for the mature warriors and one for beginners. Since all men in the tribe were warriors, clan membership did not matter, but it is said that their leader, Big Warrior, must come from a Red clan. He was, in his way, a kind of priest, for he must have had visions promising spirit aid, and he was the custodian of the sacred war bundle, containing such sacred tokens from the spirits as birdskins and animal claws which gave supernatural help.

It was Big Warrior who initiated a war party if the family of some slain warrior were urging revenge or merely if the young bloods were thirsty for glory. He literally drummed up volunteers by marching around his house drumming. The men who gathered prepared themselves for the adventure by fasting and taking emetics for three days in Big Warrior's house. In the daytime they danced, each man using all his imagination to depict the scouting and killing he hoped to achieve. Finally, they smoked the pipe, which gave binding solemnity to any ceremony, as signatures do for modern whites. He "feelingly knew," thundered a Chickasaw war chief at such a time, that "their tomahawks were thirsty to drink the blood of their enemy and their trusty arrows impatient to be on the wing and lest delay should burn their hearts any longer, he gave them the cool, refreshing word: join the holy ark (the war bundle) and away to cut off the devoted enemy."[17]

The Creek were one of the tribes who made much of close-in fighting with a club of hard wood, its knob sometimes spiked with a sharp point of stone or garfish teeth. Their rations were a few handfuls of parched corn per man, and this, mixed with water, would supply both food and drink. The party of thirty or more padded through the woods in single file, and some aver that they walked in one another's footsteps so none could know how many they were. Ahead walked the leader with the sacred bundle on his back. He never let it touch the ground, and at night, when he rested it on forked sticks, it must always point toward the enemy.

The attack was of the type used by modern commandos—a quick, destructive rush and then safe retirement. "They never face their enemies in open field," said Catesby, "which they say is great folly in the English, but sulk from one covert to another," walking silently through the forests in order to surprise some sleeping town just before dawn.[18] Throwing firebrands on the roofs of the thatched houses was an excellent commando tactic, then a shower of arrows on the escaping inhabitants, and, finally, some clubbing and scalping at close quarters. Scalps of women and children ranked as high as those of men, and, in fact, the Creek considered them more valuable, since they could not be had except by marching right into enemy country.

Scalps were not the only trophies. Like all the circum-Caribbean peoples, the southeasterners considered an arm, a leg, or a head just as good for proclaiming their achievement. Even better was a captive. The Creek did not make great use of slaves, as some other Indians did, and, if they took a few women and children or men who were not burned, these were usually adopted into the tribe. What they wanted was a warrior, in the prime of life, who could be tortured as a public spectacle. When such a man was tied to the slave post in the Creek square, he knew what was in store, and he was ready with his taunting death song. True, if he could escape to the house of the chief medicine man or to a White town, he would be safe. Still, this would have needed the connivance of some of the people, and, for them, this gruesome spectacle was one of the high points of the year, a release for emotions usually held in check. It was the women who took the chief part. Perhaps stabbing a victim with torches and cutting off parts of the body relieved the grief for their lost men which they could not assuage by active battle.

Southeasterners did not not feast on the enemy's body as did the Aztec and a number of South American tribes. The victor, however, did sometimes eat the heart of a brave foe, in order to acquire his virtues. And fighting, though "a man's chief happiness," as the Cherokee said, was shot through with ceremony and always under the guidance of the spirits.

The torture scene had to wait until such warriors as had killed an enemy were freed of danger from his ghost. This attitude, well known in northern and western America, was unusual in the Southeast. The Creek, however, felt that ghosts, anxious to be avenged, would follow the war party home and, unless exorcised, would bring disease. Therefore the returned warriors retired to the house of their priestly leader to fast and take medicine for four days. After that came the victory celebration and honors for the warriors. Those who could recount great achievements might receive such a title as Wild Man or Hardhearted Man, with special tattoo marks and with turbans of swan's feathers for the warriors and eagle feathers for the leader. That is, if the leader had been successful. Woe to him if the expedition had failed or if he had lost a man or two! Such bad judgment and disfavor of the spirits might be overlooked once, but, if it happened again, he would be deposed from his high position, even if he were Big Warrior, the great war chief, himself.

War was a business with the Civilized Tribes and, as such, a principal concern of the spirits. Even games, the "little brother of war," as the Cherokee called them, were undertaken only after fasting and with the help of medicine men. The tribal game, played with two netted racquets and a solid, hair-stuffed ball, was the southeastern version of lacrosse and probably its original. When played between two towns, it aroused as much excitement and involved as much betting as a modern college football game. It was rough enough to mean serious injury and, in fact, was instituted so that young men could distinguish themselves without risk of death in war.

Besides games, the Creek had the excitements of visiting and of trade. The southeasterners had regular trails running through the Gulf states—trails which have now become automobile highways. They could travel long distances by canoe with short portages or on foot, single file, through the forest. Whenever there was peace between tribes, little parties of men must have been always on

the move. Seashells were brought from the coast to the inland region
and copper from the Great Lakes. A crude kind of stool made in
the West Indies appears now and then among the Creek or Cherokee.
Here we have obviously the signs of contact, perhaps of long standing, and with north as well as south. The god-image in the temple
is surely a southern trait. But the Five Tribes believed also in a
number of spirits who often remind us of northern hunting tribes.
These spirits were the plants and animals, which embodied for many
Indians the mysterious force that seems to pervade all nature. Above
them were spirits of the earth and the air, and beyond them all
was Master of Breath, who had created man. This lofty conception
is found among many eastern Indians, yet it is not equivalent to the
white man's idea of God. Master of Breath had indeed given life,
but he did not cherish and guard his people like the Jehovah of the
Bible. Nor is he the master of the happy hunting ground, with some
version of a devil ruling in hell. He is only one spirit among many,
gifted with a special power. It behooves man to show respect to all
spirits, making them small offerings at his meals and his hunt, ob-
serving the ceremonies which they dictated long ago, and obeying
their laws.

Intermediaries between man and the spirits were of two kinds.
One was the priest or doctor, the wise man trained in the rituals
for curing disease, for bringing success in war, and for taking charge
of the temple. Such a man had been through the long course of
training with an older expert, but for some of the high offices it was
necessary that he belong to a certain clan. He has a general relationship to the priests of Nuclear America, who also must learn their
lore and receive their positions by appointment. Different from him
was the inspired Knower, or shaman, who received his knowledge
direct from the spirits. His is a type which we shall frequently meet
among the simpler hunting peoples and which is often more complex. With most southeasterners the inspired shaman still had a
function in foretelling events and in diagnosing disease.

This does not mean that he paid regard to symptoms, for, to
most Indians, the outward form taken by disease had little significance. The important thing was its cause, whether in the breaking
of some taboo, an evil dream, the anger of some offended spirit,
or the malevolence of a human witch. If the cause were dealt with,
the symptoms automatically disappeared. Hence the diagnostic functions of the Knower was one who must discover by trance or other

form of divination what was causing the disease and therefore which expert could dispel it with his formula. With Creek and Cherokee, especially, the animals were frequent causes of disease. The Creek considered that each animal was lord over some ailment which it could cause or cure, depending on how it had been treated. The Cherokee, with even more logic, decided that the animals sent disease in revenge for being killed by the human race but that the plants, in mercy, provided the remedies. Formulas were known to the priest-doctors, to be used in combination with rubbing the patient or spurting medicine over him from mouth or tube, for the internal administration of remedies was not common. Thus the Creek, in curing headache, which was caused by mice, chanted the words:

> Gallop away, gallop away, gallop away!
> Red rat, red cloud.
> My head is hot, is roaring.[19]

The Cherokee believed that the same ailment was caused by the Little People of the mountains. Their doctor chewed ginseng and spurted it over the patient, singsonging the hypnotic words:

> The men have just passed by, they have caused relief.
> The wizards have just passed by, they have caused relief.
> Relief has been rubbed. They have caused relief. Sharp![20]

Ailments caused by human witches might result in the loss of the soul, which was brought back by incantations. Or they could project a foreign object into the body, and this the doctor sucked out through a tube made of sawed-off bison bone. These witches were sometimes thought to be doctors gone wrong. A doctor whose ministrations often failed might be killed on suspicion of such practices, just as a war leader was deposed if not victorious. Southeasterners felt that spirit power, properly used, must always bring success.

Successful doctors, often chosen from special clans, took charge of the round of ceremonies by which the southeasterners kept the favor of the spirits. There were dances to celebrate the ripening of the various wild foods, but the ceremony which stood out above all others was that which celebrated the first eating in midsummer of green corn. The vanished Natchez had a feast of this sort most ceremoniously observed, and we can imagine that many of the Temple Mound people had done the same. All Five Tribes had something of the sort, while the Creek made this occasion, the busk, or *bosquito*, their New Year's festival, at which time each town was purified and set right with the spirits for the year. Aztec and Maya

PLATE II

A MEXICAN TEMPLE

"The Castillo" belongs to the New Empire of the Maya. Underneath this mound is another, probably older, one. The present temple was constructed by facing the accumulation of debris and the earlier structure with well-cut limestone blocks. The Castillo has impressive stairways in the center of each of the four sides which lead to the temple on the top. The temple, built by means of corbeled arches, with the spaces between filled in with gravel and rubble, was also faced with limestone blocks. The function of these temples was principally to house carved images of Maya gods. Most of the religious ceremonies took place on the pyramid platform. (From Morley, 1946; Thompson, 1932.)

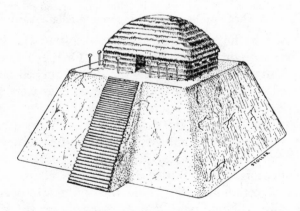

A SOUTHEASTERN TEMPLE

Southeastern temples also were a repository of images of the supernaturals. Surrounding some of them were posts with faces of the gods carved on them. This temple was built in the Lower Mississippi Valley and is part of the Coles Creek culture, a probable archaeological antecedent of the historical Natchez and Creek. The pyramid was built on fill and debris or an old mound, and the sides were covered with mud plaster. The temple was rectangular and built on single rows of posts. The whole building was covered with several layers of grass and reed mats. A stairway, made of log poles over the dirt ramp, led up to the temple. (From Martin, Quimby, Collier, 1947; Swanton, 1946.)

put out their fires every fifty-two years at the end of the Venus cycle and started afresh with a sacred fire from one of the temples. The Creek, like the Natchez, made no such elaborate calculation. Every year, in July, when the first corn was harvested, they swept their homes, put out the fires, and threw away the old dishes. New fire was made at the plaza, where the men sat fasting and purifying themselves with emetics. The Creek used a number of plants for this purpose, most frequently the *Cassine vomitoria*, which was revered by all the maritime tribes.[21] For the solemn occasion, however, two emetics were mixed, each from a number of herbs. They were handed around with the ceremonial cry, "Yahola," and the writer, who has seen this observance, can testify that a man so purified spouted like a hydrant. Nevertheless, the men thus fasted and cleansed themselves for four days, while ranged in their arbors according to rank and listening to laws and admonitory speeches from the officials.

After the purification, new fire was made, and the women, coming to the forbidden holy ground, could light their torches and start home life anew. The new corn, from which everyone had abstained, even if he were reduced to a diet of berries, was now taken to the town granary, cooked like a sacramental feast, and eaten.

At this time all crimes were forgiven except that of murder. New laws were discussed by the council and called out by the crier from the chief's arbor. Boys were scratched and received their new names. Children were lectured by visiting uncles. There were nights of dancing outside the square, sometimes by men and sometimes by women. The celebration ended with a wild, tussling game, when men and women threw a baseball-sized missile at a skull or a carved bird atop a tall pole. Finally, the whole town marched to the near-by stream, men first, then women, then children. After a purifying bath, the ceremony was over and the town right for another year with its gods.

Cherokee and Seminole also took the black drink, and it was a custom among the Timucua in Florida. Some Oklahoma Creek still hold the ceremony, with a few of the midsummer dances, while the Seminole have even more. A favorite among these is the Snake Dance, performed for pleasure and known to whites as the "stomp dance." Here men and women, their hands on each other's shoulders, circle around a fire, the leader roaring out a line of a song and the others responding antiphonally, ever louder and faster. Other ceremonies have lapsed unless they are part of a paid spectacle, to which whites are admitted, for most of the members of all the Five Tribes have been in Oklahoma for over a hundred years and are well on their way to assimilation into modern life.

CIVILIZED TRIBES

FOOD

Vegetable.—Flour and flint corn, beans, coontie, sunflower, cultivation or wild plants; seeds, berries, nuts.
Animal.—Deer, fish, turtle, fowl, shellfish.

HUNTING METHOD

Bow and arrow, fish traps, fish-poisoning; in groups or alone.

CLOTHING

Male.—Breechcloths, ankle-high skin moccasins for traveling. In winter, leggings and poncho-like buckskin shirts. Chief's robe of feathers. Tattooing.
Female.—Early: fiber skirts of twined technique. Later: skirts of cloth. In winter: shawls of skin or cloth. Some ankle-high moccasins.

HOUSE TYPES

Houses on top of mounds for chiefs. Creek: semisubterranean, mud-daubed walls. Seminole: four poles, thatched roof. Temple mounds. Sweat houses for men, oven-shaped of stone or clay. Segregation huts for women.

EQUIPMENT

Household.—Cane basketry: plaited, double and single weave, dyed. Pottery: coiled, cord-marked, punctate, mostly unpainted, effigy types. Wood bedframes, cane lacings. Wood bowls, mortars, stools. Mats of cane.
Transportation.—Canoes of charred and scraped logs.
Hunting.—Self-bow, arrows, blowgun, and darts.
Other.—Cradle: cane mat, flat board and cloth carriers. Pipes: effigy type of clay and stone, simple clay pipes, tubes, T-shaped, elbow type. Miscellaneous: fabrics of nettle, grass, and bark. Braided animal hair used for belts, straps, and garters. Dressed skin for clothing; shell for ornamentation; wood clubs with stone and garfish points. Chunky stones. Litters. Copper and fresh-water pearls for ornaments.

WAR

Bows, arrows, clubs of wood, shields, darts, slings, armor of cane, lances. Early-morning attacks, ambush, surprise, no mass open attack. Took scalps, captives of both sexes at times, other times killed everyone. Some war expeditions gone for weeks.

GAMES

Lacrosse, football, stick-ball (1 and 2 poles), chunky, moccasin game, stick and dice games. Foot races for Seminole and Caddo; "parchesi" for Alabama.

MAP I

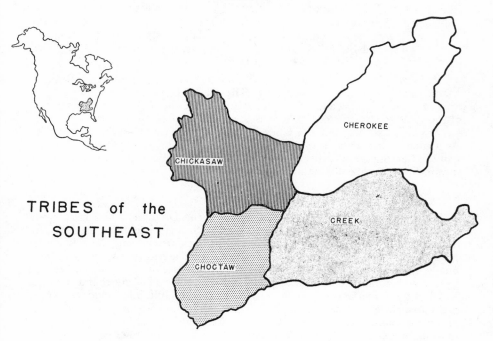

TRIBES of the
SOUTHEAST

SOUTHEASTERN TRIBES ABOUT 1700

The simplified map above shows the southeastern tribes with which this chapter is concerned as they were before the major land cessions and movements which followed white contacts. Even at this date, changes had begun, and some once-powerful tribes were being pushed out of the picture. Those with which this chapter is chiefly concerned are:

Muskogee, or Creek (*Muskogean language stock, Muskogean Division*): Located in the fine corn country of inland Georgia and Alabama. The group, properly called Muskogee, was a small one, toward the north, but with it were allied other peoples of the some general stock, such as Hitchiti, Alabama, and others. Alliance: first Spanish, then English.

Seminole (*Muskogean language stock, Muskogean Division*): Seminole were a subdivision of the Creek who left the main group about 1703 to live in the Florida swamps, by hunting and a little agriculture.

Chickasaw (*Muskogean language stock, Muskogean Division*): Located along the Mississippi River in the northern part of the present state of Mississippi. The customs of this group were very similar to those of the Creek, though their organization was not so elaborate. Alliance: English.

Choctaw (*Muskogean language stock, Muskogean Division*): Located south of the Chickasaw in present Mississippi and Alabama. Living in low, fertile country, the Choctaw were the outstanding agriculturalists in the Southeast. They were peaceful, with an organization more democratic and less formal than that of the Creek or even the Chickasaw. Alliance: French.

Natchez (Muskogean language stock, Natchez Division): Located on the Mississippi River near site of present Natchez. This group diverged in language and customs from the above Muskogean. They were conquered and dispersed by the French in 1730, and few are now to be found.

Cherokee (Iroquoian language stock): Located in the northern Allegheny Mountains, north of the Chickasaw. The Cherokee, with the Tuscarora, in present South Carolina and a few smaller groups, are the southern representatives of the great Iroquoian stock. The Tuscarora moved north to join the League of the Iroquois in 1713, but the Cherokee shared the fate of southeastern tribes. As a mountain people, they placed more emphasis on hunting than on agriculture. Sharing many customs of the Muskogean, their organization was more informal and democratic. Alliance: English.

SURROUNDING GROUPS

Timucua (Muskogean language stock, Timucua Division): This large group in northern Florida was Christianized by the Spanish beginning in 1565. In the 1700's they were practically destroyed by Creek, Yucki, and Catawba under English influence. The Calusa, of southern Florida, and the Muskogean were finally pushed to the Florida Keys, where a few may survive. The Siouan, related to the large groups in the Mississippi Valley and the Plains, are found in South Carolina, in Arkansas, and in one settlement on the Gulf. The Caddoan, whose main area is up the Mississippi and Missouri valleys, appear in Arkansas. A few Algonkian can be seen in South Carolina. Small and almost extinct groups with separate languages are Tunica (Louisiana) and Yuchi (Tennessee).

CHAPTER IV

Encirclement

DE SOTO, that explorer "who was much given to the sport of slaying Indians,"[1] marched in 1540–42 from Florida to Tennessee and then west to the Mississippi. The kidnaping and looting of that expedition went down in Indian tradition, yet it made no real change in southeastern life. It was in the 1600's that whites came to stay. By that time Spain, the first comer, had already founded St. Augustine, Florida (1565), and was spreading her villages of converted Indians both south and west as a buffer against English settlement. In 1673 the English founded their colony of South Carolina, whose huge plantations soon became greedy for slaves. In 1679 the French "took possession of the West" at Saulte Sainte Marie on the Great Lakes, and by 1679 they were at Mobile Bay on the Gulf. Thus the southeastern Indians were boxed in by France on the west, Spain on the south and England on the north. True, the European settlers at first were a mere handful as compared with the Indians. They would have been quite unable to fight either each other or the red man. The plan of each, therefore, was to gain Indian allies, to trade with them for slaves and furs, and to use them as cat's-paws to fight the other whites.

In this, despite all mistakes, they were brilantly successful. The Indians had always fought each other, rather for glory and excitement than from any actual need. As the Cherokee said: "We cannot live without war. Should we make peace with the Tuscaroras (their current enemy) we must immediately look out for some other nation with whom we can be engaged in our beloved occupation."[2] Naturally, a war party was delighted to have the help of even a few white men armed with guns and even ready to supply some. Therefore, the Creek never hesitated a moment in helping South Carolina to destroy the Christianized Spanish Indians (Yamasee, Georgia, 1680; Apalachee, Florida, 1704). The British protested that they took

47

no slaves on these raids, but there was nothing to prevent their buying the thirty-five hundred captured by the Creek.

Animosity naturally began to run high among the Indians. It was after the second Creek attack on Spanish possessions, with its tightened organization and its danger of reprisal, that one group of Creek and other Indians retired to the Florida swamps. Later (1775) they were to be dubbed the Seminole (runaways, outlaws, or separatists). In the meantime they provided a refuge for runaway slaves, both Indian and Negro, and for any other individuals who found the new atmosphere of war and primitive power politics not to their taste.

Roughly speaking, the Indian-white alliances followed geographic lines. The Choctaw and Natchez along the Mississippi were usually on the French side, until a clash in 1732, after which the Natchez were dispersed and vanished from history. The Chickasaw and Cherokee clung to their English neighbors, while the huge Creek confederacy jockeyed between the English at the north and the Spanish at the south. Each European nation attempted to court its Indian allies with trade, and soon knives and brass kettles began to replace stone implements and pots. The use of buckskin faded out as deer grew scarce with intensive hunting. Native weaving disappeared. Pictures of prominent Indians from early trading days show the feather headdress replaced by a silk turban, heron feathers by ostrich plumes, and the shell pendant by a silver medal, bearing the name of some European monarch. The Seminole, in close contact with Spain, began to decorate their cotton shirts with strips of bright-colored material, sewed on in imitation of the striped brocade worn by Spanish officials in full dress.

It was England, with her blossoming industries, which could offer the best bargains. Soon English traders were living among the Cherokee, Chickasaw, and Creek, and their influence was potent for a century afterward. These adventurers did not meet the Indians as superior beings, condescending to savages. In those days, before the machine age, a poor white man had few more comforts than an Indian. He found small hardship in eating coarse food, sleeping on the ground, and wearing the same clothes—or lack of them—day in and day out. Indeed, if he sought his fortune in the European wars, he might live through years of far less comfort than Indians knew.

Therefore a trader fought, camped, and hunted with his Indian customer as a brother and an equal—albeit a brother of chiefs, since he had such wealth to dispense. He usually married into the chief's family, and, since descent was through the mother, his sons might become chiefs. Such names of later leaders as Ross, Mackintosh, Mac-Donald, Ridge, and McGillivray indicate how often this happened. Divorce being easy, the mixed-blood children felt no disgrace if their father chose to desert to the old country. However, he had small temptation to do this unless he fell heir to an estate like Lachlan McGillivray. Quite often he settled down, planted garden and orchard, and built a log house on a new and extensive style unknown to the Indians; perhaps he taught his women to make cheese and butter or to weave on a European foot loom. As his friends and relatives copied these conveniences, a knowledge of the new ways came to the Five Tribes through natural channels and with sufficient time for smooth infiltration.

Still, the trader was never unmindful of the interest of his own nation, and often he was the guiding force in Indian alliances and wars. For the European colonies were now growing stronger, and the three-sided pressure against the Indians was increasing. There were various treaties and some gifts and sales of land. There was growing tension and sometimes bitter disagreement among segments of a tribe as to what side they should take. We begin to hear the names of prominent chiefs who were passionate on the side of peace or war, old ways or new. And here appears a phenomenon which was frequent among Indians when the white enemy hove in view. The chief gained greater power than he had had before, since crisis needs a dictator.

It was in this period that the Creek confederacy blossomed and spread, with lesser tribes, pushed out by the Europeans or their allies, clinging to the larger group for support. Perhaps the Creek would never have attained even the fluid organization reported for them if they had not had European institutions both to imitate and to dread. The Creek did not recognize the death stab given them when the colony of Georgia was founded in 1732. They even sold land to the pleasant-spoken Ogilvie, unaware that his grant from the crown included almost all their land.

Meantime the three Old World nations had locked together in Europe in the Seven Years' War (1756–63). They were getting no results, so France, Spain, and England decided to fight it out in America, using Indians as pawns. Thus began the French and Indian War (1755–63). Southeastern Indians were not deeply concerned in this war, which took place mostly to the west and north. The treaty of 1763, however, struck the first notes of their doom. France was eliminated from the New World. Spain was pushed west of the Mississippi, giving up Florida to England but receiving New Orleans from France. England got the eastern half of the continent, from the Gulf of Mexico to Hudson Bay.

The Indians found themselves British subjects, with an administrator to supervise them. They had, by this time, learned a good deal about organization from their constant contact with European negotiators. The Creek confederacy, particularly, was a powerful union so strong that it practically subjugated the Cherokee and nearly did the same to the Choctaw. This blossoming time was brief. Less than thirteen years after the treaty of peace had been signed, their protector England was at war with the thirteen colonies.

The British were ousted. They made peace and departed without a word to the Indians. Now, throughout the wilder parts of the country, there was a stirring of red men, who at last began to realize the suffocating power which was pressing against them. Tecumseh, the great northern leader whose place is in another chapter, came south to urge that all the Indians in the country should unite. It was too late. Tecumseh's plans failed, but at last the southeasterners began to understand their danger. Some of the Creek—they never could unite completely—fought brutally and furiously until Andrew Jackson quelled them, with equal brutality (1814). He had to do the same to the Seminole a few years later.

The Indian power was broken. Most tribes had already given up large tracts of land, and now they began to understand that peace and co-operation was the one hope. Inspired, perhaps, by the numbers of mixed-bloods among them, the tribes made desperate attempts to show themselves desirable citizens for the United States. Between 1817 and 1830 the Choctaw and Creek compiled written codes of laws in English. The Cherokee adopted a constitution, very much like that of the United States. Sequoyah, the grandson of an English officer, worked out a syllabary for writing Cherokee, and it is said that within a few months the whole tribe was literate in its native language. The Creek followed suit. There were now Protestant missionaries scattered through the tribes, and soon hymns and translations of the Bible made their appearance in Creek and Cherokee. In most tribes there were mixed-blood leaders, able to write letters in English and even journey to New York to visit powerful politicians and plead for their rights.

It is interesting to know that Congress at one time considered carving out an Indian state in the Southeast and admitting it to the Union. Could it have been done? Could the customs of the Indians, so different, though so reasonable, have been fitted into the plan of American government?

The proposal never reached serious discussion. The state of Georgia, which had once entered Creek country like a camel putting its head into the tent, was now clamoring for more Creek land. In 1802 the state had made an agreement with the federal government to relinquish its claims to what is now Alabama and Mississippi if the Indians could be removed from Georgia proper. Lands west of the Mississippi had now been bought from Napoleon (1803), and settlers were flooding across the Indian lands, committing depredations as they went. "What land we have left," complained Opothle Mico of the Creek, "is but large enough to live and walk on."[3] The Indians would have to go.

The better informed among them had already seen the handwriting on the wall, and, from 1780 on, some groups of Creek, Choctaw, and Cherokee had been migrating to the unknown lands across the Mississippi. In 1824 a tiny Indian Office, with a commissioner and two clerks, had been created within the War Department expressly to help with the buying of Indian lands and in assisting the dispossessed Indians. In 1830 Congress passed a law authorizing the buying-up of Indian lands and the removal of Indians, at government expense, to lands which would be purchased across the Mississippi.

This removal is the tragic event from which the Five Tribes date their modern history. It was not accomplished without desperate resistance. Chief William McIntosh, who had signed a treaty giving up Creek lands, was shot down by his people as a traitor. The Cherokee, given two years for preparation, refused to move and were finally expelled from their homes by soldiers. "Are we to be hunted through the mountains like wild beasts?" asked a Cherokee petition.[4] Some Cherokee escaped the soldiers and lived in caves until the government bought land for them in North Carolina, where they are today. Some Choctaw are in Texas, and a few thousand Seminole held out in the Everglades for five years until the United States army and navy, having lost a total of fifteen hundred men,[5] retired and let them alone.

These rifts among the tribes, lasting long after removal, were a body blow to the old communal way of life. Another was the secret diplomacy of the chiefs who made the agreements. A town or war leader had always had great prestige and had been looked upon as an aristocrat compared with the untried young warriors. Never had he had any large amount of wealth to control and especially not money. When the white men, well used to diplomatic bribery, offered the chiefs large bonuses for bringing their people into line, many of them accepted. It may be that a kindly, co-operative system cannot persist where there is surplus wealth for someone to lay hands on. At least it is on record that, of $247,000 paid to the Creek, $160,000 went to individual chiefs. They had learned what power in the modern world could mean, and the tribes were never again rid of such "grafters."

Whether persuaded by their leaders or not, a majority in each tribe finally realized that it was move or perish, and within a decade the tragic uprooting was accomplished. (The Choctaw moved in 1832, the Chickasaw in 1832–34, the Seminole in 1836, the Creek in 1836–40, and the Cherokee in 1838–39.) They sold their cattle and improvements at enormous loss, since the whites knew they could not hold on for a high price. They carried with them the temple fires or, some say, merely the ashes which were to serve as the hearth for new flames. Men with feathered wands guided the Creek travelers to make them light-footed. A few devoted Protestant missionaries trudged with their converts into the new life. Yet the journey was a hideous one, partly from mismanagement and lack of supplies, partly from the deadly haste of the escorting troops, who would not allow them to tend the sick or bury the dead. No wonder the Cherokee call it "the Trail of Tears"! Of one contingent of them, comprising twelve thousand, one-third died en route.[6] A broken-hearted Creek woman made this song, which was taken up by her companions:

> I have no more land.
> I am driven away from home
> Driven up the red waters
> Let us all go.
> Let us all die together. . . .[7]

Without their long training in agriculture and in organization, without the constant ceremonies which held them together, it is doubtful whether the tribes could have made as vigorous a new start as they did. True, the new country was a horrifying wilderness, infested sometimes by wild tribes and lawless pioneers. True, their governments suffered sometimes from venality and factionalism. Yet they did clear the woods in the new land purchased for them, which is now eastern Oklahoma. (Actually they had been granted most of the present state.) They used their government money for gristmills, sawmills, and schools. Bibles, hymnbooks, and newspapers were published in the native languages. Missionary teachers reported that busy adults begged them to hold school by moonlight. The Cherokee set up two seminaries, one for boys, one for girls, and sent emissaries east to select the proper teachers.

Their government, shorn of red tape, functioned so well that an offender, condemned to death, could be allowed to go home and settle his affairs, then would present himself for execution on the proper day. Liquor, destined for army posts near by, was confiscated and poured out if it passed through Indian territory. Nevertheless, seeds of disruption for the old life were already sown. Indian towns had usually held their land in common, allowing each family to select such tracts as it could till and keep them as long as it tilled them. When families were all about the same size, barring war losses, this worked little injustice. Now there were rich tribal members, often mixed-bloods, owning numbers of slaves and used to commercial farming. Like any white man, they hastened to claim large tracts of good farming land and even to increase them as their wealth and slaves increased. The poor, small families sought the back country, which reminded them of home and where they tilled only small garden patches. The modern division between rich and poor had begun.

This second wind of the Five Tribes was practically knocked out of them by the War between the States. The Indians had wished no part in this catastrophe, yet they were slaveholders, and many were finally drawn in on the southern side. Some miserable northern sympathizers were driven from their homes and spent months of cold and starvation. Yet war swept through the whole country, and, when it was over, there was nothing left of the Indian homes but ashes and chimneys.

Worse was to come. The United States declared that the Indians, having fought against the Union, had broken their treaties and must make new ones. In these new ones there was no hope of their retaining the huge lands granted them when all the country west of the Mississippi seemed empty and undesired. Now there were hordes of white pioneers and discharged soldiers clamoring for farms. The wild tribes farther west were being subdued and must have reservations. The Five Tribes, in the end, were forced to give up all the

western part of what is now Oklahoma, the flat prairies so good
for cattle ranches. Even a part of their eastern land had to be relinquished to accommodate some small, displaced tribes. They must
also promise to free their slaves and either admit them to tribal membership or give them land. And they must permit the passage of
railroads through their country. Life was beginning in a strange
country for the second time and on much harder terms.

We cannot follow each move in the slow lapse of old ways as new
situations and new neighbors made these unworkable. Land-hungry
whites were again at fever pitch, and it was this, as well as the desire
to remake the Indian, which inspired the next government move.
The Dawes Act appears in this chapter for the first time but will be
seen again and again, gliding through the waves of Indian history.
It provided that all lands granted to Indians might be cut up into
separate farms (generally of 160 acres, the norm of New England).
Each man, woman, and child on the rolls of a tribe might receive such
an allotment and be thereby started on the road to self-support and
self-respect. A blessing, thought the reformers and Indian sympathizers, for what white man ever received such a boon! But there
was a joker. All land left over after such allotment would be thrown
open to homesteaders.

The domain of the Five Tribes was allotted in the 1890's. It soon
became apparent that many who did not speak English or understand white ways were being cheated out of their land. A later law
therefore provided that the Indian did not attain fee simple or full
possession for twenty-five years or until he had shown himself "competent" to handle business. Meantime, he had a guardian who managed his affairs for a fee. Many were the lawyers who grew rich
on guardianship fees in Oklahoma, and some are said to do so to
the present day. Knowledgeable Indians, however, often kept their
land and made money from it. When coal was discovered here and
there (there was not much oil in eastern Oklahoma), and when the
railroads began to buy up rights of way, there was a further chance for
individuals to grow rich.

The old communal life was yielding to pressure. The future of the
Indians obviously lay in ceasing to be Indians except in memory.
Yet their move into modern life was not blocked by such a sense
of inferiority as beset some other groups. In fact, when whites first
began to enter Oklahoma, it was they who were the inferiors. These
roaming land-seekers owned no property, while some Indians had

large, well-tilled farms. The homesteaders at first had no government and certainly no schools, while the Indians had both. Mixed-blood marriages were not scorned, for many a roaming adventurer was glad enough to marry an Indian woman and, according to the custom, settle down on her family's farm. The educated and prosperous among the Oklahoma Indians have never felt inferior and do not today.

At last there were enough whites in Oklahoma at the west and Indian territory at the east, so that they called for statehood. In 1907 the two were combined as the state of Oklahoma. The tribal governments were dissolved and directed to turn their funds in to the United States Treasury. Indians are ruled now in the same way as any other citizen. They are citizens, with the right to vote both in federal and in state elections. Many Indians have held public office, and the part-Cherokee, Garner, even became vice-president of the United States. Children of the Five Tribes attend the public schools, the Indian Service paying the school boards a certain sum for each pupil, to make up for the real estate taxes Indians do not pay. It also maintains two boarding schools for children of broken homes. Many Indians go to college, either on funds borrowed from the Indian Service or sent by their families. As a result the Five Tribes can boast of doctors, lawyers, and businessmen as well as numbers of professionals in the Indian Service.

All individuals have not gone ahead at an equal pace, for that would be too much to ask. On one side we have successes like the late Will Rogers, whose Indian ancestry would never have been suspected, had he not made a jovial boast of it. On the other are poor families living in the hills and trying futilely to cling to the old ways, their old people sometimes not speaking English. It is for the benefit of these that the Indian Service maintains a force at Muskogee, Oklahoma, advising them about sale of crops and taking charge of their land. In view of abuses, all sale of Indian land has been prohibited since 1934, and these people often beg that guardianship be continued indefinitely.

That is against modern understanding of the Indians' interests. It is time now, Uncle Sam has announced, that the red man should emerge from the leading strings which have begun to cripple him. Perhaps, in the beginning, all his steps needed guidance and curbing, though that is open to question. Now that many generations have passed since he began to walk the white man's road, paternal care may be oppressive. The white man has made mistakes which glare through history. Why should not the Indian be left free to make a few dollars, even though he may lose money and take some hard knocks. Such was the government policy in the year 1951. It is planned that government management shall be removed—rapidly from some of the more advanced tribes, more slowly from the more

MAP II

SOUTHEASTERN TRIBES IN INDIAN TERRITORY

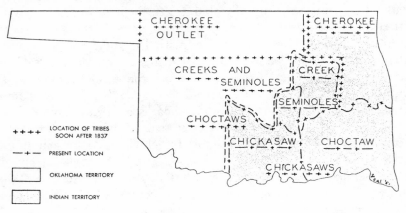

helpless ones—and the Indians, except for their treaty lands, will be placed in the same situation as any other citizen.

Before withdrawing, the government must be sure that it leaves no unfulfilled promises. Therefore a court of claims has been set up, where each tribe may bring proof of unpaid treaty moneys or of land improperly taken. The Creek have already received some large payments under this arrangement, and so may others. They will go forth from Uncle Sam's too-fostering care better equipped than some of the early white colonists. There is good hope that many of them will progress equally well, for they, too, have been for centuries Civilized Tribes.

CHAPTER V

They Have Gone

W HEN early English colonists spoke and wrote about Indians, they described stealthy footed sons of the forest whose painted faces, crowned only by a scalp lock, used to peer into log-cabin windows in New England and New York State. These were the red men who greeted the Pilgrim Fathers, who taught them to plant corn, to fertilize with fishheads, and to bake clams on the beach under seaweed. It was they who were glorified in Cooper's *The Last of the Mohicans* and Longfellow's *Hiawatha*. They left imbedded in our language such words as "squash," "succotash," "hominy," "moose," "squaw," "papoose," and "tomahawk." Their language, known to specialists as Algonkian, gave us such place names as Massachusetts, Connecticut, Illinois, and Allegheny. In fact, were Algonkian names deleted, the map of the eastern states might look like a partial desert.

The Algonkian language family, with its relatives, near and distant, is one of the most widespread in North America. On the front endpaper map it is seen stretching solidly from Labrador to beyond Hudson Bay, and once it may have reached far into our northeastern states.[1] That ancient domain has been wrenched apart, leaving two long southward streamers, one down the Mississippi Valley, and another along the Atlantic seaboard, where its southern tip joins the Muskogean of chapter iii. Algonkian country thus knows all the variations, from arctic waste to lush river bottoms, in the country which is now our corn belt. Algonkian lifeways ring the changes from that of simple hunting people, almost devoid of government, to little kingdoms, insistent on their savage pomp. They cannot be described as a unit but must be split into at least three groups: northern hunters, corn-growers of the Atlantic seaboard, and corn-growers of the Great Lakes and the Mississippi Valley. This chapter will consider only the first two, who were separated in history and, in part, in culture from their kinsmen west of the Appalachian chains and even around the Great Lakes.

PLATE III

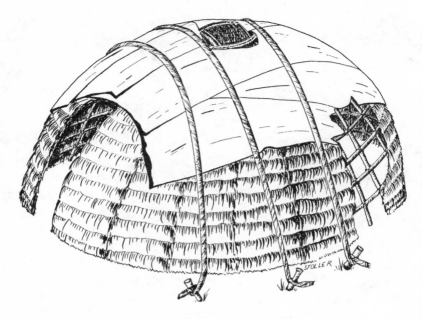

Wigwam

The wigwam, characterized by a dome-shaped top, might be round or oval and of any size. The materials used in the structure were poles or saplings, birch bark, and bulrushes; cattails and cedar bark, as well as grass, were used in mats and tied together with green basswood bark and twine.

The frame might consist of six slender poles (three on each side), set in the long diameter, and eight poles (four on each side), set in the shorter diameter. The poles were stuck firmly in the ground, with the ends twisted together overhead, thus forming an arch. The intersections of the long and short sides of the frame were tied together with basswood bark. Lengthwise and crosswise supports and two or more encircling poles serving as braces were added.

The sides of the framework were covered with woven mats or birch bark, sometimes in two layers for additional warmth, and tied inside to the framework. The top of the wigwam was covered with sheets of birch bark about 10 or 12 feet long. They were overlapped or sewed together with narrow strips of basswood bark. The corners were sometimes secured by strips of bark passed between the rushes and tied to the framework, and the sheets were further held in place by strips of bark or ropes of twined fibers long enough to extend entirely over the structure and secured to stakes or heavy stones on both sides.

The men usually prepared the poles and made the framework, over which the women fastened mats or other coverings. (From Lyford, 1945.)

Was it merely a difference in geography which caused these little Indian groups to differ almost as much as early Lapps and early Italians? Most experts think it was also the neighbors from whom they learned, after the usual Indian manner. Suppose that the earliest Algonkian immigrants were merely simple hunters, as the northernmost are still! They may well have been among the earliest arrivals, hunting

PLATE IV

PENOBSCOT TIPI

The conical bark shelter, or tipi, was built on a framework of two sets of poles, one set inside and one outside. The inner poles support the bark and the outer help to hold it in position.

Nine poles are used for the inner frame. Four of these are tied together in pairs with cedar rope and are laid one pair on top of the other. After they have been erected, the other poles are laid between them, and a hoop of flexible wood is fastened to their inner side about two-thirds of the way up for additional strength. The strips of birch bark are then added; they are lapped and sewed together and are bound to the poles.

The outside poles are then put in position, one opposite each pole inside. They are secured by tying the upper ends to the corresponding poles inside, just above the last tier of bark. The door was made of tanned moosehide and laced to the lintel. (From A. A. Orchard, 1909; Speck, 1940.)

mammoth and mastodon, for they left spear points very like those in the Plains and the Southwest. Suppose that, like the Eskimo later, they felt that big-game hunting and meat-eating was the only right way for a man. Might they then have followed the receding ice and the big animals which were known in our Northeast long after they had disappeared from drying southern countries? The Naskapi and the Montagnais, northern hunters to this day, have a system of hunting rights, hunting magic, and conservation of game which might reflect some of that ancient lifeway.

These hunting groups north of the Canadian border must be omitted for sheer lack of space.[2] However, the Algonkian of the United States cannot be seen in true perspective without some glimpse of these more primitive relatives. The United States Algonkian, it will soon appear, have adopted various forms of government and ceremony depending on the neighbors who influenced them. In following those changes, it is interesting to look back on the great spread of hunting people who were practically without ceremony or organized government. This may have been the start from which further developments were made.

The Canadian Algonkian were hunters of deer, elk, and caribou. We can picture them dressed in skins which, in early days, were put together without sewing. In the inhospitable wastes where many of them roamed, starvation was frequent. In order to keep alive at all, it was necessary to develop an almost perfect adaptation to the environment, granted the materials and the skill they had. Though much of their domain was forest country, they had no tools for hewing down great logs. Their materials were light poles and bark, and here the forest provided an asset of which they made full use. The canoe birch (*Betula papyrifera*) made the light canoe in which they traveled the streams which served as their highways. Birch bark, folded and sewed with vines, made their containers, even those for cooking, for they used an ancient device of nonpottery-making people, dropping hot stones into a liquid until it boiled. Birch bark also made the toboggan which men dragged on snowshoes. The snowshoes, we might mention, were so adequately planned for different kinds of snow that the same shapes are sold in the shops of today. All this equipment, which must have meant centuries of trial and error, was used on occasion by the Algonkian of the United States.

Northern hunters usually wandered in small bands, since larger companies would frighten and use up the game animals. In southern

PLATE V

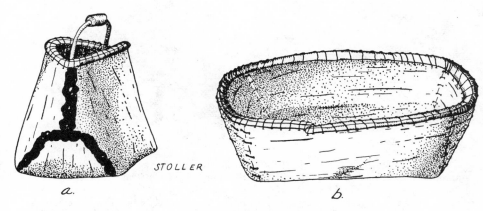

STOLLER

a.   *b.*

Birch-Bark Containers

The bark is gathered from a felled tree by peeling it slowly and carefully with chisels or wedges. The rough white outer layers and light-brown inner layers were usually used to make containers. The innermost layer—dark brown in color—was frequently used for decoration.

The two types of containers made were watertight and nonwatertight. The former was made of one sheet of material, folded with seams and fastened at the sides. The sheet of bark was heated over a small fire or in the steam from boiling water to make it pliable; then it could be bent into any shape desirable, and the shape was retained when the bark cooled. The folds were further secured with basswood fiber or skinned spruce roots. They usually had hoop rims of willow, and blades to suspend them over the fire, since one of their main uses was for cooking.

For nonwatertight containers the bark was cut out according to special patterns and sewed with roots or fiber (*b*), or they might have had pitch smeared over the seams (*a*). This also made them watertight.

The most common container is the *mocock* (*a*), which was used for storing or carrying food or water. Other containers were bowls, serving dishes, and trays (*b*), the latter used for winnowing wild rice. Containers were often decorated by scraping, with bark appliqué, with spruce root, porcupine quill, and moosehair embroidery, and beading and painting. (From Lyford and Speck, 1940.)

PLATE VI

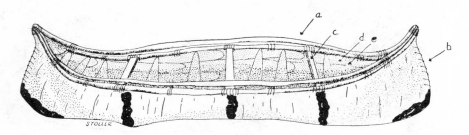

Birch-Bark Canoes

Canoes varied somewhat from tribe to tribe in the amount of curvature at bow and stern and in a few other details, but the methods of construction and the general shape were much the same everywhere it was used. (The drawing shows one made by the River Desert Algonkian of eastern Canada.) They ranged in size from small river canoes handled by one or two men to large lake canoes handled by eight or ten. If all the materials were prepared, a man and woman could make a canoe in about two weeks.

The heavy birch bark, preferably a single sheet, was laid on the ground with stones on it to hold the bark down. Two false gunwales were laid upon the bark, and the workmen bent up the sides and drove a series of stakes, arranged to flare outward slightly, around the periphery. The main rails of the gunwale (a) were then fitted into place, one inside and one outside, and sewn at intervals with spruce root or basswood fibers. Curved pieces of cedar, bent to give the bow and stern their shapes (b), were covered with bark and sewn in with spruce roots. The thwarts (c) were sewn and mortised to the inside rail.

The lining was next applied (d). It was usually made of thin cedar strips, laid lengthwise, and tightly secured between the bark and ribs. The latter (e) are also of cedar and were placed under the gunwales by a wooden mallet.

To complete the process, fir or spruce pitch was spread on the outside seams or edges.

In areas where birch trees were scarce, spruce and elm bark, or even moosehides, was used on the canoes. The extreme lightness of the canoe more than compensated for its frailty, for it could be carried by one man over several miles of portage. It could also be easily repaired.

Although typical of the Algonkian of eastern Canada, the birch-bark canoe was used by many tribes throughout the interior of Canada to the Cordillera region of British Columbia. (From Lyford and Speck, 1940; Jenness, 1934.)

Canada, where vegetation was more luxuriant and game more abundant, there were inherited family hunting territories, an arrangement to be found among many primitive peoples who hunt for a living.[3] There was almost no organized government. Some kindly patriarch acted as leader of a group, deciding on the dates for moving and making sure that all in his band or family observed the taboos imposed long ago by the spirits. For instance, every woman must segregate herself once a month and at childbirth, lest the mysterious force which temporarily imbued her should take away a man's hunting power.

As their customs unroll in this narrative, it will be obvious that the simpler groups are those which observe the most taboos and ceremonies on the subject. With others, the girl's ceremony may be overlaid or forgotten in the stress of great communal rites.

The man, too, must be aware of the spirits, whenever he would go out on the perilous task of hunting. One is inclined to attribute great age to the belief of many Indian tribes that the animals, in human form, were the first denizens of the earth. They have since donned fur, scales, and feathers, but they can take human form when they wish. "You and I have the same mind and spiritual strength," said the Naskapi conjuror in addressing them.[4] These powerful beings lived in villages, each under its chief or owner. There fortunate dreamers might be taken to visit and might see them again in their human form. The animals and especially their chiefs had to be implored for their favor with what was, for the Cree, a constant round of ceremony.[5]

Yet man was obliged to kill them. The answer was a neat theological theory, common to hunting people all the way across the continent and beyond. According to this, the slain animals did not die. Their spirits returned to their villages, but they noted with jealous care the treatment given their bones. These must be kept out of the way of dogs and of menstruating women, those beings temporally surrounded with a supernatural aura. Bones of water creatures must be thrown back into the water. Those of land creatures, at least the skull, must be hung up, often with a prayer and a ceremonial smoke. So thought almost all American hunting tribes, the belief being slightly altered according to the needs of each. One can imagine it as originating long ago when man, bereft of wings, claws, and fur, found himself decidedly the inferior of many creatures around him.

The belief in vision power from an animal was, of course, an individualistic religion, since each hunter faced his perils alone. There were almost no community ceremonies, since rarely could the wan-

derers feed a large gathering, even for a few days. Very occasionally
a hunter, with his tent full of skins and meat, would give an Eat-It-
All feast, when the visitors gorged themselves for days and each man
acted out his exploits. Naturally, the animals would have been offended at such waste of meat. So the tent openings were tightly
closed, and no one was allowed out until all food was consumed.

There were, too, occasional gatherings around the lodge of the
medicine man or "drum person."[6] Students often call him by the
Siberian term, "shaman."

> I sit down and beat the drum, he sang.
> And by the sound of the drum I call the animals
> from the mountains.[7]

Thus he drummed himself into a trance while the lodge shook and
invisible spirits arrived whistling. The people heard him question them
about the future, about lost articles and causes of illness. Finally, he
emerged, like a modern medium, stating that he knew nothing of
what had happened.

The shaman and all the group were constantly preoccupied with
the world of spirits, to which they must give offerings of tobacco
(traded into the northern country, since it could not be grown). Not
only were there the animals with their Owners and chiefs but there
was the Great Being, Owner of them all. This seems to be an ancient
belief, though the Owner was no cherishing Father but distant and
inactive. There was also a sort of primitive savior, or culture hero,
of a sort to be found in many an Indian tribe. Gluskabe (or Gloos-
cap) was a joker and trickster as well as a benefactor of mankind,
but it was he who made the world fit to live in. We shall come
upon many an Indian "culture hero" like Gluskabe, sometimes in
human form, sometimes shifting between human and animal. He is
no idealized figure but at times tricky, grotesque, and even obscene
according to white man's standards. To the Indian, he may have
seemed merely an epitome of human nature but with added powers,
which he used for good oftener than for ill.

The beginning of the world is lost, for the Algonkian, in the mists
of the past. What they know is that, when the animals assumed
their present form and the Creator made man, much in the landscape was wrong. Gluskabe went about setting it right, but there
were some monsters whom he could not conquer. Here it is notice-
able that the people of the North Woods have evolved some particularly gruesome beings whose like is not met in the sunny South.

Most dreadful was the Witigo, or cannibal monster, who devoured lone hunters and spit them out as cannibals.

Is this an ancient tale, from the time when hard-pressed hunters actually did practice cannibalism? We have few facts about the early hunters of the eastern coast, for their history is only now being deciphered. While early man was hunting mammoth in New Mexico, this region was covered with ice. We can imagine that, as New Mexico grew drier and the northern ice melted, some of the big animals might have moved north, keeping to the climate which suited them. Hunters might have followed. Perhaps the scattered spear points, as yet undated, indicate some early mastodon-hunters in the days of melting glaciers. At least, by about five thousand years ago, long-headed Sylvid hunters were shooting deer and gathering berries in central New York State.[8] Others were building fishweirs in shallow water now covered by the sidewalks of Boston.[9] After that, the story follows familiar lines. We see the Sylvids gradually spreading, and then come the revolutionary events already noticed to the south. They learn to make pottery, they learn agriculture, and they mix with an arriving broadheaded people.

The first sign of radical change is when they begin to make a rough pottery, with conical base, that same ware which is identified all the way from Mongolia, through eastern Siberia, Alaska, Wyoming, Colorado, Nebraska, and so into the Mississippi Valley.[10] Some students have suggested that it was brought by the Algonkian,[11] but the picture we have of that group does not suggest an ancient farming people. As we follow them across the country, we shall see that they did indeed learn, as all Indians did, but that their learning was added, hit-or-miss fashion, to habits and religion built up for hunters. Whether pottery was brought by a new group of people or by a second instalment of Algonkian or whether the news merely traveled by itself is a question to be answered by further digging. Meanwhile, we can follow the use of pottery and of burial mounds, or barrows, into the Mississippi Valley and then the Ohio. There grew up the magnificent civic center of Hopewell (see p. 84), which had not only pottery and burial mounds but agriculture, stone-carving, copper, mica, and, no doubt, a civic organization. The influence of that center rayed out in all directions, and we shall constantly meet it as this narrative moves west. It reached into the northeastern states somewhat late (one guess is after A.D. 900). Then began the usual change, from the nomadic hunting life of the forest to that of villagers who settled, at least for the summer,

among their cleared fields. All through the Northeast corn was raised
in the same varieties as in the Mississippi Valley. It was pounded up
in the same kind of wooden mortar and made into the same corn
soup and succotash. Settled life was now possible, at least for part of
the year, and the Indians built villages of little domed "wigwams"
(an Algonkian word), covered with bark, skin, or mats.

Here there was no starvation. The continuous forest of oak, elm,
ash, and chestnut had not the lush fertility of the Gulf states, but
still, said an old Maine man, "it was as easy then for the Indians to
pick up berries, game and fish as it is now for them to pick up snow"
in winter.[12] Even under this changed exterior, we can recognize a few
of the old hunting ways. Descent was counted in the male line, hunter
fashion. Men still went on the long winter hunt, and we hear something of hunting territories, of boys giving away their first kill, and of
careful disposal of animal bones. Families even made a food-gathering
circuit, though often in a canoe of elm bark or a dugout.

In summer, like their northern neighbors, they gathered at the fishing grounds and near by they made their cornfields. These were used
by families, for the Algonkian, we shall note, had a well-developed
sense of land rights. However, the rights to fields often went down in
the female line, for the women did most of the work. Men did pre-
pare the slash-and-burn fields and helped put in the corn—flint, flour,
dent, and pop, the first two in four, five, and six colors. Seeds were
planted in April, when little fish known as alewives swarmed up the
streams, and it was the heads of these which helped to fertilize the
stony New England fields. The plants were "hilled up" to make the
roots strong, the method which white farmers learned from the Indians, along with the recipes for hominy, succotash, corn pone, and
a score of others. Did they also learn that four kernels must be put in
every hill? Yankee farmers still recite the rhyme

> One for the beetle
> One for the crow
> One for the cutworm
> And one to grow

and they will tell you it was composed by their ancestors. But why
did the ancestors use the Indian ceremonial number of four instead
of the whites' number three?

All summer, women tended the fields with hoes of bone or shell,
while the men traveled and fished. In those days whales and seals
sported even in Massachusetts Bay, and there were plenty of clams

and lobsters for the taking. Then came fall and winter hunting, while the deer and beaver were prime and, with spring, the delicious excitement of tapping the sugar maples for syrup.

These Algonkians did not need to dismantle their houses and travel as often as did their northern kinsmen. For much of the year they might live in a village of a hundred huts or so. With some tribes, each hut held two or three families. The material was poles and bark, as in the north, but since the useful birch did not grow south of New York, often the heavier elm had to be used. Or the housewife might make cattail mats. The house was the wigwam, which means a domed frame of slender poles, covered with bark or mats. Within it were the same general articles to be found in the north plus pottery and many utensils of basketry. The seaboard Algonkian woman had a wealth of vegetal material from which to make baskets, mats, fishnets, even garters, packstraps, and long sashes.

She could put deerskin together with awl and thong, so we may picture her in skirt and loose sack and her man in a breechcloth. The long braids and dignified headdress so familiar in popular pictures of Indians were unknown here. The man's head was shaved of all but a scalp lock. Or, rather, the hairs were pulled out with mussel-shell tweezers. For war and for ceremonies his face was painted, and, in addition, there were such refinements as crowns of upright feathers, turkey-feather cloaks,[13] and necklaces of bone and shell, and perhaps that Algonkian specialty: wampum. This term, loosely used by whites to mean any kind of shell money, had for the Indians a sacred significance as the "white string," "the old dark string," or "Indian stones."[14] So highly did they regard it that the Algonkian, who have different plural forms for animate and for inanimate nouns, always rank wampum as animate.

In New England, at first, only chiefs wore the beads, but in the New Netherlands, where the shells were more common, women had rows of wampum on their buckskin skirts; they bound their hair with the strings, decorated their caps, and wore wampum necklaces, bracelets, and belts.[15] The wampum known to history was made only after the whites had brought steel tools. Then beads could be made in tubular shape, slender and smooth. Beads from the dark blue of the clamshells were combined with white in "very exact figures which have their own charm."[16]

Gradually, these figures came to be used as tribute, as ransom for captives, as compensation for crime, as payment to the medicine man,

PLATE VII

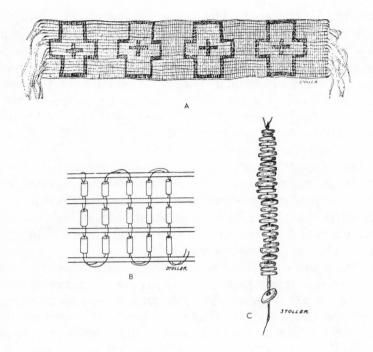

WAMPUM

The purple wampum beads were made from the colored lip of the hard clam, or quahog (*Venus mercenaria*), while the white were fashioned from the columellae of the conch. The conch, the periwinkle (*Pyrula carica* and *P. carnaliculata*), the whelk (*Buccinum undatum*), and fresh-water shells of the genus *Unio* were other sources of raw material.

Before the advent of white men's tools, the beads were probably cut and shaped roughly with stone tools. Drilling could be done by placing the bead in a simple vise—a partially split stick—and boring it with a tiny stone drill fastened to a slim wooden shaft. Or the worker could hold the bead in one hand against the point of the drill, which was rotated on his thigh by the other hand. The hole was completed by boring from both ends of the bead. They were finished by rubbing them with fine sand and were strung on cords of vegetal fibers or twisted sinew. The belts were usually woven on the bow loom.

With white men's tools and methods a good worker could make five to ten strings (fifteen to twenty beads on a string) a day and sell them for 12–15 cents for the purple and half that for the white. The average belt contained a thousand or more beads.

Illustration (*a*) shows a wampum belt; its significance is explained in the text. The next drawing (*b*) is a detail of the belt showing the method of threading the beads; (*c*) illustrates a string of disk-shaped shells. Single strings like this of disk and tubular beads were prevalent in both pre- and post-Columbian times. (From Douglas, No. 31; Speck and Orchard, 1925; Beauchamp, 1901; Schmitt and Slotkin, 1949; Bureau of American Ethnology Bull. 30, Part II, 1907–10.)

and as the Indian version of a written record for public agreements. The famous treaty belt given by the Indians of Pennsylvania to the Penn family has a white background, indicating peace, and four cruciform figures in blue which represent the contracting parties.[17] The Iroquois, inland neighbors of the Algonkian, took this idea of seaboard people and carried it to extravagant lengths, as we shall see in the next chapter.

Seaboard girls obeyed the rule of segregation like those of the north. Boys were brought up to be socially minded hunters, donating to others their first kill of every animal, even though it were only a rabbit, killed when the boy was five. The Powhatan tribe of Virginia initiated some boys into maturity with a strenuous ordeal which included purification with an emetic, so that they might start clean as men. Then came marriage, when the boy's family presented wampum to that of the girl, chosen from any village or family because of her industry. Her relatives in council might accept or reject and later might give her sisters unless he chose elsewhere. She would need to be faithful lest her husband disown her or at least cut off her hair. Death meant a quiet interment with little ceremony and few gifts. However, chiefs in the Virginia area had their skeletons preserved in a special "temple." In the Wabanaki confederacy of Maine a wampum belt was sent around to the constituent tribes, its blue sections representing mourning, the white the rejoicing to take place when a new chief was chosen.[18] For, with the seaboard people, we come to a land of chiefs, confederations, and other officialdom.

All the way from the Powhatan of Virginia, through the Delaware of the Middle States, to the Abenaki of Maine, there were small confederacies of varying pattern. Some of them were recent, and Powhatan, even under the eyes of the first colonists, increased his holdings until thirty villages paid him tribute of skins, corn, and fresh-water pearls. Each chieftain, or sagamore, was attempting something similar, even though he could collect only two or three villages as allies or tributaries.

The sagamores inherited their position in the male line (though, in the Powhatan tribe, the succession was through females). Some of them had a corps of officials, as with the Wappinger of New York, who, besides the council, had an Owl Man, or herald, and fast runners to carry messages. The sagamore's power depended much on his personality, but some of them were little despots. Remember Powhatan, who was able to order the execution of Captain John Smith, almost as autocratically as the Natchez Sun would have done! No leader in the great Creek or Cherokee confederacies would have assumed such sovereign power, and one wonders if this is the attitude of petty war leaders, lately arrived at permanent chieftainship.

Surrounded by such powerful neighbors, we could not expect the seaboard Algonkian to be peaceful. In fact, when the whites knew them, they were constantly at war. We recognize such southern customs as war honors, torture of captives, and cannibalism. After following the Iroquois through the next chapter, we shall know them even better. In fact, the Algonkian fought in the same way that their enemies fought. Their war parties were the quick, commando raids already described. The little group, stepping silently through the woods, carried bow, arrow, scalping knife, wooden shield, and the famous tomahawk, a knobbed wooden club with a triangle of bone or stone set in the end. When their chief and council decided on war or peace, they used the metaphors, so familiar in Colonial records, of "taking up" or "burying" the tomahawk.

Seaboard Algonkian seem to have had medicine men or powwows like those of the north, though without the fearsome spectacle of the shaking tent. The power they received from animal spirits was often used in blowing away disease or sucking it out through a bone tube. That last, by the way, is one of the most ancient forms of curing known to man and so widespread in the Old World that it may well have come over with the first immigrants. Among most of them we meet nothing in the way of a priest, appointed to office and reciting a memorized ritual. However, the Powhatan in Virginia, near the Civilized Tribes, had a priest guarding their temple with its effigies. The Delaware, protégés of the highly organized Iroquois, had a "longhouse" ceremony, much like that of their masters.[19]

The beliefs of the seaboard people were so early classed as devilish that we get only cloudy glimpses of the Great Spirit, or Manitou, akin to the Owner of the north. Other Manitous are the sun, moon, thunder-beings, a giant bird armored in wampum, the kindly animals, and, perhaps, any natural phenomenon which seemed strange and, therefore, endowed with power.

The story of white contact with the eastern Algonkian is a swifter and more tragic one than that of the Civilized Tribes. There were reasons. The Algonkian, even the confederated ones, had not the large groups and the organization of the Creek or

Cherokee. More important, they lived directly in the path of the newcomers. There was no time to watch them from a distance, to acquire their goods, and to learn their ways. No sooner had the first arrivals landed than conquest or infiltration began. Not only did the whites want the Indians' land and their goods, but this eastern country was to be, for a hundred years, the subject of a tug of war between England and France. Before that contest was over, Indian life on the seaboard was practically expunged.

There was fishing, trading, and some kidnaping of Indians along the Atlantic Coast in the early 1500's. Some claim that the New-foundland Banks, swarming place of cod, were known to Breton fishermen even before Cabot explored the coast for England in 1497. At least, within twenty years after Cabot's voyage, fifty ves-sels from various nations were reported there. Within fifty years, several hundred ships—Breton, Basque, Portuguese, Spanish, and Eng-lish—were engaged in fishing and whaling.[20] Crews were camping in the harbors all the way from Cape Breton down into Maine, in order to dry their codfish. White men's diseases were known on the New England coast long before our Puritan forefathers arrived there. The trade with France soon changed from fish to beaver. Coast Indians of Canada saw their opportunity, and whole bands paddled down the rivers in the spring to meet the French ships "for who, they wait upon the seashore, sitting on their rumps like apes."[21]

New France was organized, with the trade in beaver fur as its life-blood. There were few settlements, composed mostly of soldiers, trad-ers, priests, and nuns. Farther and farther west spread the knowledge that any Indian group which could bring furs to Quebec or Tadoussac could obtain untold wealth in kettles, cloth, and guns. The Iroquoian-speaking Huron, on the lake of that name, became the middlemen, milking the interior for furs and charging toll to all who passed them. The loyalty of all these Indians must be obtained for France, so, even before the traders penetrated the wilds, Jesuit priests were living in the Indian camps.

The Algonkian on both sides of the St. Lawrence, now protégés of France, were age-long enemies of the Iroquois in New York State. So King Louis's government found itself committed to some wild forays, including scalping and torture. Since the Iroquois were past masters at torture, their opponents returned blow for blow. Even the whites, in the end, had to countenance torture if they wanted Indian allies.

So we need not be surprised if the Algonkian, whose northernmost representatives lived in peace, could turn cruel when forced to it.

For a time, France had no fear of the English, whose few little settlements along the Atlantic Coast were barely able to keep alive (Jamestown was founded in 1607, Plymouth in 1620, and Massachusetts Bay in 1629). However, before 1640, there were twenty thousand English on the Atlantic Coast, mostly in New England. There were also Dutch in New Amsterdam and Swedes in New Jersey and Delaware, all plowing the land and reaching out for more. The doom of Atlantic Coast Indians was sealed. Often enough has the comparison been made between the fate of this area where the Indians were dispossessed by the English and practically exterminated and that of the Canadian hunters, with whom the French traded and made friends. What there is of truth in this statement depends greatly on the nature of the land. This seaboard land could not have sustained a fur trade for long, and it was barred by mountains from the country farther west. The English came to cultivate it and to live on it. With memories of Old World landlordism to sharpen their eagerness, they could endure no relation with the land but complete ownership. They might, indeed, profess friendship with the Indians, but, no matter what was said on either side, two bodies of such a different nature could not occupy the same space; and the only question was when the conflict would come.

It came early in Virginia. There was little time for Powhatan's people to obtain guns and trinkets, for Powhatan himself to be crowned *in absentia* by the king of England, and for his daughter Pocahontas to marry John Rolfe and go to England and die. Powhatan's successor saw that the new colonists were pushing the Indians back, clear out of the tidewater lands, and that this pressure would never cease. He countered with a desperate act of frightfulness which the English returned. By 1644 the Virginia tribes were out of the white man's way.

We cannot pause at each settlement to note the first cordial overtures, the protestations of friendship which perhaps were sincere until the speakers recognized the impassable barrier between them, then, ultimately, the clash. The period between this clash and the first warnings of doom was sometimes a fairly long one. When that was the case, Indian culture might have a brief blossoming period, an Indian summer, as the white man's tools and materials released his artistic energy along new lines.

Such was the case in the New Netherlands, where a stony little island had been bought from the Manhattan Indians for the equivalent of $24.00. Here we might pause to mention that, to an Indian, with plenty of good New Jersey meadows at his disposal, the island was probably not worth more. Near by, along the Long Island shore, was found the clam known to the Indians as *poquauhaug* and to the whites, even yet, as quahog. The deep purple and the pearly white of its shell lining were ideal for beads. Once steel awls were available, Indians could drill and polish the slender cylinders, which soon became the official form of wampum. This prolific supply was the next thing to an invention of writing, and soon no ceremonial occasion was complete without a wampum record. Ultimately wampum was used for trade, even by the whites, and the Dutch themselves began to manufacture it.

One use of wampum was in payment for scalps. There has been some argument as to whether scalping was taught to Indians by whites, but the idea is absurd when one knows how widespread and ancient the practice is. Europeans could never have taught it to so many tribes, over the two Americas, in the short time after their arrival. Nor would Indians have been likely to work up the complicated and varied ceremonies with which they surround it. What the whites did was to pay for scalps, and one of the very first to start that practice was Governor Kieft of New Amsterdam. He had become annoyed by bands of roaming and dispossessed Indians, for the Iroquois were troubling New York State as well as the Dutch. So he set a bounty on each scalp brought in, as a sign that one nuisance had been removed. The price was ten fathoms of wampum, equivalent to four dollars.[22]

The dispossessed Indians continued to roam, and once an old woman took some peaches off the land where she had once gathered berries. It was time to teach the Raritans a lesson. However, it was to the peaceful Hackensack village that the governor sent his soldiers. Eighty sleeping Indians were killed, and "infants were torn from their mother's breasts, and hacked to pieces in the presence of their parents and the pieces thrown into the fire . . . and other sucklings were bound to small boards and then cut stuck and pierced and miserably massacred in a manner to move a heart of stone."[23] Eighty gory heads were laid on view in the streets of New Amsterdam, where the governor's mother kicked them like footballs.

We will admit that there were some gentler people, like Penn in

Pennsylvania and the Swedes in Delaware. But the gentle people passed on after a brief time, and then the process of expropriation continued, like a growing tree toppling the stones of a wall. We omit, for sheer lack of space, the saga of the peaceful, civilized Delaware, as they were pushed from one refuge to another, to end islanded in Oklahoma. Or the Shawnee, landing at last among the Muskogean, or the Mahican, shifting from the Hudson River Valley to Massachusetts to Wisconsin. We turn to the Indians of school history, the red men of New England.

One believes that the Pilgrims of Plymouth, undergoing hardship for religion's sake, had really meant to treat the Indians like brothers. They paid for the stores of corn which they robbed in their necessity. They gave hospitality to the savage-looking Squanto, who wandered in during their first spring and who showed them how to plant corn fertilized with fishheads. When he had them meet Massasoit, the Narraganset chief, they expressed hearty friendship and lived on such terms with him that "there is now great peace among the Indians themselves . . . and we, for our part walk as peaceably in the woods as in the highways of England. We entertain them familiarly in our houses and they, as friendly, bestowing their venison on us."[24] The Indians bestowed more than venison, for it was they who taught the art of the clambake, of corn pone and planked shad, and of beans cooked for twenty-four hours in a warm place without fire.

The friendship could hardly have lasted, since the whites had the unconquerable yearning for land generated by living under landlords. Even had the Plymouth colony kept its vows of friendship, their less tolerant countrymen in Massachusetts and Connecticut must ultimately have pressed them into war. Such an event happened in 1637. Concerned in the clash was the Pequot of Connecticut, one of the few powerful tribes left in New England after the plague of 1616. The Pequot, according to their lights, tried to scare away the intruders by some scalping and burning. The paid military men who guarded the settlers knew these tricks and returned three or four blows for one. So many descriptions of Indian barbarity have been printed that we shall take space here only for the barbarities of the whites. When Captain Mason and Captain John Underhill made a dawn attack and burned the stockaded Pequot town on the Mystic River,

many courageous fellows . . . fought most desperately through the palisades so that they scorched and burned with the very flame . . . and so perished valiantly. Mercy did they deserve for their valor, could we have had opportunity to have bestowed it. Many were burned in the fort, both men, women and children. Others, forced out, came in troops . . . twenty and thirty at a time, which our soldiers received and entertained with the point of the sword. . . . Great and doleful was the bloody sight, to the view of young soldiers who never had been in war to see so many souls lie gasping on the ground so thick in some places that you could hardly pass along.[25]

Wrote Governor Bradford of the Plymouth colony: "It was a fearful sight to see them frying in the fire and the streams of blood quenching the same and horrible was the stink and stench thereof. But the victory seemed a sweet sacrifice and they gave praise thereof to God."[26]

The Pequot were removed from the path of colonization, and soon the other important tribe, the Narraganset, followed even though Philip, their chief, was the son of the friendly Massasoit. Philip's wife was sold into slavery in Bermuda like many other Indian captives, for the whites at last found it necessary to close all avenues of sympathy between them and the body which would occupy their space.

Yet, in spite of the approaching twilight, Indians did have a brief blossoming time. The use of steel tools, of colored cloth, needles, and beads, had stimulated them to creativeness, as it did all red men. The Algonkian had always loved the curved designs which suggested plants and flowers. Now they not only had beads with which to make them but the white man's cloth and embroidery to furnish models. The sprays of brilliant flowers which sprout up in double curves on the velvet and cloth bags, skirts, leggings, and breechcloths made by Algonkian women might almost have come from some European drawing room. When we remember how popular beadwork and flower embroidery were with white women of the 1600's, we can see where the Indians got their elaborate models. Models but not duplicates! The designs, no two alike, expressed the Indians' own ideas of form and color.

If New England Indians learned from whites, it was not through democratic companionship such as the southern tribes had with their traders. For one thing, these colonists had brought their women and had no need to live in Indian families. As for marrying an Indian and rearing half-blood children, that was out of the question. Not that the colonists felt themselves much better off than those traders had been, for often they had to live just as crudely. But the red men were heathen. This placed them beyond an impassable gulf, across which one might show justice and forbearance but never democracy.

A few men did try to practice the principles of brotherhood. One

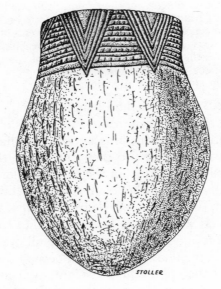

STOLLER

ALGONKIAN POTTERY

Although the Owasco culture of central New York and surrounding states cannot be definitely assigned to the historical Algonkian-speaking tribes, this Owasco pot does correspond to the early descriptions of Algonkian pottery. It dates from a period just previous to European explorations.

In general, Algonkian pottery has this elongated shape with a pointed to rounded bottom and straight to curved sides ending in a definite "neck." The construction probably followed the slab coiling and paddle method, and the clay was tempered either with pulverized granite or, near the sea coast, with crushed shell. The pots were not painted but were decorated in various ways. The most common technique was to smooth the outside of the vessel with a cord-wrapped paddle, producing the effect seen above. On many pots the neck was decorated in simple geometric patterns made by stamping, incising, or punching.

The use of this pottery was restricted to cooking. According to early records, the pots were set in a small heap of earth, ashes, or hearthstones, and fire was kindled around the base. In later periods, when the pots were made with more constricted necks and flaring rims or collars, they were suspended over the fire by thongs tied around the neck and fastened to crotched sticks. (From Ritchie, 1944; Willoughby, 1935; Martin, Quimby, and Collier, 1947.)

was Roger Williams, who lived in companionship with his benefactors, the Narraganset, until patriotism moved him to sacrifice their cause to that of the colonists. Another was John Eliot. This pastor, teacher, and Cambridge graduate conceived the idea that the Indians could not be expected to give up their heathen beliefs until they could hear Christian doctrine in their own tongue. His colleague, Cotton Mather, was outraged. "To think," he protested, "of raising these hideous creatures into our holy religion! . . . Could he [Eliot]

PLATE VIIIb

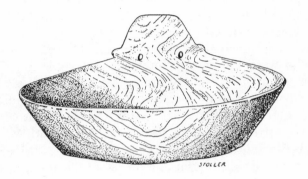

WOODEN BOWLS

Wooden bowls were used primarily as food receptacles and eating dishes. They varied in size from those used for a family to smaller ones for individuals. The bowls were made from the burls of birch, elm, maple, and other hard woods by charring and by scraping with bone and stone instruments.

This bowl, which according to its history once belonged to King Philip, is made of elm wood. The two perforations probably served for the passage of a suspending cord. (From Willoughby, 1935.)

see anything angelical to encourage his labors? All was diabolical among them."[27]

Nevertheless, Eliot took a Natick Indian into his Roxbury house in order to learn the language. He translated the Bible, the very first edition of it in the New World. By 1675, he had 1,150 "praying Indians" gathered in fourteen villages. That was the year when war broke out with King Philip and the Narraganset. Most of the converts joined their countrymen, but those who did not and were deported for their safety never showed much vigor afterward. The relic of Eliot's work is a scholarship at Dartmouth College, reserved for Indians to this day.

After King Philip's War, when twenty-five towns had been burned, eight hundred whites and nine hundred Indians killed, the Algonkian were practically cleared out of the settled part of New England. The succeeding raids and skirmishes took place on the frontiers, where settlers were pushing into the Wabanaki country of Maine and Massachusetts. These periods of killing bore the names of King William (1689–97), Queen Anne (1701–13), and King George (1744–48), after unknown sovereigns across the seas. Actually they were phases in the tug of war between France and England as the English colonists moved north and the French mobilized the Wabanaki to bludgeon them away.

We have mentioned the French drive to Christianize these buffer Indians who were still mostly forest hunters and ready, for a little pay, to swoop on any isolated farm or blockhouse. Their Jesuit mentors, who kept them in desperate fear of heresy, are said to have enjoined them, before they started for the Deerfield massacre, "to baptize all children before killing them, so great was the desire of the church for the salvation of the heretic enemies."[28] During Queen Anne's War the English began offering bounties for scalps, while the Wabanaki, led by French officers, were burning, killing, and kidnaping and dragging captured women through the woods to Montreal and leaving a living infant tied to the dead mother whose breast it was sucking.

The flames had died down even before the final explosion known as the French and Indian War. During that war most of the Abenaki, who had settled under the French wing on the St. Lawrence, were wiped out by the English. The Atlantic Coast was practically clear of Indians, from Virginia to Maine.

It is still clear. A few remnants of the ancient tribes, now much mixed with other peoples, remain near their old homes. Such are the Penobscot in Maine, the Mohegan in Connecticut, or the Pamunkey, remnant of the Powhatan confederation, in Virginia. Their status was established before there was an Indian Service or a United States government, but, in accordance with old treaties, each member may perhaps receive some yards of calico a year as a sign of the good faith of the colonies.

The known population of the eastern Algonkian today would hardly fill one moderate-sized American city. We have no census of the mixed-bloods who, for two hundred years, have been filtering into the white population. It is in this mixture, often unacknowledged or forgotten, that the Algonkian survive, though, as a people, they have gone.

NORTHERN HUNTERS

FOOD

Vegetable.—Seeds, berries, moss, bark.
Animal.—Moose, caribou, small game, birds, fish.

HUNTING METHOD

Crossbow, weirs, harpoons, calls, traps, deadfalls. Hunting tracts; group or single hunts.

CLOTHING

Male.—Skin trousers, leggings, soft-soled moccasins, shirts and robes of skin.
Female.—Slip-and-sleeve tailored dresses, moccasins, fur robes, skin capes.

HOUSE TYPES

Conical skin tent, bark houses, lodge houses of bark. Sweat lodges and female segregation huts.

EQUIPMENT

Household.—No pottery; bark vessels and dishes; wooden spoons and bowls; bark decorated with quills.
Transportation.—Bark canoe, snowshoes, sleds.
Hunting.—Sinew-backed bow, highly decorated. Crossbow.
Other.—Cradle: flat board, bow at top, carved and painted. Pipe: stone or clay, stem and bowl on one plane. Miscellaneous: drums, rattles, embroidery on bark and skin.

WAR

Rod armor, wood shields, tomahawks, war clubs, bow and arrow; sneak raids, general war parties, took scalps.

GAMES

Cup-and-pin, football, dominoes, stick game, ball-juggling.

CORN-GROWERS

FOOD

Vegetable.—Agriculture: flour and flint corn, beans, squash, pumpkin. Berries, maple sugar.
Animal.—Deer, beaver, fish, small game.

HUNTING METHOD

Weirs, calls, traps. Singly or in groups.

CLOTHING

Male.—Skin trousers, leggings, soft-soled moccasins, shirts and robes of skin, feather cloaks, lots of decoration. Tattooing.

Female.—Wrap-around skirts and blouses of skin; soon gave way to European-type dresses.

HOUSE TYPES

Wigwams, some conical, some domed. Community wigwams. Sweat lodges, female segregation huts.

EQUIPMENT

Household.—Birch and elm bark, and wooden vessels and dishes. Pottery of all sizes, coiled. Large bowls for salt evaporation.

Transportation.—Bark canoe, snowshoes.

Hunting.—Self-bow, sinew-backed bow, arrows.

Other.—Cradle: flat board, bow at top, carved and painted. Pipe: stone or clay, stem and bowl in one plane. Miscellaneous: braided sashes of bass and bark fibers, bark straps and garters. Baskets of rush coils and splint plaiting. Bedframes and rush mats. Wampum.

WAR

Rod armor, wood shields, tomahawks, war clubs, bow and arrow. Sneak raids, general war parties, took scalps and captives and killed at random.

GAMES

Moccasin game, stick games, ring-and-pin, lacrosse, hoop-and-pole, racket, dice, snow snake.

ALGONKIAN TRIBES OF THE ATLANTIC SEABOARD

(From F. W. Hodge [ed.], *Handbook of American Indians* [Washington, 1907]; Cyrus Thomas, *Indian Land Cessions in the United States*, Part II [Washington, 1899]; W. Christie MacCleod, *The American Indian Frontier* [New York: Alfred A. Knopf, 1928].)

Abenaki: A confederacy centering in present state of Maine, including Abenaki, Penobscot, Malecite, Passamaquoddy, the last two often spoken of together as Etchemin. Largely converted by French missionaries, they took the French side in French and Indian War. Abenaki tribe withdrew to Canada, where some five hundred are now. Others made peace with English and accepted fixed bounds. A few are still at Oldtown, Maine.

Massachusett: A confederacy located around Massachusetts Bay, including present site of Boston. Some thirty villages fought with Mahican; devastated by pestilence in 1617, so few were found by settlers. Gathered into villages of Praying Indians and lost separate existence.

Narraganset: Confederacy of eight villages in Rhode Island. Conquered in King Philip's War (1675), and most abandoned the country, joining Mahican or Abenaki.

Wampanoag: Confederacy on east shore of Narragansett Bay with Nauset and Saconnet as tributaries. Thirty villages. Chief Massasoit friendly to colonists; his son, King Philip, rebelled because of ill treatment. Conquered in King Philip's War, 1675–77, and tribe practically exterminated. A few Saconnet still on Cape Cod.

Pennacook: A confederacy on banks of Merrimac River, New Hampshire. Disrupted after King Philip's War.

MAP III

Pequot: Originally one with Mohegan of Connecticut; came to coast and established themselves as conquerors over most of Connecticut and Long Island. War with colonists in 1637, when they separated into small bands and joined other tribes. A few are still in Connecticut but retain little of their former culture.

Mahican: A confederacy with at least five subtribes and forty villages. Upper Hudson Valley, with extension into Connecticut. Group in Connecticut later known as Mohegan. Pushed to east bank of Hudson by Mohawk. Sold territory piecemeal and moved, some to Pennsylvania, then Ohio, some to western New York under protection of Iroquois. Some in Connecticut gathered into a mission at Stockbridge, Massachusetts, where they are still known as Stockbridge Indians.

Wappinger: Confederacy of nine tribes on Lower Hudson, including Manhattan, closely related to Mahican and Delaware. Gradually sold their lands and joined Mahican under Iroquois protection.

Montauk: A confederacy including most tribes of Long Island, New York, among them Shinnecock and Manhasset, though probably not Canarsee and Rockaway. Subdued first by Pequot and then by Narraganset. Dwindled and joined other Indians, though a few mixed-bloods are still on Long Island.

Delaware (Lenape): Most important of eastern Algonkian confederacies occupying most of New Jersey, Delaware, and eastern Pennsylvania. Called "grandfathers" by other eastern Algonkian, especially Nanticoke, Conoy, Shawnee, and Mahican, who claimed to have descended from them. Several subtribes, including Munsee, who are sometimes considered separate people. Made treaty of peace with William Penn in 1682; under dominion of Iroquois in 1720. Crowded out by whites, with sanction of Iroquois; crossed into Ohio with Munsee and Mahican. Moravian Christian Delaware massacred by Americans (1782). After many moves, some Delaware were incorporated with Cherokee in Indian Territory, others with Caddo and Wichita.

Powhatan: A confederacy in Virginia of some thirty tribes conquered and amalgamated shortly before arrival of English. Culture almost like that of neighboring Muskogean. War with colonists (1622–34), by which Powhatan were almost exterminated with further blow (1676). In 1928 two thousand individuals of mixed-blood remained on a reservation under state of Virginia, including representatives of Pamunkey, Mattaponi, Chickahominy, Nansamond, Rappahannock, and Potomac (see F. G. Speck, *Chapters on the Ethnology of the Powhatan Tribes of Virginia* ["Indian Notes and Monographs, Heye Foundation," Vol. I, No. 5 (1928)]).

CHAPTER VI

A Woodland League of Nations

A MOHAWK! A Mohawk!" When this cry was relayed from hill to hill among the New England Algonkian, "they all fled like sheep before wolves, without attempting to make the least resistance."[1] Though Colden of the New Netherlands may have exaggerated a little, he was right in voicing the universal fear of the powerful Iroquois of New York State, as represented by one of their most redoubtable tribes, the Mohawk. The Iroquois are some of the most famous Indians in American history and justly so. Their government was the most integrated and orderly north of Mexico, and some have even thought it gave suggestions to the American Constitution (Lee, Franklin, Jefferson, and Washington were quite familiar with the League). They developed what came close to an empire, with conquered nations paying tribute and taking their orders. For over a hundred years they held a pivotal position in America between the French and the English. It seems very possible that, except for the Iroquois, North America at this day might have been French.

On the front endpaper map, people of Iroquoian speech form a great wedge, pushing up from western New York and near-by Pennsylvania, to surround Lakes Ontario and Erie, the "Little Great Lakes," and, in early days, they stretched along the St. Lawrence. It was the Iroquoian who pushed the Algonkian apart, so that, as mentioned in the last chapter, a group which once filled our northeastern states was reduced to two slender streamers framing a solid clump of the newcomers. This wedge of the Iroquoian introduces a people entirely different from the Algonkian of the preceding chapter and especially from the northern hunters, who may represent the original Algonkian type. Their language is distantly related to Muskogean of the Gulf states and Caddoan of the Mississippi Valley. Their livelihood was agriculture, on a lavish slash-and-burn scale. They lived a settled life, in stockaded villages; they had mother-clans and hereditary rank; they united in a confederacy, which reminds us of those

in chapter iii. In social behavior, in war, and even in religion their behavior takes us back to Nuclear America and even to the forests south
of the Caribbean.

Most ethnologists think that the Iroquois came from the Mississippi Valley, that great highroad of southern culture. Archaeologists
are still working on their history, difficult enough to disinter in the
built-up and plowed-up East. They can assure us that there were people of Iroquoian culture in central New York and around the "Little
Great Lakes" perhaps as early as A.D. 1350[2] and that at the same time,
and even earlier, there were groups which look like mixed Iroquoian
and Algonkian spreading through most of the northeastern area and
in contact with the great blossoming center of Hopewell, already
mentioned.

With this start, the historian can reconstruct a more or less shadowy picture, in line with other Indian movements. He can imagine
groups breaking off very long ago from their kinsmen, the Muskogean, the Caddoan, and the Siouan. These would move northward
separately. The Cherokee and Tuscarora, who, we noted in a former
chapter, were strayed Iroquoians, would branch off to go toward the
coast. The others would continue, stopping at times to fight or to
settle, and, as a result, incorporating new people.

Much turmoil must have taken place as this wedge of agricultural
and civilized people spread among the Algonkian, shoving them to
east and west. The advantage, however, was not all with the Iroquois.
Those who arrived on the St. Lawrence, to set up a great village
where Montreal is now, were driven out by the Algonkian. That
group receded, perhaps to New York State, and never came back. We
cannot, therefore, think of the Iroquoian of the early 1600's as conquerors. True, they were fighting the Algonkian and had been at it
since long before the French arrived, but, says Fenton, they were
taking a constant drubbing.[3] Champlain watched the Montagnais
near the coast joyfully torturing eighteen Iroquois prisoners. When
he himself joined a war party against them, they fled terrified from
his firearms. The Iroquoian, then, in pushing among the Algonkian,
had got themselves into something like a hornet's nest. Here we may
have a vague parallel to the Aztec, who were denied a place in the
sun and therefore felt themselves forced to carve out an empire. And
to do it with the maximum of cruelty? Perhaps we should add a sense
of frustration to the hybrid vigor and increase of population which
must have impelled the Iroquoian as they spread north.

PLATE IX

IROQUOIS COSTUME

This illustration shows a Seneca man wearing a kilt, thigh-length leggings, moccasins, and woven sashes. The kilt was originally of doeskin but later was made with red and blue broadcloth. The sashes, perhaps once done with vegetable fibers, were woven with European wools. The early leggings of tight-fitting deerskin had straps which were tied to a belt worn around the waist. Later they, too, were made of broadcloth. The very distinctive Iroquois caps are described in the text. Most of their clothing was elaborately ornamented with either quillwork or beadwork. (From Lyford, 1945.)

This narrative begins with the Iroquoian as they were when white colonization started in the early 1600's. The great League of New York State was then in its infancy—if, indeed, it was born—and the largest Iroquoian group was the Huron confederacy, north of Lake Ontario. The Huron claimed to have come north ahead of the others and to have kept a purer culture. Certainly, when working out Iroquoian connections, it often pays us to find what the Huron did instead of looking only at the League, with its historical vicissitudes. South of the Huron were the Tobacco Nation, the Neutral, and the Erie. Our particular subject, the Five Nations, which formed the League, consisted of some straggling villages, buried in the forests of New York State, speaking five different dialects and with a range of different customs.

Even though surrounded by enemies, they were often fighting each other, and it was for this reason, say their legends, that they formed the League of the Great Peace. Description of its details must come later, for, perhaps, in these early days there was little more to the Longhouse, as they loved to call it, than the location of the tribes, like a number of families in one great dwelling. At its western door were the Seneca, "Great Hill People"; then the Cayuga, "of the Marsh"; next the Onondaga, "on the Hills," keepers of the central fire; then the Oneida, "of the Boulder"; and, last, the Mohawk, "of the Place of Flint," keepers of the eastern door. These people of the Longhouse, main subject of our narrative, will be spoken of, according to custom, as the Iroquois (called *Les Iroquois* by the French and the Five Nations by the English) and their kinsmen elsewhere as Iroquoian.

The Iroquois had found a rich and fertile country where they could use their knowledge of agriculture to the full and still have time for ceremony, trade, and, later, conquest. The forests and streams of central New York teemed with fish and birds, not only duck and turkey, but the beautiful passenger pigeons, now extinct, whose flights used to darken the sky every autumn. Men organized parties to the nesting place of the pigeons, where they could knock the squabs from the trees with poles. They organized to build fish dams in the streams or to manipulate a huge net made of vines. When they went on a big winter hunt, sometimes as far as the Adirondacks or Pennsylvania, they appointed a leader who directed operations and to whom all game was brought for distribution.

Farming was left to the women, whose childbearing power was

thought to be transferred magically to the crops. They did all the work except the slashing and burning, and their cornfields sometimes stretched for miles on both sides of a stream. Here grew corn as high as a man and in five colors,[4] with sixty varieties of beans and eight of squash planted between the rows. These three plants, "Our Supporters," were guarded by three spirit sisters, some of the most revered beings in Iroquois mythology. In spring all the women of a village went out under a female overseer to plant the fields of each family in turn, and in autumn they bore the corn home for a husking bee. Also they found time to comb the woods for nuts and berries, especially the sweet little wild strawberries of the eastern states. As these and other wild crops ripened, women danced in their honor while men sang for them. Even today, Seneca women dance thus in Oklahoma, dressed in calico and shawls, instead of the buckskin of ancient times.[5]

The Iroquois as far back as we know them were village dwellers. Descriptions of their settlements, with the heavy stockades of logs and the fifty or more Quonset-shaped huts of elm bark, remind us decidedly of such dwellings in the south. The Iroquois, however, specialized particularly in the longhouse, fifty to a hundred feet in length and accommodating from eight to ten families. The arrangement was something like that of a modern Pullman car, with fireplaces down the center of the earthen floor, each shared by two families (see Pl. X). Windows were lacking, of course, but there were narrow slits above each fire where smoke could escape—if the wind were right. The Jesuit missionaries complained, as one of them reported, that there were three major horrors in an Iroquois house: smoke, dogs, and noise. However, compared with a flimsy tipi, this sturdy communal dwelling, with its vestibule for storage, its sweat lodge near by, and other villagers within call, meant an advance in comfort.

It was sheathed, usually, with the tough, corrugated bark of the elm, laid on in the fashion of clapboards. Elm bark, in fact, was the Iroquois staple and used to the full, just as more northern Indians used birch. It made most of the household utensiles except pottery, and its fibers were even twisted into rope and string. Lacking the birch, men even had to put up with elm bark for their canoes. Clumsy and heavy it was, but it had the advantage that a huge slab could be shaped up in a day by merely sewing it with vines at bow and stern. Though awkward, a man could manage to carry it, and, when a ladder was needed to scale the wall of a stockaded village, the rough bark of the canoe, leaned against the palisade, served admirably.

PLATE X

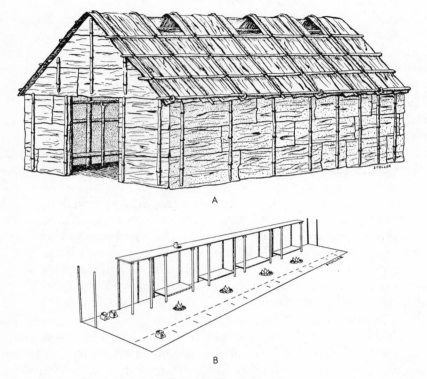

A

B

AN IROQUOIS LONGHOUSE

The men constructed the longhouse by first erecting logs with forked tops set 4–5 feet apart in a rectangle the size of the building. Horizontal poles were tied along the sides and across the top. The steep triangular or rounded roof was built by bending the slender, flexible poles in a series of rather pointed arches. This framework of logs was sheathed with bark, preferably elm bark. The slabs were about 4 by 6 feet, and, after the rough outer surface was removed and they had been dried, they were sewn to the framework with basswood withes in horizontal, overlapping strips. The roof was covered with vertical strips. A series of poles, corresponding to those in the framework, was tied outside the bark in order to secure it more firmly. The ends of the outside poles over the roof were curved up at the line of the eaves.

The diagrammatic representation shows the common vestibule and storage rooms and the two booths, one for storage and the other for living quarters, commonly allotted to each family. A continuous shelf about 7 feet from the ground ran the length of the living units. Shelves were placed in each of the larger booths to serve as beds. The fireplace in the central alleyway served two family units. (From Douglas, No. 12; Lyford, 1945.)

PLATE XI

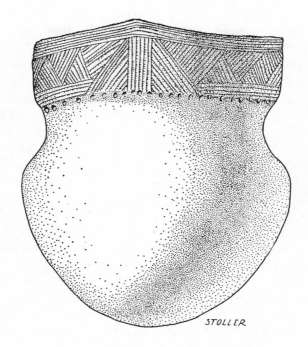

STOLLER

Iroquois Pottery

Pottery cooking utensils were made by the Iroquois women. In late pre-Columbian and early historic times pottery-making was widely distributed and skilfully accomplished. After the increase of white contacts and trade the craft decreased and was replaced by brass and iron kettles from Europe.

Characteristic Iroquois pots had globular bodies with round bottoms, constricted necks, and straight rims. The latter were usually topped by projecting collars, which were ornamented with incised geometric designs in line-filled triangular plats and chevrons, with the direction of the lines changing in each adjoining plat (like the illustration). These collars were often four-sided with an upward turn at each corner. The designs were incised with a sharp instrument (probably of bone) when the clay was still plastic. Other methods of decoration were by indentation, appliqué, and scallops.

The pottery was built up by the coiling process and smoothed by a paddle. After the pot was sun-dried, it was fired in smothered hot coals. The surface, unlike Algonkian pottery, was usually smooth, and the clay color was gray. (From Lyford, 1945; Martin, Quimby, and Collier, 1947.)

The list of Iroquois manufactures does not show them as outstanding craftworkers. In spite of their wealth and population, they make a rather poor showing in comparison with some tribes of the Southwest who had to work much harder for a living. The answer must be that they were otherwise occupied, the men in travel, politics, and, later, war; the women with their heavy load of farm work.

Women were important people in an Iroquois village. They owned the fields, an arrangement which is often found in agricultural tribes, where women do the field work. Since property went down in the female line, descent also was counted in that way, just as it did with the Muskogean of chapter iii. Iroquois women also owned the houses. A matron with her daughters, her younger sisters, and the husbands of all of them often occupied a longhouse, while the brothers and sons moved away to live with their wives. The little group of women, who were companions for life, shared work and property, named the longhouse children, and planned their careers.

A child, born into the longhouse, received a name which was owned in his mother's family and had been left free by the death of one of its members. Later, at intervals, the matrons might change it to a more important one. A girl began early to work with the women's "Mutual Aid Society," interrupting her training only for four days when she fasted in the forest to celebrate coming to maidenhood and her readiness for marriage. Boys rarely went out for lonely visions like some of the Algonkian. Instead, they worked hard to become hunters and fighters, and, when a boy had killed his first deer without help, he was permitted to accompany the men on their winter hunt.

Marriage was arranged by the women of the two families, their practical attitude usually assigning a young girl to an older man who could take care of her and a boy to some widow who shared in a good cornfield and was adept at dressing buckskin. The young man went to live with his wife's family, where he obeyed the rule of mother-in-law avoidance, surely an excellent precaution in such cases. Naturally, he could not bring home another wife unless there was a sister present and willing to take the position. One wonders if the arrangement helped to work up the tension in Iroquois life which we shall see bursting out at times. If the couple quarreled, the whole maternal family was likely to sit in judgment on them, but divorce was permitted if there seemed no other way out. In that case the husband moved out, leaving the children, as he did in the Southeast.

Death, in ancient times, was an expensive matter, or so say Iroquois traditions. It meant the saving of skeletons, somewhat after the southern manner, with a final mass burial, where immense riches of furs and ornaments were piled in a common grave. The Huron were doing this in historic times, but the Iroquois, according to legend, gave it up, when the Great League was formed, in favor of individual burial without offerings.

The government of the Iroquois has been sometimes held as an example of matriarchy, and indeed it may be the nearest approach to that legendary state which the world has ever seen. Even so, it was a distant approach. Female power was exercised mostly behind the scenes, while men held most of the offices and did the public speaking. The fundamental structure of a tribe was very like that of the Muskogean, for here we find mother-clans (three for Mohawk and Oneida, eight or more for the others) named after local animals, such as Wolf, Bear, Deer, and Snipe. Images of these "totems" were sometimes carved over the longhouses, though otherwise they received scant attention. There are echoes of the south, too, in the fact that with the three western tribes the clans were grouped in two divisions, the Turtles and quadrupeds of every tribe always on one side, the Deer and birds on the other. Members of each division or moiety must marry into the other, must perform the burials for its dead, and must play against it in ceremonial games. This is a more clearly organized arrangement than was found among the Muskogean, but it echoes a general southern tendency which we shall meet again.

It is when we look into the functioning of clan, moiety, and tribe that we meet the importance of women. In ancient days each tribe seems to have been managed by a council of sachems or chiefs, something like a House of Lords. That is, they came only from certain chiefly families within each clan. The Iroquois today speak of these as "noble," while the other families, the commoners, could never provide a chief except by special arrangement. Some clans, perhaps later additions, had no chiefly families at all. However, succession did not go automatically to the oldest son, as in European countries, for the women took a hand, choosing that man of their lineage who seemed best fitted to fill the office. Sometimes an important name was given to a boy early in life, with the expectation that it would be changed for even better ones and finally to a sachemship.

When a sachem of the tribal council had died and a new one was to be chosen, the matron of his lineage assembled all the women of household and clan and told them her choice. They usually ratified it, for doubtless much informal discussion had gone on before this final step. She next obtained the approval of her moiety, and, finally, of the opposite moiety. Then she went to the council of her tribe, which announced to the confederate council that they were ready to raise a chief. The three tribes of the opposite moiety came to condole the deceased and, on the appointed day, installed the candidate. If the chosen man failed to give satisfaction, the matron would warn him sternly three times. At the fourth time she would "remove his horns," the badge of office. In other words, she would go to the tribal council and ask to have him deposed. Women thus had the right of nomination and recall, even though they did not rule in person.

The days when each Iroquois tribe was governed separately on something like this plan are far in the past. When whites first met this people, they were already organized into the Hodesaunee, the famous League of Five Nations. Legend says that this was accomplished by the semidivine heroes, Deganawidah, born of a virgin whose face was "doubly pure and spotless,"[6] and Hiawatha. Perhaps we should explain without delay that this Thomas Jefferson of the Iroquois is not the same as Longfellow's Hiawatha, who lived by the "shining big sea water" of Lake Superior. Longfellow did indeed borrow the name of Hiawatha and even the idea of a universal Indian peace, but otherwise his hero is a refined and expurgated Ojibwa. For the Iroquois Hiawatha, each of the Five Nations has a different tale, one of the most poetic making him paddle his white canoe from tribe to tribe, urging unity for the sake of peace. At last he combed the serpents from the head of the fierce Atatarho, of the Onondaga, and won his support, on the condition that the Onondaga should have the chairmanship of the council. Legendary though the tale may be, we must admit that unity was essential for the struggling newcomers. They never completely achieved it, yet their organizing effort was so far ahead of those of other Indians that it stands unique in American history.

The organization was like that of the modern United Nations, in that it dealt only with international concerns of peace and war. Each tribe managed its internal concerns for itself unless there was a quarrel which it asked the League to arbitrate. All pledged themselves never to fight on opposite sides in a war and never to commit the League to action unless all were unanimous.

The confederacy was managed by fifty clan leaders: Onondaga, fourteen; Cayuga, ten; Mohawk and Oneida, nine each; and Seneca, eight. These were the same local leaders who had been nominated by the women from noble families and approved by their tribes. On installation, each was given the name of one of the fifty founders of the League, so that these names remained as permanent titles, chanted at every roll call.

> That was the role of you,
> You who were joined in the work,
> You who completed the work,
> The Great League.[7]

Second on the list in this primitive peerage came the name of "Hiawentha"; but Deganawidah, the other mythical founder, does not appear. It is said that he had no interest in chiefly office, and so, for him, there was instituted the title of Pine Tree, a name which could be earned by any outstanding man or woman. In later days the warriors who received this title came to overshadow the peace councilors, but that development was long in arriving.

The League met in summer, after the local sachems had long argued the questions to be discussed and when messengers had run over the well-worn forest trails, carrying sticks to indicate the number of days before the assembly. Whole villages made the journey to Onondaga country, the Pine Trees perhaps to speak and the other warriors and women to look on. If any of these latter had matter for discussion, they asked their local sachem to speak for them. Voting was done only by the sachems, each tribal group reaching its decision in private, then voting as one in the general assembly as our state delegations do at a presidential nomination. When the votes were in, the League must argue until all Five Nations agreed.

Such, at least, was the plan of organization as described by white writers. Perhaps, in early days, before this miniature League of Nations had gained vitality, the voting did not concern very important matters. The League, we can imagine, kept its status very largely through its ceremonial functions, which did not interfere with tribal independence and which were impressive enough to appeal to any Indian. In winter, when growing plants would not be blasted by mention of death, the Faceless Destroyer, the League met to instal the successor of any sachem who had died during the year. Mourning was already standardized among the tribes, which considered that one moiety should always bury the dead of the other, its "cousins," and should act as comforter.

Therefore, on these solemn occasions, the whole League considered itself as one tribe, with the Mohawk, Onondaga, and Seneca as one moiety, the Father's Line, or, later, Elder Brothers; and the Oneida and Cayuga, along with the Tuscarora and other later additions, as the Mother's Line, or Younger Brothers. With stately poetry, the moiety which had suffered death met the Clear-minded, or condolers, who came down the road chanting the roll of the Founders. A representative of the Mourners chanted the phrases of welcome, "At the Woods Edge."[8] The Mourners symbolically wiped the condolers' eyes, cleared their throats, and cleansed them from the filth of mourning. The Clear-minded then reciprocated. Then the Mourners led them to the longhouse, where, with twelve solemn speeches, each accompanied by a gift of wampum, the Clear-minded "beautified the sky"[9] so that the Mourners' eyes could rest upon it in peace. Then the Mourners produced the matron and the candidate, who, "showing his face to the assembly,"[10] was brought forward, endowed with the name of his predecessor, and symbolically crowned with the antlers of office.

This system, with its proportional representation and its approximation to two houses, the sachems and the Pine Trees, has been suggested as a model for the United States Constitution, albeit, there are many other claimants for that honor. We can probably think of the confederacy both as a kinship state and as a slow growth whose functions were largely ceremonial until pressure by the whites made unity and power essential.

One name which the League gave itself was the "Great Peace," and, supposedly, none of its member-tribes would undertake war without its sanction. When this had been given, some well-known warrior would drive a tomahawk into the war post at the meeting place. After this, small parties might be organized, each prospective leader driving his hatchet into the post, then dancing to summon volunteers. It was hard, however, to restrain the young warriors, whose chief path to glory, as in the neighbor tribes, was through war honors. In the League's early days parties were continually sneaking off, either to fulfil the behest of a dream or to quiet the soul of some slain comrade, doomed to wander until it had been avenged.

War parties carried bows and arrows, but these were only for attack from ambush. The Iroquois were noted for their close-in fighting, with the wicked ballheaded club known to the Algonkian as the tomahawk, a wooden shield, and a sort of armor made of sticks or reeds laced together with buckskin thongs. Their method was the usual

PLATE XII

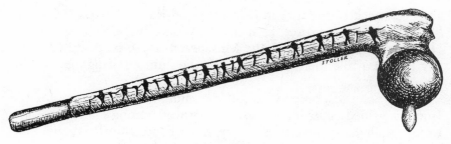

War Club

The borrowed Algonkian word "tomahawk" originally belonged to this type of war club but is more frequently associated with the trade-ax–pipe combination illustrated below. The function of each—to break heads—was the same.

The clubs, usually carved from a single piece of hardwood, were about 2 feet long, with the diameter of the ball 5–6 inches. The head sometimes resembled a face, and the handles were often carved or painted. This one has thirteen joined human figures, each with a gun, burned into the handle. For increased effectiveness a fine piece of bone, stone, or metal was attached to the end. (From Schellbach, 1928; Beauchamp, 1908.)

Trade Ax

One of the earliest and most influential implements spread by the whites was the iron ax. It usually had a broad edge for cutting and narrowed below the socket for the handle. Many of the earliest ones were stamped with three circles, each inclosing a cross, but, as the axes became more widespread, the decorations became more elaborate. The handles or stems of these weapons were often decorated with paint, beadwork, and quillwork. The axes soon met the prehistoric complex of beautiful clay and stone pipes, and so added a pipe to the other end of the blade. The illustration shows one of these tomahawk-pipes. (From Beauchamp, 1902.)

surprise attack of the region, in which, said the disconcerted French, "they approach like foxes, fight like lions and disappear like birds."[11] However, in the manner of the Muskogean, these bold warriors usually left on a tree their clan sign with the number of fighters and of slain.

It was not their purpose to kill any more than necessary, for the Iroquois valued captives, at least if they were strong and brave. The women called for substitutes for their husbands, brothers, and sons, lost either by disease or in battle, and the souls of slain warriors cried for the torture of enemies. In their treatment of captives the Iroquois followed the pattern of their neighbors, both Algonkian and Muskogean. However, they seem to have carried it to an unusual degree, both of organization and of ferocity. Each warrior carried a specially woven "slave strap" with which he bound his prisoner. Strong and brave young men who would play up to torture were the most desired, but women and children were useful as slaves. Other tribes considered women not worth torture, but the Iroquois used them in default of other victims. Perhaps this was a tribute to the equal status of the female in their system.

On the way home, the miserable creatures were beaten, bitten, burned, and, if they loitered, killed. When they arrived, they ran the gamut between two lines of excited villagers, who beat them with clubs or thorny branches. The captor received great honor for his exploit, but the prisoner was not his property. He was given by the council to some family which had suffered loss and, if old or feeble, could be used as a slave. The better human specimens were adopted into the tribe before being turned over to some bereaved family for adoption or torture. It was the matrons who made the decision, and, if death were the verdict, they provided the feast which every Iroquois gave when his end seemed near.

The final ordeal of stabbing with torches, of necklaces of hot irons, of slices cut from the living flesh and eaten, seems more varied and ghastly than those practiced by the Iroquois neighbors. During it the women, chief torturers, spoke to their "kinsman" with gentle raillery, asking if he was warm enough and refreshing him with water so that he might suffer more consciously. Even the children, in preparation for their future, were expected to take part. The torture was not considered a success unless it lasted at least a day, and often, by judicious revival of the victim, it was much longer. At its end the heart and perhaps the head were eaten by specially privileged individuals, while the body formed a feast for all. Such treatment of captives is already familiar to us. We can hear southern echoes in the demand that the victim be a fine human specimen, in the kindly treatment given him (the Huron feasted him and even gave him a wife in the Mexican manner), and in the adjurations made by the Mohawk to Aireskoi, spirit of war and hunting and perhaps of the sun: "Demon Aireskoi [so the Jesuits translated the words], we offer thee this victim whom we burn for thee, that thou mayest be filled with her flesh and render us ever anew victorious over our enemies."[12]

Plainly, the basis of the procedure was a sacrificial rite. Yet students of the Indian have suggested that this, like other sanctioned orgies, was a necessary emotional release for people whose daily life was held down to an irksome co-operation. One can imagine that the highly organized Iroquois needed such a relief even more than their neighbors. To moderns, their mere living conditions, by which fifty persons might be crowded into a single dwelling, would be cause enough for a nervous breakdown. Add to this the strain on the men, newcomers to the home and faced with a group of well-organized, houseowning women. Add, for the women, the burden of being the keepers of public morals and responsible for the tribe's good behavior without any outward power. Either sex might look forward to this one magnificent opportunity of expressing pent-up hostility. When a woman thrust a torch under the armpit of her adopted son, a psychiatrist might suggest that some of her taunts were aimed at her own men, absent for years on the warpath, while she did the heavy farm work. It has been noted that women, also, were occasionally tortured, and here the men had a chance to retaliate on their mentors.

It was only on occasions of torture that a flame of ferocity leaped onto the Iroquois scene. For the most part we see the organized groups working smoothly, with many hours for play, both among men and women. In summer, when the men were not hunting, they might make long trips in their elm-bark canoes for trade. Their huge, fertile fields supplied plenty of dried corn, which they took to the Petun on the St. Lawrence for tobacco and to the hunting Algonkian for good arrowheads and birch-bark canoes. From the Algonkian, too, they obtained wampum, whose use they were to elaborate far beyond the dreams of its makers. Furs, in early days, were not so important, since every tribe had enough for itself. The local sachems tried to keep track of proceedings, insisting that every trading party should get permission before leaving, so that all men should not be away from the village at once. One Jesuit even reported that a man could be granted a monopoly of a certain line of trade, no one else taking it up without permission.[13]

All Iroquois ventures were under the guidance of the spirits, for this tribe of fighters and organizers was as deeply reverent toward the unknown powers as any of the simpler Indians. Like the Algonkian, they believed in powerful animals and magical beings who were the "controllers" of their kind. There were also more personalized beings such as Aireskoi, the spirit of the sun, war, and hunting. Also there was the Master of Life, through whose will the world had come into being, and his evil brother, constantly trying to thwart him. This conception of a battle between good and evil powers is unusual among Indians but seems indigenous with the Iroquois. All these beings and man himself when blessed by them were foci of an invisible force which flowed through the universe. The Iroquois, unusually articulate, had a name for it—"orenda." Anything unusual was thought to be infused with orenda and especially man's inner self.

Man's contact with orenda was, as usual, through dreams. All Indian groups held slightly different attitudes toward this obvious gateway to the unknown, but that of the Iroquois seems to give more scope to the unconscious and even to approach the ideas of whites in early days. Some Iroquois boys did fast and pray in order to dream, but the unsought dream was also given tremendous value. It expressed, said the Iroquois, some need of the inner self, which would lose all strength if its behest were not fulfilled. So imperative was this need that a whole war party would turn back if one of its members dreamed of failure. In later days Chief Corn-planter dreamed that he should give up his office and did so.

Shamans dreamed more than other men, visiting animal villages and waxing strong with orenda. So far we can see a clear likeness to the Algonkian, long-term neighbors of the Iroquois. However, instead of the weird seance in the shaking tent and the emphasis on evil magic, we have here societies of those who have dreamed power to cure different diseases, or even those who have been cured and thus mastered the evil. Most famous among them were the False Faces, controlling horrible bodiless heads which were met in the woods and bewitched men to illness. Wearing carven representations of these heads, the society members entered a sick person's house, sprinkled tobacco to expel the evil, and invoked the spirits:

> Partake of this sacred tobacco,
> Oh mighty Shagodjoweh,
> You who live at the rim of the earth
> Who stand towering,
> You who travel everywhere on the earth,
> Caring for the people.

> And you, too, whose faces are against the trees
>   in the forest
> Whom we call the company of faces,
> You also receive tobacco.[14]

This direct contact with the spirits by dreamers, single or in groups, expressed only one side of Iroquois religion. As agricultural people, they also gathered the crops, domesticated and wild, and gave thanks for them at regular seasons. The maple sap, the strawberries, the blackberries, the green corn, the ripe corn—all were feted, as they were with the Muskogean. Here there was no shaman to take charge but stated numbers of male and female Keepers of the Faith, appointed in each tribe. One unusual feature at some ceremonies was a public confession of sins, made by the Keeper of the Faith and followed by all present. There was no penance. As in Mexico, this repudiation of evil was thought to give cleansing enough.

At midwinter came the renewal ceremony when old fires were scattered and, in ancient days, new fire was made. The Iroquois called this the Dream Festival, and their feeling was that, in this idle period in midwinter, people's minds were almost maddened by the accumulation of dreams experienced during the year and whose directions must be fulfilled on pain of misfortune to the dreamer.

"Now," said the messengers who announced it, "the ceremony of the great riddle has begun . . . for the Holder of the Heavens has decreed that the ceremony should be performed on earth as in the sky world."[15] He then adjured every matron to bring forward all her family who had dreamed either in years past or in this one. If the dream was an old one, they were to follow its directions, as they had done every year. If new, they were to tell its content to a committee of their moiety, and these would appoint a man to give some hint of the dream—usually, in ancient days, nothing too dangerous or expensive. Days of excitement followed, while the opposite moiety guessed the dream and made it come true by presenting some article or acting out

PLATE XIII

MASKS

The masks used by the False Face Society were carved according to a definite procedure. To give it potency and to keep the tree-spirit within it, the mask was first carved on the trunk of a living tree, usually basswood. After a three-day ceremony, during which tobacco was offered the tree, the mask was roughly blocked out and cut off. The high-relief features were carefully carved, the eyes ringed with metal, and the face painted black (if carved after noon), red (if carved in the morning), or both (called a "whirlwind"). Strands of vegetable fibers and horsehair were attached to the top as hair. The Iroquois also made masks of braided cornhusks. (From Lyford, 1945; Speck, 1950.)

some event. They might even give a dramatization of torture, thus avoiding real torture for the dreamer. Finally, the Master of Life himself received a gift. A white dog from a breed kept for the purpose was strangled and then painted with red symbols, hung with wampum, and burned. As the smoke arose, the officiant threw tobacco on the fire and pleaded with all the hierarchy of spirits that the wild plants should ever grow, the earth ever be safe for men's feet, and the streams ever flowing. At this crucial time of the year new adult names were given to those chosen by the matrons. There were dancing, both gay and serious, curing by the societies, clowning, and games. Here was another opportunity for the dignified, useful citizen to "let himself go."

This sketch gives little idea of the variety of observances in the different tribes, the extent to which the Mohawk, perhaps, leaned more toward shamanism, the Seneca more toward organized ceremony. It does show us the two streams of religious observance which we will meet again and again among American Indians: the hunters, with their dreams, visions, and magic-working shamans; the agriculturists, with their trained officiants and their group ceremonies, culminating often in the great yearly renewal of the sacred fire. The pushing, changing Iroquois had assimilated both.

This picture of Iroquois civilization relates to the days before white influence grew strong. It was only after that event that the Iroquois became the conquering imperialists of tradition, and the cause was the small furry animal which long kept the French colonists alive—the beaver. The Iroquois entered the fur trade later than their long-term enemies, the Algonkian. While the coastal tribes were already acquainted with knives, beads, and kettles, and while the French were sailing up the St. Lawrence and forming the Algonkian alliances which would last for a hundred and fifty years, the Iroquois remained in isolation in the forests of central New York. At this very date, however, the weapon which changed all Indian lives was on its way to the Five Nations. With the gun would come their role as conquerors.

Dutch traders had bought Manhattan Island in 1598. In 1614 they sailed up the Hudson and established Fort Orange where now stands Albany, the capital of New York State. Hither the Iroquois paddled their elm-bark canoes, loaded with beaver furs, one trader calculating that the Mohawk could bring four thousand a season. In return, they wanted guns, and the Dutch were willing to supply them. Here the remote position of the Five Nations stood them in good stead, for the

Hollanders were afraid to arm their closer neighbors, the Algonkian. An armed group of Iroquois, however, seemed to them an excellent device for keeping those same Algonkian in order. Moreover, it would form a buffer against the French, who, otherwise, might have streamed down into New York State. The French, too, went slowly in the arming of their Algonkian allies. So the Iroquois, by a stroke of geographical good luck, were raised to a position of potential mastery.

They took full advantage of it. At first, however, the old life-pattern continued, while the Five Nations adjusted to their new equipment of kettles, knives, hatchets, cloth, ribbon, beads, and rum. The usual burst of artistic vitality ran through the tribes, as women learned to make costumes of red and blue cloth, decorated with crystal beads. Their compact and orderly designs stand out as different from the scrolled flowers and leaves of the Algonkian. Were these suggested by Dutch and English models rather than French? As further decoration, the Iroquois received silver brooches, pendants, and combs and wampum. As the Dutch began to manufacture the neat, cylindrical beads, the Iroquois seized on them as an accompaniment to their formal contracts and speeches of condolence. The presentation of a string of wampum after any public statement came to have somewhat the same function as the white man's affixing of a signature. The League ultimately had a Keeper of Wampum, who was something like a recording secretary, since he must remember the significance of every string in his care. Ultimately, the French and English became wampum-givers.

There were war parties during this early trading period but of the traditional type whose chief aim was the taking of captives for the peace of a dead warrior's soul and the honor of the captor. Then, by about the mid-1600's, the beaver of Iroquois country began to give out. The same thing was happening in Canada, and we have mentioned how the trade moved west, leaving poverty-stricken and degenerate tribes behind it. Those tribes were not organized in a league and were vulnerable accordingly. The Five Nations, instead of pulling apart, had been slowly cementing their alliance. Perhaps they actually thought of it as the Great Peace which their speeches proclaimed. Certainly they had kept their people together except for a few scattered episodes, and now they had a united force with which to fight for commercial advantage.

This they did with as single-minded a purpose as any modern nation. Since they had no furs, they had either to loot furs directly from other Indians or to force those others to trade through them as middlemen. Careful historical study has gone into the reconstruction of this situation,[16] though it is here an impressionistic sketch. The Indians richest in furs were the Huron, kinsmen of the Iroquois who had been long and peacefully settled north of Lake Ontario, had treaties of friendship with the French, and had received French missionaries. The Huron themselves had few furs and almost no agriculture, but they gained all these things by trading. Their men followed regular circuits during the year, going to their western kinsmen, the Tobacco and Erie nations, for corn and tobacco, then to the northern hunters for furs, which they carried to the French. In 1646 eighty canoe-loads landed at Montreal.

Would the Huron share this gold mine with the Iroquois? No negotiations to that effect were successful. The Huron were growing richer and the Iroquois poorer, so the last resort was destruction of the Huron. It was done. On a March dawn in 1649 a thousand yelling warriors swooped down on a Huron village which had lived in peace for decades. Three hundred Hurons were killed; one village was burned, with captives tied in the cabins; two Jesuit priests were tortured, one for fifteen hours. The Huron fled. Next came the Tobacco Nation, or Petun, allies of the Huron. Their warriors had hopefully gone out to attack the Iroquois but came back to find their village burned and their wives and children dead or in captivity. "For half a day, they sat silent on ground, without raising their eyes, without moving, and seeming hardly to breathe, like statues of stone."[17]

This devastation of their own kinsmen marked a turning point in Iroquois history. Henceforth, their wars gradually ceased to be commando attacks, made by a few dozen men whose aim was glory and captives. The torture of a few captives would hardly alter the course of the fur trade. Therefore the Five Nations began to send out armies of from five hundred to over a thousand men. Their aim was complete annihilation of tribes handling the fur trade or else conquest and tribute. In the former case, they could hunt the abandoned territory themselves. In the latter, they could collect a toll of furs from the hunters. With this in view they forged west, wiping out Huronia from 1648 to 1649, liquidating the Neutral Nation by 1651, the Erie Nation in 1654, and the Susquehannock of Pennsylvania in 1653. For some fifty years their attacks were carried on with such violence that sometimes not one canoe-load of furs came to Montreal, and the shores of Lake Huron, once populous, harbored not a single Indian.

Even Montreal was attacked (between temporary treaties of peace), and for the trading post of Three Rivers "it was evil upon evil and sorrow upon sorrow."[18]

The dispersed tribes fled in all directions, and future chapters will often mention the turmoil caused by Iroquois conquests among Indians who, perhaps, had never seen an Iroquois. Yet we should not be surprised to find that some of these people, notably a large group of Huron, found refuge among the Five Nations themselves. In fact, they were welcomed. When a tribe ceased to be a rival in the fur trade, it became eligible to build up the Iroquois population, dreadfully diminished by war. Especially was this true of those who already spoke an Iroquoian language. The custom of adopting captives into the tribe was already established. Now whole villages might be received at once, and their children, at least, endowed with full tribal rights. The Iroquois also learned the French custom of exchanging prisoners and began to find it more profitable to keep their prizes alive than to sacrifice them. The claims of Aireskoi were giving way to those of economics.

The French tried on the Iroquois the same gentle and effective persuasion they had used on the Huron. They sent missionaries. True, some Mohawk were converted, but, when anger blazed again between French and Iroquois, they fled to Canada, where they are yet. The Iroquois kept much more constantly to their other ally, the English. In 1668 these late-comers to the scene replaced the Dutch in the New Netherlands. New Amsterdam became New York and Fort Orange, Albany. Then began the situation familiar wherever English and French traders were in conflict. England, the vigorous young trading nation, had better goods and gave better prices. Even had she not promised eternal friendship, the Iroquois must have been swayed. They kept to the English alliance through thick and thin up to the American Revolution. That did not mean that they allowed the English a monopoly on their trade. Old New York records are full of flowery speeches in which the canny sachems suggested that their English fathers should "wipe their eyes and clear their throats" with gifts and then proposed the same thing to the French before they totted up the score and decided on the better bargain.

It was in these days of astute diplomacy that the League may have reached its highest point of organization. While the worst fighting was going on, the Five Nations often disagreed, even though they never fought each other. But, as the white man's power increased, there came to the Iroquois the same need that impressed all Indians. They must tighten their organization or be overwhelmed. The eastern Algonkian had been completely unprepared for this task. The Muskogean had taken steps toward it, under the inspiration of brilliant individuals, but the Iroquois had the organization ready, and they handled it with wisdom. While keeping the balance between French and English, so that neither could count on their help against the other, they enlarged their League to take in Younger Brothers, or "outhouses to the finished house [the Longhouse]."

Their kinsmen, the Tuscarora, fled from the incursions of the North Carolina colonists in 1713. They were permitted to join the League as the Sixth Nation. Then came the Tutelo and Saponi of Siouan speech. The Algonkian Delaware, Shawnee, and Nanticoke were all subdued and placed under Iroquoian overlordship, the Delaware, for a time, being made as women, with no right to fight or make treaties (a sidelight on the actual importance of women in Iroquoian polity). Here was no drunken lust for power, as some writers have supposed. An Iroquois envoy told the Creek: "Take Care that you oblige all Such as you make a peace with That They immediately Remove and Settle near To oppose your Enemies. . . . That is the Method that We take and we would have you do the Same."[19]

As the 1700's moved on toward the American Revolution, a number of tribes in New York, Pennsylvania, Ohio, and Ontario looked to the Iroquois as their guardians. The Five Nations even talked of a league of all Indians against the whites—with themselves, of course, at the head. But the Creek were too confident of their own power; the seaboard Algonkian were near their end; the Algonkian of Canada could not be detached from their French allies. The French and Indian War burst out, and the Iroquois, the buffer state, were very near to having the decision as to which side should win. Had they been on the French side, the scales might have been turned. Had they even allowed the French to stream down through the waterways into New York State, the blow to the English would have been severe. They refused, even though the Seneca and Cayuga sympathized with the French. King George II instructed that money be poured into the New York colony in an attempt to win them over, but this never succeeded completely. However, some Iroquois did aid the English in the taking of Fort Niagara. The French route to the seaboard colonies was barred.

Except for those few bands on the English side, the Iroquois did not fight, thus showing far more wisdom than the Indian cat's-paws, many of whom never recovered after this struggle. When it was over and their most favored ally, England, was in power, there was a heyday of peace and civilized living for the Iroquois. Even before the war the English had appointed a superintendent of Indian affairs for the northern tribes near their colonies. They could not have had a better man than the young Irishman, William Johnson, who made friends with the Indians, learned Mohawk, and, finally, was knighted for leading a group of Iroquois at Lake George in the French and Indian War. Johnson built himself a "castle" of logs and two fine mansions in Mohawk country; he took a Mohawk maiden, Molly Brant, as his "Indian wife"; he educated her brother, Joseph Brant, at a mission school—which afterward became Dartmouth College—and then made him his assistant.

During these years after the French menace was gone, there were no war whoops or war ceremonies except those acted out to honor Sun and Thunder and to bind friendships. The Iroquois under Sir William's charge were now a mixed people, eleven different nations living with the Seneca, while a number of French had also married among the Onondaga. They lived in log houses with stone fireplaces, gardens, and orchards. They dressed in cloth and calico, though with touches of the beadwork, ribbon, and feathers decreed by Indian taste. Iroquois silversmiths now made their own brooches, sometimes on an ancient Scottish pattern, sometimes copying the Masonic emblem worn by Sir William. It is true the white settlers near them were beginning to make the inroads which are part of any Indian history, but the jovial and diplomatic Sir William was able to "keep the chain of friendship bright" between him and his Indians. It was even brighter when Joseph Brant, in the year 1775, accompanied Guy Johnson, Sir William's nephew, on a visit to England, where he had his portrait painted by Romney.

In the next year the Revolutionary War broke out. This was the most serious crisis which had ever faced the Five Nations, and it proved their undoing. The League declared for neutrality. Brant, of course, wished to fight on the English side, and he, with Molly's help (Sir William had died just as the war loomed), persuaded the Mohawk, Seneca, Cayuga, and Onondaga to come with him. The Oneida and Tuscarora held out for the Americans. This was the first time that members of the League had actually planned to fight on opposite sides, though there were occasions when they had failed to aid one another.

The League was disrupted, the Great Peace ended; the council fires of the Six Nations were put out.

> Woe! Hearken! We are diminished.
> The cleared land becomes a thicket
> The clear places are deserted!
>
> Alas! Woe! Woe!
> They are in their graves,
> They who established it,
> They who established the Great League.
>
> Yet they declared
> That the Great League
> Would endure forever. . . .
>
> But woe!
> The League has grown old.
> Thus are we miserable.[20]

Brant led groups of Tories and Indians, who burned villages and tortured captives in the ancient Indian manner. Monuments among the meadows of New York State commemorate the massacres of Wyoming and Cherry Valley, where, it is said, the angry British officers showed even more savagery than the Indians. The carnage had to be stopped. Washington sent General Sullivan, known to the Indians as "Corn-cutter," to overawe the Iroquois. He found the villages deserted, but he burned forty of them, destroyed 160,000 bushels of corn, and "left no single trace of vegetation upon the surface of the ground."[21]

The war ended, and the British made peace but, as we have seen before, with no reference to their Indian "brothers." Brant with most of the Mohawk went to Canada, where they were given land on the Grand River in Ontario. Others from all the Six Nations afterward joined them, and the tract was known as the Six Nations Reserve. There were already settlements of refugee Catholics at St. Regis and Caughnawaga. These Indians are mostly farmers, later rafters on the St. Lawrence; and now the Caughnawaga and St. Regis Mohawk have distinguished themselves as structural steel workers, in demand all over the country. At first, since all Six Nations were represented, the Grand River Iroquois revived the League with all its governmental paraphernalia. In 1924 the Canadian government ended this arrangement and established a biennial election, under the supervision of a superintendent. But the spirit of the League lives on at Grand River, the life-chiefs still holding council on the first Tuesday of the month.

Most of the Oneida moved in 1832 to Wisconsin on invitation of the Algonkian Menomini. The Stockbridge Indians, Mahican who had been loyal to the American cause, moved with them. Since the tract given to them by the Menomini included some excellent forest land, they are well off. Their men, educated in Protestant mission schools, often rise to high positions in the Indian Service. A mixed group of Seneca, including some Huron and captives from various tribes, moved to Oklahoma, where they still carry on the old ceremonies.

Those who remained in New York were principally the Seneca, with a few Cayuga, Oneida, and Onondaga. They suffered tragic losses of land through political red tape and the maneuvers of land companies. Disorganized as they were, with drink supplying the place of contentment as it often does, the Seneca seemed near dissolution. Then occurred one of those revelations of which we shall hear often as an Indian group reaches the point of despair. A Seneca had a vision, bidding his people return to the old, upright ways. In May, 1799, a Seneca, belonging to one of the noble families and bearing the sachem's title, "Handsome Lake," had a vision. He was, by that time, aging, poor, and a victim of drink, but he was visited by a dream in true Indian style. Four emissaries from the Creator appeared to him, bidding the Seneca to return to their ancient ways and also to give up liquor, gossip, and all unseemly behavior. Handsome Lake preached his gospel far and wide, and even President Jefferson was impressed by the change made in Iroquois life. At present the messages of Handsome Lake, a hundred and thirty in number, are recited during three successive mornings at the midwinter festival. Such Iroquois as keep to the old ways follow Handsome Lake, while the others are Christians.

The New York Iroquois are on six reservations at Tonawanda, Cattaraugus, Allegheny, Onondaga, St. Regis, and Tuscarora. They are organized in a republic of modern form, with president, vice-president, and other elected officers. They are not officially under the United States Indian Service; however, New York State holds the lands at Tuscarora, St. Regis, and Tonawanda in trust. Congress recently conferred on the state criminal and civil jurisdiction over the Iroquois. (The Tonawanda Band has a separate government of life-chiefs with certain civil officers elected annually.) One faction of the Iroquois still consider themselves a separate nation, senior to the United States, which has made them citizens, an honor which they deny. In the first World War they separately declared war on Germany, sending a runner in native costume all the way to Washington with their declaration. Since they never officially made peace, they considered the second World War a mere continuation, for which no declaration was necessary.

WOODLAND LEAGUE

FOOD

Vegetable.—Fifteen varieties of corn, many varieties of beans and squash. Strawberries, greens, maple sugar, herbs. Definitely agricultural.

Animal.—Deer, beaver, small game, fowl, fish foods.

HUNTING METHOD

Nets, fish dams, stalking, individual and group shooting.

CLOTHING

Male.—Skin leggings, soft-soled moccasins with cuff, skin shirts, head-dresses of the stand-up feather type.

Female.—Wrap-around skirts and poncho-like blouses of skin. Soft-soled moccasins with cuff. Later: European cloth with the same type skirts and varieties of blouses.

HOUSE TYPES

Village dwellers. Log stockades, "longhouses" for communal dwellings. Sweat lodges.

EQUIPMENT

Household.—Barrels, baskets, trays, carrying frames of elm bark. Splint basketry. Bowls and ladles of wood. Plain gray pottery, worked down by hand and finished with a textile-covered paddle, with overhanging collar. Cornhusk trays, plaited baskets, house mats, mattresses, and pillows.

Transportation.—Elm-bark canoe, snowshoes.

Hunting.—Self-bow, arrows, masks, and also charms.

Other.—Cradle: flat board, low wood sides and footboard, bow at top. Pipes: small clay with reed tube. Miscellaneous: Carved wooden masks, corn-husk masks, no weaving. Braided sashes and straps, some plaiting. Quillwork, later fine beadwork.

WAR

Armor of sticks and reeds, wood shield, tomahawks, bow and arrow, clubs. Anyone could organize a war party. Had raids, surprise attacks, massacres, took prisoners and scalps.

GAMES

Dice, hidden ball, hoop-and-pole, lacrosse, snow snake, snow boat, racket, races.

CHAPTER VII

People of the Calumet

On the Mountains of the Prairie
Gitche Manitou the mighty . . .
Stood erect and called the nations
Called the tribes of men together. . . .

And, erect upon the mountains
Gitche Manitou the mighty
Smoked the calumet, the Peace-Pipe.[1]

L<small>ONGFELLOW</small>'s *Hiawatha* is a saga of the Great Lakes Algonkian, re-shaped, renamed, and embellished to suit the white man's idea of a god-hero. Nevertheless, in this prelude, the poet has sensed facts which are basic to our history. The Mississippi Valley, bed of the river which flowed from the footprints of the Great Spirit, was indeed a meeting place of Indian nations. Already we have named it a highway of culture, and this chapter takes us into the jostling and turmoil produced by those who moved up and down it. These people did indeed pay reverence to that remote deity, the Great or Kind Spirit. They did indeed smoke the stone pipe with feathered stem known to the French as *chalumeau*, or calumet. It was their most sacred object, so potent that, says Marquette, "the sceptres of our kings are not so much respected."[2] Perhaps we may be allowed, in seeking a name for these tribes of different languages and customs, to call them People of the Calumet.

The huge waterway, consisting of the western Great Lakes and the Upper Mississippi with all its tributaries, provided a travel route far more inviting than forest or mountain. From the time when the ice receded, early people must have passed that way, and the skeleton of a young girl, known archaeologically as "Minnesota Man," is thought by some to be among the most ancient of human remains in America, though it has not yet been dated. Certainly Indians have been in the area for some seven or eight thousand years. Their relics have been

110

PLATE XIV

CALUMET

The term "calumet," strictly applied, refers only to the long, elaborately ornamented stem; later the name has come to mean the stem with a pipe attached. Formerly, in place of the pipe bowl, the head and neck of a duck might be used.

The stem, made of light wood, was painted, adorned with different feathers from beautiful birds, carved, or received wrappings of quillwork or beadwork. The pipe bowl was carved in various ways from catlinite, or pipestone, which, when first quarried, can be carved with a knife but hardens after exposure to the air. It was usually red.

The calumet was used in the ratification of treaties (hence frequently referred to as a "peace pipe"), to greet strangers, as a symbol in the declaration of war or peace, to insure its bearer safety among alien tribes, and as a medium of appeal to their gods for blessings or appeasement of anger.

This calumet, of Ojibwa-Sioux origin, is ornamented with a fan of eagle feathers, quillwork, and bright feathers fastened with red cloth and has a sheep's head, a turtle, and an elk's head carved on its stem. (From West, 1934.)

traced through a period of hunting, fishing, and gathering and then the
making of pottery—that same rough ware which is found all the way
west through Alaska and back into Siberia.[3]

Gradually the knowledge of agriculture and its ceremonies spread up
the Mississippi Valley from the south. In the valley of the Ohio, a
tributary of the Mississippi, the famous Hopewell blossomed, with
agriculture, pottery, barrows, and, later, public plazas and complex
burials in earthen mounds.[4] The elaborate organization and ceremony which must have formed part of this mound-building civilization have left their traces throughout the Mississippi Valley and
far beyond, reaching our area about A.D. 500. Just which peoples were
responsible is still under debate. We can say, however, that, at a date
before this chapter opens, the Ohio Valley was occupied by people of
Siouan language. This does not mean the buffalo-hunters of popular
literature but settled village tribes whose elaborate organization and
poetic ceremonies have disappeared all too quickly. Before the whites
came, most of these tribes had scattered. Owing to an Iroquois invasion? Here is another misty spot in Indian history. At least we know
that, when the Algonkian arrived, there were only a few Siouan tribes
along the Mississippi (see Map IV).

For the Calumet People, according to their own stories, are newcomers to the valley. Most tell of wandering from the East, the Ojibwa even having traditions of the Atlantic Coast.[5] Their equipment is
the same as that of their kinsmen living in New York and Ontario,[6]
and their languages are intimately connected with those of the seaboard.[7] We can picture them as part of that wave of westward migration which had its start on the Atlantic Coast, when the first eastern
Indians traded their fish and furs for guns. Armed tribes soon began
to push west in search of new hunting country, those who were still
unarmed fleeing ahead of them. Map V shows how they streamed
around the Great Lakes and down through Wisconsin and Illinois.
The early history of Chicago reports that region occupied by almost
every one of the Calumet tribes before another arrived to oust it. The
map (p. 142) and its legend list the tribes of the Calumet region
with their varied histories. For convenience, they can be divided into
People of the Lakes, who, as a rule, lived by hunting and fishing much
like their kinsmen on the St. Lawrence, and People of the Prairie,
who found river valleys for agriculture and who might even reach the
buffalo plains for a summer's hunt.

If we begin first on the flat and windy shores of the Great Lakes,

PLATE XV

Snowshoes

Snowshoes were essential to most of the tribes of the Great Lakes because of the heavy snows and the necessity for long hunting trips in winter. There are several types of snowshoes in this area: the round or bearpaw, those with a pointed heel, the snowshoe with a turned-up toe, and a fourth kind consisting entirely of wood with a thong to hold the foot. The variety of types also shows an even greater variety of techniques. Some were made with a single piece of wood (like the above); others with two pieces. Netting techniques were also numerous, the two most common types in the area being the rectangular one, like this shows, and the hexagonal weave which consists of three sets of parallel strands crossing each other at a 120° angle. Some snowshoes were made without a crossbar, others with one, two, or more. The illustration is of an Ojibwa "bearpaw" snowshoe, the name coming from its shape. They are also referred to as "old woman's shoes," since they are most commonly worn by old women. It is made of a single frame with rectangular netting and a single crossbar. The crossbar was attached by splitting both ends and lashing the bent parts to the frame. The frame and crossbar were usually made from green strips of ash wood made pliable by steaming over a fire. Narrow strips of rawhide from the moose or deer were used for netting. The strips were called *babiche* by the French. A thong of the same material was carried through the netting and wrapped across the instep from the front. (From Densmore, 1929.)

we shall find the Ojibwa and their kinsmen pushing in from north
and east to find the Algonkian Menomini,[8] the Siouan Winnebago,
left from some earlier migration up the Mississippi, and the nomadic
Santee Sioux, camping by the lakes of Minnesota. All were forced by
nature to the same yearly round of hunting, gathering, fishing, sugar-
making, and a little gardening in sheltered spots. This country, cold
and rough though it might be, was generous with food. At Sault
Sainte Marie, between Lakes Superior and Huron, the Salteaux (a
branch of the Ojibwa) had a permanent fishing village where they
and visiting tribes sometimes took a hundred whitefish in one net.
The huge sturgeon was speared by a man standing in the bow of a
canoe while another man paddled. (Hiawatha, according to Longfellow, got the giant sturgeon by his own heroic efforts.) In late summer the Lakes People sought some pond or slow-moving stream to
gather wild rice (Zizania aquatica). Some are even thought to have
planted a little. Rice was particularly important with those who had
little agriculture, and these frequently had family gathering territories, just as they had hunting lands and sugar bush.

Doubtless, when the Ojibwa, Ottawa, and Potawatomi pushed the
Sauk, Fox, and Kickapoo out of the forests teeming with deer and
elk and the shallow lakes where wild rice grew like grass, and when
these, in turn, pushed out the Miami and Illinois, the conquerors felt
that they were keeping for themselves the best food country. They
had never seen the lush river bottoms of Indiana and Ohio, where
corn would grow six feet high. Even less were they aware of that rich
meat supply, unknown in northern forests, the buffalo. It is true that
some of the bison family penetrated as far east as Pennsylvania, but
not to New York and the St. Lawrence, whence these migrants had
come. Never had they been seen in such enormous herds as those
which roamed west of the Mississippi and even reached the prairies of
southern Illinois.

The Algonkian immigrants who reached this rich food country
changed their whole plan of life to suit the new conditions. More
than this! They were now in touch with old Valley residents, having
cultures far more organized than their own. Across the Mississippi
were the Siouan Osage, Iowa, and Missouri, with whom they traded,
fought, and exchanged prisoners. Straight down the river were the
Chickasaw and Choctaw of chapter iii. Pressing them on the east
were the Iroquois, and soon arrived two Iroquois satellites, the Shawnee and Delaware. The Prairie People thus had several models to

follow, and they did follow them, some choosing one item for change, some another. Who knows to what extent they would have developed if left undisturbed?

The first explorers reported them in the fertile valleys of Illinois and Ohio, raising enormous crops of corn, beans, and squash; those of one Miami village extended for two leagues (five or six miles) along the Wabash.[9] As usual, women tilled the fields, while the men hunted and fished. However, there were some weeks in the year when the whole village moved out into the prairies or even across the Mississippi to hunt buffalo. This, before the days of horses, was no easy matter. It was done in the fall when the grass was dry and could be fired. Then a herd was surrounded, and bowmen could pick off the animals as they tried to escape. The Miami told La Salle that they got two hundred a day by this method.[10] Women were usually taken along to pack in the meat, dry it, and tan the hides. Some tribes report going out immediately after planting, leaving a few old people to tend the crops, and returning for harvest. The Sauk and Fox, before this exodus, held ceremonial feasts, clan by clan. The Illinois, who claim they got as many as twelve hundred in a day,[11] appointed camp police, who chastised any man hunting alone and scaring the herd. Thus, between Lakes and Prairie tribes, we have progression from the well-known round of winter hunting, summer fishing and gathering, to the new, luxurious life of summer crops, fall buffalo-hunting, and often a winter of ease.

Clothing, housing, and equipment were in the usual Woodland style. The birch did not grow south of Michigan, so women made mats for their house covering or used the heavy, corrugated elm bark. In summer they moved into spacious gabled houses, open at one end. Two or three hundred such houses might be gathered in one village beside their huge cornfields, as Marquette saw them on the Illinois in 1680.[12] Only the Lakes tribes, of course, could have light, graceful canoes of birch bark. The Prairie People made dugouts or pirogues of butternut wood, such as were used all the way down to the Gulf. Since they were too heavy to carry from river to river, they were kept on the home stream. The Prairie People did most of their traveling on foot, the women carrying the burdens with a packstrap, while armed men guarded them.

Men also made "platform" pipes for smoking, in the style of those dug up at Hopewell. From prehistoric times there had been a quarry in Minnesota controlled by the eastern Sioux and at a few other north-

PLATE XVI

OJIBWA BEADED POUCH

Before the seventeenth century and the introduction of glass beads, porcupine quills and moosehair were used for embroidery. After the advent of the

ern spots. Here deputations from a score of tribes came to dig up the smooth, blood-red stone, now known as catlinite after the artist who first publicized it. When the pipe bowl was carved and fitted to a long reed, it became the famous calumet, the peace pipe. Around the Lakes it was actually smoked, just as short pipes were, the "tobacco" being kinnikinnick (Algonkian for "mixture") and usually consisting of red osier bark, scraped and dried with perhaps some dried sumac or the leaves of a small evergreen shrub.[13] On the Prairie and all the way down the Mississippi the pipestem was magnificently decorated with feathers, red for war and white for peace. Sometimes there was no pipe attached, the dancer or ceremonialist merely waving feathered wands.

Calumet women also were famous for their craft, with bark and fiber as their medium. They spun it into yarn on the bare thigh, much as we can imagine southeastern women to have done; they dyed it with soft vegetal colors and twined the result into bags, sashes, and headbands. Later, when the whites brought colored worsteds, these were to develop into veritable works of art. Particularly important was the braided sash, with its one hundred or so warp strands intricately crossed. This form of textile is known all the way from the eastern Woodland to the Southwest and was probably the earliest form of Indian weaving. Another sash was made in a kind of loopless netting which can be seen in Canada to this day.[14]

In the matter of family rites the Algonkian again found themselves in contact with more complex ways. They segregated the mother at

---

beads, which were one of the most common trade articles, decoration with this technique ran riot. Even saddles were heavily beaded. In bead embroidery the beads were strung on a thread of sinew, laid in position according to color and design, and a second thread was overlaid at irregular intervals to secure the beads more firmly. It also produced a fine mosaic effect. Broadcloth, velvet, and other woven textiles supplanted hides after their introduction. The designs of the Great Lakes area are quite distinctive—elaborate floral motifs which were taken partly from their indigenous style and partly from French influences. Frequently the designs were worked on a white beaded background, as the pouch is done. Bead strips could be woven on a simple loom, often referred to as the bow loom (of the same type used to weave the wampum belts discussed in previous chapters). The illustration is a bandolier or beaded pouch worn by the "well-to-do" on ceremonial occasions. It was a large square bag with a broad band long enough to go around the neck. That such pouches served the purpose of a container is doubtful; they were simply a prerequisite for "full-dress" costumes. (From Lyford, 1942.)

childbirth, as always, but now, as shown in Table 1, many of them had clans with lists of names. A boy born into the Sauk or Fox Buffalo clans, for instance, must look for one of these names not in use, such as Straight Horns or Hooves Spread Out. When puberty arrived, they held to the ancient idea of the personal vision, and one wonders if it was not these devotees of the spirit helper who introduced it to neighbors such as the Santee and the Winnebago.

PLATE XVII

MORTAR AND PESTLE

Wooden mortars and pestles were principally used to grind corn but might also be used to pulverize other dried foods such as fish. These implements reduced the corn to coarse flour or meal, and then it had to be sifted through baskets to remove the chaff.

The mortar was made from a short horizontal section of a log, hollowed by fire and with stone and bone adzes. It usually had a handle on either side. Mortars averaged from 18 inches to 2 feet in length and were about a foot thick. The pestle resembled a "dumbell," for it was double-headed. Pestles were smoothed with stone or bone adzes; they were about a yard or less long.

Vertical mortars, made in the same manner only with a log set on one end, were used in the East and Southeast. (From Skinner, 1921.)

In this part of the country the vision was a grim affair, beginning before childhood was fairly over and applying often to girls as well as to boys. At about the age of ten a child was called before his father one morning and given the choice between his usual breakfast of cornmeal mush or a stick from the fire with a blackened end. If he had the stamina of a true tribesman, he refused the mush, blackened his face with the stick, in sign of fasting, and went forth to implore the spirits. In childhood the ordeal lasted only a few hours, but, as the magic-fraught time of puberty approached, it must be carried on for days on end. Girls were not asked to carry the process so far, but they must tame the miraculous power of childbearing by the usual monthly segregation.

When the time for marriage arrived, most tribes had clan relationships to avoid (see Table 1). Young men who were making choice among suitable maidens wandered about on summer evenings playing the flute, a crude wooden instrument, played from the end, whose few notes were more a bird call than a tune. There were even love songs sung by both girls and boys, a thing rare among Indians, despite the white man's belief. Like most of the red man's songs, these contain only a few suggestive phrases, their very lack of articulateness giving a haunting quality. Witness this girl's song from the Ojibwa:

> Oh, I am thinking,
> Oh, I am thinking,
> I have found my lover.
> Oh, I think it is so.[15]

When the mate was chosen, the young man brought a gift of game to her family. (Remember Hiawatha and the deer he carried to Minnehaha's father?) In time, he might take other wives, preferably the girl's sisters, and all would live in the same wigwam. The buffalo-hunting Prairie tribes, like their neighbors farther west, were particularly strict in the matter of wifely fidelity, and an unfaithful wife might have the tips of her nose and ears cut off. Death meant a period of frantic wailing, which gave a thorough emotional release. Afterward, people could go back to work. Sometimes the corpse was buried and the grave heaped with gifts, but, where prairie soil was hard to dig, it was placed on a scaffold. Often a family filled the void by adopting someone of the same age and sex as their lost member. The Fox had an adoption feast when the clan bundle was opened and the blessing of the spirits secured for the new relationship.

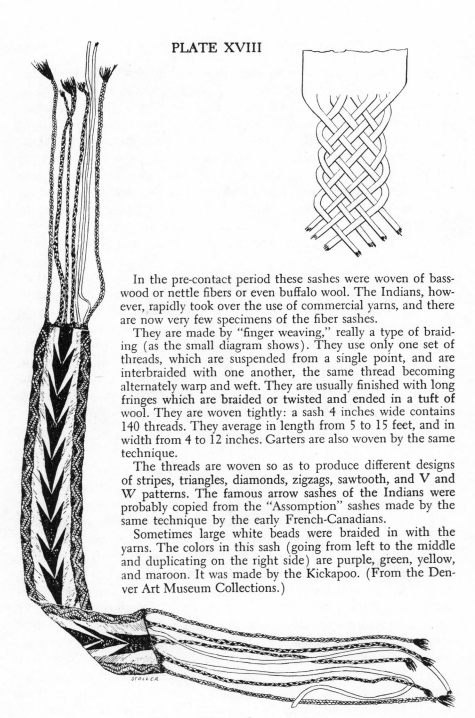

PLATE XVIII

In the pre-contact period these sashes were woven of basswood or nettle fibers or even buffalo wool. The Indians, however, rapidly took over the use of commercial yarns, and there are now very few specimens of the fiber sashes.

They are made by "finger weaving," really a type of braiding (as the small diagram shows). They use only one set of threads, which are suspended from a single point, and are interbraided with one another, the same thread becoming alternately warp and weft. They are usually finished with long fringes which are braided or twisted and ended in a tuft of wool. They are woven tightly: a sash 4 inches wide contains 140 threads. They average in length from 5 to 15 feet, and in width from 4 to 12 inches. Garters are also woven by the same technique.

The threads are woven so as to produce different designs of stripes, triangles, diamonds, zigzags, sawtooth, and V and W patterns. The famous arrow sashes of the Indians were probably copied from the "Assomption" sashes made by the same technique by the early French-Canadians.

Sometimes large white beads were braided in with the yarns. The colors in this sash (going from left to the middle and duplicating on the right side) are purple, green, yellow, and maroon. It was made by the Kickapoo. (From the Denver Art Museum Collections.)

WOVEN SASH

Clans were a new departure for the Algonkian, for most of those in Canada had no suspicion of such a thing. However, they took it up in the new environment, and Table 1 shows that they had father-clans, complete with totems or guardian animals,[16] clan ceremonies, and a list of names for clan members. A few tribes even adopted a custom of the Valley Siouans, that of grouping all clans in two divisions or moieties. That part of the arrangement they never understood very well, for, instead of making moiety membership hereditary, they assigned their children alternately, first to one moiety, then the other.

Officialdom, too, was intensified as life grew more complicated. We have seen how the Algonkian of the eastern coast turned their chiefs into little kings, after the manner of the Muskogean and Natchez. Here, the Miami did the same thing, if we may believe French reports. Others followed the example of their Siouan neighbor, the Winnebago, who had two leaders of equal power, the war chief and the peace chief. The war chief was the usual volunteer brave, functioning only in time of battle. The peace chief was chosen for wisdom and generosity and held office for life. His house was an asylum for the pursued or the wrongdoer, where even a sacrificial dog might take refuge and escape his fate.[17] In cases of murder which, as usual, was dealt with by the families concerned, the chief would go with a calumet to the victim's family, begging them to accept a payment in goods rather than death of the murderer. Tales even speak of his having himself bound like a victim to incite pity and so prevent a feud in his village.

The pipe was the medium in international relations, as wampum was with the Iroquois. The solemn assemblies when it went the rounds, clockwise, as visitors were entertained or alliances made, might be thought of as secular. To the Indians they were like an oath taken before the deity, for "any injury done to any enemy from whom they had accepted the belt and the pipe was an insult to the Great Spirit."[18] A calumet was not only a sign of alliance, like the signature on a treaty, but also a passport. "Carry it about with you and show it," said Father Dablon, "and you can march fearlessly amid enemies who, even in the heat of battle, lay down their arms when it is shown.[19] Marquette was given a calumet by the Illinois and, by grace of it, passed the whole Mississippi River in safety.

PLATE XIX

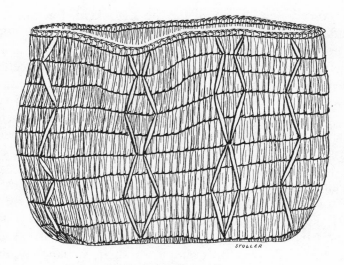

MENOMINI FIBER BAG

The bags were woven by suspending the warp fibers from a horizontal cord which had been looped around two sticks set vertically in the ground. The fibers were evenly spaced and were not fastened at the bottom. The weft threads were twisted around the warp in several ways. The maker (always a woman) left the end of the warp fibers long enough so that they could be twisted together, three to five at a time, into a heavier strand which was braided all the way around to form the rim of the bag. The work was done from the top downward, and, when completed, the top is the bottom of the bag. There were no side seams, since the weft threads were carried continuously around the warps. The method of weaving the warp and weft is technically called "twining," and there were three varieties of it practiced: plain, diagonal, and wrapped.

The most common material was fiber from the basswood tree, although other fibers were used. These bags are now woven from colored commercial yarns.

The designs could be very simple, as these are, or they could be geometrical figures arranged in bands or even conventionalized life-forms. The designs were different on each side. The bags were used for food storage or for the keeping of ceremonial paraphernalia. (From the Denver Art Museum Collections.)

TABLE 1

ORGANIZED GROUPS AMONG THE CALUMET PEOPLE

Tribe	Moiety	Clan	Totem	Link or Pair	Band	Clan Rank
Ottawa		Patrilineal clans	Matrilineal totem		4 bands	
Ojibwa		Patrilineal clans	Animal totems	5 phratries	Bands grouped into subtribes	
Menomini	Bear and Thunderbird	Patrilineal clans	Ancestors, animal totems	5 or more phratries	Developed under whites	Bear chief = peace; Thunder = war
Winnebago	Exogamous with different functions	Patrilineal clans with duties, bundles, animal names	Animal totems			Thunderbird is chief
Sauk	Dual division, not exogamous	Patrilineal clans, set of names, duties, taboos	Animal totems	Pairs serve each other		
Fox	Dual division, not exogamous	Patrilineal clans, set of names, duties, taboos	Animal totems	Pairs serve each other		Bear is leader; Hawk, war leader
Kickapoo	Dual division, not exogamous	Patrilineal clans				
Potawatomi	Dual division, not exogamous	Patrilineal clans	Animal totems			
Mascouten	Dual division, not exogamous	Patrilineal clans		6 phratries		Fish clan supplies chief
Miami	?	?			6 bands	
Illinois	?	?				
Eastern Dakota	Exogamous patrilineal clans with officers				3 bands	

This was the peace calumet. The red-feathered one for war was also well known and used, since war with the central Algonkian was a normal state of things. Say the Menomini: "When there were many of them, the Indians began to slay each other: the Menomini, the Ojibwa and those of all languages were always fighting. . . . They never ceased. . . . In every way did the Indians do grief to one another."[20]

We recognize the war procedure, which was much like that of the Southeast, with its volunteer leader, the feast of incitement,[21] and the usual commando attack. Here, too, there was a sacred bundle, carried by the leader; but often the bundle belonged to a particular clan, and the leader was the clan headman. With the Sauk and Fox and perhaps others, he was a sort of priest who remained behind the battle line, the sacred pack spread out before him, while he carried the attack forward psychologically with his prayers.

Some of the tribes (Miami and Ottawa) made a point of bringing home prisoners for torture, like the Iroquois. Here, however, we set foot in a different culture area. No grown man could be taken prisoner if he preferred to die, and many of these valley tribes lacked the belief that death by torture was the noblest possible. The Sioux would even kill themselves rather than be taken. So the most frequent captives were women and children, intended for use as slaves. Even those tribes which took men rarely reached such imaginative intensity of torture as did the Iroquois. Warriors still brought home scalps, which they immediately handed over to the women or to the clan leader, but such trophies were not of first importance. What the careerist wanted was to change his name, to wear special insignia (cf. the Muskogean), and to have the right of boasting, all his life long, that he had performed an act of derring-do. Far more dangerous than scalping was touching a live enemy, surrounded by his fighting comrades. The first four Sauks to do this might have their names changed even on the battlefield, provided they took some name owned by their clan. A Sauk who had scalped might wear scalp-fringed leggings. Later, at the scalp dance, where all the village joined, he would chant of his doings:

> In this manner I shot (or clubbed) him down.
> He cried out and begged for mercy
> But I had no pity for him
> He was my enemy.[22]

Ever afterward, at village feasts, the warrior might be asked to tell again the story of his prowess, thus bringing pride and confidence to all his hearers. Miami warriors, one by one, danced before the calumet, mimicking the tracking of the enemy, the attack, the scalping, and then the whirling elation of victory. This dance, whose origin is too ancient to be remembered, has been taken up by most western Indians and can be seen at many a paid performance. The Miami warrior, having danced, usually told the story of his exploits, striking a post with a stick at each one.[23] Woe to him or to any of the Calumet tribes if they deviated one iota from the truth! Comrades would shout their refutation, and the boaster would be disgraced for life.

These tribes, which traveled so far and wide for war, also journeyed for trade. Copper from the Great Lakes region has been found in southern mounds, and shells from the Gulf in the north. The French reported that the Ottawa went five hundred leagues to get paint, shells, and woven girdles. In the intervals of war and trade, they played the usual games of chance and athletic skill, with lacrosse, the chief one, played with much ceremony between moieties and villages.

Doubtless, these traders were entertained with calumet-smoking, for that passport was accepted from the Sioux on the west to the Iroquois and Delaware on the east. All these tribes had some belief in its sponsor, the Great Spirit, or Manitou, known variously as the Master of Life, the Giver of Breath, or Earthmaker. The Menomini called him the Gentle Manitou;[24] the Ojibwa, the Kind Manitou.[25] Under him, with the Calumet People, were Grandmother Earth, the Thunderers, the Water Monsters, and the spirit ancestors of all the animals. Unique among these is Manabush—or some similar name—the Great Hare. This clownish being, of a type familiar among western Indians, was a helper and defender of the people, even a minor creator. (It was from Hare's adventures that Longfellow distilled his tale of the divine Hiawatha.) The greed and credulity of Manabush have no repulsiveness for the Indian, who loves to tell how catastrophe overtook the Hare, time after time, while, nevertheless, he could cause sap to flow from the maple trees, punish men for presumption, and institute the Medicine Rite. (The Winnebago—an exception, as usual—separate Hare, the culture hero, from Manabush, the clown.)

When the Gentle Manitou brought all these beings to life, his last and poorest creation was man. In order that this feeble creature

might have some way to gain spirit favor, Manitou gave him the tobacco plant, which he had withheld from all the spirits and even
from himself. The spirits yearn for this strong incense, and therefore
man has always at hand the gift which will win their favor. So, on
ceremonial occasions, the offering was a smoke or a handful of tobacco. Men eager for a vision, instead of beating the drum, went forth
with tobacco in each hand, wailing and begging pity until some powerful being appeared to them.

Such ordeals, in ages past, had been the origin of the clan bundles.
We need a more poetic word for these skins, claws, and beaks of
animal helpers, which, to their owners, were something like a sacred
ark. Each had been vouchsafed to some clansman long ago, and now
it brought safety and good fortune to the whole clan, especially in war.
Among the Sauk, Fox, and Winnebago, where there were such bundles, we hear nothing of village rites for planting and harvest. Such
sacred duties seem to have been turned over to the clans, whose one
form of ritual was the opening of the war bundle. There was no temple. The only priest was the bundle-keeper, descendant of the original
recipient. He summoned his clansmen to his house, then called members of his "friend clan" to cook and serve a feast whose main item
was a sacred white dog.

While the invited guests ate to repletion, the host clan sat before
the open war bundle, drumming, offering tobacco, and singing such
vision songs as:

> Yonder person is whom I summon.
> Yonder person is a Thunderer.[26]

Such was the procedure at spring planting, at harvest, and at adoption. We suggest that, here, a group of hunters and fighters was
adapting itself somewhat awkwardly to the calendric ceremonies of
agriculturists.

Our Algonkian had kept their traditional medicine man, that visionary with a host of spirit helpers who could find lost objects and
prophesy the future. Among the Calumet People he performed minor miracles, such as thrusting his hand, unharmed, into boiling water
or holding seances, when his closed tent shook with spirit power.[27]
He also divined the cause of disease, but the actual cure was usually
performed by a different practitioner who sucked a maleficent object
out of the body or gave herbal remedies.[28]

This type of lone-wolf medicine man sank into the background, often under a charge of sorcery, in the presence of the Midewiwin, the Grand Medicine Society. There has been some discussion about this impressive organization, with its grades for initiates and its lore drawn in symbols upon birch bark. It appeared first among the Ojibwa, then the Winnebago and other Lakes and Prairie tribes, down to the Omaha. Dr. Radin, who has made a particular study of it,[29] contends that this elaborate organization was not worked out until the whites came and was an attempt to offer something in opposition to the French priests. If it was indeed a modern concoction, it was made with Indian materials. The scene when members dance around their mat-covered lodge, killing and reviving each other by means of a magic shell, is a shamanistic contest, such as we shall hear of often. Yet, Christian elements appear also, as when an Ojibwa said: "The principal idea of the Midewiwin is that life is prolonged by right living."[30] The Winnebago declared that their rites made life eternal through transmigration of souls[31] decreed by Earthmaker, the Giver of Life, himself. Says their ritual: "Earthmaker created this ceremony for us. . . . Earthmaker loved us and, for that reason, we have been brought into connection with life. We are thankful and grateful indeed, more in fact than we can express. Let the depth of our thankfulness and gratitude be proportional to the new life which has been vouchsafed to us."[32]

The Grand Medicine Society, like other institutions of the Calumet Indians, has changed and faded under more than two centuries of white influence. These Indians were not summarily dispatched, like their kinsmen of the Atlantic seaboard. They survived years of change as the fur trade undermined their economy and white contacts altered their government. They struggled through the swirl of white man's contending policies during the French and Indian War. They kept afloat, though changed and disorganized, through the Revolution and the War of 1812, and only in the nineteenth century were they finally dispersed to live in small groups west of the Mississippi.

In the early 1600's, while the fur trade was booming near the Atlantic Coast, the Huron stood guard over the western Great Lakes, keeping the French and even the Iroquois from sharing their trade with the "western savages." True, Champlain, seeking a waterway to the Pacific, got to Green Bay, on Lake Michigan, in 1615, and his henchman, Nicollet, followed him in 1634, carrying a damask robe in which he planned to meet the emperor of China. Such visitations were merely a matter of passing wonder to the Indians until the Huron barrier was removed in 1649 by cruel Iroquois conquest. Then, both whites and Iroquois flooded through the gap.

By 1670 the trader Perrot was smoking the calumet with the Fox and the Potawatomi, urging them to live at peace so that French trade could be facilitated. In 1675 Father Marquette was addressing some two thousand chiefs and warriors at the great village of the Illinois, on the river of that name, halfway down the Mississippi. Already these southernmost of the Algonkian had been receiving goods from tribes closer to the French, and one of their chiefs was even acting as middleman for tribes remoter still. In 1679, when La Salle paddled down the river, the Illinois attempted to persuade him from going farther by telling stories of frightful monsters. They were trying to keep French trade in their own hands. The Iroquois, who considered themselves the middlemen par excellence, could not brook this rivalry, and in 1680 they destroyed the Illinois village. La Salle then gathered some Illinois refugees, with bands from several other Prairie tribes, and attempted to form a federation. Thus early were the Calumet People confronted with the desirability of union.

These incidents keynote the themes of life in the Mississippi Valley for the next sixty or eighty years. The Indians wanted trade. In fact, before very long, they had to have it, since they were losing their old crafts. They were afraid of the Iroquois. Their history alternates fights and alliances dominated by this powerful tribe. Tribal unity was already broken. Since they had been dislodged from their ancient hunting grounds, most tribes had wandered in separate groups, and these were reported by the Jesuits at such scattered points that their migrations are difficult to follow. They were learning the necessity of alliance, both because of urging by the French and because their isolated bands often had to make common cause with the nearest neighbors. It is no unusual thing to learn of bands from three or four different tribes hunting or wintering together. Perhaps the huge villages like the 460 wigwams reported by Hennepin for the Illinois were the result of some such union.

These results took shape gradually. At first, as the flood of trade goods poured in, the Indians experienced that revivifying which often took place when new tools and new materials brought stimulus to the ancient crafts. With firearms, more game could be killed and more war honors won. With steel tools, wood and birch bark could be carved and etched in designs more elaborate than had been possible before. Chiefs began to wear trousers, shirts, and silver medals donated by the French officials or sometimes by the Spaniards across the Mississippi. Costumes of the Calumet People, labeled in museums as "old," often have the shape of a full-skirted French coat, though its color comes from paint and beads instead of figured satin. Buckskin costumes might be decorated with trade thimbles, a handsome substitute for elk teeth. Coarse woolen "strouding" and blankets of all colors began to replace buffalo robes. Buffalo skin also was more plentiful, for now the Prairie tribes were hunting on horses received from the south and were tipping their wooden lances with old Spanish sword blades. "With these things they had a good life."[33]

The French traders also lived a good life. They had learned from the Indians the snowshoe and the canoe, used almost unchanged to the present day, and with these they ranged all through the Lakes and Prairie country. Less frequently now the Indian flotillas come to Montreal, though the French government took various measures to induce them. Instead, the adventurous young *coureurs de bois*, the forest rangers, spread through the Indian country, buying up furs in the fall, wintering with the Indians, and taking their booty to the coast in the spring. Though required to have a license, of which, supposedly, only twenty-five were given out, these adventurers slipped out of civilized Canada by the hundreds, selling property and deserting wives and children. In 1680, of a population of ten thousand, over eight hundred men were ranging the forest.[34]

They changed the life of the Calumet People even more, perhaps, than English traders changed that of the southeasterners, for they were far more numerous. La Hontan said that, at every post in the Illinois country (1688), there were thirty or forty who used it as winter quarters. Few led a bachelor's life. Whether or not there was a wife at home, they took Indian mates, paying a bride price to father or brother according to custom. They could also leave according to custom, since divorce was easy. Yet few had the urge to go back under the rule of church and law. Hundreds of Frenchmen, dressed in buckskin and girt with braided sashes of cedar bast, roamed the North Woods for life. Some married the daughters of chiefs and sired a line of leaders like Langlade of the Ojibwa (see p. 133) or the Winnebago chiefs.[35] Others merged with the tribespeople. The Ot-

PLATE XX

Woman's Costume

The woman's costume is composed of a silk-appliquéd, broadcloth shawl,
a similar skirt, a silk or calico blouse, short leggings, and moccasins. The

tawa and Ojibwa, particularly, are permeated with French blood, as their lakes and forests are sprinkled with French names.

The late 1600's marked the high point of French power in America. Before the turn of the century which was to see that power lost, France had a string of forts from Frontenac at the eastern end of the Great Lakes to St. Louis, south of Lake Michigan. The plan was to extend these defenses all the way down the Mississippi, thus encircling a great portion of the eastern United States, which was bounded on its other two sides by gulf and ocean. The Spanish holdings along the Gulf of Mexico were negligible, while the English, who clung to the Atlantic Coast, might, with Indian help, be pushed back into the sea. At least they could be kept behind the Alleghenies, which walled the Mississippi drainage from the coast, thus isolating an empire for France in the heart of the continent.

Here the Ohio River flowed through deep woods and lush meadows where once the Mound-builders had raised their corn. It provided other prospects than fur-hunting, and, by 1700, French peasants were tilling the soil in two villages: Kaskaskia and Cahokia, now in Illinois. They got along well with the Indians and with the traders who wintered and caroused among them and at the near-by fort. In vain were they upbraided by the missionaries who followed them, preaching a very different kind of life. The forest rangers made a specialty of brandy, so easy to carry, so valuable in trade. This was the dark side of the picture, for in 1718 a French official grumbled: "The Savages no longer think of hunting in order to clothe themselves but only to get drink. Brandy is making them poor and miserable: sickness is killing them off."[36] The Jesuit missionaries complained, and there were proposals to keep brandy away from the Indians, but the traders always had a ready answer. If they did not supply it, the English traders, now slowly seeping across the mountains, would fill the need. Then, let

---

square of broadcloth, used for a skirt, is lapped around the waist and held in place with a woven yarn belt. The blouse is decorated with many native-made metal brooches. The leggings reach only to the knee and are either beaded or have silk-appliqué decorations. The soft-soled, beaded moccasins have a broad vamp set in, and the uppers are puckered to this. The cuffs are large and have a drawstring to fasten them to the ankles. A beaded hair tie is fastened about her braids in back. Many bead and shell necklaces are worn by the women. (From Skinner, 1921.)

the Jesuits take warning, for the Indians would become heretics! The liquor trade went on.

And the English menace drew closer. Far from being penned behind the Alleghenies, traders from the coastal colonies were pushing across into the Ohio Valley, and soon settlers would be following the traders, with mule, ax, and plow. At first, the Indians did not object, for the traders brought English goods, better and cheaper than France could supply, hampered as she was by the regulations of an absolute monarchy. The traders were backed by the Iroquois, friends of the English, who claimed the whole Ohio Valley, the "beautiful" in their language, by right of conquest.

Also in the 1700's came members of the Iroquois empire, albeit disaffected ones. The Delaware had been pushed out of eastern Pennsylvania by encroaching whites. The Shawnee had wandered in two divisions, one going far to the south, but now they, too, braved the mountains to find a less settled country. These two, while Algonkian, were no western savages. They had long experience with the whites and with organized tribes like the Iroquois and the Creek. They were not impressed with promises by the "French father," and they knew the value of English trade goods. The big Shawnee town of Pickawillanee, on the Miami, a tributary of the Ohio, soon became a rendezvous for English traders, with bands from many other tribes camping near. The Miami moved a whole village to be closer to the trading post. It was plain that France and England must soon fight with weapons other than trade.

The Indians had to choose between two powers, each of which promised peace and plenty if the other were driven out, but destruction otherwise. How were the red men to decide, when all they wanted was a continuation of the old life—with the addition of a good trading store! One Delaware told an Englishman, about this time, that his tribe would like nothing better than to have English families live with them, teaching the white man's arts. Would that some tribe had been left unmolested until the twentieth century, so that such a thing might be tried! The struggle for power made it impossible that any Indians should be left alone. The French and Indian War began, with the Iroquois and their subordinates, the Shawnee and Delaware, more or less on the English side, and the Lakes and Prairie tribes, again more or less, with the French.

In 1755 General Braddock marched his redcoats, his Virginia militia, and his Indian allies over the mountains to Duquesne, key French fort on the Ohio. There the commandant, ill supplied with troops, had gathered some eight hundred warriors of the Lakes and Prairie tribes, with the mixed-blood Langlade, son of an Ojibwa trader, as leader. It was these Indians, with their French firearms and their Indian surprise tactics, who routed Braddock's army and kept Duquesne French until the commandant could no longer feed them. Young George Washington, Braddock's subordinate, would have known how to oppose them, but Washington had no chance to command until the general was killed and his army in flight.

The war in the West frayed out into scattered attacks on settlers, bloody and merciless in proportion to the Indian determination that these invaders should be frightened away once and forever. The scalpings, torturings, and burnings left a scar on the white man's memory which has lasted to the present day. Yet the white men also scalped. Leaders on both sides found it simpler to pay settlers and Indians for this sort of piecework, which could be done in their spare time, rather than to keep them fed and disciplined in the army. Even the citizens of Philadelphia were urged to go out after scalps—and who was to tell to whom these belonged?—at the rate of 130 pieces of eight for a male, 30 for a female.[37]

Quebec fell in 1759, with Langlade there at the head of twelve hundred Indians. A treaty of peace was signed in 1763. Suddenly, France was stripped of all her New World possessions. Under Sir William Johnson, now superintendent for all the northern Indians, the Calumet People learned that they were to give back all captives, even the white wives they had married. They were to have few gifts, despite the losses they had suffered in the war. They were broken. Poverty and its temporary remedy, drunkenness, were everywhere. Worst of all, the frontiersmen, driven from farms by the war, were now flooding back, no treaty or proclamation seeming able to stop them. At this juncture rose one of the prophets who were to appear often during the days of Indian disorganization. He was a Delaware whose name is now forgotten, and his message was the same which has appealed to many people in time of misfortune: "We must go back to the old ways. Under them we were happy, and, because we have neglected them, we are now suffering." He bade the people throw away their guns and cease to wear white man's clothes and eat white man's food. Then by magic, so the Great Spirit had told him, the good old days would return.

The prophet did not preach war, but he prepared the way for Pontiac, the Ottawa war leader, who proposed to bring back the good old days by driving the English from the country. Pontiac was well prepared for his mission. He had fought against Braddock and was familiar with French campaign tactics and with the French plea that Indian tribes should unite against the Iroquois or other enemies. He tried to gather all the Calumet People and did succeed in allying the Ottawa, Ojibwa, Shawnee, and Delaware, along with the Mingo and Wyandot, fugitive Iroquoian from Canada. For a year this "little United Nations" was successful, taking all the English forts, except the key ones at Pittsburgh and Detroit. But Indian strategy and temperament were not suited to long campaigns. After a few failures, the allies began to fall away. In 1763 Pontiac smoked the pipe of peace with Sir William Johnson. In 1769 he was murdered by a Kaskaskia Indian at a drinking bout.[38]

Could Britain, if left in power, have handled the Indian situation? She now had three superintendents for the north, south, and middle areas. The king, by a proclamation of 1763, had reserved the coveted land west of the Alleghenies for Indians. Yet a mere proclamation meant nothing to the frontiersmen, who had hacked their way through the wilderness and held off Indian attacks, each with no help but that of his own ax and long rifle. These individualists scarcely felt themselves subjects of the king or, later, of the American nation. Treaty-makers for years to come complain, like Lord Dunmore, governor of Virginia, that all authority was "insufficient to restrain the Americans and that they do and will remove as their avidity and restlessness incite them."[39]

Dunmore had two suggestions about handling these recalcitrants, and here, again, we glimpse possibilities which might have made Indian life different from what it is now. The usurping whites, said Dunmore, might be simply cut loose from the mother-state of Virginia and forced to look after themselves. In that case, might they have had to come to some terms with the red men, like the French did at Kaskaskia? Dunmore thought so and considered that they could be allowed to incorporate with the Indians and form a separate state.[40] Neither plan was adopted. The boundaries promised the Indians were successively moved north, from river to river, the Iroquois, absentee landlords, taking payment for the forfeited territory and keeping their hapless subordinates quiet.

The American colonies revolted. The war rolled to and fro along the eastern coast while, again, its expression in the West was scalping attacks by the Indians on the farms of the invading "buckskins." The British governor Hamilton, at Detroit, was known as the "Hair-buyer." Indians expecting scalp bounties would march their prisoners carrying booty to the walls of Detroit, then kill them and present the hair. There was only one American victory on this frontier, the swoop of George Rogers Clark on Kaskaskia, Cahokia, and Vincennes.

The war was over, and again the Indians had a new master. This time it was a hated one, for the Indians could make no peace with the "buckskins" who usurped their land. Homeless Mingo, Wyandot, and even Cherokee roamed the country, killing and looting where they could, and the whites reciprocated. A band of angry Kentuckians, out for any Indian they could get, fell upon a peaceful Moravian settlement, killing ninety Christian Delawares. When the Shawnee were nearly starving because of the loss of their hunting grounds, one of their chiefs, holding the Stars and Stripes in one hand and the treaty in the other, approached a band of whites. They shot him dead.

It was a time for Indian union, if ever such a thing could be achieved. And who was better qualified to achieve it than the Six Nations, with Joseph Brant, now in Canada, at their head and Sir John Johnson to cheer them on! Under these auspices there was a series of councils involving as many as thirty-five nations. The world knows now how difficult it is for peoples of differing backgrounds to agree and to act together, even when their lives are at stake. We need not be surprised that the Indians, after a little flurry of victory over Governor St. Clair of Indiana Territory, were discouraged and dispersed when defeated the following year by Anthony Wayne. The Ohio Valley became farming land for the whites.

"Do not give us money," urged the Indians who were being evicted, "for we do not know how to use it. Give it instead to the land-hungry people who are moving in and add to that the sums you promise for our support every year and the expense of your armies that keep us quiet. Then perhaps these settlers will go elsewhere."[41]

It was no use. The money was paid, and the Indians moved. Disorganization, drunkenness, and banditry were added to the ravages of smallpox, which had swept through the country in 1781, from the

Great Lakes to the Pacific. Then again arose a prophet. This time he came from the Shawnee, that tribe which had suffered most pitiably by white encroachment. Tenskwatawa—to use one spelling of his name—preached, like his Delaware predecessor, that the people should give up all white man's goods and live in the old Indian way. And, as before, there was a man of action to implement his words. Tecumseh ("Crouching Tiger"), the brother of the prophet, has been called one of the greatest of American Indians because of his general-ship, his oratory, and his humane and generous attitude. Tecumseh, in his early forties, had already fought on the English side in the Revolution as well as taking many a scalp in Indian feuds. He was acquainted with English army discipline; he knew the power of the white man's union under the English king; and, as a Shawnee, he had grown up under the shadow of the great Iroquois organization. He took up the labor of confederation which Brant had relinquished when he retired with his Mohawks to Canada, and Tecumseh worked at it with zest and fury. "It is my determination," he told Governor Harri-son of Indiana, "nor will I give rest to my feet until I have united all the Red Men."[42] He and his brother settled at Tippecanoe, in the present Indiana, where they collected some thousand Shawnee, Dela-ware, Wyandot, Ottawa, Ojibwa, and Kickapoo. There the prophet and his followers practiced the old Indian life, while Tecumseh went up and down the country preaching union and revolt. "His voice," reported General Sam Dale,[43] "resounded over the multitude . . . hurling out his words like a succession of thunderbolts." Before 1811 he had visited and revisited the Lakes and Prairie tribes on both sides of the Mississippi. Governor Harrison of Indiana wrote to Secretary of War Eustis that, if it were not for the presence of the United States, Tecumseh would found an empire rivaling Peru or Mexico in their glory.

In 1811 the great leader had gone to the Creek, the tribe of his mother. This ancient confederacy was undecided, but, before Tecum-seh could return, the Prophet had precipitated a battle. The devotees at Tippecanoe were defeated and dispersed. Tecumseh joined the British in the War of 1812, in which, as a brigadier general, he led two thousand warriors.[44] When he was killed in one of the last battles of that war, American soldiers are said to have peeled off strips of his skin as souvenirs.[45] Thus the famous and civilized tribe of the Shawnee fades out of history, and with it go the Delaware, the Miami, and the

Illinois, to be represented hereafter by small groups domiciled across the Mississippi or by individuals absorbed into the life of the whites.

With the northern tribes, whose land was not yet in great demand, the picture was somewhat brighter. Fur-trading had been good during the British regime and even afterward. By about 1800, Indians were receiving not only necessities with a few gewgaws but a wealth of materials which provided a brilliant blooming of craftwork. Red and blue cloth was taking the place of buckskin, and soon this was decorated with gay satin ribbons, discarded in France after the revolution of 1790 and "dumped" on the American trade. There was colored yarn for the bags and sashes once made of cedar bark, and this art would flourish as the American traders brought more and more bright worsted. Sashes would even be decorated with the glass beads which traders now imported from Venice. Like the eastern Indians, the Lakes and a few Prairie tribes blossomed out in great floral figures on shirts, breechcloths, and moccasins. The Menomini, in time, adopted a little loom for bead belts. Also, the Iroquois and Delaware had brought from the East their thin silver jewelry, and men and women now could deck themselves with earrings, bracelets, pendants, combs, or belts.

After 1812 the British slowly withdrew from the country south of Canada. The new United States, scarcely yet a nation, made plans and promises about Indian lands which it had no power to carry out. The next thirty years saw treaty after treaty in which both Lakes and Prairie tribes ceded their huge hunting territories for the benefit of settlers who expected to farm or cut timber on almost every square foot of it. By 1840 all the tribes of this chapter had moved across the Mississippi, usually in several stages, each of which both they and Congress thought would be the last. In return the government had paid the Calumet People, including the newcomers Delaware, Wyandot, and Shawnee, over $15,000,000 in money and goods. In addition, they received land owned by the government but set aside as reservations where they might live free of real estate taxes. Also, some $50,000 was spent for education, mostly through the churches. The young and unformed America, itself in need of funds, should have credit for an attempt at friendly dealing seldom shown by conquerors to the conquered. True, the payments made to Indians were usually wasted by a people unused to handling money, and the assumption that warriors and hunters should settle down to farming proved a mistaken one. The tribes stagnated and dwindled.

One flare-up of hostility took place in 1832 when Black Hawk, a Sauk, led a band of his people who refused to move, saying they had not been party to the treaty which the rest approved. It was too late. The Winnebago, Potawatomi, and Kickapoo, on whom he relied for help, soon fell away, and the Winnebago even delivered the fleeing Black Hawk to the whites. He was released after a time and even honored. Still, kindness to one man could not help a whole people in the leap from one way of life to another. Black Hawk had tried to express his own attitude when he was placed in chains on board a Missouri River boat: "We told them (the whites) to let us alone and keep away from us but they followed on and beset our paths and they coiled themselves among us like a snake. They poisoned us by their touch. . . . We were becoming like them, hypocrites and liars, adulterers and ladrones, all talkers and no workers."

Once again, in the 1880's, there was an attempt to find the good life by religious means, since all others had failed. The Dream Dance was organized in several of the northern tribes (Santee Dakota, Potawatomi, Ojibwa, Menomini). This time there was no connection with war and forceful ejection of the whites. The dance around a sacred drum was one of fellowship, even with the whites, and a mutual gift-giving to prove good will. Some of the tribes practice this dance still and also the Indian's approach to Christianity, the peyote religion, which has its place in the next chapter.

Table 2 shows the present numbers of the Calumet People, and the reservations on which they now live, scattered from Oklahoma to Michigan and into Canada. Of them all, it was the most remote from "civilization," the Ojibwa, who have the most land and the largest population. Their forest lands have been looted by lumber companies; they have suffered from drunkenness and disease. Many of them still elect to live as close as possible to the old Indian way, fishing (at Red Lake they have a co-operative cannery), lumbering, and acting as guides. There are educated people from the Ojibwa and other Lakes tribes in the Indian Service. The Winnebago even provided a reservation superintendent.

The Prairie tribes have dwindled, partly because of the deadly smallpox epidemics which swept them several times, partly because many have left the reservations and been absorbed by whites. Not the Kickpoo! A band of them decamped to Mexico, where they could lead the old, wild life, and later some others followed. The Fox, objecting to the land assigned to them, took their payment money and bought land in Iowa which they still own. The Miami, sharing a reservation with the Siouan Quapaw, fell heir to lead and zinc mines which provide some of them with an income. The rest live in frame farmhouses on their allotments in Kansas and Oklahoma. Their children go to school and take jobs in the cities. Some of the older people find comfort in the peyote cult. Seated in an old-style brush shelter or a tipi, they sing to the sound of drum and rattle:

When I die, Jesus will be waiting at the gate.

TABLE 2

PRESENT RESERVATIONS AND NUMBERS OF THE CALUMET PEOPLE

Tribe	State and Agency	Population, 1945*	
Delaware.........	*Oklahoma:* Wichita Reservation	165	
Kickapoo.........	*Kansas:* Kickapoo Reservation	360	
	Oklahoma: Kickapoo Reservation	291	(651)
Menomini........	*Wisconsin:* Menomini Reservation and Agency	2,551	
Miami...........	*Oklahoma:* Miami Reservation	305	
	Peoria Reservation	414	(719)
Ojibwa..........	*Michigan:* Bay Mills Community	150	
	Isabella or Saginaw Reservation	435	
	Minnesota: Bois Fort or Nett Lake Reservation	754	
	Fond Du Lac Reservation	1,417	
	Grand Portage Reservation	402	
	Greater Leech Lake Reservation	2,333	
	Mille Lac or purchased land	428	
	White Earth Reservation	9,377	
	Red Lake Agency and Reservation	2,484	
	Montana: Rocky Boy's Agency and Reservation	568	
	Wisconsin: Bad River Reservation	1,375	
	Lac Courte Oreille Reservation	1,790	
	Lac Du Flambeau	968	
	Mole Lake Reservation	205	
	Red Cliff Reservation	689	
	St. Croix Reservation	241	(23,616)
Ottawa...........	*Oklahoma:* Ottawa Reservation	460	
Potawatomi.......	*Kansas:* Potawatomi Reservation	1,188	
	Michigan: Hannaville Community	161	
	Oklahoma: Potawatomi Reservation	2,974	
	Wisconsin: Forest County, Potawatomi County	319	(4,642)
Sac and Fox......	*Kansas:* Sac and Fox Reservation	128	
	Oklahoma: Sac and Fox Reservation	992	(1,120)
Shawnee..........	*Oklahoma:* Eastern Shawnee Reservation	305	
	Shawnee Reservation	730	(1,035)
Winnebago........	*Nebraska:* Winnebago Reservation	1,365	
	Wisconsin: Public domain allotments	1,520	(2,885)
Wyandotte........	*Oklahoma:* Wyandotte Reservation	824	

* Numbers in parentheses are totals.

LAKES TRIBES

FOOD

Vegetable.—Wild plants, wild rice, seeds, berries, maple sugar.
Animal.—Deer, elk, bear, fish, beaver, dog.

HUNTING METHOD
Fishnet, spear, bow, poisoned arrow.

CLOTHING
Male.—Soft-soled moccasins with and without cuffs, leggings, shirts of skin, breechcloths, skin robes.
Female.—Skin wrap-around skirts, soft-soled moccasins, robes of skin in winter; later, blouses.

HOUSE TYPES
Domed, gabled, or conical wigwams, birch bark or mat covered; lodge houses. Segregation huts for women.

EQUIPMENT
Household.—Plaited baskets, mats for coverings, rugs, bedding, and containers. Crude gray pottery. Cedar-bark textiles and bags. Wooden spoons and bowls.
Transportation.—Birch-bark canoe, snowshoes.
Hunting.—Self-bow of hard wood, arrows, wood lance, and spear.
Other.—Cradle: skin-covered, U-shaped frame. Pipe: platform of catlinite, decorated reed stem. Miscellaneous: cedar-bark textiles, bags, sashes, headbands, carriers—all twined. Quillwork in floral designs. Flutes, drums of wood.

WAR
Bow and arrow, lance, spears, elkskin shields. Sneak raids, little actual battle-formation fighting.

GAMES
Dice, double ball, hidden ball, hoop-and-pole, racket, ring-and-pin, shinny, snow snake, tops.

PRAIRIE TRIBES

FOOD
Vegetable.—Wild plants, wild rice, flint and flour corn of many colors, beans, squash (*Cucurbita pepo*).
Animal.—Buffalo, elk, fish, dog.

HUNTING METHOD
Bow, lance, some nets.

CLOTHING
Male.—Soft-soled moccasins with and without cuffs, leggings, shirts of skin, breechcloths, skin robes. Tattooing.
Female.—Not much clothing in summer. Skin wrap-around skirts, soft-soled moccasins, robes of skin in winter, tattooing; later, blouses.

HOUSE TYPES
Wigwam, elm bark or mat covered. Longhouse and large gabled houses. Female segregation huts.

EQUIPMENT
Household.—Plaited baskets, mats for coverings, rugs, bedding, and containers. Pottery, crude, gray. Cedar-bark textiles. Wooden spoons and bowls. Elm-bark vessels.

Transportation.—Dugout, snowshoes.

Hunting.—Self-bow of hardwood, lance, and spear.

Other.—Cradle: skin-covered U-shaped frame. Pipe: calumet in its full form. Miscellaneous: quillwork; later, silk appliqué. Cedar-bark bags. Buffalo hair added to other fibers used by Lakes tribes. Flutes, drums of wood.

WAR

Bow and arrows, lance, spears, skin shields. Sneak raids, little actual battle-formation fighting.

GAMES

Dice, tops, cat's cradle, double ball, hidden ball, hoop-and-pole, popgun, racket, ring-and-pin, shinny, snow snake.

CALUMET PEOPLE

LAKES TRIBES

Ojibwa (Chippewa in United States government reports): Closely related in language to Ottawa and Potawatomi. Their legend is that all three once were one people and migrated from the Atlantic Coast, north of the St. Lawrence, guided by a magic shell. Arriving at Michilimackinac (modern Mackinaw), they separated, some remaining for some time at Sault Sainte Marie, where the French called them Saulteaux, or People of the Falls. Others went south of Lake Superior, arriving at its extreme end (La Pointe, later a French mission) and spreading beyond. In the course of this migration they fought constantly with the Fox and the Santee Dakota, ultimately driving them from the wild-rice fields.

Ottawa: Originally formed one people with Ojibwa and shared the above migration. They stayed at Michilimackinac and, when French built a fort and trading post there, became known as Ottawa, or traders. (A. E. Jenks, "The Wild Rice Gatherers of the Upper Great Lakes," *19th Annual Report of the Bureau of American Ethnology,* Part II [Washington, D.C., 1898], pp. 1029 ff.)

Menomini: Apparently an earlier migration than the Ojibwa, their language being most closely related to the Cree-Montagnais to the north, also to Sauk, Fox, and Kickapoo of the Prairie tribes. Their earliest known home is Green Bay, Wisconsin, on Lake Michigan.

INTERMEDIATE

Potawatomi: Third member of the Ottawa-Ojibwa group. They moved southward, stopped at Chicago, then followed the French to Detroit, with some finally going to Michigan. They are intermediate between Lakes and Prairie tribes. In their forest country they did not hunt buffalo but had intensive agriculture and a number of social traits like the Prairie tribes.

PRAIRIE TRIBES

Mascouten (or Prairie Potawatomi): A division of the Potawatomi which moved into Prairie country, hunted buffalo, and shared many customs of the Prairie tribes.

Winnebago: A Siouan-speaking tribe, perhaps a relic of a northward migration from the Mississippi Valley. In their elaborate organization, they show relations with the southern Siouans: Omaha, Osage, Oto.

Sauk (French, Sac): Sac and Fox or Renards (name given by French; own name Meskwaki). Closely related to Fox and Kickapoo, also to eastern Algonkian. Probably pushed west by the expanding Iroquois in prewhite days, arriving before Ojibwa. Originally lived farther north but were pushed south by Menomini and Ojibwa. After 1730 they were in Illinois and out of the rice country.

MAP IV

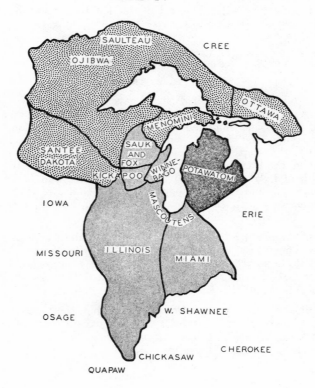

CALUMET PEOPLE

PRAIRIE PEOPLE

LAKE PEOPLE

INTERMEDIATE PEOPLE

Kickapoo: Closely related in language to Sauk and Fox. Probably moved with them from the east. Sites resembling modern Kickapoo found in western New York and Ontario. All three tribes learned much from older Algonkian, Miami, and Illinois.

Illinois (own name Iliniwek—"men"): Large confederation, among component tribes being Cahokia, Kaskaskia, Tamaroa. Scattered through Wisconsin, Illinois, and at one time across Mississippi River in Iowa. Seem to be old residents of the Prairie country and long in contact with more southern tribes.

Miami (Twightwees, an English spelling of their own name, which simulates the cry of a crane): Old residents in 1658 were at Green Bay, Wisconsin, then moved south, stopping at Chicago, finally spreading over northeastern Illinois and northern Indiana.

NEIGHBORING TRIBES

Shawnee: Language is halfway between that of Fox and eastern Algonkian. They are latest of all arrivals from the east, having wandered in two separate groups. One group went south, where they had much contact with Creek and Yuchi. The other went west to Pennsylvania and about 1730 moved to escape settlers into Upper Ohio Valley, where they were finally joined by the southern branch.

Santee Dakota: Eastern branch of the large Dakota (Sioux) group living in Minnesota on wild rice and some agriculture. Wandered into Michigan and Wisconsin (Jenks, *op. cit.*, p. 1043). Were gradually pushed west by Ojibwa.

CHAPTER VIII

The New-Rich of the Plains

To THE average white American and to the European as well, the typical American Indian is the buffalo-hunter of the Plains. Every school child can picture him, in beaded vest and leggings, galloping bareback on his mustang and aiming his iron-pointed lance straight at the buffalo. Yet Plains Indians have only had horses for about two hundred years, iron for a little longer, and beads for considerably less time. These were goods the white man brought, and without them the picturesque and vivid culture of the buffalo-hunters would not have flared up like a bonfire, to die out almost as quickly.

For the Plains way of life is actually the most recent of all those followed by American Indians. It hinged on the possession of horses, which were not ridden by Indians until some time after 1600. But, when once this magnificent new find came into use, it was like the discovery of gold in modern days, drawing people from every language and every background. The buffalo Plains became a melting pot where the most diverse tribes joined together in pursuit of the new wealth. The way of life which they evolved was compounded of customs drawn from the east, west, north, and south. The Plains Indian, far from being the typical red man, was a modern product, a nouveau riche.

The Plains, from the geographer's point of view, is that great flat hiatus in American scenery which stretches from the Mississippi to the base of the Rockies. In a really detailed picture we should divide it into three parts. At the east is the rolling prairie land where the Mississippi Basin tapers off into the flats and which is now rich corn and hog country. At the west are the foothills of the Rockies, barren and rugged, but not flat. In the middle are the true High Plains, ancient domain of the buffalo, modern cow country, and, sometimes, dust bowl. Each of these has had a slightly different history, and the fate of its people has depended on the nature of the land.

That land has changed completely since Folsom man hunted the antique bison amid lakes and forests, leaving his spear points all the way from Colorado to Texas. Even after drier times began and those incredible hunting days were over, there have been cycles of lesser drought and lesser moisture which kept primitive people moving in and out of the Plains as some moderns are doing even today. After most of the big mammals and, probably, most of their hunters had departed, there were thousands of years of meager living. During this time groups whom we shall not venture to identify lived in caves or pitched their shelters in the open, leaving stone points and other tools to testify that the Plains were not vacant.[1]

By the time the Christian Era commenced in the American Southwest, both corn culture and pottery had begun, coming from the south. In Alaska the Eskimo, last comers to the continent, had already made their settlements, with fine ivory tools and pottery from Asia. The Plains had been backward, perhaps due to their recurring dustbowl habits, but now, again, the climate seems to have relented and a new type of settlement sprang up. The people were still hunters, it is true, but they had a kind of equipment never seen in that region before—pottery. It was of the crude, unpolished type, with wide mouth and pointed bottom, which we have so often spoken of as Woodland. So much we know about the newcomers, and also that they collected the bones of their dead at intervals and interred them in mounds.[2] New immigrants? That is possible. And did they bring pottery? It has been suggested.[3]

The highest development of the so-called Woodland pottery, whose origin may not have been in the woods at all, was in the lush meadows of the Ohio Valley, already a prosperous farming country (see chap. vii). We left it, in the last chapter, peopled with incoming Algonkian, but in those early days it was the heart of that culture popularly known as Mound-builder. We have mentioned it already as the Hopewell culture (see chap. vii, n. 4, p. 112), famous for its pottery and copper, its burial mounds and agriculture. It is tempting to imagine Hopewell as a happy union between pottery-and-burial-mound people who had traveled east across the northern Plains and those users of corn who had come up the Mississippi. Such a possibility, let it be understood, exists so far only in the imagination. Much of Indian prehistory is still behind a curtain, not of iron but of earth to be excavated.

We know, at least, that the influence of Hopewell and its cornfields radiated for a thousand miles around and that the Plains, too, had their share. By A.D. 1200 or 1300 corn, beans, and squash were being

PLATE XXI

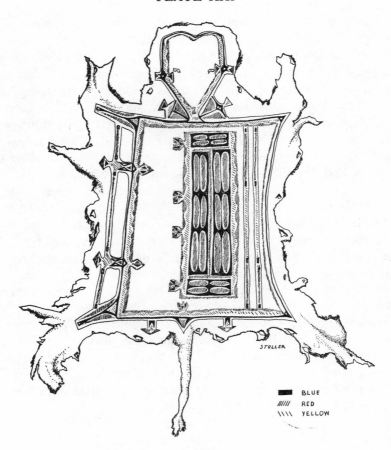

BLUE
RED
YELLOW

PAINTED BUFFALO ROBE

Robes were commonly worn throughout the Plains. They were made of a whole buffalo skin, dressed with the hair on. The weather determined which side of the skin was worn outward. The two general categories of painted decorations are geometric and representative. The geometric forms were carefully combined in well-defined patterns. The representative paintings are of three types: (1) time counts or calendars; (2) personal biographies; and (3) records of visions. The women painted the geometric designs, and the men did the representative. Hide dressing and painting are described on pages 153–55. (From Ewers, 1939.)

raised along the streams all the way from South Dakota to Oklahoma and Texas.[4] Perhaps it was at this early date that the Plainsmen—or Plainswomen—of the past began to breed corn suited to the short, northern summers. Perhaps, too, these corn-growers were ancestors of some of our historic Plains Indians. Not the buffalo nomads, who were practically a modern development! No, the Plains were settled, somewhere between A.D. 1200 and 1600 by sturdy agriculturists, known as the Village Tribes, or, more colloquially, the Old Settlers. They belonged to two language stocks new or almost new to this narrative. One is the Siouan, a word which to most people stands for befeathered fighters. Yet the Dakota warriors (see list opposite Map V, p. 184, for the location and history of the Plains tribes) ranked once only as a crude offshoot from a great civilized group whose home was the Mississippi and Ohio valleys and whose habits included agriculture, high organization, and elaborate ceremonies. The Winnebago, met in the last chapter, were a remnant of this organized group, left by a receding tide of immigration. Related to them were the Mandan, high up on the Missouri and perhaps the earliest agriculturists of the Plains. Later, and farther south, were the Omaha and Osage, with some of the most poetic rituals recorded for Indians. The list (p. 183) gives the names of others once influential but now almost extinct.

The other language stock is the Caddoan, closely related to Siouan and Iroquoian. This stock, too, spread out from America's agricultural heartland—the Arikara, like the Mandan, moving north. The Pawnee followed slowly, spreading and splitting. The Wichita, met by Coronado in Kansas,[5] and the Caddo, a true Mississippi tribe with reed houses and dugout canoes, scarcely enter this narrative.

The Old Settlers in their fields along the river bottoms raised beans, squash, tobacco, and corn in several varieties, growing shorter and hardier toward the north. The Arikara, in North Dakota, had varieties of flint, flour, and sweet corn, red, blue, and white.[6] They were such famous gardeners that their name, in the sign language, was the motion of grinding corn. The gardens, as usual, were women's work, while the men hunted for deer and elk, and, now and then, the whole village trooped out to the buffalo Plains. The ancient *Bison taylori* had died out, but the modern *Bison bison*, now the largest animal on the American continent—six feet high at the shoulder and weighing sometimes as much as 1,800 pounds—represented a source of wealth ideal for a hunting people. However, it was no easy matter to follow the buffalo on foot with only dogs to carry the baggage on their backs

PLATE XXII

MATO-TOPE, A MANDAN CHIEF

Mato-Tope was made famous by some of the early artists in the Plains area. Costumes such as the one he is wearing were strictly for formal occasions and could be

or tied to a frame of poles dragging from their shoulders, known to the French as a travois. True, the Spaniards in 1541 met one group who "travel the plains with the cows," living in tents "like Arabs";[7] but these perhaps were Apache, who had never been anything but nomads. The Village people sallied forth only once or twice a year, in summer for meat and in winter for skins. It was hard enough to handle the great beasts on foot, and they used every device known to primitive man. The method of surrounding a herd and driving it over a cliff or into a pen may even have come down from Folsom days, as witness the great heap of bones at Plainview, Texas. In summer they fired the prairie grass, and in winter they tried to trap a few animals in the snow. Lone hunters sometimes crawled up on a herd, disguised as wolves. All this meant hard work and plenty of danger from the stampeding herd. So the villagers stayed for most of the year in their solidly built houses, only venturing out occasionally to camp in skin tents on the plains.

For house covering they had not the elm and birch bark of the Woodland or the plentiful reeds of the Lakes country. They used the earth lodge, a standard type of primitive dwelling known all the way across northern America, through Alaska, Siberia, and far into Europe. It meant a framework of logs, large or small according to the resources, built over a shallow pit and perhaps provided with a long entranceway. The covering was poles and brush and finally a deep layer of earth. No better insulation was known until the invention of modern materials, and many a white pioneer has been glad to build a "soddy" after the Indian manner. The fashion is old in the Plains and perhaps came in with the first agriculturists, for some of their sites show earth lodges as large as fifty feet in diameter.[8]

These agriculturists were well to do and well organized. Table 3 shows their system of clans, each with its properties and its duties.

---

worn only by men of great honor. His cap consists of strips of white ermine and feathers. The wooden knife is a signal of a heroic deed. The rest of his headdress consists of buffalo horns and a long trailer of black-and-white eagle feathers. His face is painted in red and yellow. The painted buffalo robe has quill embroidery, tufts of human hair and horsehair, and more ermine on it. His leggings and moccasins are also embroidered with quills. His breechcloth shows slightly under the robe. Besides the feathers on his lance, there is also a scalp, mounted on cloth, which is attached by leather thongs. (From Maximillian, 1843, portfolio.)

TABLE 3
VILLAGE PEOPLE

TRIBE	MOIETY OR PHRATRY	CLAN	BAND	CHIEF	SOCIETIES	
					War	Other
Arikara	Confederacy of villages	Mother, weak exogamy	Villages	Village leaders	Warrior; entrance by purchase and desire; age grades	Secular societies; female Goose Society by purchase, other not
Hidatsa	Moieties	7 mother-clans, weak exogamy	Villages	Village leaders	Warrior; age graded, member by purchase, oldier society	Social and clan societies; 1 female society, connected with buffalo, age graded and fee
Iowa	Moieties, winter and summer	6 father-clans exogamous, caste tendency	4 bands	Hereditary from bands, also moiety chiefs and 1 from bundle-keepers	Military and clan war bundle; ungraded, no fee	Social, animal and mystery, shamanistic, membership through vision
Kansa	Moieties with phratries that cut across	Mother-clan exogamous, totemic with caste tendency	3 bands	5 hereditary chiefs from clans, 3 from bands, 1 elected for life	Warrior and bundle-owners; ungraded	Dance and religious, not well defined, membership through vision; female social
Mandan	Village moieties, left and right	7 mother-clans	13 villages	1 peace, 1 war, and 1 village leader, bundle-owners	Warrior and soldier; age graded, membership by purchase	Social and shamanistic; 7 female societies, 1 connected with buffalo and 1 age graded, membership by purchase
Missouri	Moieties	Father-clan exogamous, totemic	Lodges	?	?	?

150

TABLE 3—*Continued*

Tribe	Moiety or Phratry	Clan	Band	Chief	Societies	
					War	Other
Omaha	Moieties	Father-clan exogamous, totemic	Bands	Hereditary; 2 principal, many subchiefs and council	Warrior; 7 age grades, member by purchase	Secret and social, no female societies, but could join men's; member by vision
Osage	Moieties, peace and war	Father-clan exogamous, caste tendency, special duties	3 subtribes	Chief appointed for life by village chiefs	Soldier; no age grading	Social and medicine
Oto	Moieties	Father-clan exogamous	Bands	Moiety chiefs	?	?
Pawnee	4 phratries	Mother-clan endogamous	Bands or villages	Inherited chiefs and 4 bundle priests	Warrior; not age graded, take turns as hunt police	Lance, hunt, and medicine, shamanistic; bundle-owners; vision membership
Ponca	Moieties, Earth and Sky (Thunder)	Father-clan exogamous, totemic		Hereditary for men of clans, also elected for merit	Warrior; 3 age groups, membership by purchase	Medicine and social; shamanistic; membership through vision; 3 female societies
Eastern Dakota		Mother-clan endogamous		1 head chief and 8 selected by council of clans	Soldier; no age groups, no fee or adoption of members	Dance society by vision; shamanistic medicine society, by adoption into group; 1 female society, connected to buffalo, membership by dream

Sometimes the clans were divided into Earth People and Sky People, or right and left, each with its assigned place in the circle of tipis made on the buffalo hunt. Among their war customs, we should recognize many from the Southeast, such as warriors' rank and insignia, warriors' boasting, and war bundles. These villagers were actually a fringe of the Mound-builders, and so they might have gone down in history except for a geographic accident: they were near the buffalo Plains, and they had access to Spanish horses.

Without the horse, the buffalo might never have been more than an incidental source of food, for America's horses had died out thousands of years ago. But, in 1598, Spanish colonists came to New Mexico bringing sheep, goats, and horses. (We can disregard the earlier expeditions of Coronado and De Soto, since their horses all died or were taken home again.) The horse bred on the huge Spanish ranches was the Moorish horse, brought originally from Arabia to Morocco and there accustomed to the hot sun and sandy plains so like those of the New World.[9] It was ridden with the Moorish saddle of tooled leather, with high back and cantle and silver trimmings, which later became our western saddle.

The Spaniards did not allow their subject Indians of the Pueblos to own horses, since this meant independence. However, they soon began to trade horses to the more distant tribes, by way of keeping the peace. At first, the Indians ate the animals, but it was not long before they saw their advantages. By 1676 the Indians of Coahuila, in Mexico, were following a regular trade route up through Texas, bringing loot, including horses, to the Caddo and other tribes. Soon the wild Navaho and Apache were creeping up on the haciendas of New Mexico, howling like wolves and waving blankets to stampede the horse herds. In 1680, when the Pueblos rebelled and drove the Spaniards away for twelve years, many a ranch was abandoned, and the Indians took what they wanted. Numbers of horses went wild and roamed the Plains in herds, as their primitive ancestors had done. The Spaniards later called these horses "bronco," or *mestenyeno*, meaning "wild," and thus we get our word "mustang." The Indians called them "mystery dogs."

Decade by decade, the horses passed north, traded, stolen, or caught wild on the prairie. No sign here that the Indian by nature was "unadaptable" or averse to learning! Not only did the Indians tame and train the new animals but they made all their equipment. The elaborate Spanish saddle, sometimes presented to chiefs, was beyond their means. So they worked out saddles of leather bags stuffed with grass, or they rode bareback, guiding the horse with their knees, the only rein a single rope of horsehair. They developed tricks never known to whites, such as tying a loop of horsehair to the animal's mane and, with one foot thrust through this, throwing themselves along the horse's side, shooting arrows under his neck.

The village tribes were among the first to own the wonderful animal, but, for them, this was not an unmixed blessing. True, they could now spend months on the Plains camping in their well-ordered circles, with Sky People on one side and Earth People on the other. True, they worked out rules for the hunt, such as we have already heard of among the Illinois and which would be adopted and elaborated by later comers. But, as rivalry on the Plains increased, they had to give more and more time to fighting both Indians and whites. Their agriculture suffered; their pottery deteriorated. A culture which had been developing handsomely along its own lines was practically cut short.

Not so with the wandering hunters dwelling north, east, and west of the Plains. Tables 4 and 5 show how they came from every part of the country. Blackfoot, Arapaho, and Cheyenne moved out from the eastern Woodland, forsaking their cornfields, their pottery, and the beginnings of a settled civilization. Comanche came from the western foothills, Crow from the Mississippi, and Kiowa we know not whence. Last of all, in point of time, were the Teton Dakota, or Sioux, most famous of them all. Trekking out of the woods of Minnesota, they did not reach the Missouri until 1775, the date of the American Revolution. There they traded for horses with some of the oldest settlers, the Arikara, and their life as Plains Indians began.

It ranked them among the richest Indians in America, since, to primitive people, wealth is expressed not in money but in food. The buffalo meat, including the vitamin-rich internal organs, gave food in plenty, and hundredweights of it could be sun-dried as jerkee and so kept for months. Pounded fine and mixed with fat and dried berries, it became the staple, pemmican. The tough skins, impermeable as tin, made an ideal covering for the movable tipi, once painstakingly swathed in birch bark. Moreover, with the "mystery dog" to drag long poles and heavy skins, it could now measure as much as twenty-five feet across. Skins, with the fur on, made mantles or bedding. Scraped skins furnished shields, boats, meat bags, pipe-holders, or just material for painted records. Sinew was used for sewing, bones for tools,

TABLE 4

NORTHERN PLAINS PEOPLE

Tribe	Moiety or Phratry	Clan	Band	Chief	Societies	
					War	Other
Assiniboine	Moieties	Father-clan exogamous	Several	Village chief acclaimed	Military; age graded, membership by purchase	Social and medicine; Horse Dance by purchase
Blackfoot	Phratries	Father-clan	Bands	Leader of each band for council; 1 chief elected	Soldier society; age graded, member by purchase, take turns as police	Social, religious; female organization connected with buffalo
Crow	6 phratries	Mother-clan exogamous	3 bands	Camp chief, herald	Military; ungraded, take turns as police	Social and dance; Tobacco society by purchase
Gros Ventres	?	Father-clan exogamous	Local bands similar to clans	Band chiefs	Soldier society; age graded, member by purchase	Social and medicine; 1 female society
Plains Cree	Phratries	Mother-clan exogamous	Bands	Band chiefs	Warrior society; ungraded	Dance and hunt societies
Plains Ojibwa	?	Father-clan totemic exogamous	Local bands	Band chiefs in general council elects 1 chief	Warrior society for male and female; ungraded	Dance and hunt, for male and female
Sarsi	?	?	?	?	No age groups	Dance societies by purchase; females with males
Teton Dakota (Sioux)	Phratries	Father-clan	Bands	4 headmen and society of old men elect 1 chief	Short-term police warrior society; age graded for very young	Chief's society, social societies, female shield society

and horns for cups. Even the stomach was cleaned out and served as
a container for cooking or for carrying water. Given a little deerskin
for clothing and some herbs and roots to balance the diet, the Indians
needed nothing else. And the buffalo seemed inexhaustible. On their
yearly migrations they blackened the Plains as far as the eye could see
and took three days to swim the Missouri. Soon a lifeway began to
crystallize around the buffalo—and around the horse, which made the

TABLE 5

SOUTHERN PLAINS PEOPLE

TRIBE	MOIETY OR PHRATRY	CLAN	BAND	CHIEF	SOCIETIES	
					War	Other
Arapaho		None	Local bands	4 chiefs chosen from Dog Society	Warrior society; age graded, membership by purchase	Women's society connected with with buffalo; social, lance, and shamanistic for men
Cheyenne	Phratries	Mother-clan exogamous		Council of 44 elects 4 headmen and 1 chief	Warriors and soldier, ungraded	Social, dance, and medicine, shamanistic
Comanche		Mother-clan endogamous	Bands	Band chiefs	Police, ungraded	Hunt and social
Kiowa	Phratries	Mother-clan endogamous		Tribal chief hereditary, elected if no heirs	Warrior; Rabbit is only age grade, other by prestige and rank	Social; 2 female

buffalo attainable. It scarcely came to full flower, at least in the north,
until almost 1800, and it began to wane by 1850. A meteor-like culture, based on one of those awakenings so common after the coming
of white man's tools but stifled by white man's own presence!

In the early 1800's the white man was still absent, except for a few
traders, French and Spanish stealing out from New Orleans and St.
Louis and English from the north. Any Plains Indian who cared to
collect a few buffalo robes and smoked tongues could tip his lance
with a murderous Spanish saber or even use a gun. His wives could
cut up the meat with steel knives and boil it in brass kettles. They

could make a wealth of buckskin clothing and handsome horse trappings, embroidered with beads which the unseen white man sent from Venice. There was no limit to possessions, for the supernatural dog would carry them all.

Few of the tribes had had much organization in their former life, and they needed little now. In winter they separated into bands or even families who camped in sheltered valleys, living on their dried meat and hunting deer. When the grass was green again, and the migrating herds could be expected, the tribe, or division of a tribe, came together, and suddenly it was an organized body. Tipis were pitched in a circle with some of the rigid etiquette of the Omaha. A head chief, or council of chiefs, took charge, and scouts were sent out to locate the buffalo. Old Indians still love to tell of the impressive way this was done, how the appointed youths, having smoked with the chiefs, ran whooping all around the camp while the drums beat and the people sang. Compared with such satisfaction, a weekly paycheck from the Indian Service has little virtue.

It might take days or weeks to locate the herd while the people feasted one another on their slender supplies and indulged in the Indian's most beloved pastime—laughing, singing, and gaming in the company of relatives. Perhaps they moved camp several times before, on a distant hill, a scout was seen running back and forth to indicate a large herd. Then came the march to the chosen camping ground, chiefs in front, warriors keeping order at the side, women guiding the laden horses, and the youngest wife holding up her husband's banner or his sacred shield. When they camped, there was no hunting until the councilors, or perhaps an elected chief of hunt, gave the word. When the right day came, hunters on horseback surrounded the herd, or a part of it, then each, on his trained pony, ran down the chosen animal, preferably a cow, shooting an arrow toward the heart and perhaps finishing the work with a lance. While the animal was being butchered, the trained pony stood, much as a cow pony does now during roping, and its pricking ears gave warning of any danger. The whole technique was partly Indian, partly Spanish and Moorish, and much of it, applied to cattle, has come down to the present day.

The summer months, while the buffalo ran, were a time of full-fed enjoyment, culminating in the Sun Dance, which kept the buffalo coming and the world in order. Now and then a party of braves might rush off to steal horses from an enemy tribe, or a whole tribe or band might load its baggage and ride off a hundred miles or so to visit a

group with whom they were temporarily at peace. Then came trading, courtship, athletic games, and the learning of new songs and ceremonies. Language was no barrier, for, very soon, they invented the
sign language, good for most purposes of news and trade.

We can hardly imagine a more dramatic melting pot than this,
which threw together tribes of five different language families, with
original homes thousands of miles apart. Each brought its own customs which were mixed and changed in the general brew. They invented little that was new, for human lifeways usually consist of new
combinations rather than new acts. They took the pattern provided
by the Old Settlers, long familiar with the buffalo Plains, and around
this ranged their own contributions of shamanism, the vision, and
general fighting tradition. It seems to this writer that the Old Settlers, with their customs stemming from the Mississippi Valley, have
received far too little credit for their share in the brilliant Plains culture. If we remember their warriors' rank and warriors' boasting, their
sacred bundles and secret societies, we can see how the newcomers
seized upon these and elaborated them. For the newcomers were
eager and had leisure from subsistence worries. They developed a dramatic lifeway, based on the buffalo and therefore on the horseman,
the hunter, and the warrior.

There was little importance for women in such a lifeway, even
though they worked harder than their gallant lords at erecting or dis-
mantling the tents, drying meat, and dressing skins. Such, we might
notice, is the case with most cattle-owning tribes or even with modern
societies of a few generations ago where men ranked as sole "bread-
winners." Owing to the wide-open opportunities of the Plains, during
the halcyon days before white dominance, men could acquire huge
wealth and reputation. The result was ambition and competition not
too unlike that of modern days. Naturally, then, Plains Indians life,
from the cradle to the grave, swung around the importance of the
brave young man.

After the mother's segregation at childbirth, came a carefree life
for children, with as little discipline as the most extreme "progres-
sive education." Plains Indians today are amazed at being asked to
send their children to school. "He doesn't want to go" seems to them
sufficient reason against it. Very soon, the keynote of ambition and
competition made itself felt. Little boys were expected to kill rabbits
and, as soon as possible, a buffalo calf. At each exploit the father gave
a feast, distributing gifts so as to insure his son's position in the band.

This usually meant a new name, and that of Sitting Bull, by the way, alludes not to the hero himself but to the killing by his namer of a sitting buffalo calf.

The girl was bred to work hard though not at the really tough jobs, which were left to old women. She learned to do beautiful quillwork and to decorate moccasins for her honored brother, who would one day dispose of her hand in marriage and bring her horses from his raids. Yet, after the age of eight or so, she was never left alone with that brother. Plains Indians respected virginity almost as much as Victorian whites, though they did not punish its opposite so cruelly. The maiden was so carefully chaperoned that she scarcely spoke to any man, for her husband wanted to show off a virtuous wife quite as much as a fine horse. In this masculine society the girl had no coming-of-age ceremony. However, her father, in the course of establishing his importance, might give a great feast and have her clothed in a robe trimmed with the elk teeth which took so long to get. Something of the sort had been an old Omahan custom,[10] with the prerequisite, of course, that the maiden must be virtuous.

Plains Indian men, like modern whites, were not expected to marry until they had achieved a position in the group. This was done by earning war honors (see below) and acquiring horses. In fact, the youth must make a sizable gift to the girl's brother—in this society it was the young man who counted, not the retired father—and before he could do this he might have reached the late twenties. So there was time for dreaming and courtship, though this was carried on by gestures and flute-playing rather than by words. Too, the Plains youth put emphasis on beauty rather than the industry which appealed to agriculturists. So the maiden kept her hands soft by doing pretty quillwork, while the hard job of skin-tanning was left to old women. This was, indeed, a culture for the young.

Marriage often involved the mother-in-law taboo met with in the Southeast, and this even if the groom was not living with his bride's family. If he was a good provider, he had a right to all his wife's sisters without further payment, and, if he died, his brother or cousin would be expected to take them over. We gather that women did some quiet flirting and even eloped at times, but this meant losing reputation in the tribe. Plains wives had no such right of easy divorce as did those of the Pueblos (chap. ix), who owned the houses, or even the hard-working food-gatherers of Nevada, co-breadwinners with their husbands. The virtuous wife could boast of her good behavior as men boasted of their war deeds, while the erring one might have the tips of her nose and ears cut off. Her lordly husband, however, gained even more status if he showed complete indifference to her doings, and, to prove how far he was above such things, he might even "throw away" a decent wife at a feast, just as he would hand out gifts of horses.

The Plains Indians rank high among tribes who make it a point of etiquette to show an unmoved demeanor in public. Yet they let go after a death, wailing loudly and gashing themselves. Even men would do this for a beloved child, though scarcely for a wife. Women released their pent-up feelings in an orgy of gashing and of wailing which might last a year. Then the corpse, at least in later days, was placed on a platform, out of reach of wolves, while gifts were heaped about it and a favorite horse perhaps killed beside it. Here widows might come to mourn or a father sit silent planning a war party where he would take out his grief on the enemy.

There were other outlets for strong feeling, for the Plains Indians, with limitless opportunity before them, were not calm and humdrum people. In family life there were usually certain relatives set apart— brothers and sisters-in-law and mother's brothers[11] with whom joking and even horseplay were expected. While a white man chooses for himself the people with whom he dares be familiar, the Indian had them listed for him as well as those to whom he must show respect.

He could display strong feelings, too, when he went out to implore the spirits for help in his career. We are familiar already with this custom of northern hunters, but, in the Plains, it reached fantastic proportions. A man had, literally, no hope of success unless he convinced himself, through a trancelike experience, that some Power was with him. Not only in boyhood did these bold fighters go out to "cry for pity" but all their lives whenever some important act was in prospect. Though the northern Plains, at least, did not torture prisoners, they did torture themselves. After fasting and thirsting, a youth might cut off a finger joint with his stone knife, begging Sun to take pity and give him horses. As he grew older, he might go through such extreme forms of torture as having himself suspended over a cliff by cords threaded through his flesh or dragging buffalo skulls about the camp in the same way. Was it the insecurity of their new life that made these wealthy and doughty fighters call for pity? Or was it frantic yearning for the new wealth just appearing within their reach?

Of course wealth was to be obtained by war, and no man worthy of the name thought of anything else. Yet, on the wide Plains, with

the seemingly inexhaustible buffalo, war was not necessary for survival or even for territory. Perhaps we can credit some of this belliger-
ency to old traditions, from both northeast and southeast. Some must
have come from the opportunities which fired these new-rich, as the
opportunities for wealth in America fired past generations of white
men.

In such a simple society war, whether necessary or not, gave one
opportunity for advancement, so young men thirsted for it. Their fathers and their sisters urged them to join war parties and to take fantastic vows of bravery, even when these meant death. Youth and
physical courage were at the top of the world, and many a tribe sang
with the Blackfoot society of Crazy Dogs:

> It is bad to live to be old
> Better to die young
> Fighting bravely in battle.[12]

The war technique of the Plains was one with which we are already
familiar. We recognize the self-chosen leader with his spirit powers;
the war bundle or the individual vision; the sneak attack with a few
trophies and great blame for the leader if any man was lost. Finally,
the triumphant return, with honors, name, and insignia for the warrior. All these had been used in the Southeast and the Mississippi
Valley, but there, war, though important, was only a part of the tribal
life. Southeastern Indians had their ceremonies to hold and their living to get, with no such easy source of supply as the buffalo. Nor, in
early days, did they have that overpowering reward—horses.

True, parties sometimes went out to avenge a slain tribesman, but
the reason for slaying had usually been a horse raid. Every important
man needed at least forty or fifty animals for gifts, display, and bride
price, and several hundred was not unusual. But this war for wealth
had few of the grim features of a war for survival. For one thing, there
was little cruelty. The nomads rarely tortured, or even took prisoners,
though some of the Old Settlers did both.[13] The nomads, especially
the northern ones, out of touch with southern cultures, seem to have
been quite lacking in the sadistic delight which formed one of the
psychological outlets for the Iroquois. Was it because they felt satisfied and free from frustration?

At least they went into the war game with the zest of medieval
knights, and here we shall change our parallel from that of a modern
businessman to that of the knight-adventurer, hungry for deeds of
derring-do. Those knights saddled themselves with all sorts of rules

PLATE XXIII

STOLLER

LANCE FROM A WAR SOCIETY

This lance is one of the emblems of membership in one of the most famous of the Plains Indians' war societies: the Kit-Fox. This particular staff was used among the Blackfoot tribe, but staffs decorated in various ways were part of the ceremonial equipment for every society, no matter which tribe, throughout the area. Membership in war societies depended on the accumulation, by each warrior, of war honors—usually "counting coup" on the enemy (see text). The societies were age-graded, and within each society there were special officers. This staff belongs to the third ranking men within the Kit-Fox Society.

The hooked lance was about 10 feet long and was wrapped almost the entire length with otter-skin. At four equally spaced places it was also wrapped with gooseskin which held on two eagle feathers. The straight end was sharpened so that it could be stuck in the ground. (From Maximillian 1843.)

PLATE XXIV

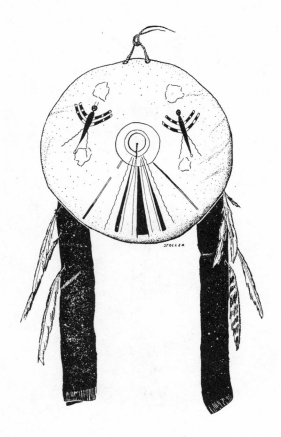

WAR-SHIELD COVER

Shields were made from the breast of the bull buffalo. The skin was smoked and allowed to contract to the desired thickness, then shaped and decorated. Some tribes gave it a convex surface by staking it, when damp, over a mound of earth. All shields were convex so as to provide an inclined surface to the impact of the weapon. They were excellent protection against arrows but, of course, no match for bullets. It was carried on the left arm by means of a strap passing over the shoulder, thus allowing freedom to the left hand.

The shield was made usually by old men, according to the owner's directions. The designs had come to the owner from a dream and were considered "protective medicine." The shield was a sacred possession and was usually buried with its owner. Covers for the shield were made of a softer skin of the buffalo, elk, or deer. A cover was left on the shield until the moment of going into the fight, when it was removed. Both the cover and the shield were painted with mythical figures or geometric designs bearing the symbolism of the dream. Both could also have feathers attached to them or have streamers of red cloth with feathers attached, as this one has. (From Hall, 1926.)

about whom they might fight and how it must be done—rules which would have been impractical in serious warfare. The Plains Indians did something similar. Following perhaps the example of the Oma-ha,[14] Old Settlers with a bent for organization, each tribe set up a se-ries of war exploits entitling a man to special insignia. The first, quite usually, was striking or just touching a live enemy in the course of battle. This, of course, was more dangerous than shooting him with a bow from a distance, and some men even went into battle armed only with a special stick for the purpose. Four men might claim hon-ors for this exploit, each succeeding honor slightly less. Another was touching a dead enemy surrounded, of course, by fighting comrades defending his scalp. A third was cutting loose a trained horse from within the enemy's camp, with the danger of attackers rushing out from every lodge. After these came killing and scalping, which, after all, could be done with little harm to the perpetrator.

A man who had performed one of these acts or a half-dozen others of minor importance was entitled to boast of the deed, with each boast giving a blow (the French called it *coup*) to a post erected for the purpose. We remember the boasting of the Creek and the rise of a youth from one warrior class to another. Here the whole perform-ance was raised to the *n*th degree, and the main entertainment at any feast was a recital of exploits by important warriors. Just as in the Southeast, an unjustified boast was a mortal blot on a man's reputa-tion. Jealous comrades would be sure to mention it, and then a trial might be necessary.

There was a complete system of honors insignia for each tribe, including feathers upright, feathers slanting, painting on robes, on horse trappings, or tipi, and the right to perform certain acts at cere-monies, just as they had been done on the battlefield. This was the simpler part of the war system. Besides these individual honors, every tribe had war societies which a man might join, taking vows for par-ticular acts of bravery. Tables 3–5 give some idea of the scope of these societies, some of which were graded by age, so that a group pur-chased its way up the ladder, ending with the most dignified group of all. The famous feather bonnet, now claimed by every Indian as a mark of race, and the handsome headdress of buffalo horns appearing in some advertisements, were costumes belonging to these societies.

Note that membership was often purchased. So, in some tribes,[15] were sacred objects and dream songs. This was a culture where wealth counted, yet, among roving hunters who carried all their property with them, such property could not go much beyond tent, food, and clothes. Therefore, perhaps, the emphasis on gift-giving. Plains Indians to this day love to taunt the whites with their miserliness and their custom of counting the cost. "Whenever we had enough," they say, "we gave it away." True enough, but the harassed white might answer that what they had enough of was food, and food is hard to keep. Without looking for psychological complexities, we can assume that, when one had a buffalo carcass, the very best investment was to

PLATE XXV

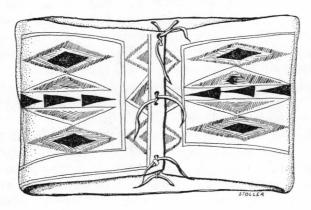

PARFLECHE

The parfleche was really an envelope made of a rectangular piece of rawhide, folded so that the long as well as the short sides met. The folds were not sharply creased, so that the capacity could be expanded. They were used chiefly for storage and transportation of food. Since the shape was convenient for packing on horses, they were often used like saddlebags and made in matching pairs.

Parfleches, as well as trunks, bags, and cylindrical cases were decorated with painted designs. The colors were earth pigments, ground to a powder, and usually mixed with a thin gluey substance made from hide scrapings which made the colors adhere and increased their luminosity. Brushes were made of the spongy, porous part of the buffalo's leg bone or willow sticks.

The geometrical designs were always painted by women. Usually just the flaps or front were painted. It would seem that the native artist viewed the field to be painted as one which could be continuously subdivided. The illustration shows a simple design; most are more complex, are almost always symmetrical, and are usually enclosed by boundary and paneling lines. They were rarely symbolic. The most frequently used colors were red, blue, yellow, and green. (From Wissler, 1934.)

bank it in the stomachs of one's friends. Later they returned the favor.

Such may well have been the origin of the great Plains give-away, a custom found throughout the Indian country wherever there is plenty. As wealth accumulated in the Plains, the feast and gift distribution included not only meat but embroidered clothing and horses. Today it may mean sheets, bath towels, and electrical supplies. The gifts were not thrown out helter-skelter. There was very careful planning, which included, first, those who had helped the feast-giver and who were now receiving public payment. Next came relatives and especially the sister, whose services must always be at the giver's command. Next came people with whom the giver would like to be on friendly terms, as a modern might issue a dinner invitation to some notable whom he hoped to know. Last were the charity gifts, a sort of informal community chest, which took care of the poor and the widows. Even these were not without return, for the recipient of a horse or a robe was expected to go through the camp singing the praises of the giver. A primitive publicity system!

It was for renown of this sort that men implored the spirits and chiefly Sun, whom most believed to head them all. The Pawnee thought of Sun as a god who gave all blessing through Mother Corn.[16] The Siouan had the belief, already met under various names, of a pervading force which could make animal, plant, or man alive with power. They called it something like "wakanda." The Plains told, too, of that primeval Transformer, foolish as any man, who had once wandered through the world, changing its features until they were fit for man's use.

The villagers had a series of tribal ceremonies, some, like those of the Omaha[17] and Mandan,[18] very similar to yearly rites in the Southeast (see chap. iii) meant to "keep the world in order." Though they are almost forgotten now, we can feel the reverence of the Osage when they "spoke to the male star who sitteth in the heavens,"[19] or the Pawnee who spoke to Sun: "Tirawa hearken, mighty one. . . . The Mother Corn stands waiting here."[20] These rites were in charge of priests, each guarding some sacred object like the cedar pole of the Omaha,[21] the various bundles of the Mandan,[22] the great tribal bundle of the Osage, enfolding life-symbols of all the clans,[23] and the feathered wands of the Pawnee, which resembled the calumet stems of the Mississippi Valley.[24]

Some of the nomads, with no tradition of tribal organization, had developed similar practices. The Cheyenne had their sacred arrows, the Arapaho their flat pipe, the Teton Sioux the calf pipe, donated in a vision by a power-giving white buffalo calf. Other "bundles" belonged to societies (see Tables 3–5) or to individual men who had won them by prayer, by inheritance, or, sometimes, by purchase. With each went a song, simple and almost wordless, so that it was easily learned. However, it was protected by an unwritten copyright more binding than any of modern days, since it was guaranteed by the spirits. No one but the owner dared use it, for fear of supernatural danger. Nor would anyone without permission dare touch the shield which a warrior had had painted with prayer and ceremony to represent his spirit power. His wife hung it daily outside the tipi and moved it around with the sun, never letting it touch the ground. A few years ago the Omaha, just getting used to white man's houses, had no use for the second story, except to keep the shield unviolated by disrespectful fingers.[25]

The melting pot of the nomads had produced one great tribal ceremony, centered around a pole, like those of the Omaha and Mandan. Old Indians have told, with reverence, about the rites for this pole, performed by a chaste woman and a warrior's society. And no robed bishop with a chalice could use more solemn gestures than the half-naked Arapaho ceremonialist with a rabbit skin. The Sun Dance included as many varied rites as the white man's Christmas, with its tree, mistletoe, and Santa Claus, all from different parts of the world. The central feature, however, was a mass ordeal by young men, who danced, fasting, looking at the sun and perhaps torturing themselves, in the hope of the longed-for vision.

The government forbade this so-called "barbarity" long ago. In the days before two world wars, a few scars on the breast, without permanent injury, seem to have shocked officials. Before that happened, the Plains culture, which had blazed into brilliance like a bonfire, burned out almost as fast. It took little more than fifty or sixty years for this way of life to reach its prime. Based on white man's movements, it was, actually, only a curtain-raiser for the coming of the white man himself. Even as it began, in the early nineteenth century, the Louisiana Purchase had been made. The United States had reached the Mississippi and was looking beyond; Lewis and Clark were sent westward to see if the Plains were passable. Mere passage, of course, was all that President Jefferson was thinking of. No one dreamed, at that time, that the wild, flat country would be other than a gap between

PLATE XXVI

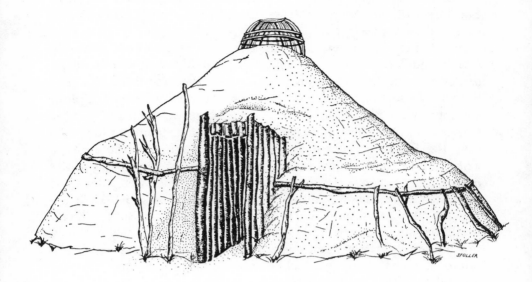

Mandan Earth Lodge

To build an earth lodge, a hole of the desired circumference was excavated 1–4 feet deep, with a ramp left leading to ground level. Outer beams were set in the hole, and supported posts were linked with them by their forked tops. Four large posts were set in a square in the center and also supported four horizontal beams. Small poles, close together, were laid at a 45° angle from the floor to the horizontal beams of the outer posts. A second set of poles were placed at a 30° angle from the first set, resting against the high inner beams and forming a circular opening directly over the center of the pit. These poles were tied to the beams and posts with fibers. On the second layer of poles willow rods were bound at right angles; on top of the willows coarse grass was laid, and, on top of this, thick strips of sod were placed in such a manner that they overlapped like shingles.

All the work was done by women, except for cutting and erecting the heavy posts. The fireplace was in the center, and frequently a circular screen, made of twigs, was placed over the smoke hole as protection against wind and rain; it could be covered with skins. The lodges, depending on their size, could accommodate forty to sixty people, and villages ranged from a dozen to over a hundred lodges. There were ceremonies to accompany every step of the building. (From Maximillian, 1843.)

the United States on the east and Spanish possessions on the west. The Indians might keep it forever, thought the average white American, and good riddance!

But America, then as now, was a country of free enterprise. No sooner had Lewis and Clark reported favorably than the fur companies and the traders began pushing into the new land. We may think of the first half of the nineteenth century as the period of pleasant contact for Plains Indians. Of course there were brushes like the one Ashley's fur-trading party had with the Arikara, or Immel and Jones with the Blackfoot. These were rather stimulating to the Indians. They proved their warlike power and, supposedly, scared the whites out of those particular regions for good. The tribes were pleasantly interested when Major Atkinson came up the Missouri in 1825, handing out gifts and urging the Indians to stop fighting so the Plains would be safe for travel. They promised, but, now that they were getting ammunition, war parties were becoming more interesting. It was improbable that they could oblige the strange white man for very long.

In 1832 mule trains began to trot over the Santa Fe Trail, carrying loads of cloth and store goods to exchange for Mexican silver. This was a new excitement for Indians of the southern Plains, and, on the first trip, so many Kiowa accompanied the party that they consumed a thousand buffalo. Soon it became more interesting to attack the mule trains than to follow them, for there was usually a herd of horses to be driven off. The Kiowa and Comanche made a war game of securing horses, booty, and scalps from the whites, and soon they were joined by some Cheyenne and Arapaho, drifting toward the south. These four tribes had once done deadly fighting among themselves, but, soon after the trail opened, they became allies. They now had a new enemy who could satisfy all their warlike desires, for, besides the mule trains, there were ranches in New Mexico and Texas. Soon they had silver on their bridles. They wore bright kerchiefs and little mirrors in their head decorations, and they used mirrors for signaling. They even had some white women and children as slaves around their camps. But the camps were still inaccessible and the buffalo still plentiful. This was the high tide of their history.

The northern Indians were not so pleased, as first the pack trains and then the wagons began to lumber over the Oregon Trail. They tried to scare the intruders by short, sharp attacks, meant to end the nuisance. They did not know that the white men thought their commando tactics barbarous and worthy of the heaviest punishment. In fact, they were unaware that the United States was waking up to the idea that it must free the Plains of the "red varmints."

A change had come over America during this first half of the nine-teenth century, even while the picturesque Plains life was reaching its apogee. Instead of a small country east of the Mississippi, glad of a buffer state to defend it from Spain, the United States now saw it-self as stretching from coast to coast. There were gold-miners in Colo-rado and California, homesteaders in Oregon. Even though they did not want to colonize the Indian country, they called for a safe stage-coach service across it and, ultimately, for railroads. Moreover, the country itself was being whittled down. By 1830 the prairie land at the east was being carved up into states, and Old Settlers like the Missouri and Osage were moving west. An Indian country had been set up in once empty hunting country, and eastern Indians were mov-ing into it. In 1849 the War Department turned the whole Indian problem over to the Department of Interior. It was understood that the duty of this department was to get all Indians settled on reserva-tions and out of the white man's way.

The Plains knew nothing about this. In fact, when the old people looked back at the high tide of their hunting life, they named the 1850's. Yet it was in 1851 that the breath of change began to blow. An agent had been appointed for the whole Plains country, and this man, Fitzpatrick, the old beaver-trapper, held a conference with all the northern tribes at Fort Laramie, Wyoming. Here, for the first time, the Indians were promised annuities—$50,000 a year for the next fifteen years. In return they were to allow roads and military posts within their country. Boundaries were set for each tribe, and it was to stay within them. Two years later, Fitzpatrick made the same arrangement with the southern tribes, managing this time to promise no more than $18,000 yearly.

To the white men this meant that the Plains were at peace. To the Indians, who scarcely understood what they had signed, it meant that a struggle to the death had begun. As they soon found out, each fort in their country meant more forts, more soldiers, more travelers. The buffalo began to disappear at a surprising rate, helped, we must admit, by the Indians. How could they know what effect this easy killing with guns was going to have! To them, the supply of buffalo was due, not so much to conservation, as to pious observance of the Sun Dance. They took the skins to the villages and trading posts and got floods of new goods, including bright ribbons, calico and broadcloth, coffee, sugar, and liquor. It was years since some Indians had petitioned Washington not to allow liquor in their country, and a law had been passed. But traders could evade it, and now some young men were getting visions by the very easy route of intoxication.

Every move the Indians made seemed to be interfered with, so they responded in the one way they knew—they fought. But the war parties now were not a mere handful of men out for glory. They were larger and larger bands of grim guerrilla fighters, throwing in their lot with some leaders as did the patriots of France and Czechoslovakia in World War II. Thus the great Plains chiefs like Red Cloud and Sitting Bull were created. Many whites think of an Indian war chief as a despotic leader, like Genghis Khan, galloping over the Plains with his thousands of devoted followers. We know that, in old Plains life, the war chief did not exist except during the few days of a war party. War was now not a game. Desperate men were making it their one business in life and clinging to a leader as their only salvation. So were born the great Indian war leaders, another result of the white man's coming.

The next thing would have been for all the tribes to unite as allies and elect a "general of the army." They did not. Whites who remember how hard it has been even for modern nations to do this may understand why. Yet the Allies of World War II had years of national governments and army training behind them, while the Plains Indians had absolutely none. So the tribes fought separately or in temporary groups, soon broken up again. If they followed any one chief, it was because he seemed to be successful, and, if he failed, they deserted him. When we read that a chief "seemed unable to control his warriors," we need not be so surprised as the white historians. Whenever Red Cloud or Crazy Horse was able to work out some strategy involving co-operation of a group, it meant something really new in Plains warfare.

For the next fifteen years or so Indian attacks and peace treaties followed each other in fantastic succession. It was the attitude of the military that the Indians should be "whipped to a standstill," then fed until they either "began to earn an honest living" or died out. The Department of Interior, encouraged and even outdistanced by enthusiastic friends of the Indian, believed that the red man could be coaxed and educated into white ways. And here we might pause to ask what should really have been done. Should the millions of acres in the Plains have been left undeveloped, in the middle of a growing country, for the pleasure of a few thousand hunters? That would have been impossible. The tide of immigration from the Old World and across the New was such that no man could stop it. When we remember that, in parts of the Old World, the population was two hundred to the square mile, the idea of leaving the Plains empty looks fantastic.

Then should the Indians have been liquidated and turned into farmers, all in one generation? That could have been done only by a dictatorship, which America had not. The time was one for large-scale, economic planning, but that science is only having its birth pangs now. The lawmakers of the nineteenth century knew nothing of it. So they made hopeful treaties which they had no ability to carry out. When treaties were broken, the Indians felt free to fight, and then the military punished them. General Harney said: "I have lived on this frontier fifty years and I have never yet known an instance in which war broke out with these tribes, that the tribes were not in the right."

At last, the Indians were thrashing out madly at any white man, treaty or no treaty. They wrecked stagecoaches; they burned ranches and killed the owners; they sneaked up on unwary soldiers. Those who have known the bombings and the commando raids of World War II cannot find this unusual. They know that men forced to such tactics can be, at heart, kind and humane. But whites of those days had never been forced to such acts of desperation, and they thought themselves justified in exterminating all Indians like wildcats. Custer surprised the peaceful Cheyenne village of Black Kettle and wiped it out. In the sandhills near Denver, Chivington's troops killed off a camp of southern Cheyenne who had surrendered and raised the American flag. Afterward, severed arms and legs were exhibited in the Denver Theatre with hoots as wild as those of any Indian.

The Civil War had ended. Hundreds of discharged soldiers were seeking land. It was evident that the Plains were not only going to be a highway to the coast. They would be needed for cattle ranches, mines, and even cities. The new treaties did not merely ask the Indians to remain within boundaries while the white men passed. They marked off reservations which were not large enough for hunting but only for farming and cattle-raising. Agents were placed in charge who would distribute rations until the new work could get started. These rations, of course, came out of the money which the Indians had been promised for their land. Sawmills were to be set up and houses built. Plows and wagons were to be imported. Schools were promised. It was time for the curtain to go down on the brief drama of horse-and-buffalo days.

A few Indians could see this, chiefly among the Village People, who were not prepared to fight. The Pawnee accepted a reservation in 1857. They tell pathetic tales of how their old men put away the medicine bundles and refused to teach the young people any Indian lore. "Better to turn around," they said, "and lead a new life." So the Pawnee became scouts for the whites. Little by little, the other village tribes followed them. They were too civilized to fight like the real buffalo Indians. Yet they were too much hunters to organize and make a good bargain like the nations of the Southeast. It was an ironic chance that oil was later discovered on Osage land, and lead and zinc on that of the Quapaw. In the twentieth century these were the richest Indians in the United States.

The real buffalo-hunters could see nothing good in the new life. Said Red Cloud, the Sioux: "Friends, it has been our misfortune to welcome the white man. We have been deceived. He brought with him some shining things that pleased our eyes; he brought weapons more effective than our own. Above all he brought the spirit-water that makes one forget old age, weakness and sorrow. But I wish to say to you that if you wish to possess these things for yourselves, you must begin anew and put away the wisdom of your fathers. You must lay up food and forget the hungry. When your house is built, your storeroom filled, then look around for a neighbor whom you can take advantage of and seize all he has." Red Cloud refused to "come in," but Spotted Tail, of the Brulé Sioux, saw the necessity, and so did Quanah of the Comanche. In 1867 the Kiowa, Comanche, Southern Cheyenne, and Arapaho promised to move to reservations. In 1868 Red Cloud, himself, had to give in, for the Sioux were promised that all whites would leave the Black Hills and that hunting ground would be theirs forevermore.

It was after these arrangements had been made that the most tragic fighting took place, for Congress could not keep the whites off the land it had promised to the Indians. Looking back from this distance, we can realize that those promises were impossible of performance. The tide of movement which was passing over America was only the expression of public opinion. One year it looked as though the Black Hills would never be wanted for settlement. The next year gold was discovered there. So, year by year, the holdings promised to the distant red men were revised downward.

Already the old Indian life was completely broken up. Instead of hunting in little bands in the winter, the tribes congregated around their agency, living on rations. There was some small excitement in having a steer turned into the corral so that they could shoot and skin it like a buffalo. But the feasts and ceremonies which should have followed lost all their savor, for the agents frowned on feasting as thriftless. When some bands left in summer for the buffalo hunt, they might wander for months without seeing more than a hundred animals. If they gathered for a ceremony, the white men feared a rebellion and sent troops to scatter them. So they changed from their healthy round of hunting and feasting to the life of drifters, fighting when they had food and ammunition, then taking rations from the agencies until they could fight again.

The worst fighting came in the seventies, just when the United States was giving full attention to Indian welfare. A commission had decided that the red men were not hostile nations to be dealt with by treaties. They were wards of the government to be civilized as quickly as possible. President Grant had perceived the corruption in the Indian Service and had asked the churches to nominate agents, so that he might have men of kindness and honesty. But of what use was a kind agent when supplies did not come, Congress did not get around to voting the money for annuities, and white squatters kept sneaking onto Indian land! In 1874 the southern Plains broke out in a blaze of raids and murders. Three Kiowa leaders—Satanta, Satank, and Little Wolf—were accused, and Satank gladly boasted that he had been down to Texas, once enemy of the United States, and done much killing. The three were condemned to imprisonment as murderers, so Satank sang his death song and leaped from the army wagon. The Kiowa tell to this day how the manacles dropped magically from his hands and a knife appeared there by spirit help. But he died under the soldiers' bullets. Later Satanta, again accused of murdering white men, threw himself to death from his prison window. In the northern Plains, Crook and Custer made ready to chastise the Sioux. Every school child knows the story of how Custer came to surprise an Indian camp, helped by scouts from the Pawnee and Shoshoni. Instead, the Sioux and Cheyenne surrounded his little command, leaving not one man alive.

The years after these revolts had been quelled were a time of deep-

PLATE XXVII

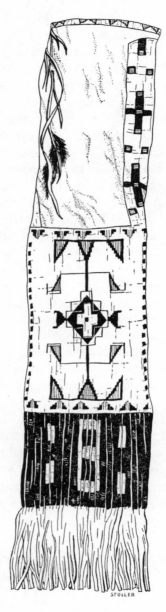

SIOUX PIPE BAG

These soft bags were usually made of the skins of antelope or deer. They held tobacco, the pipe, and stokers. The mouth was drawn tight by a thong. They were ornamented with a band of beadwork around the middle, with a strip of beads up the side and sometimes around the mouth. The long

est depression. Older Indians had lost all hope, so they had no goal in life to give their children. They waited listlessly for government rations, scarcely listening to the unskilled and halfhearted officials instructed to start them in farming and self-support. Farming was women's work, and the Plains warrior looked upon it as a modern businessman would on washing dishes. He had no longer any way to win fame, nor could he get spirit help. The Sun Dance had been forbidden as cruel, and, in any case, the spirits had obviously lost power.

It was at this stage that the Ghost Dance swept the Plains country. We have already heard of the Paiute, Wovoka, and his vision, only one of many which had aimed to lift the white incubus by supernatural means. Of the many Indians who visited Wovoka, some returned shaking their heads and deciding that the new gospel was not for them. But the Plains Indians were desperate. Arapaho, Cheyenne, Kiowa, Comanche, and Caddo took up the new religion and danced until they fainted. Most eager of all were the Teton Sioux. In 1890 they were dancing on two reservations: Pine Ridge and Rosebud. When white authorities tried to stop the gatherings, they left the reservations in frightened crowds. Probably both Indian and white had a right to distrust the motives of the other, and hostility mounted wildly. Sitting Bull, an Indian leader, was killed resisting arrest—killed by his own people, acting as police for the whites. Then soldiers surrounded a great group of fleeing Sioux, and, somehow, shots were fired. The end was piles of Indian bodies—men, women, and children—shoveled into

---

fringes were frequently decorated with quill embroidery. This decorative technique is one of the most typical of all American Indian crafts, for it is found nowhere else in the world. After the quills have been softened in water and flattened, they present a smooth, glossy surface. They were sewed on with sinew in many different techniques and patterns.

Decorative art in the Plains was usually done in geometric patterns. These patterns could serve only the purpose of decoration or could be highly symbolic. The basic design elements were rather limited, so that the symbolism attached to each piece relied for interpretation on its owner. Therefore, the same design element could represent many different things. These bags, made by women, were used only by men, and the symbolism embroidered on the bag was frequently connected with their military exploits.

Design elements and the patterning of their combinations varied from tribe to tribe. Of the three general styles found in the Plains, this, the Sioux style, is characterized by rather light spread-out designs. The background was usually white. (From Wissler, 1934; Douglas and D'Harnoncourt, 1941.)

trenches. The massacre of Wounded Knee gave Custer all the revenge he could have asked.

That ended the Ghost Dance for all the Plains Indians. The lost generation which had tried it as a last hope lived despairingly on. But at the south, where the Kiowa and Comanche were raiding into Mexico, another religion arose which lives to the present day. The ancient Mexicans had long made ceremonial use of the top of a cactus root, called by the Aztec name "peyotl" and by modern Indians "peyote." Once a year, on important occasions, they chewed the dried root or boiled it as a tea. The result was magnificent hallucinations in which the world turned glorious and all objects were surrounded by rainbows. To the Plains people it meant rescue from spiritual helplessness. Here was a substitute for the lost vision and obtained without fasting or self-torture. "Peyote is the savior of the Indians," say some of those who have adopted it and organized ceremonies around it. "It is our plant, unknown to whites, and it came to give us spiritual help."

Whites look upon this artificial vision with horror. Yet they need to remember how tremendous was the exigency for spiritual outlet among a despairing people. They must remember, too, that the white man's religion had its revelation in the minds of white men, on the basis of white customs and traditions. Indian religion had no place for penance, forgiveness, and hell-fire. White teachers might have helped the red man more if they could have forgotten this side of their belief and got down to essentials. "You believe in a revelation from the spirits which gives strength for all a man's life. So do we. But while you believe in many spirits, we have One, all good. While your vision is for hunting, gambling, or war, ours is for the wider task of loving our neighbors as ourselves." No one knew the Indian religion well enough to make this connection. Indians were asked to accept Christianity whole, and only a few were able to do so. The others found that the Peyote church gave them solace and a spiritual return to the old way of life.

Today the Peyote church is organized in a number of different ways, sometimes with old Indian songs to fire, air, and water, sometimes with Christian hymns and visions that lead to Christ. It has its abuses, and there are some who take the "diabolic root" with no religion at all. But modern young Indians are not looking in that direction to get their new hold on life. After generations of despair, they are beginning to deal with reality.

It was in the time of the great railroad boom that the new Dawes plan for helping the Indians was proposed. Its motives were not un-selfish. Ostensibly, they were to give incentive to the discouraged Indians by letting each one have a farm of his own, the chief desire of every human heart, thought the white man. But practically, he knew that, when a reservation had been cut up into farms, there would still be a stretch of unoccupied land which could be thrown open to home-steaders. Over the protest of the Indians, in many cases, this was done. Many Plains Indians became proprietors of small, barren farms, for the buffalo country was not adapted to planting. On these farms the government often erected frame houses which Indians were supposed to use instead of the tipi. But a tipi requires no maintenance. When it gets dirty, the Indian picks up and moves. He had no idea of all the scrubbing and repairing required by a house. Usually, the houses became hovels.

The farms were as bad. Braves did not realize the patience and hard work required before a crop could mature. They did not love the soil as a farmer does, and most felt with the Comanche: "The earth is my mother. Do you give me an iron plow to wound my mother's breast? Shall I take a scythe and cut my mother's hair?" It seemed better to lease the land to whites who liked that kind of work. The amount of money this brought was very little, but it kept a family alive. When they grew sick, from malnutrition and insufficient cloth-ing, the government must help.

These transition years, through the turn of the century, were the low point for Plains Indians. Today we recognize that a man who has been completely geared to the life of a fighter needs help from a psy-chologist before he can adjust to the ways of peace. Yet our soldiers who receive such help have only fought for three or four years and have a whole childhood of peacetime ideals behind them. The Indi-ans who tried to settle down had been guerrilla fighters all their lives. Even their old chivalrous ideals had been lost to many of them. And the whites who tried to help knew nothing of war psychoses. All they could say was: "Your old way was wrong. This is right." Often, they ended with the conclusion: "Indians won't work, and they can't learn. They are made that way."

Nevertheless, the United States spent thought and money in trying to take care of its wards. Slowly, the Indian Service was made into a business-like organization. Good schools were built, and the teaching standards raised higher and higher. Farmers and range experts were brought in. Various crops were tried. The Indians were given cattle in

PLATE XXVIII

A Plains Tipi

The cover of a tipi was made from ten to twelve buffalo hides sewn together. It was laid on the ground—roughly a half-circle with two "ears" projecting from the straight sides—and the foundation poles (three or four) were laid over it to determine where to tie them together. When the poles were tied and erected, the other poles were tied to them. There were twenty to twenty-five poles to a tipi. The cover was raised by the last pole and was pulled around the structure until it met in front. The laps were pinned together with wooden pegs. The poles were pushed out against the cover to make it tight, and then it was staked to the ground. The cover was placed so that the two "ears" dropped down in front, one on either side of the smoke hole. To hold them upright, a pole was placed in a pocket of each "ear," and these could be moved over the smoke hole in accordance with

the hope of turning former hunters into cowboys. Often, the Indians looked with listless eyes on the activities prescribed for them. Their tragedy had produced one lost generation and, perhaps, two.

In 1934 government policy took a new turn. We have already described the Indian Reorganization Act, meant to throw responsibility back on the Indians by allowing them to organize in communities, borrow money, and manage their local affairs. It did not mean betterment all at once. Old people kicked like steers at having their aimless, quiet life taken away from them. Selfish individuals played politics. No one knew how to organize an efficient, voting democracy, for never, in Plains history, had this been done. The new governments are still in the formative stage, and, if we remember how long it took the United States to shake down into a working unit after adopting a constitution, we need not wonder.

Today, Indians of the tribes who used to live on the High Plains number some thirty-five thousand, and they are increasing. They are on thirteen reservations, in the states of Montana, the Dakotas, Utah, and Oklahoma (see the back endpaper map and Table 6). Most of their lands have been allotted, so that each family owns its 160 acres or so, but these may not be sold to anyone but another tribal member. Thus the land the Indians still own is assured to them. We have all learned, since dust-bowl days, that this prairie land is not meant for agriculture. So most Indians are encouraged to be cattlemen, and the schools specialize in range management. The government has brought large herds of good cattle and distributed them to Indians on the principle of getting one calf back for every cow. On the Pine Ridge Reservation there is one community herd, managed by a number of families together. This kind of co-operation for large-scale business looks like

---

the wind. All the work was done by the women. The finished tipi was about 15–18 feet high and 15 feet in diameter.

The tipis were decorated with either quill or bead trimmings; some were painted. This Blackfoot tipi was painted with two yellow buffaloes. This signifies that its owner possessed a sacred bundle and the ritual associated with it. The design, as well as all the ceremonies that went with it, came originally through dreams and belonged exclusively to that person. The symbols commonly fell in one of three classes: the mythical originator and his wife, their home, or their trails. The darkened area at the top represents the night sky; the white disks are stars. (From McClintock, 1936.)

TABLE 6

PRESENT RESERVATIONS AND NUMBERS OF THE PLAINS TRIBES

	State (or Province) and Agency	Population, 1945*
Arapaho.........	*Wyoming:* Wind River Agency and Reservation	1,346
Arikara	*North Dakota:* Fort Berthold Agency and Reservation	782
Assiniboine.......	*Montana:* Fort Belknap Agency and Reservation	792
	Fort Peck Agency and Reservation	1,718 (2,510)
Blackfoot.........	*Montana:* Blackfeet Agency and Reservation	5,164
Cheyenne and Arapaho..........	*Montana:* Tongue River Agency and Reservation	1,719
	Oklahoma: Cheyenne and Arapaho Agency and Reservation	3,102 (4,812)
Comanche.......	*Oklahoma:* Kiowa Agency	2,694
Cree............	*Montana:* Rocky Boy's Agency and Reservation	252
Crow............	*Montana:* Crow Agency and Reservation	2,488
Gros Ventres......	*Montana:* Fort Belknap Agency and Reservation	1,013
	North Dakota: Fort Berthold Agency and Reservation	849 - (1,862)
Iowa............	*Kansas:* Iowa Reservation	540
	Oklahoma: Shawnee Agency	114 (654)
Kansas..........	*Oklahoma:* Kaw Agency	544
Kiowa...........	*Oklahoma:* Kiowa Agency	2,692
	Texas: Kiowa Agency	368 (3,060)
Mandan.........	*North Dakota:* Fort Berthold Agency and Reservation	387
Ojibwa..........	*Montana:* Rocky Boy's Agency and Reservation	58
Omaha..........	*Nebraska:* Winnebago Agency	1,840
Osage...........	*Oklahoma:* Osage Agency and Reservation	4,612
Pawnee..........	*Oklahoma:* Pawnee Agency	1,149
Ponca...........	*Nebraska:* Winnebago Agency	404
	Oklahoma: Ponca Reservation	926 (1,330)
Wichita..........	*Oklahoma:* Wichita Reservation	460
	Canadian Reservations	
Assiniboine.......	*Saskatchewan:* File Hills-Qu'Appele Agency	....
	Moose Mountain	....
	Alberta: Stony Sarcee Agency	....
Blackfoot.........	*Alberta:* Blackfoot Agency	....
Blood and Piegan..	*Alberta:* Blood and Piegan Agency	....
Plains Cree.......	*Alberta:* Lesser Slave Lake Agency	....
	Saddle Lake Agency	....
	Ontario: Moose Factory	....
	Saskatchewan: Duck Lake Agency	....
	File Hills-Qu'Appele Agency	....
	Moose Mountain-Onion Lake Agency	....
	Edmonton Agency	....
Sarcee...........	*Alberta:* Sarcee Reserve	....

* Numbers in parentheses are totals. Populations for Canadian reservations are not known.

a good possibility for the Indian, and officials are hoping to see it get started in other places.

Perhaps the greatest stimulus to a new life has been World War II. Here the Plains fighters came into their own and distinguished themselves. Moreover, they fought side by side with whites and were treated as comrades. Many of them rose from the ranks to be officers, and the Osage had a general. The kind of pride and self-reliance that comes from this achievement is more life-giving than any amount of rations. As we watch to see what the Plains Indians will do in the future, we realize that there have been lost generations at many other times and in many races. Yet these have rarely meant that a whole people must go under. Sometimes, in fact, they have meant a renewal of strength and a breather for a new start.

OLD SETTLERS

FOOD

Vegetable.—Corn: some hybrids, flint and flour in several colors, sweet and pop. Beans and squash (*Cucurbita pepo*); sunflowers, seeds, herbs, roots.
Animal.—Buffalo, small game, birds.

HUNTING METHOD

Circles, drives over cliffs or into pens, fires, disguises.

CLOTHING

Male.—Breechcloths, hip-length leggings, soft-soled moccasins; later an occasional shirt in north, buffalo robes, deerskin robes. Headdresses and war bonnets with eagle-feather streamers and, in certain societies, buffalo horns on crown.
Female.—T-shaped dresses (made by sewing two full skins together on shoulder and down sides, without tailoring; ankle length), soft-soled moccasins without cuffs, short leggings, buffalo robes, and deerskin robes.

HOUSE TYPES

Early: bark, grass, or earth shelters. Later: skin tipis of twelve skins, twenty or twenty-five supporting poles, and about 20 feet in diameter.

EQUIPMENT

Household.—Early: plain pottery, not coiled, hand-shaped, sun-dried then fired, sometimes made in mold. Not decorated. Wicker baskets, gambling trays, gambling baskets, and carrying baskets. Later: skin containers, parfleches. Cooked in buffalo stomach or hole in ground.
Transportation.—Dog travois, round hide bullboat; later, horses.
Hunting.—Self-bow; north, compound bow of horn and wood sections.
Other.—Cradle: east, flat board with willow rods or bow in front, both painted; west, fur or skin bag. Pipe: catlinite, T-shapes, elbow pipes. Miscellaneous: skin painting, many small skin ornaments and articles such as pipe bags, pouches, etc., porcupine quillwork and, later, beadwork.

WAR

Bow and arrow, lances, coup sticks, circular shields of thick buffalo rawhide. Rarely involved pitched battle but were sneak raids; counted coup rather than kill.

GAMES

Archery, dice games, handball and football, hoop-and-pole, races, snow snake, hand games, shinny, shuffleboard, tops.

NEW-RICH

FOOD

Vegetable.—Berries, cherries, camass root, prairie turnip, greens, little gardening. Crow had corn from Hidatsa, plus beans and squash, also cultivated tobacco.
Animal.—Buffalo, deer, elk, antelope, fish.

HUNTING METHOD

Drives, impounding, cliff drives, deadfalls, pits, snares, fish traps, deer-head disguises.

CLOTHING

Male.—Early: very little clothing. Later: occasional skin shirts, hip-length leggings, breechcloths, and soft-soled moccasins (after horses, moccasins were hard-soled), eagle-feather war bonnets and fur headbands and caps. Buffalo robes.
Female.—South, wrap-around skirts, knee-length boots, sometimes poncho-like upper garment; north, T-shaped dresses (two full skins sewn together on shoulder and sides, no tailoring, ankle length); soft-soled moccasins and short leggings; belts. Skin robes. Some tattooing.

HOUSE TYPES

Conical skin tipi of three- or four-pole foundation variety. Pitched in glades in winter; in circle on Plains in summer. Sweat lodge.

EQUIPMENT

Household.—Willow backrests, wood, horn, and skin vessels, horn spoons and cups. Paunch vessels, pemmican pounders.
Transportation.—Travois, first dog, then horse. A type of raft.
Hunting.—Self- and sinew-backed bow and arrow. Crow used some compound bows.
Other.—Cradle: Blackfoot, curved board, fur-lined pocket with rawhide sides; Crow, tapering rounded board, skin-covered, flaps for fasteners instead of thongs. Arapaho, quilled skin bag on U-shaped rod frame; general northern, ovoid board, skin-covered to make pocket; general central, ornamented skin bag on forked frame. Pipe: Tubular soapstone (Crow traded for pipes), later used catlinite. T-and elbow shapes. Miscellaneous: quillwork, beadwork after 1800, bags, pouches, rawhide containers, parfleches, carriers. Many saddles and horse trappings, saddlebags but no pack saddle.

WAR

Coup stick, bow and arrow, spears, stoneheaded clubs, circular buffalo-hide shield. Many raids, counted coup, took scalps and prisoners, plunder.

GAMES

Archery, dice games, hand games, handball and football, hoop-and-pole, ring-and-pin, shinny, a form of snow snake, swings, tops.

TRIBES OF THE NEW-RICH OF THE PLAINS

NOMADIC TRIBES: SIOUAN LANGUAGE

Dakota: This is the largest group speaking the Siouan language and is divided according to its movement into Eastern Dakota, or Santee (Midewankton, Wahpeton, Sisseton). This division lived in Minnesota until reservation days and was noted among the Lakes tribes of chapter vii. The middle group, using the form Nakota (Yankton, Yanktonai), lived in eastern Dakota. The Western Sioux (Teton or Lakota), west of the Missouri River, was divided into bands known as Upper and Lower Brulé, Ogalala, Sans Arcs, Shihasapa, or Blackfoot (not the same as the Algonkian Blackfoot), Mineconjou, Oohinanpa, or Two Kettle, Hunkpapa. All may once have lived in Minnesota, where the Santee remained as forest and canoe people. The others were forced west by the Ojibwa, who had guns from the French.

Assiniboine: An offshoot from Yankton and Yanktonai living in Canada.

Crow: The Crow and Hidatsa once formed one tribe. Their history is uncertain until they reached the Missouri, where the Hidatsa remained with Mandan, while the Crow went west.

NOMADIC TRIBES: ALGONKIAN LANGUAGE

Blackfoot: Three divisions: Pikuni (Piegan), Kainah (Blood), and Siksika (Blackfoot proper), now called North Blackfeet. Separate tribes with same language but each with its own organization. They may have migrated from the northeast but have no such tradition. Early in the 1700's they were found living on the northern Plains in a huge area east of the Rocky Mountains. Got horses from Shoshoni enemies about 1730 and became one of the most powerful of nomadic tribes. Peace treaty with United States in 1855, territory defined, roads and forts allowed there, Blackfoot to receive $20,000 annually for ten years and to have schools and missions. In 1873 and 1874 boundary was moved north; in 1877 to Canadian reservations. In 1883–84 the last buffalo died. In 1888 United States Blackfoot with some Crow sold much land and accepted three small reservations in Montana. The Blackfeet Fort Belknap land was lately sold to the government for the Missouri Basin improvement.

Cheyenne: Before 1700 in Minnesota living in villages with agriculture and pottery. Pushed west by Sioux and joined a tribe of similar speech, Sutaio. On obtaining horses, they gave up agriculture and became nomadic hunters. In 1832 when Bent's Fort built on Arkansas, the tribe divided, some going south, others remaining in the north. Division was made permanent by treaty with United States in 1851. Constant fighting of northern Cheyenne with Kiowa until peace in 1840. In 1860–78 they were prominent in border warfare; in 1874–75 they joined in the outbreak of southern tribes; in 1878–79 Dull Knife's

MAP V

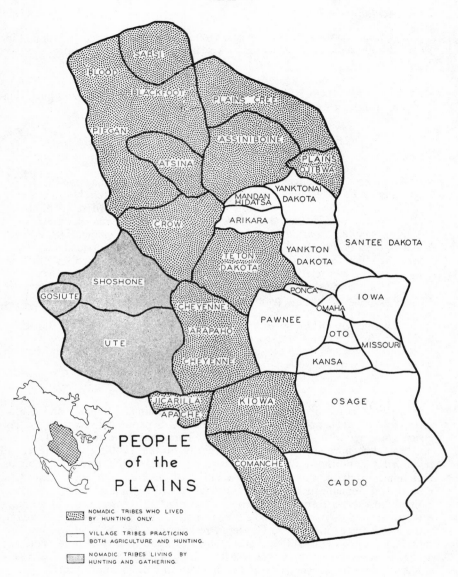

SARSI
BLOOD
BLACKFOOT
PLAINS CREE
PIEGAN
ASSINIBOINE
ATSINA
PLAINS OJIBWA
YANKTONAI DAKOTA
MANDAN HIDATSA
ARIKARA
CROW
SANTEE DAKOTA
TETON DAKOTA
YANKTON DAKOTA
SHOSHONE
PONCA
IOWA
GOSIUTE
CHEYENNE
OMAHA
PAWNEE
ARAPAHO
OTO
UTE
MISSOURI
CHEYENNE
KANSA
JICARILLA APACHE
KIOWA
OSAGE
COMANCHE
CADDO

PEOPLE of the PLAINS

NOMADIC TRIBES WHO LIVED
BY HUNTING ONLY.

VILLAGE TRIBES PRACTICING
BOTH AGRICULTURE AND HUNTING.

NOMADIC TRIBES LIVING BY
HUNTING AND GATHERING.

band escaped from Oklahoma to Montana. Northern Cheyenne reservation is in Montana. In 1867 southern Cheyenne removed to reservation in Oklahoma. In 1875 most prominent hostiles were deported to Florida for three years.

Arapaho: Once sedentary and agricultural in Minnesota, the Arapaho moved west about same time as Cheyenne, with whom they have had long alliance. Divided into northern and southern groups, like Cheyenne, around 1830–50. By treaty of 1867 southern Arapaho took reservation in Oklahoma with Cheyenne; northern Arapaho with Shoshoni in Wyoming, who later paid for receiving them. Atsina branch of Arapaho with Assiniboine at Fort Belknap, Montana.

Plains Cree: A Canadian tribe closely related to Chippewa and once living west of them. One group obtained horses and moved out to the Plains. Long alliance with Assiniboine.

VILLAGE TRIBES OF THE PLAINS: SIOUAN

Nebraska culture, contemporary with Upper Republic but more advanced. Oneota (1600–1700), Chiwere Sioux, Iowa. Something like Upper Mississippi of Wisconsin.

Mandan: Up Missouri to South Dakota, then by 1350 built earth lodges and had corn, beans, and squash. Maybe earliest Siouan on plains. Language belongs to Mississippi Valley Siouans, maybe related to Winnebago. Tradition says that they came west and upstream. Had much influence on later comers. Lewis and Clark found population of 1,250; after smallpox of 1837 there were 150.

Cegiha Sioux: First lived on Ohio and Wabash and worked west. At mouth of Ohio, Kwapa went down Mississippi, others up. Omaha up Missouri in Great Bend until whites came. Hunted to Minnesota River. Also includes Osage and Kansa.

VILLAGE TRIBES OF THE PLAINS: CADDOAN

Whole family includes Arikara in North Dakota, Middle Pawnee and branches in Nebraska and south, Caddo, Wichita, Kichai, on Red River of Louisiana and its tributaries in Arkansas and Oklahoma, also into Texas. Southern groups used conical straw hut; northern, earth lodges. All had confederacies of villages with chief.

Arikara: Split from Skidi Pawnee. Derived from generalized Upper Republican culture in northern Nebraska; this mixed with Nebraska culture (Omaha and Ponca?). Omaha ethnology indicates close contacts with Arikara, but both remained distinct. Joined by Mandan coming from north and east—when, we do not know, or which was dominant. Arikarees known to all Plains tribes as corn-planting Indians par excellence and shown so in sign language.

Pawnee: Oldest Nebraska tribe. Came from Southeast Woodland. Had life along lesser rivers of central loess plains. When Caddoan moved to northeast, Pawnee brought up rear in groups. Best period in pottery before they got horses (1540–1682). At first they spread out for agriculture but later consolidated in a fortified village.

CHAPTER IX

The Peaceful Corn-growers

THERE was Indian corn in New Mexico some three thousand years ago and perhaps earlier.[1] This is the report from Bat Cave,[2] near the Mexican border, where under layers of stone tools, animal bones, and charcoal there were found the remains of a primitive plant which is both pod and pop corn.[3] Its discovery does not mean that we have found the actual birthplace of maize, for much more digging is needed before that crucial question can be settled. It does mean that we have tracked down, in the United States, a group of corn-users earlier than any so far known, even in Peru.[4]

Who were they? It will be remembered that, some six thousand years ago, when Mexico was still a hunter's paradise, there was in this very locality a group whose grinding stones prove that they had more interest in vegetable food than in hunting.[5] Tools of these Cochise people have been found in Bat Cave along with primitive corn.[6] So now we can follow the history of at least one group from earliest food-gathering days, through the coming of agriculture, and, thanks to recent investigations,[7] far into the Christian Era. During that history the southwestern landscape changed from one of lakes and forests to bare hills and sandy plains with only a few streams. The bison departed, and, we imagine, most of the bison-hunters with it. Now the chief food was rabbits, with only an occasional deer, killed after ancient manner with snare, club, or throwing spear. The Cochise and other wandering tribes who chose to stay and grow up with the country might have remained as undeveloped as some of their neighbors to the north, except for the coming of corn.

The first kernels, dating from at least 1000 B.C., may have been brought from the south, since there is as yet no sign of the plant growing wild in New Mexico. Perhaps, too, there came with it some of those ceremonies for planting and harvesting which, to most southwestern Indians, seem just as important as tillage. Surely the plant

186

had great care, for in the millennium from 1000 B.C. to about A.D. 1 the lumpy oval seed heads grew longer, the pod covering fell away, and the short stems on which each kernel was perched began to disappear. Then came the mating with teosinte (see chap. ii), perhaps again brought from the south, and from their descendants evolved the corn of today.[8]

During this early agricultural stage the Cochise were fading away, and their place was being taken by two daughter-cultures, the Mogollon and Hohokam. Also squash and kidney beans had come from the south, and the people had begun to live in pit-houses, a smaller version of the earth lodge we have already seen. By A.D. 1 the news of corn was spreading north, and, in the next centuries, three, four, or perhaps five different groups took up agriculture. Different though their traditions may have been, they were slowly developing the distinctive lifeway of the American Southwest.

Southwest, for our purposes, includes most of our states of Arizona and New Mexico, with northern extensions into Nevada, Utah, and Colorado. Accurately speaking, there should also be southern extensions into Mexico, for the international border which makes our southern boundary is a white man's creation, dating from a treaty scarcely a hundred years old. From the Indian point of view, the arid, sunny country on both sides of the line is the same. So are the dwellings, the crafts, and the Indian languages. Cultures very like those of our Southwest are, in fact, scattered all the way down to Mexico City, and it is only lack of space and information which forbids their inclusion here.

From earliest times there was constant communication up and down this area. True, we shall get some glimpse of movement across the Plains, but, by and large, when we study the Southwest, we turn our backs on the Plains, the Woodland, and the Mississippi and consider this particular portion of the United States as a peninsula of culture, jutting north from Mexico. It reaches only a little way past the northern boundaries of Arizona and New Mexico and, at periods in its history, not that far. There is good reason. This area of the southwestern corn-growers is the region which, during most of its history, could count on summer rain. It is subject to cycles of drought, as will soon appear, but in most years there are six weeks, beginning in late July, when pelting cloudbursts bring to the corn the moisture it must have.

Compared with the gentle and reliable rains of the east, this is a barely acceptable blessing. Yet the rigors of the situation have given to southwestern farmers an impetus which pushed them far ahead of their neighbors to west, north, and east. Only here do men devote their working lives to agriculture, instead of leaving most of it for women in their spare time. Only here is every ceremony, even that of war, oriented toward the boon of rain and corn. Special varieties of maize have been developed to withstand intense heat and tearing winds. Colors have been segregated, until some villages can show at least six, with ceremonial significance. In spite of the large fields of the Iroquois or the Mississippi Tribes, these hard-working southwestern farmers can be spoken of in several senses as our first corn-growers.

This was no country for poles and bark, like the eastern Woodland, or for skins, like the Plains. The chief source of material for dwellings was the desert earth and rocks; clothing and equipment were from scanty vegetation. The house was a "pit-house," sometimes covered with insulating earth (see Pl. XXIX). Clothing was of woven fiber, a breechcloth for men and a short skirt or merely two aprons for women. There were basketry sandals instead of moccasins. In place of hide mantles, there were blankets made of ropes of rabbit skin, twined together with cedar bark in a basketry technique.

Sometime in the years before A.D. 900, when southwestern culture came into its full flower, other equipment and arts must have come from the south. The first was pottery—pottery of a style and technique quite unlike those of the east and north. Heretofore, our mention of first steps in ceramics has concerned a rough, uncolored ware, patted into shape with a paddle, and decorated with scratching and punching. Mogollon and Hohokam wares, already being made about A.D. 1, were smoothed and colored.[9] The brownish scraps, which are the earliest found, may not look impressive, but they are indicators of a craft which reached its flower in South America and later in the Pueblos. It is built up of clay coils, laid one upon another, then scraped smooth, painted with a color wash, fired, and then, perhaps, given a further design. When the Mogollon and Hohokam women began to make such brown or buff pottery with red designs, they were starting a new fashion north of the border.

Another new fashion of this period was loom-weaving, known in Peru since at least A.D. 1. In the areas so far studied there has been no sign that a true loom was used, even the simple waist loom which was the first in the Southwest. Nor have we heard before of the raising of cotton. Many of the corn-growers, however, raised a variety of cotton

(*Gossypium hopi*) which is also native to Mexico and Central America.[10] Add the bow and arrow, perhaps brought in by immigrants from the north, and our southwestern culture is well on its way.

This culture, in all its variations, has been intensively studied, perhaps more than any other in the United States. The dry climate and the many caves have preserved houses, pottery, textiles, human bones, and even some desiccated bodies. The science of tree rings, evolved in the Southwest, has been able to work out dates in certain regions, almost back to the beginning of the Christian Era. By comparing the growth rings of modern trees with those of older trees and still older, its experts can tell when some kinds of ancient woods were cut.[11] Best of all, there are Indians still in residence and still practicing the lifeways, which must be centuries old.

HOHOKAM AND PIMANS

Every group concerned in it merits detailed description, but there is space here for only two of the most important ones, the Hohokam (later Pimans) at the south and the Anasazi at the north.

PLATE XXIX

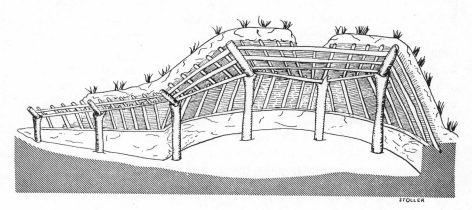

MOGOLLON HOUSE

All houses of this period were round and had floors of gravel and adobe. Many pits for cooking and storage were dug in the floor. The lower walls were dug into the native earth. The upper walls and roof were made by setting large poles out from the walls and covering them with smaller poles, branches, and mud, leaving a smoke hole in the center. A long entrance passage was built to the east. (From Martin, 1940.)

The Hohokam have already been mentioned as probably direct descendants of the Cochise. Their home was a torrid plain, broken by
volcanic hills, stretching across the southern part of Arizona and into
Mexico. Here are gravelly flats, dotted with creosote bushes, hillsides
bristling with a dozen kinds of cactus, and gullies or "washes" which
have water only for a few weeks in summer. At the north of the region is the one source of water other than the summer rains, the Gila
River, formed by the union of the Salt and the Verde and flowing
toward the Colorado. It was near these streams that large-scale corn
culture developed, even before the beginning of the Christian Era.
Perhaps it was new arrivals from the south who brought the idea of
digging irrigation ditches from the rivers as was done by so many Mexican Indians. By A.D. 900 or 1000, the Hohokam ditches had reached
a length of ten and even sixteen miles.[12] The wide shallow canals were
dug out, probably with a stone hoe, wielded by men who knelt and
scraped up the dirt while women carried it away in baskets. Villages of
pit-houses stood near the cornfields; the people were dressed in coarse
cotton woven on a horizontal loom. They were making handsome
painted pottery, figurines, and shell ornaments.

Then came an invasion, from other settled farming Indians,
who were already building large communal houses of stone or clay. A
group of them moved in among the Hohokam, but here was no in-
ternecine war such as we found among the Mississippi tribes. They
built their huge dwellings, one of which still rears many feet of crum-
bling adobe wall at Casa Grande, near Phoenix, Arizona. They may
have helped with the canals, which grew bigger and better. They
seem to have brought some new kinds of corn and something even
more valuable to Indians—new songs and ceremonies. Then, about
A.D. 1400, they departed. Perhaps it was incoming Apache who frightened them, so that some fled north and some south, thus further in-
terweaving southwestern customs.

Those remaining are thought to be the Pima and Papago or, for
brevity, Pimans. They belong to a language family which, so far, has
not appeared in these pages, the Uto-Aztecan. As the name implies,
members of this family are found all the way from the Ute of Utah
and Colorado to the Aztec of Mexico. They live in the basin and
plateau country west of the Rockies, and, in the United States, only
a few like the Comanche have ever moved out past that barrier. Piman
territory in ancient days ran from the Gila River in Arizona, past the
Altar River in Mexico, with a desert stretch between. On the rivers

were the irrigators, with their great houses. They were known as Pima, which means "I don't know," their usual response to the Spaniards. In the desert lived the Papago, the Bean People, so nicknamed after the only crop they could grow in bad summers. The Pima of Mexico have long since disappeared. Those of the Gila kept their canals until a few years ago, but now, as English-speaking farmers, they have lost most of their old customs. Description must focus on the Papago.

Their name for themselves is Desert People. They are descended from a long line of hunters and gatherers which may go back to the Cochise, those early seed-users.[13] In fact, their life, until a few years ago, involved as much gathering as agriculture.

In summer, when the late rains drenched their desert flats, the Papago planted their ancient yellow flour corn, their tepary beans of a kind native to northern Mexico, and their round pumpkins.[14] Meantime, parties of women tramped the plains gathering every variety of cactus, for the stems, fruit, thorns, and woody skeleton would all be used. When the rains ceased and the ponds could not even supply drinking water, families wandered to the mountains to hunt or to the Pima or the Mexican Indians for trade. In early summer each family sought its grove of giant cactus (Cereus giganticus), that huge candelabrum-like growth which is found only in the hot country of southern Arizona and near-by Mexico. The fruit of this plant made a cider, one of the very few fermented drinks made north of Mexico, and the solemn drinking of this ushered in the new year.

The Papago kept the tradition of simple hunting people in having a special hut for women at childbirth and for girls at puberty and every month thereafter. When the young mother emerged with her infant after a month's seclusion, the child received a special southwestern ceremony, presentation to the sun. Then he was given a name of good omen from the dreams of the officiating shaman. The adolescent girl had a four-day seclusion, when she guarded herself against supernatural danger by not touching her head, the most sacred part of her, and by eating with special dishes, afterward thrown away. This ordeal over, the whole village danced every night for a month, two rows walking backward and forward, arm in arm, while they sang songs about wind, flowers, and butterflies. Boys were expected to have visions in the manner of the northern hunters.

Then came a peaceful and industrious life, the young man and his successive wives occupying a hut near his father and brothers. When death came, there was an affectionate goodbye to the loved one with

PLATE XXX

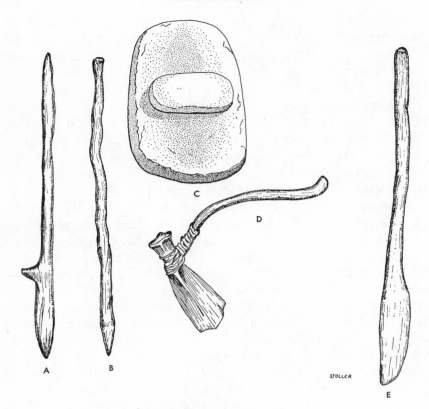

STOLLER

Agricultural Implements

a) The digging stick with a footrest is made from a juniper branch, flattened and sharpened to a round-nosed, blade-like point with sandstone. A branch made the footrest. About 3½ feet long. (From Cushing, 1920.)

b) The straight digging stick, of heart wood of ironwood, peeled and having the sapwood removed from the point, furnished the Pima with their planter. The chisel-like edge was made by abrasion on sandstone. About 4½ feet long. (From Castetter and Bell, 1942.)

c) Mano and metate. The metate, or grinding stone, is made of hard, coarse-grained sandstone (granitic stones were sometimes used), 18 inches long and 10 inches wide. The milling surface is ground down from this flat surface to the usual trough shape by use. The mano, or muller, also of sandstone, is 10 inches long and 4 inches wide. It is made with a pecking tool and has a groove on the vertical side for a finger hold. (From Kidder, 1932).

d) Hoe with deer scapulae for a blade, a juniper wood handle, and fastened together with fiber twine or sinew. Common among the Pueblo Indians of the period. About 4 feet over all. (From Cushing, 1920.)

e) Straight hoe. Made of a Juniper limb, with fire-hardened blade, shaped and ground on sandstone. Approximately 5 feet long. (From Underhill, 1946.)

an adjuration to be content in the land of the dead and not return to frighten the living. Then, after four days' silence, while the spirit flitted to its new home, the brush house might be torn down or burned, and the name of the dead was never mentioned again. Otherwise the ghost, thinking itself called, might come and take some loved one for companionship.

The Papago father ruled his little family like a business manager, even though they counted relationship on both sides. They had father-clans and moieties, but this system long ago fell into disuse. The important unit within which one must not marry was the village. That is, the summer village, a sprawling array of brush huts, surrounded by cornfields. Each village often had its own dialect and its own version of the ceremonies. Spread around it might be "daughter-villages" founded by groups of relatives who needed new farmland but always returned to the mother-town for important ceremonies. At a little distance from the town, where it would not be disturbed, was the "big house," a special brush hut containing the town's sacred objects and inhabited by the "big man," its ceremonial leader.

Here were no great confederacies, no ambitious warriors rising to power. Each little community aimed to live in peace, looking after its own affairs and perhaps those of a few daughter-villages. Rather, it saw that its affairs were looked after by the spirits. All had much the same list of needs which must be taken care of: rain, war, hunting, health, sometimes public discipline. All had officials or societies whose duty it was to keep the good will of the spirits in these matters and, often as a secondary duty, to lead the people.

The Papago had this arrangement, at its least systematized stage, with few hereditary rights and no organized societies. The village "big man," for instance, worked up to office through being chosen as one of four assistants by his predecessor, generally a relative. Through years of listening to them, he learned the beautiful rituals which brought rain and the words to be recited when the village fetish, consisting of sacred stones or feathers, was removed from its plaited basket. He lit the cane cigarette (southwesterners did not have the calumet) when the men of the village gathered at night in council. When the old leader died, the council chose his successor from among the four assistants.

War, with the Papago, was surrounded with as many restrictions as childbirth. When they had been raided by the wild Apache, until retaliation was necessary, the man to whom they looked for leadership was the "hard man," the "angry man," who had proved his worth by going on many raids and taking scalps. No Papago enjoyed such exploits and no warrior boasted of them. War songs and orations rarely mentioned killing but dwelt on the mystical belief that this disagreeable experience would bring rain. When the leader referred to enemy country in an effort to enthuse his men, he said:

> There did I seize and pull up and make into a bundle
> Those things which were my enemy's
> All kinds of seeds and beautiful clouds and beautiful winds.[15]

PLATE XXXI

PIMAN HOUSE

This dome-shaped structure, 7 feet high and 15 feet in diameter, is constructed about a circular excavation 12–18 inches deep. Four poles with crotches at the top form a square, two heavy roof timbers are put through the forks. Other lighter timbers are laid crosswise, others in the opposite direction, and then they are all covered with earth. Against the roof poles wall timbers are leaned slanting. These are tied together with withes, then thatched with brush and perhaps covered with earth. A small door faces east. (From Curtis, 1908.)

The self-sacrificing volunteers, thus adjured, mended sandals and made extra bow strings, while a few specially rugged fighters looked to their wooden clubs and shields of mountain-sheep hide. Above all, each man chose a sponsor to see him through the ordeal of purification in case he should be a killer.

Here we meet an attitude foreign indeed to most northern and eastern Indians—dread of the enemy's ghost. The hero who ventured into the magically evil land of the Apache never took booty but must bring back at least four hairs to show what he had done for his village. During the usual commando-type attack only one or two men might kill. They would then blacken their faces and walk home at a distance from the others lest they spread danger.

While the nonkillers were feted and the villagers danced around the so-called "scalps" for sixteen nights, the scalp-takers remained in quarantine, far from the village, their polluted weapons beside them. They observed precautions against supernatural dangers which are found, in special strength, through most Indian country west of the Rockies. That means seclusion, diet taboos, keeping silent, not looking at the sun or at fire, and using special dishes which are thrown away when the danger is past. The old guardian who brought the warrior's meager rations and taught him ritual adjured him with each interview:

> Verily, who desires this?
> Did not you desire it?
> Then must you endure many hardships.[16]

It was like the initiation into a priesthood, and in other parts of the Southwest such priesthoods existed. However, the unorganized Papago merely presented the warrior at last with the purified scalp, which he called his "prisoner," and which he must feed with tobacco. The ritual he had been taught would serve to cure insanity and excessive lovesickness, which was akin to it. For war, to the Papago, meant insanity.

The men who became skilled hunters had a milder initiation. They merely learned the songs which called the deer, learned to make the deer-head disguise under which a man moved close to his prey, and learned, of course, that men must keep away from women before a hunting trip and must make large gifts from every kill. One special hunt priest, who passed his lore down to a relative, took charge of the surround hunt when a deer must be run down and smothered, without blood, for ceremonial use. Another lit the fire and recited the ritual without which rabbits could not be surrounded, and another brought the luck and the rain which attended intervillage games. There were ritualistic experts, too, for the arduous pilgrimage which brought salt from the Gulf of California. Each of these activities, if properly conducted, would result in blessing which, to the Papago, meant only one thing—rain.

In addition, they had, like all good corn-growers, a series of special ceremonies celebrating the birth, maturity, and death of their most important citizen—the corn. Perhaps their first ceremony should be called "impregnation" rather than, "birth," for it was at this time, just before the summer rains, that the juice of the giant cactus was fermented and drunk with solemn ritual. Such ceremonial drinking, we have mentioned, was widespread in Mexico and South America, but, before white arrival, it was not practiced north of the border except by the Pimans. Their belief was that, as men saturated themselves with liquor, so the earth would be saturated with moisture. In a short time after the drinking festival, the rains came.

Then followed planting, months of "singing up the corn" by hamlets or individuals, and harvest, at which time the corn sang to its gatherers:

> Truly most comfortably you embrace me,
> I am the blue corn.
> Truly most comfortably you embrace me,
> I am the red corn.[17]

With their minds free of worry, the Papago gambled without restraint at intervillage games of kick stick or relay racing. Every fourth autumn, when the ponds had dried up and they prepared to leave the summer village, they held a great pageant with masked dancers and with songs and images to honor the rain and clouds and to keep the "world in order." This particular pageant has strong echoes of other corn-growers to the north. It is a relic of the great housebuilders and a sample of the constant interchange that went on in the Southwest.

The spirit world of the Pimans dominated the animal spirits with which we are so familiar and, apart from these, their special hero, Elder Brother, who had made the people out of clay and taught them their arts. The animals gave dreams, and each man—even sometimes a woman—might meet them for himself, gaining power for running, gambling, war, or curing. Elder Brother never appeared in dreams. Long ago he had brought the rain, gathered salt, taken scalps, hunted deer, and left accounts of his exploits. Ceremonies consisted of reciting these accounts, after which songs were sung and offerings made. The offering was the famous prayer stick, of which we shall hear much in the Southwest. With the Papago, it was made of eagle down, which, to them, represented clouds. Attached to an unpainted wand of willow, this was set up on the dance ground or placed beside springs on the salt pilgrimage. Placed with eagle down in the sacred baskets, belonging to a village or to a scalp-taker, were tails of the black-tailed deer—to the Desert People a symbol of wealth.

All these ceremonies were dangerous as well as beneficial. That is, a dancer or a priest could easily make some slight error and then would be taken ill. The remedy was to have the ceremony, or part of it, done over again in the proper way. Most curing, however, went back to the ancient idea of animal visions and the medicine man. As with the Cherokee, each animal was thought to control some disease which it sent to those who had shown it disrespect or mistreated its bones. To its favorites, however, the animal would give a song, curing the ill it sent. There were numbers of these curing singers, sometimes with songs from several animals. They did not form a society, but each kept his songs for himself, singing for his meals if called upon by the medicine man.

With the medicine man, we find ancient beliefs in full force, for his power came not from a learned ritual but from dreaming. True, he sometimes went through a special warrior-like initiation, by killing four eagles in four years, then being "sung over" each time by former eagle-killers. Still, during the four-day seclusion before the singing, he expected to be visited by the eagle's spirit and to learn songs which would diagnose disease and help him to suck harmful objects from the patient's body. If disease came from animals, he called in the curing singers. If the cause was some failure in ritual, he would have the offended ceremony done over again. If it was an intrusive object in the body, he might suck it out himself. The cause of an intrusive object was witchcraft and its agent another medicine man. Or was it the practitioner himself? If too often his patients died, this was suspected, and many a medicine man was publicly clubbed to death as a sorcerer.

This same loosely organized village life, in close co-operation with the spirits, was carried on by the Pima in the irrigated Gila Valley. They had ditch bosses and a careful apportionment of duties in cleaning the canals and using the water. They also held the drinking festival for rain, and, when the Yuman Maricopa came from the Colorado River to join them, these followed suit. Among other corn-growers we shall find the same priestly leadership in all life's practical affairs but variously organized.

In the history of the Southwest we leave the realm of English and French influence and of the fur trade. The white conquerors were the Spaniards, moving up from Mexico as early as 1540. That spectacular march of Coronado scarcely touched the Pimans, though it had lasting effects on Indians farther north. The Spaniards, in fact, were not interested in this hot desert country. They left it unvisited until 1678, when the dynamic Jesuit missionary, Father Kino, began establishing his string of missions in northern Mexico. He decided to carry them north to the Gila River and, to that end, made several whirlwind "entries" when he baptized Pima Indians by the hundred, gave them Spanish names, some staves of office, and, better still, some wheat and cattle. This is the ideal form of what anthropologists call "acculturation," for the Pimans were left to use the new acquisitions as they chose. The baptism and the names they regarded as added magic. The cattle they bred, and the wheat they raised by the acre, threshing it by the trampling of cattle after the ancient Spanish method. The Papago, in the western desert, were scarcely visited, but they too received the baptism-and-name magic.

Then, for over a century, the Pimans were left alone. The Pima raised more and more wheat, and the Papago contracted the habit of a yearly pilgrimage to Mexico, where, at one of Kino's mission stations, they could renew the baptism-and-name magic. Then the United States warred with Mexico, Arizona became American, and the fates of Desert and River peoples divided. The Pima, the River People, were directly in the path of the white men going west. General Kearney passed through their country, buying tons of wheat and using the friendly Pima as scouts. They served as scouts later when the Apache were deviling the ranchers of Arizona and would have been invaluable except for the sixteen days when each must stop fighting after killing an enemy.

Strong, brave, and industrious were the Pima in those days. Then came the settlers, pushing in with pioneer individualism to grab what water and land they chose. The Pima never fought with the whites. They do not, they say, know the color of a white man's blood. They did not object to a reservation as the roving hunters did. They accepted reservations though they did not want individual allotments. Still, all their friendliness did not prevent whites from taking water out of the rivers until Pima canals ran dry. The oldest and most extensive farms in the Southwest had to be given up. The Pima could go to the towns to beg or do odd jobs, or they could cut down the tough little desert trees and take a day's drive to Phoenix to sell wood.

From the late 1800's until 1934, this was Pima life. We can hardly condemn the sullen apathy which took hold on the tribe, as they watched the whites grow prosperous around them, while their position was on the lowest rung of the ladder. They spoke English, they wore white man's clothes, and they changed their houses from the "half-orange" covered with brush to square adobe in the Mexican style. Their children went to the Indian schools, and they themselves often joined the Presbyterian church, the quiet decorum of whose prayer meetings reminded them of their own council.

Then the Coolidge Dam was built, bringing water to the whole valley. The Pima were outraged at first when they found that the new canal system of concrete and machinery could not be maintained by their pleasant communal labor. They must do commercial farming like the whites and thus earn money to pay a maintenance tax. They do it now, and they use the extra acres which the government cleared for them. They are chartered as a corporation, and they have borrowed money to buy cattle and farm machinery. Those who need quick money work in the cotton fields, for which the area around Phoenix is becoming famous. The Pima are coming back. They had the boon of most agricultural tribes—work to which they were accustomed and which they could continue. They were not left in a vacuum like the unfortunates of the Plains.

The Papago had even better fortune. For almost two hundred years after Father Kino departed, they were left practically alone. They had time to grow used to wheat, horses, and cattle. They could trade in Mexico for knives, pans, and cloth. True, the Apache raided them now and then. The villages had to consolidate, and the men had to keep their fighting ability. Yet their village system and their patriarchal families continued even when reservations were set up and Catholic missionaries arrived.

The drought of the thirties was an ordeal, and it was then that the government began to dig some wells for them and make recommendations about soil conservation. The quiet Papago objected to being whirled off their feet, but slowly they accepted the government arrangements. They organized. Now they are rapidly moving into white man's ways, without the lost generations which some Indians suffered. Not that the change is entirely without suffering! One wonders if it can ever be so. When whole families migrate to the cotton fields to work for the whites as once they worked for the Pima, they live with a minimum of physical decency and with little steady school attendance by the children. Employers are only beginning to notice the need of better conditions for these Indian migrants who will supply some of our future citizens. With the changed economic situation, change is going on slowly in that stronghold of Indian tradition—the family. As young men make money, they and their wives are no longer subject to their fathers' orders. The co-operative family is broken up, and some may even move away to the white towns. But life there lacks the warm friendliness of home. There is prejudice against Indians, who soon begin to feel that they cannot rise. Then why not drunkenness and delinquency, for those outlets at least are as open to an Indian as to a white!

It is only some Papago who feel these pains of dislocation. There are many who live industriously, using the money from the cotton fields to build adobe houses and save for kerosene stoves and furniture. Their craft guild sends baskets all over the Southwest. The Papago are workers, and their lot is a kinder one than that of the erstwhile fighters. They are asking the government for more education, better hospital care, and better conservation of their arid land. They know what they want.

THE ANASAZI

The other important development of the corn-growers to be considered here was in the north, on the arid plateau which runs diagonally down across Arizona and New Mexico, from northeast to southwest. Here, where the squared edges of the two states meet those of Utah and Colorado, there grew up a culture known by the Navaho name "Anasazi" (the "old peoples"). It began with the usual wandering groups, living in pit-houses and making so much use of the desert vegetation that they have become known as "Basket-makers." Corn came to the Basket-makers about A.D. 200, some thousand years after the first rude cobs had appeared among the Cochise.[18] Perhaps it had taken all that time to establish communication with their relatives farther south. Then came pottery, merely sun-dried at first as though trying a new art from hearsay. Later it was coiled, fired, and painted in the true southern manner. No influence from Siberia here!

Lacking the right water supply, the Basket-makers could not develop great canals like the Hohokam, and their cornfields remained small.

Their efforts went into houses, which changed from the pit-house, with its wooden superstructure, to rectangular dwellings of poles and mud. They were indeed using the earth for all it could give them. Toward A.D. 900 these houses were made partly of stone; they were gathering into groups, with the old pit-houses still kept and used as a place for ceremonies. This conservatism in religious matters reminds one of the way a great silver communion cup was used in some churches long after private individuals had taken to separate drinking vessels.

In the centuries from about A.D. 900 to 1300 the Anasazi civilization came into flower. This was the period of the famous "cliff dwellings" and of the terraced apartment houses, each a pueblo, or village, in itself. These used to be thought of as the remains of an ancient and vanished people, but now we know that the builders were the ancestors of our present Pueblo Indians and that the buildings, now deserted, are no older than many of the cathedrals of Europe. Nevertheless, they are remarkable works of architecture for a people without iron tools. In Chaco Canyon, New Mexico, where hundreds of the great houses lined a flowing stream, now dry, the sandstone slabs were coursed and fitted with the most meticulous care. The great underground kivas seem planned for magnificent ceremonials. It is true that this very time of great building in cliff and canyon seems a time of concentration, as though there were enemies within or without the Anasazi territory. Of that, more later. In the matter of craft and of the ceremony which it often served, this was a high point in the history of the villages, known later to the Spaniards as "pueblos."

The Pueblo Indians comprised a number of groups, of different dialects and traditions, but all shared to some degree in the general culture. This meant fields of varicolored corn and of squash, beans, cotton, and tobacco. It meant handsome pottery, coiled, polished, and painted, the designs being different for each small area. It meant cotton clothing with blankets now woven on a tall, upright loom, which is still used by the Hopi, as well as the narrow waist loom of early days. It must have meant many of the masked ceremonies to bring rain which are still given.

Several situations put an end to this "classic" period of the Pueblos. For one, a creeping drought cycle, such as attacks the Southwest every so often, forced the abandonment of villages toward the edge of the rain country. For another, there may have been internal dissensions, not to mention the prowling nomads, who will loom large in the next chapter. One by one the great classic villages were deserted, and Pueblo people took up much the same position they now have along the Rio Grande drainage with extensions east and west.

Then came the Spaniards. We pass lightly over the early "entries," even Coronado's flash in the pan of 1540, which has left legends of terror to the present day. The event which permanently altered Pueblo life was the arrival of Don Juan de Oñate, in 1598, bringing sheep, goats, horses, and 129 colonists, many with their families. He settled

PLATE XXXII

PUEBLO—OLD ZUNI COURT

Large stones, chinked with smaller stones to make them level, are plastered with adobe annually. The walls vary from 2–4 feet in thickness. As the walls approach the top, beams are put in, crosspoles are laid at right angles, then brush, grass, and adobe. Stone drains are put in. Some of these houses are two and three stories high. (From Mindeleff, 1886–87.)

his capital, ultimately, at Santa Fe in about 1610, and, from then on, the eastern Pueblos were a subject people. They paid taxes of cloth, corn, or labor; they had Catholic churches placed in their villages, and their own masked ceremonies were forbidden. On the other side of the ledger, they learned to grow wheat, peaches, and peppers (the latter brought up from Mexico). Horses were not permitted then, but they kept donkeys and sheep; they wove and embroidered woolen garments.

They had one violent break with the Spaniards when a reformer arose preaching, as so many Indians had before, that they must give up white man's goods and return to the old ways. Popé, however, demanded violent action, and, in 1680, the Pueblos achieved it. They drove the Spaniards out and kept them out for twelve years. Meantime, many Pueblos left their ancient sites and camped in the forested hills of north-central New Mexico. There they were joined by some nomads known as *apaches*, "enemies," and one particular group who became *apaches de navahu*, "enemies of the cultivated fields." That association was highly important for both groups, and its consequences will be told later. The Spaniards returned, and so did the Pueblo refugees—those who had not married Navahos. Pueblo life continued with little change through Mexico's independence in 1823 and the acquisition of New Mexico and Arizona by the United States in 1848 and 1853. When white Americans began to visit and describe the Pueblo Indians in the late nineteenth century, all indications were that they had changed but little since the coming of the Spaniards or even before that. Our picture of the Pueblos, then, is a composite of very ancient customs, firmly interwoven with a few new ones.

Map VI shows how they are now ranged down the Rio Grande Valley, with a long extension west into the deserts of Arizona. They speak four languages, mutually incomprehensible, and with several dialects. Still, all but the Keresan are somehow related to that western plateau group, Uto-Aztecan. The lifeway of all of them can be recognized as similar in that they were closely knit, agricultural villages with a government which may be called "priestly" and with a round of elaborate, costumed ceremonies which kept the rain falling and the crops growing. Within this framework there are enough differences to demand study not only of each language group but of each pueblo. In the present sketch we shall divide them merely into Pueblos of the Desert (Arizona and western New Mexico) and Pueblos of the River (the Rio Grande drainage).

DESERT PUEBLOS

The desert is the region least touched by white influence and therefore keeping more of the old customs. Hopi and Zuni are its representatives, with Acoma, the ancient "sky city" on its mesa top, and Laguna, a refugee village built after 1700, as intermediates between the desert

PLATE XXXIII

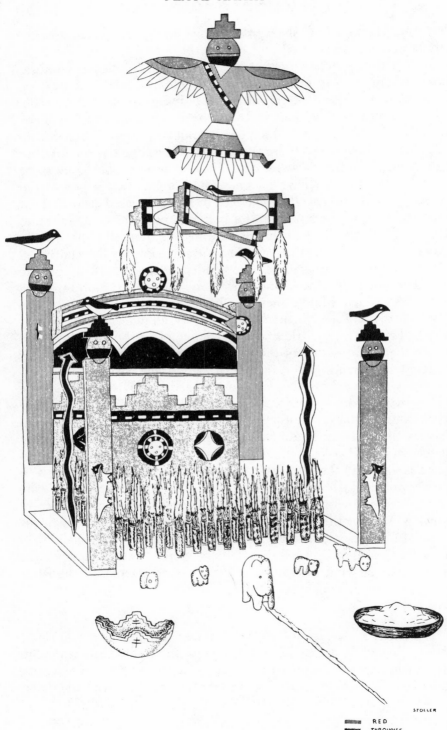

STOLLER

RED
TURQUOISE
BLACK

and the other Keresans on the river. All these villages have been described so often and so well that we need scarcely do more here than enumerate the traits which make them stand out as among the most picturesque and interesting Indians in the United States.

The men put in long days at their agriculture, which was done without irrigation and, with the Hopi, particularly, on tiny fields chosen for underground moisture and often miles from the pueblo. We can imagine them in Spanish times, dressed in cotton kilts and yucca sandals, while the women, kneeling over their pottery at home, wore a tightly wrapped blanket of dark wool fastened on the right shoulder with their left arm free. (The dead, they say, do it the opposite way.) On days of ceremony these costumes were enlivened with bright embroidery, done with Spanish needles; with necklaces of turquoise, which the Pueblos had dug and worked from earliest days, and with only a dot of red on each cheek and with their long black hair washed in suds of *amole* (*Yucca baccata*), Pueblo people give an appearance more consonant with white taste than some eastern tribes with their tattoo and scalp lock.

The close-knit village life, with its succession of splendid ceremonies, gave little time for the rites of birth, puberty, and death which are so prominent with hunting people. Indeed, says Dr. Bunzell, "in contrast to the ceremonial recognition given to natural phenomena—the solstitial risings of the sun, the alternations of summer and winter, the perpetual dearth of rain—crises in personal life passed almost unnoticed."[19] They do send the men out of the house at childbirth, and the Hopi keep the mother in for twenty days. Then comes the impressive southwestern custom of presenting the child to the sun, the father's kinswomen, among the Hopi, giving it a name from those owned by their clan. The child has been admitted into the close Pueblo network, and, almost immediately, he will have duties toward kinfolk, then toward the village and its spirit helpers. Almost all Pueblos, as shown in Table 7, have some general society into which a boy must

---

ZUNI ALTAR

The altar is composed of painted backboard and front pieces. The various prayer sticks and plumes and offerings are placed in this quadrangle. The knife-god, or flint-god, with his directional representations hangs above the altar. On the floor in front of the altar are the animal fetishes, the ceremonial pottery bowl and basket containing corn meal. This drawing shows the altar just prior to the final sand painting. (From Stevenson, 1904.)

TABLE 7

PEACEFUL CORN-GROWERS

Pueblo	Clans	Moiety or Phratry	Society	Kiva	Priests	Town Ceremonial Leader	Required Initiation for Males
Hopi	Matrilineal exogamous; grouped in phratries; owns property and ritual; provides leadership for ceremonies, and others join	Phratries	Associated with clan priesthood; function: rain and curing; membership voluntary; 3 female societies	Owned and used by clan and society	Hereditary in clans	Town chief member of particular clan; priestly duties	4 societies, war, hunt, fertility; male and female kachina cult; sponsor unrelated
Zuni	Matrilineal exogamous; lineages in some clans own sacred objects and rain ceremonies; provides priesthoods	None	12 societies curing and magic membership voluntary; male and female	Owned by kachina (dancing) groups	Hereditary in lineages	Houses chief, with ceremonial duties; chosen by 6 important priesthoods; Sun watcher—hereditary	6 kachina groups; sponsor is husband of woman who picked child up at birth
Acoma and Laguna	Acoma: matrilineal exogamous; Laguna: not after 1880	Acoma, none; Laguna, 4	8 curing societies; membership voluntary	Owned by the kachina groups and Antelope clan, which furnishes town ceremonial leader	Volunteer society members	Priestly duties; Acoma: Antelope clan member; Laguna: optional	Acoma: kachina required; Laguna: optional

206

TABLE 7—Continued

Pueblo	Clans	Moiety or Phratry	Society	Kiva	Priests	Town Ceremonial Leader	Required Initiation for Males
East Keres	Matrilineal exogamous; no property	Moiety; patrilineal	4 curing societies	Owned by the moieties	Volunteer society members	Head of 1 curing society	Several dance societies, joined by invitation
Towa	Matrilineal exogamous; owns sacred objects	Moiety; wife joins husband's	2 curing societies; membership voluntary	Owned by the moieties	Volunteer society members	Hereditary in 1 clan	1 of 2 kachina groups of moiety; 4 societies, war, hunt, curing; sponsor unrelated male
Tewa	Very weak; bilateral kin system; male owns house	Moiety; patrilineal, endogamous	2 curing societies; moieties control ceremonies	Owned by the moieties	Volunteer society members	1 each moiety for one-half year	No required membership
Tiwa	None; bilateral kin system; male owns house	Moiety; children assigned alternately Taos: unknown	2 curing societies; moieties control ceremonies	Owned by the moieties	Volunteer society members	Isleta and Sandia: office filled in rotation from corn groups Taos: unknown	Isleta: 5 corn groups; child initiated or adopted into mother's Taos: 1 of every 6; no restrictions

207

be initiated before he can have ritual knowledge and can take part in
the ceremonies which keep the village prosperous. At Hopi and Zuni
when they are eight years old the boys, and now and then a girl, meet
the masked rain spirits and are soundly whipped as a form of exorcism.
Later, for the boys, comes the initiation into one group or another
which involves the duties of dance, song, and prayer for the benefit
of the village. Women's duties are less dramatic. They include providing food for all the feasts, guarding and feeding ceremonial objects
in their homes, and variously assisting the ceremonial performers.
While the men take charge of the spiritual life of the village, women
are honored and satisfied with their responsibility on the material side.

In marriage customs the Pueblos differ from almost all other Indians
in the United States, for a man has but one wife—at least only one
at a time, for divorce is easy and frequent. There are several reasons
for monogamy, the first being that the houses belong to the women
and that the young husband comes to live at his bride's home. It
would be difficult to bring an extra woman there unless it were her
sister. Another reason may be that the lack of war and hunting keeps
the male population from being depleted. And, perhaps, since women
have no farm work or even weaving to do, they do not need help in
the home. At least, the fact is that a man's real home is his mother's
house. There he keeps his important ceremonial property, there he
directs and advises his sister's children, and there he returns in case of
marital trouble.

If his marriage lasts, he may come to be a friend and adviser to his
children rather than a stern family head. At Zuni, when he or his wife
dies, the other will mourn for a year, sitting away from the fire and
scarcely speaking. In former times the corpse was buried with gifts,
each pot "killed" with a hole in the bottom, so that it would be useful
only to the dead. These Pueblos did not fear the names or memory of
the dead but thought that they became clouds which sent the supreme
blessing of rain.

The western Pueblos until lately were thoroughly matrilineal. Wom-
en owned the houses and all the food after it came into the house.
Descent was counted through women, and the tribes were divided
into mother-clans. Most activities at Hopi and Zuni are connected
with the clan system or, at least, with certain families within the
clan. Priests must come from certain families. Gifts and counter-
gifts are assigned by clan. The whole intricate mechanism works on
a basis of relationship, and it is no wonder that a citizen of the

western Pueblos feels lost when expected to act as an individual in the white man's world.

Table 7 shows how the Desert Pueblos organized to take care of their needs in town government, weather control, war, hunting, and curing. Each function was in charge of persons who knew the ritual, with no visions needed. These officiants were not, as with the Papago, unattached individuals who had worked up to the position. All but the town chief were organized in societies, and very often these societies were managed by some clan which supplied the chief priest and owned the sacred objects used. All but the curing societies! Curing, always the last function to be altered, had given up its prerogative of visions, yet any person cured by the society might join. These Pueblos, in spite of their professions of brotherly love, were not democracies. They were ruled by a group of interlocking directorates with privileges, duties, and ceremonies which kept most of the adult males constantly busy. This is the southwestern framework at its most systematized.

As with the Papago, almost every activity, even war, was focused upon rain, and the scalp-taker went out

> . . . to win the enemy's waters
> his seeds
> his wealth
> his powers. . . .[20]

In fact, we must assume some connection between the Pimans and the western Pueblos who both abhorred war and who, each in his way, purified the warrior and gave him priestly powers.

Pueblo theology was more rounded and complete than that of most Indians, perhaps because their priesthoods in their long retreats had opportunity to discuss and elaborate it. Their "Book of Genesis" started, as befitted agriculturists, with the union of Mother Earth and Father Sky. Thence came the people, generated deep in the fourth womb of Earth and climbing out with the help of two children of Sun, the War-Gods. These supernatural brothers were unknown to the Pimans, though we could find something like them in many other parts of America. The Pueblos held ceremonies for them and called on them at need, but their reverence for them was mixed with fear, like their reverence for the Bow Priests.[21] The supernaturals most loved and enjoyed by these agriculturists were the cloud-beings and rain-beings called, by the Hopi name, "kachinas." "Enjoyed" is the correct word. These beautifully costumed apparitions—

or, rather, men wearing the masks they had given—danced frequently in the plazas to make people happy and to bring the rain, which was their other self. Was it the bright sunlight, the lack of danger in Pueblo life, which produced a religion so free from fear and subservience? The rain-beings were thought of as companions with whom the villagers exchanged favors.

> Now this very day
> For the rite of our fathers
> We have prepared plume wands. . . .
>
> Yonder from the north
> The rainmaker priests
> Bring their waters
> Will make their roads come hither.[22]

So the chief of the Zuni Fire Society explains that he has done his duty and that the rain-beings will now do theirs.[23] With the rain spirits usually came the Clowns, grotesque figures who feared neither obscenity nor blasphemy, so great was their supernatural power. The Clowns were sometimes used, especially by the Hopi, to ridicule some citizen who needed rebuke.

The Pueblo contribution to the spirits was the prayer stick, which was far more elaborate than that of the Pimans:

> With the massed cloud robe of our grandfather
> Male turkey
> With eagle's mist garment
> With the striped cloud wings
> And massed cloud tails
> Of all the birds of summer.[24]

These wands were planted at springs and other holy places as offerings or, one might almost say, in trade with the spirits for their favors.

Each act of the procedure was deliberate and reverent, even to the most humdrum preparations. In their kiva, or their secret ceremonial room, the appointed priests or the society members set forth sacred objects, sometimes contriving an elaborate altar, with ground painting and images of the spirits. (The Hopi Snake Priests brought in live snakes instead of images.) Usually, there were eight days of such preparation before the public ceremony in which the masked spirit figures or the priests, with live snakes held in their mouths, danced all day to bring blessing. Zuni priesthoods went into retreat, one after another, all summer long, while the initiated men of the town, in sanctified masks, impersonated the dancing spirits. Both had a specially important ceremony at the winter solstice, when the Hopi made new fire, and the Zuni entertained representatives of the spirits who came to promise their blessing for the next year.

In these organized villages we look in vain for the solitary medicine man who sucks out disease. He does exist at Hopi, but he visits in secret and is often suspected of witchcraft. Such is often the fate of this sort of healer when religion becomes ritualized. Curing, with the Hopi, is properly done by the priestly societies, each of which controls some disease, to give or to take away. In highly collectivized Zuni individual effort is suspect, even in religion. So we find the "doctors" gathered in societies into which one enters by initiation and goes up through various grades. True, anyone may enter, man or woman, and he usually does so through being cured of a sickness. This is as far as the western Pueblos go in democracy, a far cry indeed from the Plains, where anyone can communicate direct with the spirits and even sponsor the Sun Dance.

THE RIVER PUEBLOS

Life in all the pueblos was so outwardly similar that early writers rarely made much difference between those of the Desert and those of the River. However, a few variations are so apparent that even this brief sketch cannot overlook them. The River Pueblos, in Spanish days, covered an immense extent all the way from Taos, near the border of Colorado, to San Marcial, near that of Texas. All the far southern pueblos and an eastern extension toward the Plains were later abandoned because of Apache raids. There was ample contact with the Apache and other Plains peoples through the centuries. Tanoan, the language spoken by many of the River Pueblos (see front endpaper map), has been thought related to Kiowa, a well-known Plains speech. Tiwa, one of its subdivisions, may even have belonged to some of the early residents before the Four Corners emigrants arrived.[25] Keresan, spoken by Pueblos between the Tanoans and the Desert Pueblos, is classed by some linguists with the great Siouan-Iroquoian group.[26] We can surely imagine some mixture here, whether early or late. We know that in Spanish days, Taos, the northernmost River Pueblo, was the market town, where Pueblo people came to trade with Apache and Comanche. Some Tiwa people even ran away from the Spaniards into the Plains and remained for years. All these influences we should expect to produce a different kind of life from that of the more isolated Desert Pueblos.

One difference, due partly to geography, was that the River Pueblos could have irrigation. We can trace signs of this all the way from Mesa Verde. Even today, in many pueblos, the opening of the ditches is a religious festival, and every citizen gives to them a yearly quota of work. Another difference is the building material. The river valleys could offer little stone, so even the early houses of these Pueblos were often of poles smeared with clay or lumps of adobe, patted into shape by hand. In clothing there was much use of buckskin, since the northern Pueblos could raise no cotton. In later days the women began to wear wide-topped, Spanish-style boots, quite different from the puttees of the Desert Pueblos. Their ancient wrap-around blankets received the addition of petticoats, silk blouses, and silk shawls.

These are outward differences. Much more striking is the change in government and ceremony which takes us away from the tightly organized religious oligarchies, away from hereditary privileges, and back toward the realm of individual endeavor. These Pueblos who moved farthest from the homeland of the Four Corners probably suffered much breakup in the process, not to mention the influence from individualistic nomads. True, secular and religious activities were still intermingled, according to the pattern of the Southwest. However, most activities were open to everyone, with no inherited family rights. Mother-clans, as Table 7 shows, faded away, and, where relationship mattered at all, it was counted through the father. In most cases it did not matter at all. One joined any group which he or his parents chose and, quite often, could work up to be the head. The head of the Keresan Flint Society, who was its member of longest standing, becomes automatically head of the village.

All this means a different outlook: more democracy, more individualism—and more war. We hear nothing in the River Pueblos about warriors' purification. Instead we find the war chief, or two chiefs, representing the war-gods, as the executive officer of the village dealing with outsiders and policing ceremonies, while the priestly leader remains in seclusion. True, all the Pueblo Indians must have done some fighting, or they would not, so carefully, have preserved their war organization. Still, we can imagine there was more emphasis on it among these River People, jostling one another for desirable land and facing hostile foreigners.

They have the myth of emergence from Earth's womb, but some of the Keres make it a mother-goddess who emerged, then brought them to life and taught them. Their ceremonies no longer include public masked dances, since the Spaniards forbade masks as representing the devil. Masked dances are now held in secret, their beautiful drama forbidden to all whites. In public there is often a ceremonial of racing and, in secret, pilgrimages to sacred spots. Such dances as whites may see are performed by both men and women, costumed in the height of the ancient style, in handwoven wool and cotton and strings of turquoise. Women wear upright on their heads a *tablita*, or thin slab of wood, carved and painted in rain symbols. Men wear ruffs and armbands of spruce, the tree that is always green. The dancers are silent, waving their feathers or spruce twigs, while old men, in the loose shirt and cotton pantaloons of Spanish days, sing to the beat of a drum. Between dances the ceremonial Clowns, belonging to one or two permanent and honored organizations, make their usual instructive fun.

A "Corn Dance" of this sort is given on the day of the saint chosen for each pueblo in the 1600's by its Spanish priest. Before the dance the villagers attend Mass, honoring the new spirits brought them by the whites and added to their own. The saint is then carried forth and placed under a green arbor to watch the dance. The River Pueblos also have eagle dances when members of the Eagle Society, almost as honored as warriors, strut and whirl in eagle costume. In the hunting season costumed game animals prance around the Mother of Game as she leads them to the plaza. On Christmas Eve, at San Felipe, I have seen the deer impersonators leap into the church and up to the altar, the sound of their drum mingling with the Christian hymn.

HISTORY

These River Pueblos have had over two hundred years of Spanish rule, followed by another century when Spanish-Americans continued to live close to them and even entered their villages, often as husbands and wives. It is no wonder that they have Spanish names and speak Spanish and that many are good Catholics as well as good followers of their own religion, never abandoned. All obeyed the Spanish command that they should elect a secular governor, and proudly they show the staff of office which Spain's authorities provided for him. Beside it is the "Lincoln cane" donated by President Lincoln to confirm the promise that the Pueblos, under American rule, were to retain all their former privileges.

One of these privileges was the land grants which Spain had made to all the Pueblos except the Hopi, at that time considered too remote for white encroachment. These, the American government confirmed and, for a long time, was oblivious of the fact that much of the land had been occuped for years by outsiders and also, as with the Pima, that water rights had been seriously interfered with. In the 1930's, when much was done to right Indian wrongs, large sums of money were spent in securing a livelihood for the Pueblos. Before this, a reservation was set aside for the Hopi, who had been sharing land with the

TABLE 8

PRESENT RESERVATIONS AND NUMBERS OF THE
PEACEFUL CORN-GROWERS

Tribe	State and Agency	Population, 1945*
Pueblo............	*New Mexico:* United Pueblos Agency	
Acoma..........		1,398
Cochiti..........		365
Isleta...........		1,374
Jemez...........		812
Nambe..........		146
Picuris..........		118
Pojoaque........		28
Sandia..........		137
San Felipe.......		740
San Ildefonso.....		156
San Juan........		728
Santa Ana.......		278
Santa Clara.......		561
Santo Domingo....		1,083
Taos............		867
Tesuque.........		145
Zia.............		252
Zuni............		2,443
Hopi.............	*Arizona:* Hopi Agency	3,685 (18,065)
Maricopa..........	*Arizona:* Gila River Reservation	295
	Salt River Reservation	138 (433)
Papago...........	*Arizona:* Sells Agency	5,752
Pima.............	*Arizona:* Gila River Reservation	4,702
	Salt River Reservation	1,113
	Sells Agency	27 (5,842)

* Numbers in parentheses are totals.

Navaho, their ancient enemies. New tracts of land were bought for many of the others, so that they now claim both land grants and reservations. Usurping whites were bought out where possible, and, if not, as was often the case with River Pueblos, the villages were given money for irrigation, cattle, and other improvements. Around the pueblos may now be seen sheep, cattle, tractors, and harvesters, even though there are occasional threshing floors where horses trample out the grain as in Spanish days. Such new possessions are working an interesting change among the mother-right clans of the Desert Pueblos, where men, who scarcely owned anything in former days, now own sheep, cattle, and horses. Will alterations stop with one change of this sort, or are others inevitable?

As with other tribes, the government has offered to the Pueblos the possibility of incorporating under a charter. Understandably, these ancient theocracies are unwilling to change. The Hopi accepted but are having hard going in uniting some dozen villages, great and small. With the River Pueblos, only those torn by factions have accepted or considered the project. Toward schools, the attitude is different. The pretty stone Pueblo day schools have a higher standard, both in equipment and in teaching, than many of the rural schools around them. There are high schools at Oraibi, Zuni, and Taos, and the big boarding schools at Albuquerque and Santa Fe give opportunity to the other pueblos or to children from broken homes who must be boarded. We may note that in the ancient days of close family organization, no child was ever without a home among relatives, near or distant. That was before money economy made a child more a liability than an asset. We can hardly complain, because Indian life is slowly following the pattern set by the rest of the country, nor can we hope to stop the process.

Today most pueblos look like clean and attractive Mexican villages. Only Taos keeps the terraced apartment house (and rightfully charges admission to tourists who wish to see it). Only Hopi and Acoma retain their aeries, and that of Acoma is kept mostly for ceremonies. In the others one may look through the windows of one-story houses to see oilcloth, kerosene stoves, and modern furniture. In those near the highway there is a craft shop or public market. The Pueblo Indian had one kind of renaissance when the Spaniards brought them new crops and materials; they have had another in recent years, owing to the stimulus of the white Americans.

The stimulus given to other Indians was usually a by-product of military alliance or trade carried on for selfish reasons. The Pueblos, more fortunate, saw little of American whites until the 1890's, when such activities were in the past. By this time, when the Southwest was American and pacified, when the railroad came within distant reach of the Pueblos, white archaeologists penetrated the region to study and admire. At Awatovi in Hopi country, at Puyé of the Tewa, they unearthed scraps of an ancient pottery style no longer made. In each area an Indian woman was encouraged to re-create the neglected art. Nampeyo of Hano and Maria Martinez of San Ildefonso both had creative talent. Yet why should they labor at coiling, polishing, and firing pots when more durable and watertight containers could be bought in the stores? The white scholars encouraged, exhibited their work, and found sales. In time, scores of Pueblo women were making pots. Tourists were buying them by the thousands, and organizations of art-loving whites were holding exhibitions and giving prizes for fine work. Pottery in the Pueblos has taken the step inevitable for all hand-

PLATE XXXIV

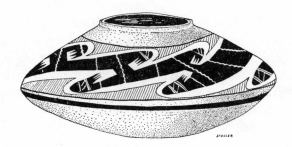

HOPI POTTERY

Hopi pottery, made of fine clay, sand- and grit-tempered, is coiled. Starting with a pat of clay, coils are laid on and smoothed with first a rind-scraper then smoothed and polished with a stone when it is dry. The vessel is painted with highly conventionalized designs after it is polished, then fired to a high degree to make it waterproof. It is easily recognized by its cream-to-orange background and the blackish designs. (From the Denver Art Museum Collections.)

work. From a necessary product made by everyone for use, it has changed to a luxury article, made by the skilled few, for sale.

Pottery is a revived art, but painting is one which has only just reached maturity. Centuries ago Pueblo people painted murals on the walls of their kivas and scratched figures on rocks. They had never had the range of opportunity provided by paper and water colors. It took only little stimulus from scholars and government schoolteachers to set young Pueblo employees and pupils to painting the jewel-bright scenes which are now sold and exhibited all over the United States and even abroad. The school at Santa Fe has classes in painting, with an Indian teacher.

For silverwork, the white Americans cannot take credit. That art was probably learned from Mexicans in the late nineteenth century and combined with the Pueblos' own taste for turquoise beads and inlay. With the sale possibilities of recent years, it has taken a leap, and traders, white art-lovers, and the Indian Service have all helped by suggesting adaptions of old designs which will appeal to modern purchasers.[27]

All this means change, but slow change. Pueblo people, like the Papago, and the southeasterners, were blessed with an occupation which they did not have to abandon. More fortunate than the south-

PLATE XXXV

BLACK
YELLOW

ACOMA EMBROIDERED SHAWL

Made of handspun cotton in a plain basket weave, this woman's manta is 41 by 50 inches. The embroidery, in a backstitch, is composed of two elements of handspun wool. The colors are natural black wool and native vegetable-dyed yarn. It was made about 1850. The black shawl used as a dress is herringbone weave in the center and diamond weave at the end. (From Mera, 1943.)

easterners, they were never hustled off their own land or fed on rations. Never did they cease to earn their livelihood. Farmers for two thousand years, they have the pride consonant with that record and a natural fear that change may be for the worse. Because their own sense of values was so firm, they have been able to take from whites what they wished and to reject the rest.

Until lately! With the second World War, two forces have loomed before them, one threatening, one beneficent, and both, perhaps, be-

PLATE XXXVI

ZUNI SILVERWORK

The use of large masses of several colors of stone and shell, the presence of silver-wire trim, and delicate elaborations are the identifying features of Zuni silverwork. This modern pin, 4 by 3½ inches, represents the knife-god or flint-god as depicted on a Zuni society altar. (From the Denver Art Museum Collections.)

yond any handling. Pueblo boys were drafted into the armed forces like other Americans. With whites who received them as equals, they traveled over the world. For the first time they realized what money can buy and what must be done to get money. They came home to ask the village leaders for more liberty, more outside contact, than was planned by the little theocracy. Mostly, the leaders stood firm. Their system had worked. If even one item was removed from it, who could tell how soon the whole might crumble? So at last the theocracies are threatened with disruption.

To many of the River Pueblos, such change does not look frightening. They are near a great atom-bomb center, now a city of highly trained and intelligent whites. These experts need unskilled help, and they are willing to pay wages incredible from the Pueblo point of view. Will one who has had such wages and bought what they permit be

PLATE XXXVII

PIMA BASKET

The foundation of bear grass (*Nolina erumpens*) is split by teeth or fingernails when dry and formed into bundles as shown in the small drawing. A center is plaited and the coils started by an interlocking stitch of fine willow splints. The spine of a cactus or a fine-pointed wood awl is used to make the holes for the stitches. Devil's-claw (*Martynis probosidea*) is the black used in the design. The stitching material is soaked in hot water and kept wet while the work is in progress. (From the Denver Art Museum Collections.)

willing to go back to living in a self-sufficient pueblo? That self-sufficiency which held a pueblo together through poverty and persecution melts under that kindly companionship of interested whites. For the scientists do not scorn the Pueblo Indians or try to govern them. They have presented the opportunity of a whole white society willing to make friends. Where is the value of self-sufficiency now?

PLATE XXXVIII

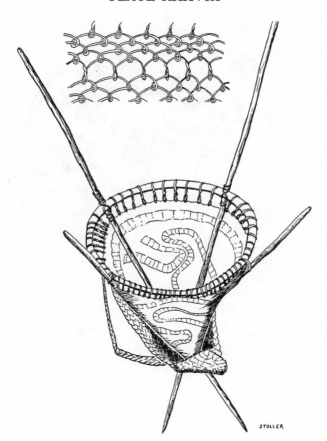

PIMA CARRYING BASKET

Made by lace coiling (small diagram) of maguey (*Tasylirioni wheeleri*), twisted into twine. The rim is a wood rod. The back protector and carrying strap are of plaited yucca splints. The long rods, projecting above the head, are 4 feet long and the smaller ones about 26 inches. Huge loads can be carried in this *kiaha*. (From Mason, 1902.)

MOGOLLON AND HOHOKAM

FOOD

Vegetable.—Hohokam had flour corn, cultivated pumpkin (*Cucurbita moschata* and *C. maxima*), cactus buds and leaves, mesquite, greens, wild fruits. Mogollon had pod and pop corn, later flour corn.

Animal.—Deer, small game, rabbits, bear, bighorn sheep (Hohokam), antelope, birds.

HUNTING METHOD

Bows and arrows, spear-throwers; Mogollon had snares of all sizes.

CLOTHING

Male.—Mogollon: sandals of yucca, robes of rabbit fur and deerskin. Hohokam: breechcloths, rabbit-fur blankets, cotton blankets, and robes of both, sandals of woven fiber and wickerwork. Poncho-type skin and cotton shirts.

Female.—Mogollon: yucca fiber aprons and sandals, fur and feather robes. Hohokam: similar to men, except for cord apron-skirts, belts.

HOUSE TYPES

Mogollon: round, semi-pit-house, in open or cave. Hohokam: first, round, semi-pit-house in open or caves; later, puddled adobe house of one to many stories with first story filled in solid, this and other buildings of previous residents surrounded by adobe wall.

EQUIPMENT

Household.—Mogollon: coiled pottery, plain and painted, red-on-buff, black-on-white. No basketry found. Hohokam: pottery coiled, some use of paddle, plain and painted, bowls, jars, etc. Corn-grinders, stone vessels, bone and horn spoons. Plaited and coiled basketry, pitched jar.

Transportation.—No evidence.

Hunting.—Throwing spear, self-bow, arrow, grooved club.

Other.—Cradle: sticks laced together for Mogollon; no Hohokam found. Pipe: pottery, stone tubes, cane cigarettes. Miscellaneous: Digging sticks, wooden spoons, nose plugs, rings, beads, cordage, netting, prayer sticks (Hohokam). Flutes. Hohokam loom was belt loom with figure-8 warp, horizontal. Also plain and gauze textiles.

WAR

Not known.

GAMES

Guessing game of disks, dice, gaming bones, pin-and-ring.

PUEBLO

FOOD

Vegetable.—Flint corn, many colors, flour corn. Later: beans, squash (*Cucurbita moschata*), wild plants, sunflower, agriculture.

Animal.—Deer, small game, domesticated turkey.

HUNTING METHOD

Rabbit sticks, communal hunts, some individual. Deer-head disguise, ceremonial rundown of game, smothering. Antelope drives.

CLOTHING

Male.—Kilts of cotton, sandals early, later ankle-high moccasins. Cotton blankets, later of wool. Robes of rabbit fur and turkey feathers. Braided cotton sashes.

Female.—First cotton, then wool rectangle dresses, cotton shawls, wool robes. Sandals first, then high moccasin boots. Later: embroidery on wool and cotton shawls and sashes.

HOUSE TYPES

Village dwellers, huge community dwellings of stone and adobe, some on cliff sides. Underground ceremonial rooms.

EQUIPMENT

Household.—Pottery first sun-dried, now coiled and fired. From plain gray cooking pottery to polychrome (many colored), polished. Basketry of coil and wicker types, now almost gone.

Transportation.—None.

Hunting.—Self-bow, arrows, spears, lances, deer-head disguise.

Other.—Cradle: flat board type, some sideboards, also swing type. Pipe: pottery tube, cigarettes. Miscellaneous: weaving of cotton by men on vertical loom with heddle rods, wool after about 1600. Belts, robes, blankets, dresses. Galaxy of masks, kachinas, painting on kiva walls, prayer sticks (feathered), flutes, drums, and rattles.

WAR

Bow and arrows, spears, basketry shields. In charge of a priesthood. Organized parties for offensive wars, also defensive fighting. Some raids.

GAMES

Races, kick race, bowling, tops, balls, hoop-and-pole, double ball, archery, bean-shooters, cat's cradle, shinny, stilts, quoits.

THE DESERT PEOPLE

FOOD

Vegetable.—Tepary beans, flour corn, squash (*Cucurbita pepo*), winter squash, tobacco, mesquite, cactus, wild greens.

Animal.—Deer, rabbits, other small game.

HUNTING METHOD

Stalking, rundown, ritual hunts, rabbit surround.

CLOTHING

Male.—Breechcloths, sandals of yucca, rabbit-skin robes, later cotton robes.

Female.—Wrap-around skirts of cotton or deerskin, rabbit-skin robes, tattooing on chin.

MAP VI

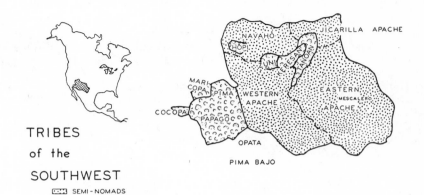

TRIBES
of the
SOUTHWEST

JICARILLA APACHE

NAVAHO
HOPI
ZUÑI
KERESAN
TANOAN

MARI-
COPA
PIMA WESTERN
APACHE

EASTERN
MESCALERO
APACHE

COCOPA
PAPAGO

OPATA

PIMA BAJO

☷ SEMI-NOMADS
☷ AGRICULTURISTS

TAOS

NAVAHO   NEW MEXICO

PICURIS

SAN JUAN

HOPI

SANTA CLARA   POJOAQUE
SAN ILDEFONSO   NAMBE
TESUQUE

FT. DEFIANCE ●   ★ SANTA FE

JEMEZ
COCHITI

ZIA
SANTA ANA   SANTO DOMINGO

ARIZONA   SAN FELIPE
SANDIA

LITTLE COLORADO R.

LAGUNA

RIO GRANDE R.

● HOLBROOK   ZUÑI

● ALBUQUERQUE

ACOMA   ISLETA

Neal '51

MODERN PUEBLOS

☷ RIVER PUEBLOS
☷ DESERT PUEBLOS

HOUSE TYPES

Semispherical pit-house; conical ritual house; female segregation hut.

EQUIPMENT

Household.—Plaited baskets and mats of yucca and bear grass. Coiled baskets for all purposes and of all sizes. Pottery coiled then paddled, red-on-buff.
Transportation.—None.
Hunting.—Self-bow; Pima sinew-backed bow, arrows.
Other.—Cradle: slat type. Pipe: stone cloud-blower (Pima); cornhusk cigarette and cane pipe (Papago). Miscellaneous: unpainted prayer stick, ritual equipment, gourd masks, reproductions of birds and mountains. Belt loom: horizontal, figure-8 warp, heddle rods, like Pueblo.

WAR

Bow and arrow, war clubs of mesquite, rawhide shield. Defensive fighting mostly, no captives.

GAMES

Kick ball, relay races, *ginyeskut* (like parchesi), stick dice for women, archery, double ball, hoop-and-pole, quoits, ring-and-pin, shuttlecock.

CHAPTER X

Late Arrivals

In the centuries around A.D. 1000 there was a series of upheavals around the edge of the corn-growers' country. It began at the east, as early as A.D. 900, when some frontier hamlets in New Mexico were burned out and driven out.[1] Others suffered the same fate in 1294, and, from the number of skeletons found, they died fighting.[2] About A.D. 1000 corn-growers at the north began to concentrate and move south. Those on the northernmost frontier built the famous cliff dwellings whose purpose must surely be for fortification. By the 1300's even these retreats were deserted, Betatakin after only fifty-eight years of occupation. By 1400 the Hohokam, at the south, had left their great houses and disappeared.

We can think of reasons why any one of these desertions might have happened. But to explain so many, all within a few centuries and all on the frontier, one possible cause stands out above all others—incoming nomads. We know that the Navaho and the Apache, once a single people, roamed around these very frontiers somewhat later and that, in 1700, a whole string of pueblos along the Rio Grande was abandoned for fear of them. Advance the incursion a few centuries, at least for some of the bands, and the whole picture is clear. It is true that, in A.D. 1000, the nomads had no horses and could not have marched like an army upon a well-built pueblo. Still, they could have prowled in small groups, as nomads will, stealing corn and women. Mobile groups, with nothing to lose, would be a nuisance to settled people, guarding their possessions, and doubly dangerous if they had better weapons. That they had, for it seems probable that it was these very nomads who brought from the north the sinew-backed bow, a late importation from Asia and far more powerful than the simple bent sticks the Pueblos used.[3]

Navaho and Apache speak a language which, up to this time, had been foreign to the Southwest. The singsong Athapascan, with its

225

three tones which can give different meanings to the same syllable, is spread widely through western Canada and interior Alaska. One could almost imagine the Athapascans as camping along the trail from the Old World, with a few outliers in Oregon and California and one great detached fragment in the Southwest.

They must have reached the Southwest almost empty-handed except for that useful sinew-backed bow. The North Woods, their original home, has, of course, no agriculture. The Athapascans there lived by hunting and fishing, too busy and too mobile for either craft or ceremony. Their dwelling was of logs and earth, and some, like the Sekani, may have used the tipi shape, familiar in the North Woods, with a covering of bark and leaves. Their clothing was of skin, including moccasins. Was it they who introduced this new form of footgear to the sandal-wearing Pueblos?

We can picture them seeping south in little groups, whose progress was spread over centuries. Some may have followed the foothills of the Rockies. Some may have penetrated the passes and found the Great Basin country, where Indians wore cedar bark, lived in brush huts, and ate birds and lizards, as some Navaho say they once did. Some, on the other hand, may have wandered east into the Plains, where the Spaniards found them in 1541.[4] Somewhere they picked up the tall gray pot which we have noticed in the east and which the Navaho, at least, regard as ancient and sacred. As they filtered into the Southwest, awed and excited, doubtless, by the buildings, the fields, the clothing, and the ceremonies they saw, the wanderers received from the Tewa the name apachu, which means "stranger" or "enemy."[5] It must have been some time before they sorted themselves out into the groups we know now, which include at least nine divisions of Apache and one of Navaho, many times larger than all the others put together. This last group settled among Pueblo people, in north-central New Mexico. There they became known as apaches de nabahu, "enemies of the cultivated fields." They had begun their career as some of the outstanding learners among American Indians.

Their history is obscure until the late 1600's. Then we find the typical Navaho dwellings scattered on the ledges above little streams in north-central New Mexico[6] known as Dinetkah ("Home of the People"), or Old Navaholand. This type of dwelling is the well-known forked-stick hogan, nothing more or less than a tripod frame of logs covered with earth and with a sort of vestibule added. Old Navahos can recognize even its ruins because of the two flat stones which mark the doorway. After 1680 the hogans are interspersed with small stone Pueblo dwellings and surrounded with scraps of pottery from almost every pueblo known. The story is plain. This was the period after the Pueblo revolt when whole families and even villages left their homes to escape Spanish vengeance. The refugees lived for some sixty years among the Navaho, and the learning possibilities for the newcomers can hardly be overestimated.

Say that the Navaho—and perhaps some Apache not yet separated —already knew about agriculture. Say that they had stolen some

PLATE XXXIX

NAVAHO FORKED-STICK HOGAN

With the entrance always to the east, these homes are constructed of three to five forked piñon logs, 10–12 feet long as the center support. The poles are set in place, the sides filled in with smaller limbs, brush, and cedar bark. Earth is thrown over this to a depth of 6 inches. A smoke hole is left in the center of the house. Two long poles, supported by the center poles, form the sides of the doorway. It is constructed in the same manner as the house. (From Mindeleff, 1895–96.)

sheep and horses from the fleeing Spaniards. They still had everything to learn about weaving, costume, myth, and ceremony. The signs are that they did learn. By 1706 a Spanish expedition reported the Navaho—for they now bear the name—as keeping sheep and weaving wool.[7] Their loom and their earliest blankets are exact replicas of those of the Pueblos, so there can be no doubt as to how they learned.

Yet in the next century Spanish reports which used to extol Pueblo weaving have praise only for Navaho. They adopted a variation of Pueblo woman's dress, though with two blankets instead of one, perhaps in imitation of the two-skin dress of the Plains woman. Old pictures show men wearing belted blankets in addition to their buckskin leggings. In the matter of dwellings they were more conservative. Right to the end of this period of mixture, the hogans and the little sweat lodges stand among the square masonry buildings. The forked-stick hogan is used by many Navaho to this day.

Ceremony may have taken longer to evolve, but we cannot mistake the pattern of eight days' preparation, with offerings of prayer sticks and tobacco, then a public dance on the ninth day. In one ceremony, the famous Yebitchai, the dancers wear the mask and kilt like Pueblos, a strange sight on the lean, rangy figures of the Navaho. However, not all the People, as they call themselves, are lean and rangy. Thousands of them show the neat, plump bodies, the small hands and feet, which characterize Pueblo people. During the long period of association, marriage, the great agent of social change, must have done its work. Tradition says that many a mother-clan of the Navaho started when a Pueblo or even a Mexican woman married one of the People.

During the 1700's the Navaho slowly moved away from their hidden, wooded hills. There were several other settlements where they mixed with Pueblo refugees, but, in the end, these latter either returned home or became definitely Navaho. Meantime, the People had been acquiring horses and sheep, by means lawful and unlawful. They had no idea of keeping horses in a corral outside a village as the Pueblos did. They mounted them and rode away, family by family, the horses carrying extra baggage, the sheep bringing both food and weaving materials on the hoof. During the 1700's they spread over a large part of the plateau country west of the River Pueblos, which is now their reservation. The Hopi and Zuni were surrounded. Though they have tales of fighting, it is plain that these swift and daring nomads did about as they wished in the country between the four mountain groups (Mount Taylor, San Francisco Peaks, La Plata Range, and Jemez Range).

Spanish ranchers felt the new menace almost as much as the Hopi and Zuni. The government alternated between desperate punitive expeditions, treaties, and presents to those whom they thought of as leaders. Nothing touched the Navaho greatly. There were deep canyons where they could hide with their stolen sheep, sometimes a thousand at one raid. When the Spaniards decided to give bribes of silk handkerchiefs, velvet breeches, and silver ornaments, they accepted them with pleasure. Meantime, they had plenty of slaves to do their work and also to be traded for horses. Their women had leisure to weave more and more beautiful blankets, sometimes with threads unraveled from the precious red baize, or *bayeta*, which the Spaniards used in trade. When Mexico won her independence (1823) and Spain no longer sent troops against the nomads, life was even better. For some twenty years the Navaho, the Apache, the Ute, and the Comanche rode high, wide, and handsome. They pillaged New Mexico ranches and even towns. They had a regular slave route along which

PLATE XL

BLUE
RED

NAVAHO BLANKET

This blanket, 55 by 72 inches, was made about 1840. It has white handspun warp, with while, indigo-dyed blue handspun and raveled red bayeta (baize) designs. The vertical Navaho loom, with figure-8 warp, was used in its manufacture. (From Amsden, 1949.)

they took Pueblo and even Spanish girls, trading them for horses. It was a life which many white people had led in the Middle Ages, but this was the nineteenth century. Sooner or later, civilization was bound to interfere.

This event took place in 1848, when Mexico turned over the Navaho and Pueblo areas to the United States. Innocently, the new government accepted all the obligations of the previous one, including that of subduing raiding Indians. There followed some twenty years when blue-coated troopers made futile attempts to chase the Navaho and Apache through the canyons. Then came the War between the States, and the troopers were removed. Yet, since gold for the troops passed across the country where the Navaho and Apache plied their occupation, this brigandage had to be stopped. The task was given to Kit Carson, an illiterate trapper, guide, and, finally, Indian agent, who had made a success of every mission he had undertaken. With a few New Mexico regiments of "dismounted cavalry" he went first after the Mescalero Apache and soon had four hundred of them ready to cease raiding and go on a reservation. The one provided was forty square miles on the Pecos River in eastern New Mexico, where, it was thought, both Navaho and Apache could soon learn to till the soil and become self-supporting farmers.

The Mescalero attended to, Kit went after the Navaho. He could not hope to chase them into the canyons, so he simply killed their sheep, burned their corn, and cut down their peach trees. Soon the people were starving. They came in droves to Fort Defiance, found that they would be clothed and fed, and finally some eight thousand consented to go in relays to Fort Sumner or Bosque Redondo—in their terms, "the Long Walk." There they remained for four years. These were the most tragic years of Navaho history, and even today few Navaho can make a speech which does not begin with the woes of *huelte*, "the fort."

It is the opinion of this writer that the Navaho, during this Babylonian captivity, learned practically nothing. They were given modern seeds and iron tools. They were shown how to dig an irrigation ditch. As their clothes gave out, the army provided them with trousers and coats never worn before, and charitable organizations sent barrels of men's and women's clothing. Still the Navaho plaint, as translated by a modern scholar, was: "Oh beloved Chinlee . . . that in the Springtime used to be so pleasant. . . . Oh beloved Black Mountain! Would that one were at these so-named places."[8]

The project was a failure. In the fourth year they planted no crops at all. General Sherman, sent to investigate the situation, reported that it would be cheaper to board the whole tribe at the Fifth Avenue Hotel in New York. The Navaho still tell how they embraced the general's knees, begging: "My father, my mother, let us go home!" There was nothing else to do. A treaty was signed in 1868 which stands as the Navaho Magna Carta. They promised never to fight again, and they have not done so. They promised to acknowledge the authority of the United States, to till the soil, and to send their children to school. In turn, the government promised to provide a school for every thirty children, "in so far as they could be induced or compelled to attend." Also it promised to replace the sheep Kit Carson had killed, to provide rations until the Navaho were properly started as farmers, and to distribute clothing and tools.

These promises were not all kept on either side. It is true that, after some delay, the government was able to provide sheep and goats at the rate of three animals per person. That is, until the last Navaho who had evaded the Long Walk began to come in, and donations had to be reduced. The rations were provided and for longer than the ten years expected. The seeds and tools came late or not at all. As for the school, it was of the one-room variety at Fort Defiance, but never thirty children. Why should the Navaho send their children to school? They did not expect to share the white man's life. Children were needed to help plant the fields, to rebuild the ruined hogans, even to hunt rats and prairie dogs, so the family need not eat their sheep.

All these things they did. For the next twenty years after their return from the fort, the Navaho worked as they never worked before. Like the Pueblos, they had an occupation, never abandoned. They had now been raising sheep for at least a hundred years, and, through misery and poverty, they planned to continue. Children tended the animals and hunted small game. Women wove blankets for trade; men, instead of raiding, toured the country, trading blankets for horses with the Mexicans, the white settlers, and the Mormons now established in Utah. Also, men had a new art. They had long possessed Spanish silver ornaments but had been too busy to make them. Now a traveling Mexican taught a few Navaho whose descendants practice the art today.[9] Knowledge spread, and soon a number of men were hammering out American quarters, cutting out shapes with tin shears and scratching designs with a crude file. The items they made were the Spanish pomegranate flower, the silver buttons, bracelets, rings, conchas, and the *naja*, the two-horned sign against the evil eye which had been known in Europe for untold centuries. These and the women's blankets were traded. The sheep increased. The corn patches were replanted. Slowly the Navaho began to move toward prosperity.

This determined, upward climb is in striking contrast to the mournful inactivity of many Plains tribes who resigned themselves to idleness, to the Ghost Dance, or to peyote. Had the Navaho suffered less? Had they more tradition of industry due to their Pueblo intermixture? If students of government could make sure of the facts here, they would own a valuable tool for understanding minorities. For the Navaho, in 1868, merely a small tribe of raiding Indians like many others, are now the largest tribe in the United States, famous for their weaving, their silverwork, and their ceremonies.

The government can take little credit for the change, at least in the first years. That was the period after the Civil War, when the United States was changing from a small country to a large one, with enormous areas to populate and develop. No care was given to the choosing of Indian agents. Their pay and their quarters were miserable, and they themselves were often incompetent or dishonest. It was the traders who guided the Navaho into the new life, filling the role of teacher, guardian, and friend. Traders sold their silver and their wool and sheepskins. They persuaded the weavers to change from a light blanket to a heavy rug, suitable for eastern floors. They imported aniline dyes, then yarn. They suggested designs and colors suitable for sale. There was a bad period when the puzzled women went overboard with strange patterns and colors. Not entirely Navaho? No, but also not entirely white. The combination of Indian taste with white man's materials and requirements has often produced this kind of new, vigorous art.

Traders also introduced the Navaho to new materials. Now that they could get steel saws, they began to build log cabins like those of their new friends, but these must be circular, like the ancient forked-stick hogan. When the railroad was built and the Navaho worked on it, they got strong wooden ties, of exactly the right length to construct an eight- or six-sided dwelling with cribbed roof. This is the most common type of Navaho house seen today. Clothing changed too. The double woolen blanket was now too expensive, since the Navaho weaver must sell her work. She took to calico skirts like the trader's wife and finally, about 1900, to the full-flounced skirt and velveteen blouse worn today. White ladies had but just given up velveteen "basques," and one wonders if the wholesale houses had a surplus stock to dispose of.

Meantime, there had been little schooling and little government help. The Navaho were living the life of twelfth-century peasants and felt no need of nineteenth-century learning. In fact, when one badgered agent tried to collect children for boarding school, they besieged him in the trader's store and nearly frightened him to death. The tribe was increasing, and so were the sheep. The herds of some rich men now numbered in the thousands, and a few hundred horses for such a man was nothing unusual. The reservation had already received some additions, but it could not support the growing population. Agents asked for more land. Then, as this grew difficult, they tried to improve the water supply. But the Navaho country, with its glistening plains and crimson-red rocks, could not, at best, supply much corn or pasture. After the period of about 1890, when the tribe reached its peak in sheep production, the pinch began to be felt.

Our description of their lifeway must come from that time, carrying with it echoes from Pueblo, Spaniard, and American white but yet standing out clearly as an expression of the *Diné*, the People themselves. At this time every family owned sheep and moved with them from the flat lands in summer to the mountain springs and the shelter of trees in winter. There was a hogan of sorts at each locality, with a corral where the sheep were brought in every night. Ruinous to pasturage, the experts were later to explain, but thus the Navaho had laid their plans when they had needed to keep sheep near by for fear of hostile raids. Besides plenty of mutton and goat, with corn, squash, and perhaps watermelon from the garden, they bought coffee and canned peaches at the store and wheat flour to make the "fried bread" they had learned from Mexicans. Their furniture was mostly sheepskins; their clothing the velveteen blouse for all, with blue jeans for the men, flounced calico skirts for women.

Babies were carried upon cradleboards, and a mother had no hesitation in sitting on a horse for long distances, her infant in her lap. Children ranged the mesas with the sheep. Boys, at about eight years old, were given initiatory strokes of a whip by a masked god, reminiscent of Pueblo initiations except that it was out of doors. Girls at maturity had an imposing ceremony when guests gathered for four nights of singing while the maiden ran every morning toward the east, perhaps a symbol of industry. Then the gathering ate an enormous cake, baked in a warmed pit, the Indian version of a fireless cooker. At marriage the youth wooed his chosen one with gifts of horses and, then, if accepted, came to live with her in a hogan next to that of her parents. He strictly observed the taboo against speaking to his mother-in-law, for neglecting it might mean that he would go mad and jump in the fire. In time he might take his wife's sisters as additional brides, but he and they both had rights of divorce. A saddle placed outside the door was enough notice from his wives that he should now return to his mother's house.

The Navaho had as much horror of death as we could find among Pimans or Mohave. In fact, such horror is widespread in the northern country also. After a death, the house must be burned, and, to avoid this, old and sick people were often moved, with their consent, into a shelter outside the house. Goods were left at the grave, and perhaps a favorite horse was shot, that the dead might have all he needed and not be tempted to return. The relatives returned by a zigzag route, then purified themselves in a cedar smoke. Later, when they found that the government, or missionaries, would bury their dead, they accepted gladly.

War was over, but the Navaho still remembered how they had gone out with lance and shield under a picked and successful leader. Boys had to be trained for years for these exploits, doing the camp work, using special language, and sleeping in prescribed positions. The warriors took plenty of booty, since that was their main purpose. They also took scalps, which were kept hidden in the rocks, and the scalper purified himself by taking sweat baths and singing songs. Sometimes, even so, the miasma of enemy contact would make him ill, and, years afterward, he might need a singing of the Enemy Way. White visitors today see the last act of this symbolic battle and victory, ending in three nights of "Squaw Dance," when the maidens dance with the warriors and are rewarded. Since stranger and enemy are so nearly the same in Navaho thinking, the children who go to boarding school or the men working among whites often have this ceremony.

After dancing most of the night, the Navaho are still ready, during the day, to race their horses or to play the gambling game in which some small object is hidden in one of several moccasins. In this, men cheerfully lose their silver belts and necklaces, then borrow toward another ten-hour session the next day.

There is no gambling during the solemn nine-day ceremonies, for then everyone present is expected to keep his mind on sacred things

PLATE XLI

STOLLER

NAVAHO SAND PAINTING

Sand paintings are actually altars, composed of the representations of the divinities used in the particular chant. They are made on the floors of the ceremonial hogans of dry sands colored with clays and ochers and black from soot made by ritualistic burning. This painting, from the Shooting Chant, representing the Hero in the Eagle's Nest, shows the two eagles at the top; a basket, an antelope, a mountain sheep, prairie dog, and rabbit around the nest; the figure of the Hero is in the blue nest with other personages and young eagles. (From Reichard, 1939.)

that he may share with the patient in the blessing obtained. All ceremonies, with the Navaho, are for the benefit of a suffering individual.
Rain is needed here as much as in Pueblo country, but there is no
gathering of the people to pray for this common blessing. As with
the hunting tribes, man's great interest is in health and good fortune.
Brief illnesses can be handled by a short rite, but a serious illness,
whether it means physical pain or mental discouragement, calls for a
nine-day ceremony. There are a number of these, organized on a pattern which combines northern myth and ceremony with Pueblo ritual.
The myth is the well-known adventure of an individual who is taken
to a village of animals or other spirits and there given power. However,
such adventures were not required of living youths, as they were in
the Plains or the Great Lakes. They had all happened long ago to
some god or protégé of the gods who had acquired not only songs and
talismans but the ancient southwestern art of sand painting.[10]

This theology shimmers with reminiscences of other Indian tribes
described here, yet it has been reworked into Navaho form. The songs
are often magnificent poetry; the sand paintings are more elaborate
and colorful than anything dreamed of by the Pueblos. The eight-day
private ritual, held in a newly constructed or newly cleansed hogan,
is solemn with purification and offering; then the sand painting calls
the spirits, and on the ninth night they may dance in their Pueblo-like
masks, a Navaho-style Clown accompanying them. Men may dance
naked around a fire to show magic power, or there may be sword-
swallowing and sleight-of-hand. The patient must pay the chanter and
all the helpers, and, in former days, he fed the guests. It was a public
benefaction, resulting in as much spiritual benefit as a Pueblo dance
for those attending.

The chanter who managed the performance may rightly be called
a priest. He learned one myth, or more, with its attendant drama by
paying an older chanter for years of instruction. This meant that, with
the myth in mind, he could direct purification, songs, paintings, im-
personations—a whole drama of the mythical healing. When he was
paid in horses, sheep, and jewelry, he gave a royalty to his instructor.
The therapeutic myth had usually no connection with the symptoms
of the disease. Sometimes, to tell what chanter should be called, the
patient consulted a diviner with direct visions from the spirits. Otherwise he took anyone he chose, and, if he got no relief, he saved up
wealth to employ another. These myths of the Navaho bear some
resemblance to Pueblo stories. They include the emergence from

PLATE XLII

NAVAHO SILVER NECKLACE

The beads of the necklace are made by putting small squares of silver over funnel-shaped holes and forcing them into the mold with an iron bar. The half-globe thus formed is soldered with fine wire to another half. The "Squash Blossoms" (or pomegranate) are cast and a half-bead soldered to the top. The pendant, a *naja*, is cast. The necklace is 16 inches long. (From the Denver Art Museum Collections.)

Earth's womb and the exploits of the War-Gods, who here swell to Wagnerian grandeur. Then they go off into a wealth of adventure showing how one out of harmony with the world can regain well-being.

The Navaho in the early twentieth century were still contented, still felt that the spirits were looking after them, though there had been some hard years. Periodically, a wail had gone to Washington from the agent. "This was a bad year, and the Navaho are destitute!" Somehow, the tribe weathered each crisis and continued to pasture its sheep. World War I passed, with Navaho volunteering in the fighting ranks. The depression came. Finally, it was time to do something for the Navaho. But what could be done about producing more pasture? There would not have been enough even had every moist spot been lush with grass. As it was, little hooves had trampled some of the ground utterly bare, and nibbling mouths had destroyed even the grass roots. The Navaho were sad, but their solution was: "We have neglected the old ceremonies. Therefore, the spirits do not let the grass grow."

The government had another solution: there must be fewer sheep. To the Navaho, such a proposal seemed little better than if they had been asked to kill their own children. Sheep were their means of livelihood. Sheep were what kept their self-respect and their will to live during a half-century of hardship. As for the extra horses, they were to a Navaho what a fine house and a good car are to a white man. True, one could live without them, but where would be his status? Without his extra horses for gifts, gambling, and bride price, the Navaho would be like a rich white man forced to walk the streets in shabby clothes.

Still, it was the government which would have to pay the bill when the pasturage was gone and the Navaho starving. Complete responsibility for the welfare of a group is a burden which few have ever handled with complete success. When the edict went out that no Navaho might own more than a certain quota of sheep and that all extra horses must be sold, the people rebelled. Not openly! They already knew the tragic consequences of that. They grumbled. They refused to adapt. They talked as though they were being purposely starved. White men, in the past, have lost means of livelihood and have philosophically gone out to find something else. They had not been living in the Middle Ages, where money, industry, and education were practically untouched mysteries. The Navaho had suddenly met the twentieth century in bitter guise, and, for a time, they felt helpless.

Plans were made for them, as well as such things can be done when the recipients of help are not consulted. Their extra horses and sheep were bought at a good price. Soil-conservation projects were started, and Navaho employed on them. New day schools went up, even in desert places, and in them were sewing machines for the community, shower baths, sometimes a workshop. The Navaho were mildly interested in school, but even yet, however, they were unable to see why a child should sit at a desk five days a week, nine months a year. They would send one child for a few months or even a year, then another. If the white man's magic had not worked in that time, it could hardly have much power. And why should they incorporate, hold meetings, and borrow money as other tribes had done? They could manage their own business.

It was World War II which finally shook the Navaho out of the Middle Ages, as it shook other peoples in various parts of the world. They were drafted like other Americans, and a surprising number turned out illiterate or physically unfit. A literate few rendered unique and dramatic service by talking in their own language across enemy lines to give army instructions. Gangs of men went all over the world to work on ranches and railroads. Men, and women too, worked in munition plants. With their wages and with soldiers' allotments, the Navaho had suddenly the kind of income known to white Americans. This was not a situation for the Middle Ages. Boys in the army wrote home: "Send my little brother to school. I've just found out what I could do if I was educated."

The tribe was awake. The leap across the centuries was painful to people who had been living contentedly in earth-floored huts, trading wool and rugs for canned goods, and otherwise asking nothing but to live peacefully in the sunshine, with much family affection and an occasional heartening ceremony. Suddenly, they wanted education. Plenty of it! As much as any white! And they wanted money! There had been very little saving in the lush war years, for the Navaho had never thought of inedible government paper as something to keep. Many families were truly destitute. Young men had found other wives. Old parents had been deserted. Stray children who once would have been received by relatives as a matter of course were now handed over to the government as orphans. The lifeway of the Navaho was under revision.

It is still under revision, but some misapprehensions of both the People and the government are being corrected. Fortune had favored the Navaho in several ways, and one is that, when this huge tribe

(70,000 in 1951) is facing a drastic change in lifeway, the white man is awake to problems of minority group and of varied cultures. No longer does he expect that a Navaho will walk off the reservation and immediately behave like a denizen of some modern city. Even on the reservation, he knows the vital importance attached to ceremonies, signing of names which the Navaho blithely changes on each important occasion, and even food preference. Large sums are now being allocated to the Navaho. The school system has been revised and plans made for groups of young Navaho to have a quick course at many boarding schools all over Indian country. At least these illiterate adolescents will have something with which to face the world. Boarding schools are being built or repaired in other parts of the reservation, for it is obvious that the seminomadic Navaho, living such distances apart, cannot manage day school. Some of the younger adults who skipped school will be left uneducated. That is, unless they want to go out and procure schooling for themselves as whites do. For the next generation, there will be provision.

Seventy thousand people cannot, in one generation, be brought to health and economic competence. Hospital services are being improved. Social workers are in action. An employment service is seeking work for Navaho off the reservation and negotiating with railroads and ranchers for proper housing and fair pay. Some Navaho families have accepted lands on the Colorado River Reservation, where the hot, low farming country is as different as possible from their upland home. But it offers a living. Navaho, who have been United States citizens since 1924, can now vote in state elections if they fulfil Arizona's literacy requirements. They are eligible for social security payments like other citizens.

All this means more change than has already gone on. For social security arrangements are set up on the basis that a man will have but one wife and that he will keep the same name through life. Hospitals expect that a tuberculous patient will not return to his family until he has ceased to be a source of contagion. Schools expect that pupils will attend every day. Employers want to rely on an employee for at least a number of months. All these requirements go against Navaho practices, and the rewards they bring seem to many a Navaho not worth the price. The resulting uncertainty means liquor, delinquency, desertion, and a shift, by some perplexed seekers, to the peyote religion. White Americans who are outraged at such results might do well to read intimate stories of their own commonwealth just after the Revolution. Was the percentage of upright and successful people so great at that time? Or at any other crisis?

Which group reached the Southwest first, the Navaho or the Apache? This is a favorite question among students of prehistory but surely a meaningless one. The sharp division into two "tribes" was never made in early days. The wandering strangers who spoke of themselves as *Diné*, the People, were divided in their travels into a dozen or more groups, of which the *Apaches de nabahu* were only one and no more important than any of the others. Probably they all filtered into the Southwest by various routes and at various times. It is easy, then, to account for the long span of centuries during which there were eruptions along the Pueblo border.

TABLE 9

PRESENT RESERVATIONS AND NUMBERS OF THE LATE ARRIVALS

Tribe	State and Agency	Population, 1945*
Western Apache....	*Arizona:* Fort Apache Reservation	3,202
	Fort McDowell Reservation	210
	San Carlos Agency and Reservation	3,439
	Camp Verde Reservation	461
Jicarilla..........	*New Mexico:* Jicarilla Agency and Reservation	816
Mescalero..........	*New Mexico:* Mescalero Agency and Reservation	868 (8,996)
Navaho...........	*Arizona:* Navaho Agency	28,836
	New Mexico: Navaho Agency	26,268
	Canoncito Agency	364
	Puertocito Agency	309
	Utah: Navaho Agency	354 (56,131)

* Numbers in parentheses are totals.

Those of the Strangers who chose to remain aloof from the corn-growers, centering their interests as always upon war and hunting, doubtless felt that they had chosen the richer lifeway. Yet today the nine groups called Apache number all together only one-quarter as many people as the one group called Navaho (see Table 9). One reason is that they did not marry wholesale with the Pueblo and other tribes as did the Navaho. In fact, measurements have indicated that they are unusually free from foreign admixture.[11] Another is that many of them were still fighting and roaming long after the Navaho had settled down to sheep-raising. The Apache had few peaceful contacts, either with Pueblos, with Spaniards, or with white Americans, so the amount of their learning was small. None of them does any weaving or silver-work. None kept sheep or cattle until reservation days. Some, it is true, took up agriculture, and, as we look them over, we can find a gradation from part-time farmers, with some resemblance to the Navaho, to wild rovers who may be as empty-handed as when they first reached the Southwest. If we are puzzled as to what customs the Navaho brought with them and what they learned after arrival, we have but to look at this control group of their blood brothers, without agriculture, weaving, clans, or even a consistent counting of descent through the mother. Below is a list of the Apache groups as they have been standardized today, omitting some of the duplicate and local names scattered through history. They and the Navaho all speak different Athapascan dialects, but all can understand each other except the Lipan Apache, who strayed far into Mexico, and the Jicarilla of the Plains and the Kiowa Apache, who, before historic times, joined their fortunes to those of the Kiowa tribe and traveled with them.[12]

EASTERN APACHE

Jicarilla: Southeastern Colorado and northern New Mexico, east to Kansas and Oklahoma

Mescalero: Rio Grande to Pecos in New Mexico, east to Staked Plains, south to Coahuila

Chiricahua: Southeastern Arizona, southwestern New Mexico, into Chihuahua and Sonora

Lipan: Lower Rio Grande in New Mexico and Mexico, east through Texas to the Gulf

WESTERN APACHE ("COYOTERO")

From Tucson north to Flagstaff and east to White Mountains

White Mountain: Easternmost and largest around White, Gila, and Pinaleno Mountains

Cibecue: North of White Mountains along Mogollon Rim

San Carlos: West of White Mountains almost to Tucson

Southern Tonto: North of San Carlos in Mazatlal Mountains

Northern Tonto: Up to Flagstaff

The tribes summed up under Western Apache are those nearest to the Navaho in culture. Their range stretched almost the full length of Arizona, from Tucson at the south to Flagstaff at the north, with the Navaho east of them and sometimes in alliance. Each group had its several mountain fastnesses from which they issued on foot, swift as antelopes, to raid the Pimans or the ranches and towns of Mexico. Raiding was one of the chief sources of livelihood, providing cloth, tools, guns, and livestock. These last, even the horses, were usually eaten like venison, for, as the army found later, horses were of little use in that craggy country. There was excellent hunting in the mountains, and these Apache hunted with the same general devices and ceremonies used by Navaho and Hopi.

Meantime, the women planted their garden patches of corn, beans, and squash, some of them using crude irrigation ditches, after the manner of their neighbors and victims, the Pimans. Leaving the old people to tend the crops, groups of women then trudged far afield, led by the wife of the local headman, to seek mesquite and screw beans, acorns or wild green vegetables. The favorite among these was the agave, or mescal (our century plant), whose sweet and juicy hearts were hacked out with wooden spades, then roasted by the dozen in earthen pits. Cooked mescal was one of the sources of the fermented beer which the Apache made, while others came from cactus fruit or sprouted maize. These drinks, called "tiswin" by the whites and *tulibai* by the Indians, seem to have been learned by the Chiricahua in Mexico and not brought north until historic times.

Apache clothing was of buckskin, the hunter's wear. Old pictures show the men with hair hanging loose and topped with a buckskin cap or a great crown of feathers—not the long war bonnet. If they wore shirts, these might be painted with brightly colored designs or hung with scalps. When a scalp was once purified, these Indians did not hold it in awe. Except for a breechcloth, their sinewy legs were bare, but their moccasins often came almost to the knee, perhaps as protection against underbrush. A few in museums have an upturned pointed toe, after an ancient Spanish style. Were they copied from some which the Apache had plundered?

It was in their house and equipment that these Apache showed the greatest difference from the Navaho and even from the Pueblos. They specialized in basketry. Their dwelling was a domed brush hut without even earth insulation, put up by the women in an hour or so at any camp. This "wickiup" is the very hut used by desert Indians in Nevada, and it looks as though the Western Apache might have entered the Southwest by that route. Indeed, they have other equipment of the basket-using desert people, such as a seed-beater and a canteen, tightly twined or coiled of willow and made watertight with a coating of pine gum. Their most decorative basket, however, is in bold black-and-white patterns, made with willow and devil's-claw in the Pima manner. Surely some captive Piman wife must have taught this art to her daughters, who thereupon embellished it with realistic figures and buckskin fringe in a 'style unknown to the Pimans. The Apache made a few pots in Navaho style, their principal use being to be filled halfway with water, covered with buckskin, and beaten as a drum.

Among these Apache we find the familiar Navaho customs of mother-clans, residence with the wife, and the mother-in-law taboo. Birth, adolescence, marriage, and death are treated in much the same way, except that the maiden's ceremony was more highly featured and regarded not with awe but as a special source of blessing. Those ancient devices, the scratching stick and the drinking tube, were used so as to keep her hands from contact with her body, imbued with supernatural power. For four days a beautiful and virtuous woman symbolically molded her into admired shape, and the girl assured her future industry by grinding corn and fetching wood. At night a medicine man sang songs over her, and on the fourth night, after she had danced, he sprinkled her and the spectators with pollen, symbol of fertility. Meantime, during the night, rows of boys and girls had danced opposite each other, and in the intervals masked kachina-like figures also danced to bring blessing.

Though the Western Apache had mother-clans, their essential organization, like that of most nomads, was that of local bands with their influential leaders. The groups listed on page 242 were all divided into bands, each with its territory and chief. The chief, who often came from some particularly wealthy and numerous maternal family, was chosen by the whole local group for his wisdom and generosity. Beneath him were headmen of family groups. All might have acquired rites for war and hunting, but sometimes special leaders arose for these functions, gifted both with bravery and with supernatural power. In Apache life there was plenty of chance for an unknown man to rise if he distinguished himself.

Raiding was a business with the Apache. They fought on foot, armed only with bows and, in the west, not even sinew-backed ones.[13] Strategy was their chief weapon, and their aim not glory but loot. True, scalps were taken and hung on a pole at the wild victory dance, where women danced almost naked in the usual saturnalia of triumph, but the warrior purified himself only by a sweat bath. His ambition was to take horses, sheep, and other wealth and to present these to relatives and those who danced in his honor.

Western Apache belief and ceremony was very like that of the Navaho but in a dimmer, less elaborate form. The story of the emergence is vague, but Sun with his two children and all the magical people of Corn, Cloud, and other phenomena have their place as man's friends. Those powerful beings who first emerged from the earth and who dress and mask like the Pueblo kachinas are here too. There are four clans of them who live in the mountains in the four directions and who come, accompanied by a Clown, to dance at important ceremonies. Whites mistakenly call them "Devil Dancers," though their weird postures actually convey a blessing.

Instead of the highly organized nine-day ceremonies of the Navaho, the Western Apache had short rites, lasting from one to four days but often with similar myths and procedures, including sand painting. These were sponsored by a chief or subchief, who paid the officiating shaman and fed the spectators. Their purpose was usually health, but, in the summer months, they were to keep danger from the crops. All these rites could be learned from their owners for payment, as could the charms for hunting and war. Even the lightning ceremony, most important of all, could be learned (cf. the Shooting Chant of the Navaho, which was also a protection against lightning). However, here there was a chance for individual vision, and the shaman who could achieve this was revered like a chief.

The history of the Western Apache was somewhat more peaceful than that of their eastern kinsmen, who did almost nothing with agriculture and could not conceive of settling down. True, small detachments of them were raiding up into the 1870's and keeping Tucson and its environs in terror. However, as early as 1857 some bands had recognized American power and asked to be allowed to settle, with their gardens and the animals they had begun to keep. By 1865 nine hundred of them were being fed at Fort Goodwin. Reservations were established in 1871, and, though there were many changes, still, the Apache were never deported, like the Navaho, to strange country. They were finally collected on the Fort Apache Reservation in their own beautiful White Mountains with an extension to the Gila added.

Under the administration of General Crook and his humane young officers, most of them settled down to raise corn, to graze the ponies and mules stolen in wilder days, and to hunt in the hills. This life might not have kept them quiet long had it not been for General Crook's wise plan of enlisting them in the army. Five hundred Apache served as scouts, getting the same pay as regular soldiers, and with their own war leaders as sergeants. Their white officers all testified in praise of these scouts, who served the army loyally, sometimes against their own families. Some detachments which pursued the hostile Apache consisted almost entirely of scouts, the regular soldiers proving untrained for such alpine maneuvers.[14] When the army withdrew, the Apache reservations went through that period of blundering and venal politics which was a feature of many early reservations. In fact, said General Crook, "the simple story of their wrongs . . . satisfied me that the Apaches had not only the best reasons for complaining, but had displayed remarkable forbearance in remaining at peace."[15] Once they did break the peace, according to a well-known pattern. At Cibecue, in 1881, there arose a prophet, demanding that old Indian ways be revived and whites cleared from the country. The prophet was killed in a skirmish, and rebellion died. In time, abuses were remedied, and the Western Apache moved toward prosperity.

It is an Eastern Apache group which has gone down in history as among the bravest, cleverest, and cruelest of all Indian fighters. The Chiricahua should actually be called southern, for their territory was at the south of Arizona and New Mexico, with one band permanently intrenched in Mexico itself. They were bandits from earliest times, with only a few families in Spanish days who tried a little gardening. Their mountain fastnesses were alive with game, and the settlements of Mexico were, as they put it, their *rancho*, furnishing all other supplies. No Mexican and few white Americans ever thought of following them up the precipitous mountain trails to their hidden camps. So they took goods and captives as needed or made peace with one town for trading purposes while they were raiding another.

Their wickiups, clothing, basketry, and few pots were very like those of the Western Apache. So was their social life, except that here the incoming bridegroom must avoid his wife's father as well as her mother and had to observe complicated rules for the treatment of all her kin. There were no clans. The local group was the close-knit, important unit. It might have a headman who had been selected because of family and trained to his duties like Cochise, the famous ruler and general of the central Chiricahua band, or an ambitious warrior who raised up his own following, like Geronimo of the Mexican band. The ceremonies of the raid with its special language and behavior must be learned by every boy. When a well-known leader proposed an expedition, sometimes every eligible male in camp joined in the dance of incitement which was a vow of participation.

How could such a group settle peacefully to agriculture? It is true that both Cochise's and Victorio's band remained quiet for some years on reservations of their own choosing and with friendly agents and government rations. Then began the series of blunders and political chicanery which moved the Indians high-handedly from place to place without any attempt at understanding them. Perhaps understanding would have been impossible at that time, when most Arizona whites regarded the Apache as mad wolves, to be dealt with only by extermination. Bundled onto the White Mountain Reservation, the men, who left all farming to their women, had nothing to do but receive rations, drink tiswin, and gamble. A suggestion from army officers that they should be given livestock was rejected by a distant Washington, which had decided that all Indians should farm.[16] Could these early planners have looked ahead and seen how cheerfully Apache men were to work eight hours a day at road-building in gangs, they might have spent more time finding them an occupation which would satisfy the warrior's psychological needs. Instead, they merely issued orders that drinking and wife-beating were to stop. It was not long before the warrior Geronimo gathered a number of families and decamped.

Thus began the long dramatic duel between a few hundred Apache and the infantry, cavalry, officers, citizens, and scouts of the United States. The escaping Indians killed and burned without distinction between combatants and noncombatants, and the frantic whites reciprocated. Said Lieutenant Davis, who took part in that very campaign: "In treachery, broken pledges on the part of high officials, lies, thievery, slaughter of defenseless women and children and every crime in the catalog of man's inhumanity to man, the Indian was a mere amateur compared to the 'noble white man.' His crimes were retail, ours wholesale."[17]

Geronimo's band consisted not only of warriors. All his men had their families, and the women and children learned to scatter and hide as agilely as mountain goats when an enemy was sighted. For almost twenty years the duel went on, and finally it was Apache scouts who ran Geronimo down. There were army squabbles and counterplots, but finally he surrendered to General Miles in 1886.

The entire Chiricahua band, even its innocent and friendly members, was sent first to Florida, then to Alabama, and held until 1894. Then they were transferred to Oklahoma and kept, still prisoners of war, until 1913. By this time, most of the recalcitrants had died, and their descendants were given the choice of taking up land where they were or joining the other Apache. Only a hundred remained, while the others joined the Mescalero in New Mexico. They were but a tiny remnant of a band once numbering over a thousand, but such as had

survived the long captivity were inured to new ways. Both in Oklahoma and in New Mexico it is the once-wild Chiricahua who are
most ready to farm and to live in houses.

None of the mountain people so far described were horse Indians.
They used mules as pack animals and might ride them sometimes in
open country, but herds in the mountains would have been only an
encumbrance. It was the Apache of the flat land who collected horses.
We cannot give detailed histories of the Jicarilla, Lipan, and Mescalero, all distinct groups who did not cling together, as did the Western Apache, or understand each other's languages. They are first heard
of in the Plains country east of the Rio Grande, with the Jicarilla at
the north near the Colorado border; the Mescalero, diggers of the
mescal or century plant, in the mountains at the south; and the Lipan
roaming far into Texas and Old Mexico and remaining there as hunters. Coronado, in 1541, met "querechos" who have been thought to
be Apache living in skin tents and hunting the "wild cows."[18] Remains
of houses, pottery, and stone tools in Nebraska date to about 1700
and may indicate some late arrivals.[19]

Plains Apache in the fifteenth century hunted the buffalo on foot
and dragged their baggage by dog travois. Naturally, when that new
animal, the horse, was brought by the Spaniards in 1598, Apache
groups were among the first to trade for or steal it. Mescalero, Lipan,
and Jicarilla all became horsemen and used to crowd the annual fair
at Taos, bringing slaves and skin and meat to trade for more horses.
It was surely one of these groups which struck such terror into the
southern pueblos that all the Lower Rio Grande and the Salinas to
the west were deserted. They were always on the move, hunting deer
and antelope in the winter, buffalo in the summer. With their curved,
sinew-backed bows,[20] the horseman's weapon, and their arrows, sometimes poisoned, they became the terror of eastern New Mexico and
Texas and fought even the Western Apache.

They had no clans. Men did go to live with their wives, but the
law of descent through women, the avoidances, and the treatment of
relatives were all changed and varied. Loyalty was to the family, which
meant all the relatives on both sides, and, after that, to the band with
its self-appointed leader. Power came from the spirits in dreams, and
the medicine man, not the trained priest, was their mouthpiece. There
was much variation, testifying to the length of time that each of
these groups had roamed separately. The Jicarilla, who came often to
Taos, show some Tiwa elements in their ceremony, especially the yearly

relay race at harvest time. Also, they have one ceremony with a kachina-like dance and sand painting[21] reminiscent of Navaho chants. The ceremony for the adolescent girl is missing except with the Mescalero.

The Eastern Apache did some of their most destructive raiding in Spanish days when whole villages were depopulated and the governors used up much paper in discussions as to whether they should be won over or exterminated. Later the Ute and Comanche filtered in to share the spoils and give them some hard fighting. In 1845–56 Texas decided to get rid of the Lipan, and they fled to Mexico whence some never returned. In 1861 the United States sent forth its well-known edict that, if the Apache did not surrender and move onto reservations, their men would be killed and their women captured. The Mescalero, as mentioned, shared Fort Sumner with the Navaho for a year, then sneaked away. Finally, after moves and squabbles, they received their present reservation in southeastern New Mexico and the Jicarilla theirs at the north, with remnants of Lipan and Chiricahua added to the Mescalero.

The Apache have had luck in their reservation life, and, to the hardworking Navaho, this seems cruelly undeserved. Hundreds of Apache were being fed as war prisoners long after the Navaho were forced into self-support. Moreover, the mountain country where many Apache groups had lived and which was finally given them as reservations was well wooded and watered. Also it must support fewer people than barren Navaholand. There was an initial bad period when the Apache in their wickiups crowded around the agency, their frame houses and farms neglected, and when children were brought to boarding school with their feet bound so they should not jump out of the wagon. Most of that is past. The government belatedly accepted the idea of issuing sheep and cattle to the Apache on a reimbursable plan so that they might have other income besides their farms. It was hard to convince these former hunters that they should care for animals instead of chasing and killing them, and even yet a rodeo or slaughter for a feast takes precedence of other considerations. Nevertheless, under skilled white management, the Western Apache, in 1945 had nearly fifty thousand cattle, and some owners were actually wealthy. The Eastern Apache, while owning a few cattle, specialized in sheep, eight hundred Jicarilla owning some thirty-six thousand. Sales of timber from the well-wooded White Mountain and Mescalero reservations brought in nearly $200,000.[22]

The four reservations have set up their local governments under the Reorganization Act, and paternally minded officials watch their decisions with concern. When there is money in the tribal treasury, the Apache is no more anxious than the white to spend it for improvements that will benefit posterity. He demands to spend it now, and doubtless that is the only way he can learn. No one need say, however, that he is helpless in money matters. The Mescalero are considering building a motel in their pleasant mountain country, thus attracting some of the white man's cash.

NAVAHO

FOOD

Vegetable.—Early: wild plants, seeds, berries. Later: flint and flour corn, squash (*Cucurbita moschata*), watermelon, wild greens, beans. Not much agriculture, piñon nuts.

Animal.—Deer, small game, mountain sheep, prairie dogs, rabbits. Sheep-raisers after 1680.

HUNTING METHOD

Bow and arrow, lance, surrounds and rundowns, antelope drives.

CLOTHING

Male.—Early: deerskin leggings, then hip leggings, moccasins hard-soled and crimped over vamp. Native blankets after 1680. Later: cotton or velveteen shirts, breeches, hard-soled moccasins, buttoned deerskin leggings, garters, blankets.

Female.—Early: Apache style deerskin poncho waists, skirts, and moccasins. Then two oblong blankets held at shoulders and sides, belt and hair tie. Later: full calico skirts and velveteen blouses, open under arms; moccasins.

HOUSE TYPES

Early: forked-stick hogan, cone shaped; sweat house. Later: forked-stick hogan, brush arbor, then six–eight-sided log hogans, horizontal cribbed roof. Medicine lodges, sweat houses, circular forked-stick or dome. No female segregation.

EQUIPMENT

Household.—Pottery, gray, fired, coiled in "trail" style, Woodland type, pointed bottoms. After 1680 some painted Pueblo-like types. Baskets: coiled ceremonial types and pitched water jars like Basin. Famous for weaving after 1680, used vertical loom with figure-8 warp.

Transportation.—Early: wandered on foot. Later: many horses.

Hunting.—Sinew-backed bow, arrows, lance, spear, and clubs.

Other.—Cradle: wood, with tall points, skin-covered, sun shield. Miscellaneous: learned silverwork from Mexicans after 1855; some Spanish designs and some from eastern Indians. Highly decorated saddles and bridles. Wove blankets, belts, garters, hair ties, cinches. Made buckskin masks, prayer sticks and wands, drums, Buffalo-testicle rattles.

WAR

Lance and rawhide shield, bow and arrow, wood clubs; raids, took horses and slaves for trade, scalps and booty.

GAMES

Archery, ball race, bean-shooter, cat's cradle, dice, hidden ball, stick games, hoop-and-pole, quoits, shinny, running races, horse-racing.

APACHE

FOOD

Vegetable.—Early: wild plants, seeds, roots, berries. Later: flint and flour corn, squash (*Cucurbita moschata*), wild greens, beans, berries, yucca, mesquite beans, some postwhite irrigation.

Animal.—A few deer, small game, rabbits, ate horses like venison.

HUNTING METHOD

Bow and arrow, stalking.

CLOTHING

Male.—Buckskin shirts, leggings and moccasins, breechcloths, skin caps and headdresses of yucca. Western used knee-length boots.

Female.—Buckskin skirts of two skins, poncho-type blouses worn outside skirt, moccasin boots. Jicarilla, Plains type, long, skin dresses.

HOUSE TYPES

Wickiup, brush arbor in summer. Wickiup thatched with bear grass. Sweat house. Jicarilla had tipi.

EQUIPMENT

Household.—Basketry: for storage, burden, bowls, pitched water bottle; Chiricahua had twined baskets. Jicarilla had coiled pottery like Navaho. No weaving.

Transportation.—Horses after 1700, especially Jicarilla. Chiricahua used donkeys.

Hunting.—Predominantly self-bow, arrows, similar to Hopi. Jicarilla used sinew-backed bow.

Other.—Cradle: slat type and basketry covered with skin. Miscellaneous: crown dance masks and bull-roarer, drums, musical bow (post-Spanish).

WAR

Bow and arrow. On foot except Jicarilla and, later, Mescalero. Used raids, which were chief livelihood. Horses for presents and food. Took scalps and sheep. Aim was glory.

GAMES

Archery, hoop-and-pole, stick dice, hidden ball, races, cat's cradle, yucca fiddle.

CHAPTER XI

Those Who Had Little To Lose

In INDIAN days agriculture stopped short somewhere in southern Nevada and Utah. North of that, all the way to the Arctic Ocean and west to the Pacific, there was no corn grown and for good reason: most of the area was too dry or too cold to allow of planting by primitive Indian methods. Hundreds of tribes west of the Rockies were, therefore, assigned by nature to the life of hunters, fishers, and gatherers. For some, as will appear in the next chapter, such a life could mean plenty and even riches.

At present we deal with the huge stretch of intermontane country between the Rockies on the east and the Sierras and Cascades on the west. Geographers call it the Great Basin and Plateau. This country, today prosperous with mines, industries, and irrigation, was in aboriginal times a land of seminomads moving from camp to camp as the deer, the salmon, or other food offered them subsistence. They could not settle in permanent villages. Therefore, they could not take the next step toward civilization, that of organized government and regular ceremonies. Though many are related to the corn-growers in language, they were forced by the necessities of their life to lag far behind in craft, government, and ceremony. When the whites came and those Indian institutions which were not strongly rooted were swept away, these were the people who had little to lose.

Map VII shows the extent of this great, thinly populated country, cut at the north by rivers which gave some fishing possibilities and rising to mountains which provided deer. This is the Plateau which merges gradually into the low, arid land at the south, the Basin, whose mountain-fed rivers never reach the sea.

All Indians of this region were seminomadic. They moved about in bands which had regular territories, and, the poorer the country, the smaller the band. We do not find here the use of clay for houses and containers, which characterized the Southwest, or the skins of the

Plains. The chief resource of the country was the short, scrubby vegetation of the desert, and sometimes this was the only resource. So the gatherers were, above all, basket-makers. Many of their houses, crude structures of poles, covered with brush or mats, are in the realm of basketry. Their clothing was of bast fiber from cedar or even sagebrush. Their equipment was of basketry, from the mats used for bedding to the container for cooking, the baby's cradleboard and the woman's hat. Here was the one chance for craft, and the gatherers made the most of it. They used every basketry technique and carried some to high points of elaboration. With such grass, twigs, and dyes as the country produced, they made some of the most useful and beautiful baskets in America.

We begin description with the Plateau country, the upland area which stretches from the Fraser River in Canada and down through the Columbia drainage into the United States. Though it lay west of the Rockies, which we think of as the migration route for the first Americans, it may have been the scene of some early wanderings, for sandals and bits of basketry found in Oregon date some thousand years ago.[1] However, most of our relics information reflects recent times, after the passage of Lewis and Clark in 1805.

At that time the Plateau contained twenty-five tribes, belonging to four language families. The most typical, perhaps, are the Salish, whose rough speech, bristling with consonants, may, nevertheless, be distantly related to Algonkian.[2] If that is so, we have a spread of that ancient northern language from Labrador to the Pacific. North of the Salish is the tail end of the great Athapascan area, spreading into Alaska, and from which the Navaho and Apache may have broken off. South are the Sahaptin, with relatives in California and perhaps farther south, while a few Shoshoneans appear also along the southern border. This barren upland, with only a few patches of forest and lake, was cut by two great rivers, the Columbia and it tributary, the Snake. That mean salmon. Most bands and villages had rights along some stream where they built traps or, according to the season, used seine, dip net, spear, or hook and line. Even today, if one stands in the mist and roar of The Dalles, the great rapids on the Columbia, he may see Indians of many tribes leaning from their inherited platforms to swing their long-handled dip nets. The first salmon of the season, almost everywhere, was honored by a little ceremony with singing, praying, and, perhaps, dancing. Many tribes had ceremonies for other fish and for berries and various kinds of "first fruits," since these gatherers were as reverent toward the wild foods as the corn-growers were toward cultivated ones.

Women smoked the salmon on wooden racks as they do today, then continued the yearly circuit to the meadows for starchy bulbs, to the lakes for beaver, and to the mountains for deer and mountain sheep. The lifework of Plateau men was hunting, and they used almost every device known to primitives. Beyond this practical side of their work was the realm of danger and bad luck which could be controlled only with spirit help. To make sure of this, the hunter often bathed and vomited before going out, while his wife helped, in his absence, by keeping especially quiet, as he wished the game to be. There were rules as to how the meat should be cut up, how it should be brought into the house, who might eat the different parts, and where the bones should be placed. Many of the same rules would be found among northern Algonkian.

In a remote, unorganized area like the Plateau, we should expect segregations of the mother at childbirth and rigid rules for the girl at maturity. This is the case. In fact, Plateau girls had a particularly rigorous training. Often they were sent to a lonely hut for months on end; here they were kept busy carrying wood and water, or, if this was not necessary, even picking leaves off bushes so that they should not be idle at this crucial time. Some of them never touched their heads but used a scratching stick like the Apache, and a few even used the drinking tube. Nevertheless, the woman, who was a food-gatherer, had a station in life a little better than that of the rich Plains girl who was only a helper economically. True, she shared her husband with other wives, for this was necessary when men were so likely to die early from accident. Still, she could divorce him at will, and often he came to live with her parents for a while. Fear of the dead, not death, was strong in the Plateau. We are familiar with the belief that, if not banished utterly, the dead might return to call the living. Therefore all the usual preventives were practiced: purification of the mourners, taboo on using the name, and destruction of the dwelling unless it could be magically cleansed.

Most of these beliefs we have met before or shall meet later. In fact, some students have considered that the Plateau is little more than a transition zone between areas of more definite character to the east, south, and west.[3] Still, some essentials of its own ancient life stand out plainly: democracy, industry, peacefulness, and few ceremonies but an intense sense of individual need for communion with the spirits. The lack of formal organization is striking. Here, as almost everywhere west of the Rockies, there were no nations, no confederacies. The word "tribe" is loosely used for groups of people simply because they spoke the same dialect and did not fight among themselves. Each village and, in less settled areas, each wandering band managed its own affairs without regard to the others. The Plateau had no clans and no moieties. Descent was counted on both sides, an arrangement that occurs often when women are equal producers with men. The choosing of chiefs was an informal affair, depending on their achievements. True, the idea of inheritance seeped in at the west, where, as will appear, hereditary offices were usual. At the east, where Plains influence came in, office might depend on war honors. In the heart of the Plateau the ancient Salish custom was to choose a man from some honored family line but only if he were worthy. Such a chief was father, adviser, and judge rather than autocrat. Men who led war and hunting parties were simply volunteers. Only when opposition to the whites made dictatorship necessary was this informality changed.

In this nonagricultural region there was no belief about men and animals issuing from the womb of Earth. Earth and Sky were parts of the daily scene which had always existed, though not in the form now known to man. As with the Algonkian, many stories deal with how the rocks, the rivers, and even the sun needed rearrangement to meet the needs of humankind. The being who accomplished this was that all-too-human character, the Trickster. In the Plateau he was usually Coyote, greedy, selfish, clever, showing mankind by his very mistakes what was the right way to live. Many of the tales deal with the animals and how they achieved their present form, while, over and over again, the wickedness of being stingy about food is emphasized.

Many Plateau ceremonies, as already mentioned, were local rites, centering about the food supply. The scattered hunters had little time for large public affairs or the supplies to feed a gathering. Securing help from the spirits was the responsibility of each individual and especially each male. Here we meet again the belief in individual guardian spirits, on whom all success in life depends, and here the spirit quest found one of its most ardent expressions. The spirits, even those with medicine powers, might visit girls as well as boys, perhaps, because woman, as the plant-gatherer, occupied an important place in the economy. However, the girl had her own birth magic, while the boy must place all his hopes on spirit favor. Under the direction of his father or other guardian, he undertook to sleep in frightening places, to plunge into icy pools, or to lacerate his body with thorny branches. Having been told by animal, plant, or mythical being what power he would receive, the boy kept his hopes secret until he became expert in adult life. If then he was a good hunter or medicine man, he knew the vision had been right—an excellent psychological device to inspire a youth and keep him working.

A future medicine man or woman went through the same ordeals but more intensively and received stronger powers. He could, as usual, remove the stick or worm which was causing illness or even the guardian spirit which had been sent by some evil medicine man into an enemy. If the patient's guardian spirit was lost, strayed, or stolen, he could retrieve that also. This introduces a complex theology about the uses of spirits never heard of in the Plains. Some Plateau people also shared a special western belief which laid illness to the temporary loss of one's soul. Of that, more in later chapters.[4]

The Plateau people, who were so busy and scattered in summer, had worked out the belief that, when one's guardian spirit returned in adult life to certify his power, the time would be midwinter. In many places one who felt his spirit coming at this time would give a feast, lasting days, to which all who heard of it were invited. The protégé of the spirit would fall unconscious and, as he revived, would begin to sing. A medicine man interpreted the song which ever after would signify his power. Then the blessed one danced and sang, and all others who had spirits were invited to perform in turn. One who has seen these dances about a blazing fire can testify that one frantic, half-naked dancer, cedar-bark ornaments streaming in the firelight, can be quite as imposing as a file of perfectly costumed masks in the Pueblos. Finally, the medicine men, with their power, might rival and perhaps injure each other with magic tricks. Then the host and all who had danced gave gifts in honor of their spirits. Is there a suggestion here of the Plains Sun Dance? Perhaps, but with emphasis completely changed. There is nothing more historically revealing than to note the passage of an idea among Indian tribes and the way in which each makes use of it after its own fashion.

The Plateau People, remote and uncomplicated in their early days, had a dramatic history. Its first act involved the coming of the horse, which reached the Umatilla in Oregon as early as 1739,[5] moving north among Indians west of the Continental Divide. By the mid-eighteenth century the westernmost Plateau People were riding yearly to the Plains to hunt buffalo and were fighting or trading with the tribes there and especially the Blackfoot. For Plateau tribes this meant a whole new series of customs, such as living in tipis on the hunt, camping in a circle, wearing skin clothing, moccasins, and war bonnets, setting up a system of war honors, and choosing their chiefs for fighting ability rather than for wisdom and lineage. The Kutenai and Shoshoni even set up a mild version of the Sun Dance. Perhaps we should include here the Comanche, close neighbors of the Shoshoni in Wyoming and speaking almost the same dialect. They were among the first to buy or steal horses from the Spaniards, and ultimately they became some of the most skilled horsemen of the Plains. By 1719 they were in Kansas, and by the end of the eighteenth century they were raiding and buffalo-hunting through Colorado, Kansas, Oklahoma, and Texas. They harried the Spaniards all the way into Durango; they were the terror of the Santa Fe Trail and, in fact, barred the southern Plains to whites and northern Indians. As Plains Indians, they make their exit from this chapter.

Soon the new fashions in clothing began to penetrate the whole Plateau and even to reach the coast. At The Dalles, where canoe travel on the Columbia was interrupted by rapids, the Wishram held a yearly fair, exchanging skin clothing and dried buffalo meat for such coastal products as fish oil and shells.

When Lewis and Clark made their memorable transcontinental journey (1804–6), their Indian interpreter and peace envoy was a Shoshoni woman, whom they had found married among the Mandan. Who knows how much danger was averted by the presence of a woman with her baby in the party, a sure sign that they were not on a war raid! After the two explorers came fur-trappers and fur-traders, both from Canada and St. Louis. In the 1830's the Green River in Wyoming was the summer rendezvous for the bearded American trappers, who rode in often with Indian wives and families to exchange the year's catch of prime beaver for next year's supplies, including whiskey for the men and beads and other "fufarraw" for the women. Soon Indians, too, were trading their furs; hunting gradually changed from a subsistence activity to a business, and some of the ceremonies which had sanctified it dropped away.

The last great rendezvous was held in 1840. Already the buffalo were disappearing, and the Indians must somehow make a new life. Perhaps the Nez Percé had sensed this when they heard from a white man, early in the 1830's about a Holy Book which could give even more power than could the spirits. In 1831 they and the Flathead sent a delegation of seven men to St. Louis to consult their friend William Clark, now a general. Clark could not promise missionaries at this moment when the trail to the West was scarcely broken and full of dangers. The delegation leader, Rabbit-skin Leggings, is said to have told him: "I came with one eye partly opened for more light for my people; I go back with both eyes closed. I go back with both arms broken and empty."⁶ There were desertions and deaths during the journey over the mountains, across the Plains, and up and down the Missouri. Only one man returned with this sad news.

In time, the missionaries came. The Methodist church sent out two couples, Marcus Whitman and Henry Spalding with their wives, the first white women to make this journey. The Whitmans built their log cabins and set up their school at Waiilatpu among the Cayuse in Oregon; the Spaldings at Lapwai, Idaho, among the Nez Percé. By degrees, other missionaries arrived and began the hard task of coaxing the Indians into settled life and farming with white man's seeds and tools. The Indians balked at the stern new rule with its supervision over their married life and ceremonies. A Catholic mission among the Flathead had to be withdrawn.⁷ The Indians around Whitman's mission rose in 1847, killing all the whites and making prisoners of some score of Christian Indians. It was time that the Far West had law and order. In 1848 Oregon was organized as a territory.

Before that happened, the third and most dramatic act of Plateau Indian history had begun. The Overland Trail was open. Whitman himself had returned east in 1841–42 and led back a determined party on the road to Oregon. Here was no trapper's pack train but families with their women, riding in covered wagons. Up the Missouri in flatboats was their route, then along the Platte, and through the Rockies at the wide gap called South Pass. In Idaho, among the Shoshoni, they came to Fort Hall, the fortified trading post with high adobe walls, where whole bands from Plateau and Plains came in to stare and trade. There were crossings and recrossings of the winding Snake River, then Fort Boise, and, finally, for those who wished, boats down the Columbia to civilization.

After this, for forty years or more, even after railroads were operating, the ox-drawn wagons lumbered along this trail, leaving ruts so deep that in some places they can still be seen. The "great emigration" of 1843 comprised a thousand people. In 1852 there were ten thousand. None of them stopped in the Plateau. They were on their way to the rain-fed meadows beyond the Cascades and regarded the dry interior country as wasteland, fit only for Indians. Perhaps that was why most of the Plateau tribes were friendly. Chief Washakie, of the Shoshoni in Wyoming, had his people aid the immigrants across fords and help find their strayed cattle. He did not even complain when such cattle destroyed the Indian gathering and herding grounds. Washakie had a testimonial to kindliness signed by nine thousand immigrants.

Chiefs were now gaining more authority, as usual when Indians had to concentrate against the whites. They needed both negotiating and fighting power when the Union Pacific was surveyed in 1852 and the Canadian Pacific in 1854. Tribe by tribe, the Indians accepted reservations, but there were revolts and pathetic little "wars" up to 1880. The most dramatic was that of the Nez Percé under Chief Joseph in 1877. In 1855 this tribe had ceded much of their gathering territory and accepted a reservation partly in Oregon, partly in Idaho. There was rumor of gold in the Oregon country, and, as usual, the Indians were asked to cede it. Joseph and his band, the Oregon residents, resisted. They had ammunition to fight the United States troops, and, even with women and children to hide and defend, they won several battles. When it was plain that they could not hold out longer, the starving and desperate people made a heroic march across the mountains toward Canada. Within a few miles of the border, they were captured and sent out of the way to Oklahoma.

Today, the Plateau people are on reservations (see Table 10), but they are not the Indians of history. Groups have been broken up and reassembled. Leadership has been destroyed. Even the "blood," as heredity is still called in official documents, is only part-Indian. Since the days of the trappers, there has been intermarriage but without the rank and honor which resulted among Creek or Cherokee. When no white women were present, an Indian wife had status and her sons were leaders. In the Plateau, white women arrived all too soon for such an arrangment. No sooner had the covered wagons rolled in than the Indian wives of the "bourgeois" at the fort or the trapper in the wilds were reduced to the position of social inferiors, even outcasts. So their children had no honor among Indians and, of course, were not accepted by the whites. They form a caste now on most reservations,[8] a caste perhaps favored by officials but suspected by the "full-bloods," who withdraw and conduct their affairs in isolation.

These full-bloods have had all too little time to make an adjustment. In the Plateau, as much as anywhere in the United States,

TABLE 10

PRESENT RESERVATIONS AND NUMBERS OF THE PLATEAU AND BASIN PEOPLE

Tribe	State and Agency	Population, 1945*
	Plateau	
Bannock..................	*Idaho:* Fort Hall Reservation	337
Cayuse..................	*Oregon:* Umatilla Reservation	384
Coeur d'Alene..............	*Idaho:* Coeur d'Alene Reservation	616
Flathead..................	*Montana:* Flathead Agency	3,630
Kutenai..................	*Idaho:* Kutenai Reservation	103
Kalispel..................	*Washington:* Kalispel Reservation	102
Klamath and Modoc........	*Oregon:* Klamath Reservation	1,266
Nez Percé.................	*Idaho:* Nez Percé Reservation	1,525
Sanpoil and Nespelem.......	*Washington:* Colville	3,505
Shoshone..................	*Idaho:* Fort Hall Reservation	1,623
	Western Shoshone	207 (1,830)
	Nevada: Duckwater	129
Spokane..................	*Washington:* Spokane Reservation	925
Tenino..................	*Oregon:* Warm Springs Reservation	544
Umatilla..................	*Oregon:* Umatilla Reservation	121
Walla Walla..............	*Oregon:* Umatilla Reservation	623
Wasco....................	*Oregon:* Warm Springs Reservation	260
Wishram and Yakima.......	*Washington:* Yakima	3,229
Various Plateau...........	*Oregon:* Dalles allotments	48
	Basin	
Chemehuevi...............	*Nevada:* Moapa River Reservation	5
Goshute..................	*Utah:* Goshute Reservation	182
	Skull Valley Reservation	62 (244)
Paiute....................	*Nevada:* Fallon Reservation	198
	Fort McDermitt Reservation	301
	Moapa River Reservation	172
	Pyramid Lake Reservation	563
	Summit Lake Reservation	46
	Walker River Reservation	437
	Yerington Reservation	78
	Seven colonies	502
	Nonreservation	516 (2,813)
	Utah: Cedar City	17
	Kanosh	28
	Shivwits Reservation	108
	Gandy Homestead	6 (159)
Shoshone..................	*Nevada:* Duckwater Reservation	129
	Fallon River Reservation	97
	Duck Valley Reservation	475
	Yomba River Reservation	113
	Walker River Reservation	38 (842)
	Utah: Nonreservation	423
	Washakie Agency	136 (559)
Ute.....................	*Colorado:* Southern Ute Reservation	459
	Ute Mountain Reservation	499
	Utah: Allen Canyon Subagency	29
	Kanosh Reservation	21
	Koosharen Reservation	27
	Uintah and Ouray Reservation	1,470 (2,505)
Others..................	*Nevada:* Fort McDermitt Reservation	5
	Pyramid Lake Reservation	9
	Duck Valley Reservation	129 (143)

* Numbers in parentheses refer to totals.

agents made a determined effort to break down Indian customs and produce conforming citizens. There was reason for hurry. After the Civil War the Far West changed in less than a hundred years from trackless wilderness to an area of cities, ranches, railroads, mines, and waterworks. There was no time and no room for small-scale farming, even had the Indians desired it. Their land was allotted. The Indians became nominal Christians. They live now in frame houses, wear white man's clothes, and regulate their local affairs under the Reorganization Act. In Montana, Washington, and Oregon their children attend public schools. Warm Springs, Oregon, and Fort Hall, Idaho, still have Indian boarding schools.

Yet the Spirit Dance or the Sun Dance is still held. The yearly rodeo at Pendleton, Oregon, will draw Indians from any occupation to ride in their treasured buckskins while whites applaud. These hunters and gatherers like farming no more than do the buffalo-hunters. The little frame houses are empty much of the time while families go off together to work in the hopyards and orchards. Their group spirit has been fighting to keep alive for almost a hundred years. White Americans, who are only beginning to understand the need for co-operation, might do well to look at those Indian hamlets and families who regard group living as the only normal lifeway and so teach their children.

From the Plateau we move south, with no perceptible boundary line, into the low and almost rainless area of the Great Basin. A basin it was literally, in the days of melting glaciers when this huge depression, cupped between the mountains, contained sixty-eight lakes,[9] with huge Bonneville and Lahontan the most impressive. On the shores of such bodies of water, ten thousand years ago, early man sheltered in caves and hunted the ground sloth.[10] Now Gypsum Cave, Nevada, where signs of that ancient life have been found, stands on a ledge above a dry valley. Of the sixty-eight lakes, there remain only a few small ones besides Great Salt Lake, the remains of Bonneville, whose waters evaporate year by year, leaving their salt spread over desolate acres. The Basin, in fact, has become one of the driest and least hospitable areas of North America. Mountains to east and west of it keep out the rain. Since no river can find an exit through them to the sea, the streams die away in swamps or "sinks." Death Valley, lowest area of all, is below sea level, with a summer temperature which may reach 140° F.

The Indians who lived here were among the poorest in North America. "Diggers" they were called by whites who watched them digging for roots and who swore that they lived no better than animals. Yet they were all of the Uto-Aztecan language family, related to the corn-growing Pima and Hopi and to the mighty Aztec. It was lack of corn and lack of contact which condemned them to stagnation. We must admire the complete adjustment to environment which kept these Indians alive where a white man might have starved and where some, later, did starve. The Indians used a minimum of tools and the maximum of knowledge about animal habits. They drove grasshoppers into trenches where they were roasted alive, then ground into flour. They jerked rats and lizards from their hiding places with wooden crooks, then clubbed them.[11] They drove rabbits and even birds into tall nets, where their heads were caught in the meshes, carefully calculated for size. Some of these nets, made of Indian hemp, spun on the thigh, were eight feet tall and as much as thirty feet long.

It is amazing to see how much equipment was produced out of poles and twigs, grass and bark. This included the domed wickiup of poles and brush; the clothing of cedar bark, the woman's round basketry cap, the seed-beater, mush-stirrer, and all the containers for gathering, storage, winnowing, and stone boiling. There was even a canteen, made watertight by smearing inside and out with pine gum. Some of these products look almost exactly like those of the ancient Basket-makers, who once lived in this area. If the Basin Shoshoni are not their descendants, they have at least inherited their lifeway, the only possible one for the region.

The food quest kept Basin people on the move. Their flimsy brush huts or windbreaks would be grouped for a week or so at a time near some seed patch, which they would strip completely. Then they might split up and join other families or go alone, for there were no rules here except to get the food wherever and whenever possible. It seems remarkable that they observed the rules for childbirth and menstruation, but they did so without ceremony. Usually there was no separate house for the mother or the maturing girl, but there were baths, sometimes a warm sand bed, fasting from meat grease and salt, and the use of a scratching stick. Often the father of a newborn child shared these restrictions and even refrained from hunting for a time, for it was felt that he had come close to the mysterious female power and was in danger of losing his strength.

This simple, fluctuating society had no marriage rules. Young people married such neighbors as were on hand and traveled with the parents of either one. Sometimes no unmarried person was available as a mate. Then it was thought practical not only for a man to take two wives but for a woman to have two husbands. Poverty, which dictated this practice, also ruled that, when old people became too feeble to follow the traveling party, they should be left behind to die. Newborn infants were sometimes treated in this same way and not from cruelty. Where there were no doctors, beds, or medicines available, a quick end for the ailing was the most merciful. As on the Plateau, houses of the dead were burned, and the names were never used.

When their livelihood compels people to live in small bands, they rarely need leaders or government. So Basin groups had merely a fatherly adviser known as the "talker."[12] And not always that. If they gathered for a rabbit drive or piñon-picking, a temporary leader was appointed. As for war, it was nonexistent. People in a poor area have the advantage that few bother to attack them and that they themselves are too busy for aggression.

Even the mythology of the Basin shows poverty. A rich and imaginative account of origins usually results from the combining of varied traditions and from myth-tellers who have the leisure and the stimulus to work on them. Basin people tell stories about the animals, often obscene; and their story of the origin of things goes no further than to say that the world was put in order by Wolf, the Good Brother, and Coyote, the marplot. The story of the two contending brothers flits through half the myths of North and South America, but here it seems to be found at its most prosaic.

Ceremonies were rare, since these demanded not only a common interest but food enough to supply a multitude. Both conditions were fulfilled once a year, in the southern part of the area, when several groups gathered for a communal antelope hunt. Young men went out to scout for the herds, while a shaman who had dreamed antelope songs sang to bring them near. Waving torches and howling like wolves, the men drove the galloping animals into a brush corral, where they could be slaughtered. The only other ceremony was a summer gathering, when people danced around a tree, singing songs about the birds and animals. It was these very songs which later figured in the famous Ghost Dance.

Ordeals were not practiced. The dream came in sleep, and many men had none at all. The future medicine man who dreamed knew that he was chosen and might have power for sucking out evil, combating sorcerers or ghosts, retrieving a lost spirit, or stopping the deterioration of the blood.[13] Lesser technicians might have power over bears and rattlesnakes, might give love charms, or might call antelope. A confused, mixed conception of shaman's power with elements borrowed from several neighboring regions! Here is no such dramatic conception as the Plateau Spirit Dance, announced by illness and performed with frenzy.

This picture shows people practically at the bottom on the Indian culture scale. No clearer proof could be given of the strangling power of circumstances. Basin People went as far as they could with inventions, but they had not the resources for further steps, nor did stimulus reach them from outside. When these limitations were lifted, as we have seen, the Shoshoni, at the northwest of the region, turned into mounted buffalo-hunters, with organization and ceremonies like those of the Plains.

Much the same has happened to the Ute of Utah and Colorado. They fought the Spaniard, the Navaho, the Apache, and, after 1846, the white American. Even in 1879, after they had settled on reservations,[14] the White River Ute killed the agent who was forcing them into farming. At present the Ute, like hundreds of other tribes, are working with the government in its gigantic project of settling all Indian land claims before ending their status as wards. The government has allowed a claim of this group for some thirty-two million dollars when an acceptable plan for long-range spending has been submitted, but some of the funds are to be held back for reservation improvements. Apparently the Ute will get the money. Then their white brothers will watch with interest an Indian's first real essay in economic independence.

For most people in the true interior of the Basin, horses were of little use, since there was no pasture. They continued their laborious life, while the eastern Indians were being exterminated or removed and the Plains Indians were joyously raiding. The Apache and Navaho often chose the Paiute as victims,[15] for this docile and unarmed people were helpless when armed horsemen kidnapped their children and sold them to the Spaniards. Later, the raiders took their captives to the kind-hearted Mormons, who bought them.

Until the mid-1840's Basin people rarely saw a white man except for a few explorers and trappers, including the famous Frémont and the equally renowned Kit Carson. In 1843 Frémont opened up a route from the Oregon Trail through the Basin to California. A few wagons passed along it toward the Sierras, sometimes presenting the

Indians with coffee and flour which they threw away as inedible. They kept the flour sacks, however. In 1847 occurred the Donner tragedy, which points up, as nothing else could, the complete adjustment of the Indians to their difficult land and the maladjustment of the white newcomers. This party of eighty-one, victualed with bacon and flour as usual, were belated in reaching the foot of the Sierras where they wished to cross before winter. If they had been Paiute, they would have realized the situation in time and would have hunted, stored food, and built themselves earth-covered dwellings for winter. As it was, they pushed doggedly on until snow overtook them, then camped in flimsy shelters while their food diminished. Thirty-six died of starvation, and the desperate survivors were forced to eat some of the bodies.

In 1847 California came under the government of the United States, and in 1849 gold was discovered there. Now the traffic across the Basin became constant, with no one even aware that the Indians used the seed plants which were being crunched by oxen and the sagebrush which was being burned lavishly in campfires. In 1847 great deposits of silver were discovered in the Nevada mountains, and Virginia City sprang up overnight. The country which had barely been able to support a few hundred Indians was to make white men millionaires. Nevada was hastily organized. In 1861 it was separated as a territory from that of Utah and in 1864 became a state. This was during the hectic years of the War between the States, when the government gave little attention to any Indians except those who were impeding the war effort.

Nevada Indians, with their regular gathering route broken up, wandered in small groups. They had no organization or experience for war, and their brief resistance around Pyramid Lake was soon quelled. Some tried to find new gathering areas unoccupied by whites. Most attached themselves to some ranch or mining camp, where they lived by begging or casual labor. Around 1874 two small reservations were set up for the Paiute in Nevada and a few others for the Shoshoni and various mixed groups. None was large enough to permit the old nomadic routine. So they evolved a new round, with part-time hunting and gathering, part-time working for whites. Slowly the Basin groups were being extinguished, with no one to care.

We have learned to expect that, at this point in the history of an Indian people, a prophet often arises, preaching salvation through a return to the old ways. So it happened in Nevada. Strangely enough it was the Paiute, a people with so little ceremony, who produced a belief and a series of rites which swept Indian country. This was the famous Ghost Dance. We have seen its tragic consequences among the Sioux, but in the vision of Wovoka, or Jack Wilson, it involved only peace and brotherhood, even with the whites. Wovoka, in true Indian fashion, had a trance and "saw God," as his father, it seems, had done in 1870. As a result he urged his people to return to the old ways, to love each other, and, also, to dance in a circle five nights in succession. This was the old Basin dance, and the dream songs which Wovoka bade them sing were the old songs about wind, cloud, and animals, with the old monotonous tunes.[16] If all this were done, the whites would disappear, and the dead Indians return.

The miracle did not happen. The Paiute quietly abandoned their belief, and now, though the circle dance goes on, they will not acknowledge that it has anything to do with the ghosts. Their bands were now broken up, their livelihood disappearing, and they were living in "shanty towns" near the white settlements. This quick and tragic loss of their culture might have been an incentive to adaptation, that is, if they had been offered any share in the white man's life. To the miners and ranchers, however, the "Diggers" were still quite as lowly as old plantation slaves. The Paiute had to struggle for themselves. Yet, to this writer, it seems that they have as much to show today as some of the hostiles who have sat mourning on their reservations. The Paiute case has somewhat resembled that of the Negro, who was left to struggle without help and who, instead of sinking, is swimming.

In due time the government did take cognizance of the Basin plight. It was too late for any large reservation, but after 1934 a number of small ones were set up and, also, "colonies" of decent homes for workers in the towns. Here the residents settle their affairs under the Reorganization Act. Their children attend public schools and have a boarding school for the homeless at Carson City. There has been little attempt to remain isolated or to retain Indian ways. Basin people have slipped unnoticeably into the life of the whites, though sometimes on its lowest economic level. It remains to be seen whether this sink-or-swim treatment will produce a better adjustment than the careful guarding of the Plains Indians who have held to the old lifeway so tenaciously.

BASIN

FOOD

Vegetable.—Seeds, roots, nuts, sunflower seeds; "Diggers," no farming.

Animal.—Rabbits, rats, lizards, caterpillars, grasshoppers; very few deer, antelope, fish, and birds.

HUNTING METHOD

Drove grasshoppers into trenches. Crooks, clubs, and very large nets for rabbits. Brush inclosures for antelope.

CLOTHING

Male.—Early: very scanty. Later: skin shirts, some fiber sandals (yucca splints and twine), rabbit-skin robes and blankets, leggings.

Female.—Early: cedar-bark fringe aprons, basketry caps, and shell beads. Later: sleeveless tunic, fringed except around arms, yucca sandals. Chin tattooing. Some later had Plains type dresses.

HOUSE TYPES

Domed wickiup of poles and brush. Brush windbreaks and huts. No steambath huts, only a place set aside for both sexes. No general use of female segregation hut except the southern Ute. The Paviotso developed hut later.

EQUIPMENT

Household.—In general, the basketry was coarse, marginal types quite fine. Coil and twined types: seed-beaters, mush bowls, cooking baskets, pitched canteens. Mush-stirrers. Early: Paviotso made some stone pots. Owens Valley made molded pottery. Mats for beds and coverings. Southern Paiute made pointed bottom clay pots.

Transportation.—Mostly on foot, wandered in search of food; some pack sacks on dogs. Balsas of tule (cattails) for river tribes.

Hunting.—Sinew-backed bow (Paiute used horn strips), crooks, clubs, nets.

Other.—Cradle: crude, V-branch with cross-rods and fiber pad. Northern tribes used board with skin cover. Pipe: tubular wood cigar-holder type, or entirely of stone, some had stone bowls. Some catlinite used. Miscellaneous: many gaming devices and gambling equipment. Bull-roarer.

WAR

War very rare and generally a defensive type. Took scalps, no coup counted. Some chases and raids. Used twelve-foot spears with a long blade. Bow: short, recurved, with sinew wrapping in center. Thick hide shields, poison arrows. Paviotso used rawhide armor.

GAMES

Ball-juggling, hand games, hoop-and-pole, ring-and-pin, double ball, shinny, football, four-stick game, tops.

MAP VII

THOSE WHO
HAD LITTLE
TO LOSE

SHUSWAP

LILLOOET

THOMPSON

KOOT-
ENAY

SAHAPTIN
TRIBES

COEUR D'ALENE

YAKIMA

KLIKITAT

FLATHEAD

NEZ
PERCE

BANNOCK

NORTHERN
PAIUTE

WESTERN
SHOSHONE

SHOSHONE

WASHO

UTE

MONO

SOUTHERN
PAIUTE

CHEMEHUEVI

WALAPAI

HAVASUPAI

YAVAPAI

☐ BASIN

▨ PLATEAU

PLATEAU

FOOD

Vegetable.—Bulbs (camass), bitterroot (*Lewisia rediviva*), berries, wild plants, and seeds.

Animal.—Mainly salmon; fish, deer, elk, beaver, and mountain sheep.

HUNTING METHOD

Fish: seines, dip nets, spears, and hooks. Animal: annual trips for game; used dogs, nets, snares, deadfalls, calls, disguises and decoys, blinds and corrals.

CLOTHING

Male.—Early: nothing or rabbit-skin robes. Later: complete skin clothing, soft, gathered-at-the-instep moccasins, no cuffs; skin caps, woven rabbit-skin robes.

Female.—Early: small fore-and-aft aprons and socks made of cedar and sage fiber. Fez-shaped basketry hats. Later: tunics of skin, belted and fringed. Basketry hats and caps, skin and rabbit-fur robes, skin leggings.

HOUSE TYPES

Early: winter earth lodges and summer gabled arbors. Later: gabled pole structures with cattail mats or brush cover. Smoke hole and skin doorway. Four to six families. Male sweat house. Female segregation huts.

EQUIPMENT

Household.—Baskets: high elaboration, coiled and imbricated, highly decorated. Stone cooking in baskets. Pottery not known in historic times. Mats for bedding and coverings. Few bark vessels, stone mortars, and wooden pestles. Horn spoons. Soft twined bags.

Transportation.—Crude dugout canoe, some bark in northwestern section. In East, bullboats of skin over willow frame, shaped like large tub.

Hunting.—Sinew-backed bow, club and spear.

Other.—Cradle: general; flat elipsoid board, skin-covered; Lower Columbia River—top cut so that it resembles a stone arrowhead. Fraser-Thompson: imbricated basket type. Pipe: tubular, cigar-holder type, stem of wood with clay or stone insert. Later: Plains elbow and rectangular. Miscellaneous: many gambling devices, ornaments of bone, stone, and copper. Bone flutes, reed pipettes, drums; bags of skin, some painted, some of undressed hides.

WAR

Bow and arrow, lances, rod and slat armor, heavy skin shirts, wooden clubs. Later: very large shields. Central Plateau largely pacifist. All mainly marginal defense fighting within a fortress. Offensive in marginal, sneak raids at night. Seldom scalped, did not cut off heads. Hair cut from prisoners used in place of scalps.

GAMES

Ball-juggling, dice games, double ball, handball, hand games, hoop-and-pole, ring-and-pin, shinny, stilts, tops.

CHAPTER XII

West Coast Medley

WEST of the Basin, across the Sierra, or Sawtooth, Mountains, lived a medley of tribes now included in the state of California. Seen on a map of Indian languages (see front endpaper), this state would be spotted with different colors, for, of the six language families in America north of Mexico, all but the Eskimo are represented. This is in striking contrast to the East, where great stretches of country, covering several states, were all occupied by tribes of the same stock, such as Algonkian or Muskogean. Only one explanation seems to fit. This country at the edge of the Pacific must have afforded a stopping place for many migrating groups. The majority probably went on, for their representatives can be found in the Northeast, in the Plains, and in Mexico. Only small detachments, perhaps weary, adventurous, or quarrelsome, were left pocketed here and there.

And in pockets they have remained ever since. The independence of California's local groups, their hostility to one another, and their tenacious grip on their own particular territories have become familiar to students of the subject. The tribelets have adopted customs from east, north, and south in varying degrees and have developed customs of their own until no summary will fit them. They must be referred to as the "West Coast medley."

From the Indian point of view, which is also that of natural resources, California should be divided into several states. Maps VII and VIII show that its northern portion belongs partly to the Plateau, just described, and partly to the wooded coast, subject of the next chapter. The Basin overlaps it on the east, and, on the south, Basin country and Basin people cut a wide swath toward the sea. At the southeast, the rich valley of the Colorado River is shared with the land of the peaceful corn-growers. Each of these areas deserves volumes to itself, and many such have been written.[1] Here we can give only such glimpses of the West Coast medley as serve to set it off from Indians on three sides of it. The following pages may point up the customs, particularly the death customs, which make it possible to group California Indians in the California area rather than with the Southwest or the Basin.

A group which is not usually treated with other Californians is that of the Yuman-speaking peoples on the Colorado River. They are corn-growers whose place would seem to be with the other agriculturists of the Southwest. Yet this writer, who has spent many months among them, is prepared to contend that they have none of the customs of genuine farmers. In the first place, they leave the work to the women, as none of the peaceful corn-growers do. In the second place, they lack that series of ceremonies to foster the crops which is so fundamental in southwestern life. Instead, their interest is in war and the great California obsession—death. They have the appearance of people who found themselves by chance in marvelous planting country and were practically forced to take advantage of it.

In the ancient days there were Yuman groups on both sides of the Colorado, from where Needles, California, now is, down to the river mouth. Others were pushed away by their warlike neighbors and went to live with the Pimans on the Gila. Still others were wandering hunters and gatherers living in upland portions of the Southwest, much as gatherers lived in the Basin. However, they were no relation to the Basin People. Their language is related to that of the Siouan, Muskogean, and Iroquoian, thousands of miles away. Are they an offshoot from a migrating mass which turned east while they turned west? Some archaeologists have thought that their early settlements may have been on the west of the Pueblo area (chap. ix, n. 25, p. 350) or among the Hohokam (chap. ix, n. 26, p. 351). Even if that were so, their later history took them into very different lifeways.

The River Yuman, settled on the Colorado, could hardly help planting. This great stream, before Boulder Dam days, was the Nile of America. Every summer, gorged by the melting snows of the Rockies, it overflowed its channel, sometimes for miles, and its recession left silt-covered flats in which all sorts of seed-bearing weeds sprang up. Some of these, now lost, were apparently cultivated by the early Yuman residents. Later, the women planted corn and teparies like those of their near neighbors, the Pimans,[2] but a different type of squash.[3] Also they gathered wild greens and seeds, especially the beans of the mesquite, most of the trees being owned, as the river plots were. Here we meet a different psychology from that of the mild-mannered Pueblos and Pimans. Land among these later was assigned to clans and families who cultivated their little plots or subdued new ones without interference. The land in the narrow valley of the Colorado was richer than anything in the desert, but it was limited. Patrilineal families laid claims to their narrow plots, running straight back from the river; they marked the boundaries and fought with any who trespassed by so much as a foot.

Yuman houses resembled those of the Pimans but were much larger, housing a man with several wives, plus his male descendants and their wives. These were the winter houses, set above the flood plain, while arbors below sufficed for the family in summer. They fished in the river and hunted small animals, and occasionally the men got a deer. We hear nothing of the solemn ceremonies used by the Pimans and Pueblos for their deer hunts. These men seem to have centered their interest upon fighting. Often, they went naked, and old pictures show them tattooed from top to toe. Otherwise, they wore breechcloths and sandals. Women, tattooed on face and breasts, wore a variation of the fore-and-aft apron common in California. That means two aprons made of fiber—in this case shredded willow bark. A short one hung in front with a very large bustle-like one in back.

The daily life was different from that of other corn-growers, as was the treatment of life-crises. True, the childbearing woman was segregated as is usual, but the girl at adolescence received far more notice. She was required to remain quiescent for four days, without touching her head, while she received the usual treatment given invalids. She lay on a bed of sand, previously warmed by a fire, while arrowweed and sand, or perhaps merely sand, was heaped over her. Every day her head and those of all the women guests were washed with boiled mesquite bark, and the women sang joyful songs. As often, when girl ceremonies are features, the boy was let off lightly. Four days of running, about the age of eight, with piercing of the ears, was considered enough.

Death was the occasion on which we find the greatest difference from the other corn-growers. The Yuman cremated. Their funeral pyre was a house-high mass of logs, carefully selected and oriented. Upon it lay the dead, dressed in his best and loaded with gifts, while his father-clan danced back and forth all night, singing the clan legend and sometimes throwing gifts.[4] After this, the house of the dead was usually burned. Once a year, or perhaps oftener, relatives of the recently deceased assembled after a fashion common in California and held a mourning celebration. Here, for four days, there were songs and speeches, then a mock battle, and, in recent years, the burning of images representing the dead.[5] With the Yuman the mention of dead relatives or stating that one is an orphan is considered a deadly insult.

The Yuman have father-clans, each owning a series of descriptive names which are borne only by women. Even though the Deer or Mustard clan may remind us of the Pueblos, clans have no leaders and no ceremonies. Yuman leadership was political rather than priestly. There was a civilian head for tribe or district who might be hereditary[6] and whose duties were of the advisory kind we shall meet often among seed-gatherers. There was Brave Man, the War Leader, who had risen to his position with the help of dreams, and the Scalp-keeper, an important official who guarded the enemy scalps by right of dream power and called the people to dance for them each month.

Obviously, the warriors were important people. Old accounts tell how the Yuma or Mohave would march out in formation, issue ceremonial challenges, and sometimes watch duels fought between their leaders before a general battle.[7] Only a man with the proper dream could take the scalp of the slain, and he must be purified with a four-day rite. The Yuman took prisoners, who must also be purified, after which they could be enslaved or killed. Dreams were needed for the running and wrestling games in which the Yuman were expert, as they were at swimming. They ran or jog-trotted for immense distances to trade with tribes on the Gulf of California or the Pacific Coast and to hand on shells and feathers to people farther inland.

The dream, it will be seen, was of immense importance with all River Yuman. It gave a man power to fight, to make speeches, to learn the clan songs. In fact, it has been stated that almost nothing could be done without dream power.[8] This did not mean a vision obtained after ordeal. It was an experience which often came to the infant in its mother's womb, picturing the future event or, for a shaman, re-creating the past, when Mastamho or his equivalent taught the people their arts. The Yuman consider that all things were born of earth and sky, but they have no long myth of emergence like the other agriculturalists. Instead, their tale is of the dying god, Matavilya, or his like, the son of earth, who was poisoned by his daughter and provided the first cremation. Then came his son or younger brother who made the Colorado River and set up the sacred mountain and built upon it the house where shamans dreamed before they were born.

Much of this is California mythology with no rain-beings, no masks, no prayer sticks, no cult of the corn. The chief ceremonies are those for death and war, with some jollifications at harvest, where the speeches are informal and the songs are clan songs.[9] These songs are an interesting production, being long, detailed accounts of the ancestors' wanderings, in stereotyped verse and prose.[10] A man or woman must dream the power to learn them and thereafter can lead the singing at cremations and mourning ceremonies. If one is more ambitious, he may dream power to learn the esoteric tales of origin which belong to the shaman. The shaman known to the writer, having dreamed such power, then paid an older shaman to teach him. His cure is by herbal remedies, rubbing, singing, or bringing back a lost soul as he learned to do before birth.

It is strange to see this fierce, inspirational attitude so close to the peaceful Pimans and the Pueblos. The Yuman are, in many ways, equally different from the California seed-gatherers to the west of them. They must stand alone as a pocket of different culture and tradition left, by chance, in the corn country. Only lately has their fate merged again with that of their neighbors. In the 1860's a large reservation was set apart for "Indians of the Colorado drainage." Up to a few years ago, it was occupied only by some eight hundred farming Mohave and their neighbors from California, the Chemehuevi. (Yuma and Cocopa have allotments; Maricopa, a reservation on the Gila.) Now the lush, torrid land which gives five or six crops of alfalfa a year looks promising to government officials, seeking more room for Indian farmers. It was used once for a Japanese relocation camp and has now some good buildings and soil well tended by the Japanese gardeners. The Mohave, after many meetings, have decided to turn over half their area to other tribes in the drainage. The government will dig ditches for irrigation, clear and fence the land, and plant the first crop. Indians can borrow money for their equipment which must be paid back within a term of years. A few Hopi and a few Navaho families have taken advantage of the offer, even though it means a life very different from that of their past. What will evolve when Indians of two or perhaps more tribes are thrown together to set up such institutions as they choose?

Leaving the Colorado, we enter the domain of typical California food-gatherers. That lifeway is ancient indeed, for shell mounds along the coast date some seven thousand years ago.[11] In the Mohave Desert and near-by areas were found stone tools which may have been left in the Ice Age, when this withering hot area contained a lake, with people camping on its shores. From the grinding stones found, it looks as though they might have done seed-gathering as well as hunting.[12] In historic times a wide stretch of country, contiguous with the Basin and stretching to the Pacific, was occupied by people whom some whites called "Diggers" and some, "Mission" Indians. Most were named after the Spanish missions of later days so that their own titles are forgotten, even by modern young Indians. They were a number of small tribes, one a strayed Yuman group (see Map VIII), the others closely related to the Basin and speaking the same language, Shoshonean, of the Uto-Aztecan family. As far as workaday life goes, they could be described with the Basin people, for they wore the same vegetal clothing, brief or nonexistent; they built the same brush-covered huts; and they wandered over a circuit, gathering every edible thing they could find.

However, California provided food opportunities almost unknown to the Basin. Chief of these was the acorn, the great staple of all the trans-Sierra country. Pounded to meal and boiled with stones in a basket, it made a mush which was as much a staple for California food-gatherers as corn mush for agriculturalists. Yet, to make it, years of experiment must have been needed, since acorns contain tannic acid, which is bitter. The Indians solved this problem by placing the acorn meal in a basket and pouring water through it until the tannin was leached out. The whole process of gathering acorns, cracking them, pounding, stone boiling, and storage, required six or eight baskets, all made for the purpose. One of those used for pounding, in southern California, was specially interesting, since it made use of the native asphalt. What process of experiment went on, one wonders, before the Indian women discovered the gluelike asphalt, then realized that they could cut the bottom out of a basket bowl and glue the rest over a rock hollow, thus making a convenient hopper with rock bottom and basketry sides!

Another advantage for the southern Californians was their outlet to the sea. Only a few of the tribelets had territory along the coast, but others came yearly to trade for fish and clams. Sometimes they obtained the ceremonial dishes made of soft steatite or soapstone on the coastal islands. Also they got shell money. This product is not called wampum, although it was made from clamshells and was used, much like the eastern wampum, for ceremonial payments. The coastal Gabrieliño hacked out circular disks from huge white clamshells, then perforated them, strung them on a cord, and ground them on stones until they had much the shape of the modern peppermint disks.

Such clamshell beads are worn by Pueblo and Navaho people to the present day and must have been obtained in trade.

More important than the new foods and the new equipment was the contact with other peoples. At this point in the narrative it should be plain that contact stimulus is an absolute necessity for a group's progress. The Nevada food-gatherers, cut off by mountains from a knowledge of other lifeways, remained as primitive as any Indians on the continent. Their relatives of southern California, who touched the Yuman on one side and the tribes of central California on the other, developed systems of organization, ceremony, and mythology far beyond those of the average American food-gatherers.

Like the Paiute, they wandered in small groups in the summer and congregated in villages for the winter. Unlike the Paiute, they were organized in father-clans, each of which had its priestly leader and its ceremonial house where he lived and carried on the clan rituals. He also kept the sacred bundle, which, with this basket-making people, was a roll of matting. Two of the tribes ranged their clans in moieties which intermarried and which helped each other in ceremonies.[13] This moiety, or dual division, which was so prominent in the Mississippi Valley, seems to have appealed to many California Indians, and we shall meet it again, often with ceremonial duties which one division performed for the other.

With the Mission Indians, as with many food-gatherers, ceremonies clustered around the events of personal life, particularly puberty and death. They made a public ceremony for a girl's puberty, at maturation, laying her on a warm bed of sand, as the River Yuman did, while they fasted ceremonially, used a scratching stick, and old women sang for her. After this, there was a solemn admonition by the clan chief or the moiety chief. He made a rude diagram on the ground, explaining to the girl that it was the disk of the earth, with the encircling sea and the overarching sky. Within it she must take her place as a grown woman, fruitful, industrious, and kind. If she failed in such duties, which meant good living for the entire community, then there were evil monsters which would devour her. In view of the sand paintings of the Pueblos and the Navaho, this crude design is interesting. It seems to have precursors among the Yaqui and Mayo of northern Mexico[14] and suggests that the art of ground painting had a slow and widespread development.

For boys there was also a ground painting and a speech of admonition. Before that, however, there was a ceremony most unusual for

Indians north of Mexico—the taking of a drug. The Mission Indians wished their young men to have dreams and guardian spirits, but, instead of asking them to fast and pray for a vision, they produced it by a drink made from the pounded root of Jimson weed (*Datura stramonium*). It was the tribes nearest the coast, especially the Luiseño and Diegueño, who did this, perhaps learning from older tribes, but they made of it a solemn ritual. Each boy was cared for by a man who had himself taken the drink in his youth. This guardian held his head that he might not drink too much out of the magical steatite bowl, then marched and sang with him, and finally laid him down with the others in a little inclosure, where they were to sleep and dream. Some might have dreams so powerful as to make them shamans.

Later came the ground painting, the admonition to be unselfish and not to hoard food, and the threat of what might happen to the stingy. The Luiseño had ordeals for a youth before he could be considered a man, one being to lie naked on a hill made by huge biting ants.

Marriage, of course, did not take place within one's own clan—or moiety if there was one. It meant an exchange of gifts between the two families, for these Indians were not rich enough for any great marriage price. There was a speech of advice by the local chief whose duties seem to have been largely preaching. The couple camped with the husband's clan and divorced without ceremony at the wish of either party.

It was after a death that the most imposing ceremonies were held. We have noticed before how much death impressed the Californians. Even though they feared the return of the departed and never mentioned his name, sometimes changing a number of their terms of relationship thereby, nevertheless they exerted themselves to the utmost for a great funeral ceremony and an even greater mourning anniversary afterward. Most of them cremated their dead, like the Yuman, but no group attended to its own. They sent for the opposite moiety or another clan which they called their opposite.[15] Thus they avoided the danger of too close contact, while giving the dead all possible honor. The house and many possessions were burned at the same time as the corpse. Shell money was sent by the officiants to the mourners (later to be returned, for the Californians were extremely careful about counting costs). A year later there was the mourning anniversary, when the relatives of the dead beggared themselves by making gifts in his honor, and a few tribes burned images as the Mohave did. The mourning chants, sung at this time, were tragic epics telling how

Eagle, one of the first people, flew north, east, south, and west to escape death but found that it was everywhere in the world. Or they tell of the god Wiyot, killed by his own daughter, asking every month as he saw the flowers and the fruits change: "Shall I die this month?"

This story of the dying god, so different from most myths we have met, is shared with the Mohave. So is the story of an actual beginning

PLATE XLIII

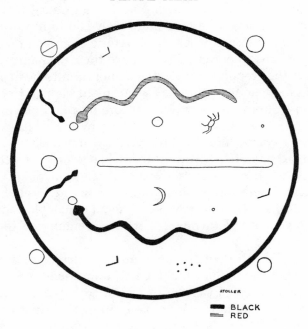

STOLLER

■■ BLACK
== RED

DIEGUEÑO GROUND PAINTING

This is a map or diagram of the Dieigueño world, used in the latter part of their boy's puberty ceremony. The inner circle is made of powdered white soapstone, as is the line through the center. The outer circle is made of ceremonially burned and powdered charcoal. The inner figures, representing the all-powerful snakes, moon, sun, and various animals, are made of red oxide of iron and variously colored seeds. It is approximately 15 feet in diameter. (From Waterman, 1910.)

of the world when Mother Earth and Father Sky emerged from the void, then generated both men and their ceremonial objects, beginning with the stone bowl from which Jimson weed was drunk. The head-man of clan or moiety chanted it at ceremonies when the first fruits of different wild plants were honored or when chained eagles were ceremonially killed. Some of the Coast tribes added a strange myth about a savior who descended from on high and returned there. To this writer, the story of Chinigchinich sounds like some early Jesuit preaching seen through Indian eyes.

No such story was told by the medicine men, who got their power either from Jimson weed visions or from an old-fashioned dream. It was spectacular power, for, besides sucking out disease, it allowed them to walk through fire and throw it about with their feet.

These tribes have been called Mission Indians with good reason. All but the Serrano and Cahuilla, living back in the mountains, were converted by Franciscan missionaries less than two hundred years ago. The picturesque Spanish missions of California are looked upon as ancient, yet the first one, at San Diego, was founded in 1769, and the last, at San Francisco, in 1823, only twenty-six years before the famous gold rush. Though they existed in full power for only about sixty years, they changed the life of the Indians forever.

The Franciscans were devoted missionaries, vowed to poverty and service. Their solution for the Indians was to gather them in villages around a mission which should consist of church, school, and shops. Here they would be taught Christianity and civilized trades and at last would live like white people. This might have worked with an agricultural people, used to living in one place, and perhaps such people could have appreciated the oranges and grapes which the fathers planted in California. Wanderers grew sick with the unusual confinement and the heavy clothing, though many accepted it because their own lands were being overrun. The worst tragedy came when Mexico, which then included California, gained her independence and ceased to support the missions. The Indians were turned out to support themselves, but they had lost all capacity for it. Used to taking orders and having all plans made for them, they were helpless against the whites who were now occupying the land.

When California became American, these Indians were scarcely remembered at all. There was almost a century when they wandered, finding any living they could, while white ranches occupied their wild lands. When our government realized the tragedy, it was too late to set aside large reservations. Small parcels of land were bought here and there, and Indian communities were established on them (see Table 11). There some of the old ceremonies have been revived, even though the men who conduct them may have graduated from public high school or from the big government school at Riverside. That school trained aircraft workers during the war and had well-paid positions for all it could send out. Now many of the workers are still at San Diego and Los Angeles. One group has had some of the unpredictable luck that sometimes befell Indians. Their land is near Palm Springs, the fashionable winter resort, and can be sold for an enormous price.

North of the Mission country we meet the true diversity of California Indian life. Here are tribes related to the Algonkian of the Northeast, the Siouan of the Plains, the Navaho of the Southwest, and the Sahaptin of the Plateau. The population at some points is as dense as in the agricultural pueblos,[16] showing that, even in ancient days, California was a desirable place to live. One such vanished tribe, the Chumash, of the Santa Barbara coast and near-by islands, is still a puzzle to students, because of an ocean-going canoe found on their coast and made of planks sewed together in a technique something like that of the Northwest Coast and also the South Pacific.

All these tribes were hunters, gatherers, and basket-makers. In fact, we are here at the very heart of the basket industry in the United States. With more vegetal material than the people of the Basin, more leisure and more occasions for display, the women of the Pomo tribe especially produced baskets so fine that a microscope is needed in order to count the stitches. They worked in decorations of beads or of tiny brilliant feathers, in an extravagance of artistic expression which the hard-worked Basin could never have afforded.

Each of these central tribes would repay study because of the perfect adjustment of their lifeway to natural resources.[17] Here we shall concentrate on the central valley, home of five important tribes of the Penutian language, related to peoples of the Plateau (see Map VIII). This valley, where Sacramento and Fresno now stand, in a network of highways, towns, and ranches, was once a land of meadows and small streams, bordered by foothills. This was the acorn country above all others, but also there was enough fish and small game so that its residents had time for extra ceremony and for warfare. Not the eastern warfare, where whole tribes were constantly on the move and every man's career depended on killing enemies! Rather, these populous tribes, each with its well-marked gathering territory, were like established nations which preferred to keep the peace unless invaded. It is interesting to see that, in Indian days, it was the Far West which was crowded with small groups with settled boundaries while the East was the new, wild land where people were fighting for place.

Yet these little western groups, old though they must be, had not developed any elaborate organization or ceremony. One reason, perhaps, was their very provincialism. They were so afraid of trespass on their gathering rights that the Maidu even kept sentries on the hills to ward off strangers. Another was the fact that, though they had plenty to eat, the gathering of food kept them busy and on the move

PLATE XLIV

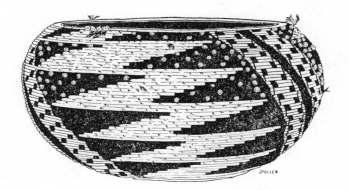

POMO BASKET

Made in very fine three-rod coiling technique, using *Cares barbarae* splints for the three rods and finer sections for the sewing material. The decorative elements are blackroot sedge (*Carex sp.*), quail topknots (*Lophotyx californicus*), and woodpecker crest feathers (*Melanerpes formacivorus*) and clamshell (*Saxidomus nuttallii*), native-made beads. At times the entire basket would be covered with these woven-in feathers and be dripping with sewed-on pendants and beads. These baskets were made for gifts, weddings, and ceremonial purposes. This one is 14 inches in diameter and 7½ inches in depth. (From Mason, 1902.)

for most of the year. They could not plan a calendric series of ceremonies like the Pueblos. Yet ceremonies they did have, some perhaps acquired long ago from southwestern neighbors, some centering around that obsession of California Indians—death.

They lived much like the Mission Indians, in clusters of hamlets in the winter and wandering bands in summer. Here, however, there were groves of trees, so that houses could be larger and more solid.

Often, they were semi-underground, with a conical roof of logs or redwook bark. Most valley groups had a large house where dances were held and where men could lounge and sweat. These gatherers were like the Basin in secluding the mother at childbirth and even asking the husband to share some of her taboos. Their adolescent girls, while secluded, must use a scratching stick, but often the end of their re-

PLATE XLV

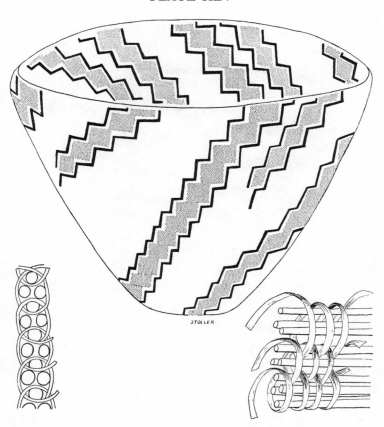

STOLLER

TULARE BASKET

The distinguishing features of this basketry bowl are the three-rod coil (small diagram), its diagonal designs, and the brownish background. The foundation is stems of grass (*Sporobolus vilfa*). Roots of slough grass (*Cyperus virens*) is used for sewing, and the red and black designs are redbud (*Cercis occidentalis*) and common fern root (*Pteridium*). This one is 10 inches high. (From the Denver Art Museum Collections.)

tirement meant a ceremony and dance. We can more or less calculate when such things will occur. People who are too poor, like the Basin gatherers, have no time for them. Those taken up with big communal gatherings do not bother. It is those in between, like the Yokut of the California foothills, who feature the girls' coming-of-age. With some tribes close to the Mission Indians, boys too had an initiation, including the use of Jimson weed. The easier circumstances in California and especially the use of shell money led to larger marriage payments. In some places there was a mere exchange of gifts, but in others the shell money was paid for the bride, and she and her children felt themselves socially important in proportion to the amount expended.

Most of these central tribes cremated their dead, like the Yuman and the Mission Indians. California, in fact, is divided half and half between cremation and burial, practices which can be referred partly to tradition and partly to the difficulties of digging in certain kinds of soil. In our particular area the Maidu and the Yokut burned their dead along with house and possessions. Later, the mourning anniversaries for all the dead of the year were among the most elaborate of their kind. There was burning of images, as with the Yuman. The Yokut held a masked dance and a shaman contest. The Maidu had an elaborate system of shell-money exchange between mourners and their friends. Also, they burned property, including exquisite baskets, often made especially to be consumed in this way. Until such honor had been paid to the departed, their names must not be spoken.

Simple though their living was, these central Californians had much more organization and ceremony than their neighbors of the Basin. There were father-clans and sometimes moieties who contended in games and helped each other at funerals. Each group of hamlets had a chief and sometimes a herald, offices which were inherited in certain clans. There was no war chief and no system of war honors. When a feud started, because of trespass or suspected witchcraft, the two sides were likely to line up and appoint champions—a very economical way of fighting. When peace was made, there were often money payments, a modern touch probably due to the existence of shell money. Captives are rarely of any use to food-gatherers, who can neither use nor support them. Therefore the few males taken were tortured and killed in the dance-house. When scalps were brought home, they were good-sized ones, including the ears.

We can make no simple summary of the mythology of these diverse groups, but it is interesting to find that, at least among the northern ones, there was some idea of a single creator. Sometimes the marplot Coyote interferred with his plans, as when, in a touching Maidu myth,[18] he persuaded the benevolent one that it would not be good for mankind to have either eternal life, easy livelihood, or painless production of children. Some of the central tribes also had a ceremony which contains echoes of the Pueblos. One is tempted to think that migrants from that highly organized population which underwent

PLATE XLVI

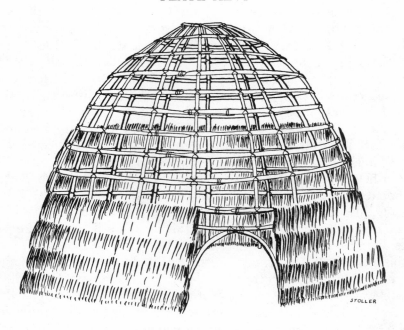

SOUTHERN CALIFORNIA HOUSE

The usual house of the southern California Indian was 9 feet high and about 16 feet in diameter; however, communal houses up to 60 feet in diameter were used. After clearing a place, protected from high winds and having good drainage, the first six poles of young sycamore were set up. Lighter poles were set between these. The tops were then drawn together and lashed with wild-hemp cordage. Beginning at the bottom, the house was thatched by tying bunches, or even whole clusters, of plants (roots and all and usually deer weed) to the crosspoles. Other poles were tied on horizontally over each row of thatch. The southern houses had no smoke holes as did the northern houses, but the two entrances, about 30 inches high, to the north and south, were common to both. (From Woodward, 1949.)

such shrinkage about the 1400's might have arrived here, bearing traditions which they tried to preserve. Stone houses and agriculture, they could not have, but the kachina dances which promoted agriculture and all good living might still be recalled. That, think some students,[19] might be the origin of the mysterious figures which appeared singly at the yearly Kuksu dances. Here was no woven cotton or strings of turquoise, but California had wild riches of which the Indians took full advantage—its brilliant birds. The redheaded woodpecker and the yellow warbler furnished crowns as well as basket decorations. The magpie gave striking black-and-white plumes, while eagles and owls were plentiful. So Kuksu dancers, instead of wearing masks, were draped and crowned with feathers.[20] There were other societies, particularly the Ghosts, which seems to have been a men's cult, intended to scare the women. Also there were ceremonies to increase the wild crops and the salmon, for such "first-fruits ceremonies" must long have antedated those for corn.

California had also its full quota of medicine men, gaining their power from dreams of animals or ghosts. Here there seem to have been more specialists than usual, for we hear of sucking shamans, weather shamans, rattlesnake shamans, and a much-dreaded variety, those who had power from the bear and could actually turn into that animal. The shamans were reverenced, both as users of witchcraft and as great magicians. One of their practices was a public contest when each tried to overcome the others, even to death.

This part of California, too far north for most of the Spaniards, was left almost undisturbed until the gold rush of 1849. Suddenly, then, the Indians were overwhelmed and pushed aside. In the 1850's large tracts of land were ceded and some reservations set up, many of them later withdrawn or divided into individual allotments. These Indians, at least in an organizational sense, were among those who had little to lose. As their land was overrun, they, like the Paiute, simply took to working for the whites. Since their money requirements were small, they could manage something of their old seasonal arrangements, working in the summer and congregating in the winter, in hamlets or in small hunting or fishing parties. They had the usual religious revival. If we were not already aware that man turns to the supernatural in times of unbearable stress, we should have the proof in this regular appearance of Indian dream prophets. In 1870, twenty years before the better-known Ghost Dance, a Paiute Indian, precursor of Wovoka, announced a doctrine of much the same sort, involving the disappearance of the whites and the return of the Indian dead. It spread into California and Oregon, generating new cults, some of which have lasted to the present day.[21] It is interesting to see that, when Christianity does get a foothold, it is the more revivalistic forms of Protestantism which appeal to the Indians. They have some likeness to a shamanistic experience.

All California Indians now live under one state agency. They attend public schools along with whites and share the same social security payments. Their obvious future is absorption in the white man's culture, but we must regret that the start was made under such a handicap of injustice and contempt on the part of the intruding race.

YUMAN

FOOD

Vegetable.—Flour corn, tepary beans, pumpkin, winter squash, seeds, wild plants.

Animal.—Some deer, mountain sheep, fish, small game.

HUNTING METHOD

Fishnet, trap, and snare; deer, mountain sheep, and rabbit with bow. No communal hunts.

CLOTHING

Male.—Mostly naked, some breechcloths, full tattooing.

Female.—Front and back aprons of shredded willow bark, later the front apron of cotton cord. Chin tattooing.

HOUSE TYPES

Large dome-shaped brush huts, some earth-covered.

EQUIPMENT

Household.—A few coiled baskets. Pottery crude, paddle and anvil, plain buff or painted designs, not polished; Maricopa, highly polished red with black designs in Piman style.

Transportation.—Rafts.

Hunting.—Self-bow and arrow.

Other.—Cradle: slat type. Pipe: cane and cornhusk cigarettes. Miscellaneous: not much.

WAR

Bow and arrow, potato-masher club, feather staves, shields for heralds. Defensive and offensive fighting. Hand-to-hand combats and raids. Female captives.

GAMES

Hoop-and-pole, ball race, dice, hand games, shinny.

SOUTHERN CALIFORNIA

FOOD

Vegetable.—Seeds, acorns, wild plants, greens, and nuts.
Animal.—Deer, fish, shellfish on coast, rabbits, caterpillars, grubs, grasshoppers, birds.

HUNTING METHOD

Nets for small game, fish, and birds. Bow and arrow, hunting crook, snares, stone fishhooks.

CLOTHING

Male.—Mostly naked. Breechcloths of bark or a skin wrapped around waist. Tattooing, rude skin or bark sandals for travel. Rabbit-skin robes, sea-otter furs, feather headbands and "crowns."
Female.—Two fringe aprons, back one of bark, front of cordage. Tattooing, rabbit-skin robes, some basket caps for burden-carrying. Crude sandals of fibers.

HOUSE TYPES

Summer or traveling: tule mats over framework of poles. Permanent: domed pole and brush, covered with earth. Sweat house. Female segregation huts.

EQUIPMENT

Household.—Coiled and twined basketry: cooking, carrying, seed-beaters, mortar baskets, bowls. Pitched water bottle. Steatite or soapstone vessels. Pottery, coiled and sometimes painted. Tule (cattail) mats.
Transportation.—Plank boats, balsas.
Hunting.—Long self-bow, arrows, rabbit sticks, nets, clubs, hunting crook.
Other.—Cradle: ladder-like frame. Pipe: tubular, stone and pottery, 6–8 inches long. Miscellaneous: gourd and rawhide rattles, turtle-shell rattle, straight flute. Wooden headrest. Jimson weed rites.

WAR

Long bow, arrows, few lances or spears. War mainly for revenge. Took heads and scalps, female and child slaves.

GAMES

Dice games (pitch inlaid shells), hand games, shinny, hoop-and-pole, tops, quoits, ring-and-pin.

CENTRAL CALIFORNIA

FOOD

Vegetable.—Seeds, acorns, wild plants, nuts.
Animal.—Deer, fish, rabbits, grubs, grasshoppers.

HUNTING METHOD

Fishweir, scaffolds, spears, and nets. Deer fence, game pits, deadfalls, bow and arrow.

CLOTHING

Male.—Mostly naked. Breechcloths or skin wrapped around waist. Feather blankets and robes, rabbit-fur robes. Clumsy soft-soled, ankle-high moccasins and fiber sandals, footgear rarely worn. Hairnets of iris fibers. Crown of feathers from yellowhammer and woodpecker.

Female.—Fore-and-aft aprons, shredded bark or cordage. Many caps of basketry. Moccasins like men. Same type robes.

HOUSE TYPES

Semi-underground, conical roof, logs, bark-covered. Center pole. Brush arbors. Multifamily roundhouse, frame thatched with tule or grass. Sweat house. Female segregation.

EQUIPMENT

Household.—Fine basketry, twined and coiled, with lattice twining for Pomo, wicker for Maidu; one- and three-rod coiling; many types; Pomo decorated with feathers. Burden baskets, cooking bowls, mush bowls. Mats, a few wooden bowls, mortar baskets, seed-beaters.

Transportation.—Simple dugouts, rush balsas, log rafts.

Hunting.—Fishing equipment: weirs, nets, hooks, spears. Other: throwing sticks, sinew-backed bow, arrows, snares.

Other.—Cradle: basketry, sitting type; also ladder type. Pipe: wood, bulb end. Miscellaneous: rattles of deer hooves and cocoons; bull-roarers, bone whistles, stick-clappers. Clamshell disk beads.

WAR

Bow and arrow, war spear, and war club.

GAMES

Cat's cradle, dice games, hand game, hoop-and-pole, racket, ring-and-pin, acorn tops, ground coasting arrow—like snow snake.

TRIBES OF THE WEST COAST MEDLEY

AGRICULTURAL RIVER TRIBES

Yuma (*Yuman*): Among first tribes to be discovered.
Mohave (*Yuman*): Agricultural people.
Diegueño (*Yuman*): Mission Indians; two dialects.
Kamia (*Yuman*): Mission Indians; practically extinct.

COASTAL TRIBES

Esselen (*Hokan, related to Siouan, Muskogean, and Iroquoian*): Possibly a remnant of a larger group; first California group to become extinct.

Chumash (*Hokan*): First group discovered by whites; five missions established, dialect for each mission; only eight to ten left who speak language.
Salinan (*Hokan*): Practically extinct.

BASIN-LIKE TRIBES

Washo (*Hokan*): On boundary between Basin and California with Basin culture.

TABLE 11

PRESENT RESERVATIONS AND NUMBERS OF THE
WEST COAST MEDLEY TRIBES

Tribe	State and Agency	Population, 1945*	
Chemehuevi....	*California:* Colorado River Agency	325	
	Nevada: Nevada colonies	8	(333)
Cocopa........	*California:* Colorado River Agency	88	
Maidu.........	*California:* Carson Agency†	3	
Me-Wuk......	*California:* Me-Wuk Agency	90	
Mission........	*California:* Augustine Reservation	17	
	Cabazon Reservation	28	
	Cahuilla Reservation	93	
	Campo Reservation	125	
	Captain Grande Reservation	168	
	Cuyupaipe Reservation	3	
	Inaja Reservation	31	
	La Jolla Reservation	235	
	La Posta Reservation	0	
	Los Coyotes Reservation	91	
	Manzanita Reservation	63	
	Mesa Grande Reservation	241	
	Mission Creek Reservation	20	
	Morongo Reservation	316	
	Pala Reservation	223	
	Palm Springs Reservation	58	
	Pauma Reservation	66	
	Pechanga Reservation	211	
	Rincon Reservation	191	
	San Manuel Reservation	49	
	San Pasqual Reservation	9	
	Santa Rosa Reservation	53	
	Santa Ynez Reservation	87	
	Santa Ysabel Reservation	279	
	Soboba Reservation	137	
	Sycuan Reservation	37	
	Torres Reservation	202	
	Others	4,052	(7,088)
Mohave.......	*California:* Colorado River Agency	575	
	Fort Mojave Reservation	343	(918)
Pomo.........	*California:* Sacramento Agency	411	
Tule River.....	*California:* Sacramento Agency	205	
Washo	*California:* Carson Agency	150	
	Nevada: Washo Reservation	80	
	Washo colonies	461	
Wintun........	*California:* Sacramento Agency	58	
Yuma	*California:* Fort Yuma Reservation	979	

* Numbers in parentheses are totals.
† Others grouped with other tribes and uncounted.

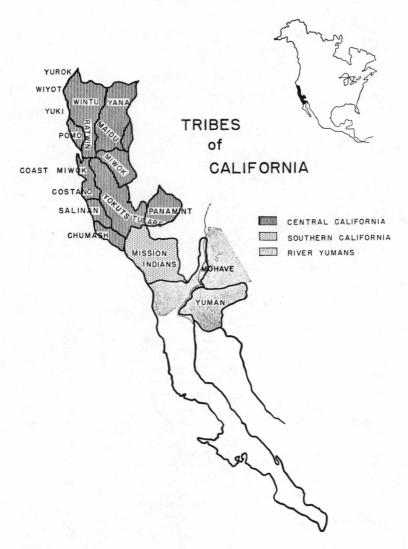

MAP VIII

TRIBES
of
CALIFORNIA

YUROK
WIYOT
YUKI
POMO

WINTU
YANA

PATWIN
MAIDU

COAST MIWOK
MIWOK

COSTANO

SALINAN
YOKUTS TULARE
PANAMINT

CHUMASH

MISSION
INDIANS
MOHAVE

YUMAN

▨ CENTRAL CALIFORNIA
▨ SOUTHERN CALIFORNIA
▨ RIVER YUMANS

Mono (*Shoshonean*): Two divisions with two dialects; now most numerous in California.

Koso or *Panamint* (*Shoshonean*): Very few left of original five hundred.

Kern River (**Shoshonean**): About a hundred and fifty left; offshoot of Cheme-huevi but definitely Californian in culture.

CENTRAL TRIBES

Costanoan (*Penutian*): Now extinct for all practical purposes. Originally Spanish recorded seven thousand people, with a hundred villages and as many dialects.

Maidu (*Penutian*): Three language groups; originally nine thousand, now only a few left.

Miwok (*Penutian*): Three large groups; originally over a hundred villages but few left now.

Yokut (*Penutian*): Unique for California as divided into forty or fifty true tribes, each with name, dialect, and territory.

Wintun (*Penutian*): Three dialects with minor variations within each.

Yuki (*Yukian*): Small isolated speech family with four dialectically distinct groups: **Yuki proper, Coast Yuki, Huchnom, and Wappo.**

SOUTHERN CALIFORNIA TRIBES

Serrano (*Shoshonean*): Two groups: Kitanemuk, related to Kawiisu, and Alliklik, now extinct.

Gabrieleño (*Shoshonean*): Ancient Mission Indians; now practically extinct.

Luiseño (*Shoshonean*): Ancient Mission Indians; now practically extinct.

Cahuilla (*Shoshonean*): One of the important tribes of California.

CHAPTER XIII

The Potlatch-givers

IN ALL America north of Mexico there were no more wealthy Indians than those on the Pacific Coast from northern California into the "panhandle" of Alaska (see Map IX). Wealth, from the Indian point of view, meant plenty of food, and that usually involved agriculture. However, such need not be the case, for we have already seen that the Plains Indians had tons of wealth which presented itself on the hoof, with no planting and digging needed. Indians of the Northwest Coast were in even better condition, for their wealth was in salmon. This lusty fish, carrying fifteen pounds or more of rich, oily meat, swam up the rivers from the Pacific every summer in such numbers that, as white pioneers said, "you could walk across on their backs." An Indian family in a few months could catch and dry enough fish to supply food for a year.

Besides this there were the deep-sea cod and halibut; the shellfish on beach and rocks; the smelts in the surf. In the ocean there were sea otter, sea lion, and whale. From some of the northwestern tribes[1] a dugout canoe containing eight men might put out into the Pacific to harpoon a fifty-foot humpback whale and tow it to shore. Even the climate was kind. The Japan Current, sweeping up the coast of Asia, was deflected by the Aleutians so that it flowed down past southern Alaska, making Sitka and even Juneau sometimes as warm as Boston. The Rockies at the north and the Cascades farther south caught the moist winds so that the coastal strip was bathed for weeks on end with fog and showers. As a result, marshy meadows were blue with blossoms of the edible camass bulb, and from the beach nearly to the mountaintops stretched a dense, almost impassable forest. The Douglas fir at the north, the redwoods farther south, and the California pine furnished soft, straight-grained wood far more workable with primitive tools than the elm and hickory of the East. So the river and coast people could build houses larger and more commodious than

292

any we have met among agriculturists. They could fashion great sea-going canoes and, in some villages, the totem poles which have become known the world over.

Many tribes were attracted by this wealth of natural resources, some moving out from inland, some—or at least the influence of some—moving north from Washington and Oregon. Map IX and the list of tribes accompanying it (p. 318) show at least three language families with their subdivisions, and whole libraries of monographs have described their various customs. Here, we can point only to the obvious distinction between north and south. The south, which means from northern California up to about the Canadian border, was the home of poorer people. That is, they were poor in comparison to the north, though Basin Indians would have looked upon them as plutocrats. They may be called Inland tribes, since they lived on rivers and bays rather than the coast. Most Inland tribes did not go whaling. Their woodwork was mostly unpainted; they made no great masks, feast dishes, or totem poles. Many of them spoke Salish, a Plateau language. It would be easy to see how many of their customs could have developed from those of Plateau people, moved to a richer environment. Students feel that this rather simple version of Northwest life may represent its origins, while the art and ceremony of the more northern tribes may be an extravagant and perhaps recent development.

Three tribes on the northernmost margin of the Inland people are real coast dwellers and, except for an arbitrary international boundary, would not be considered here. They are the Quinault, Quileute, and Makah on the actual Pacific Coast, forming a transition between the Inland people and the full-blown Maritime tribes farther north. Whalers and seagoers, they often form an exception to statements made about tribes south of the border, and, when set apart in this way, they will be called the Maritime fringe.

North of them are the true Maritime People,[2] living mostly on the coastal islands of British Columbia and Alaska. They included such famous sea raiders, whalers, and totem-pole builders as the Nootka, Haida, Tlingit, and Tsimshian. They are outside the scope of a book which deals only with United States Indians, yet, without a glance at them, the full flavor of Northwest Coast life would hardly be apparent. Some space, therefore, must be given to their extravagant display of wealth, their art style—unique in North America—and their elaborate mimetic and sleight-of-hand performances. How did a development so intense and perhaps recent supervene on the Plateau-like culture of the Inland tribes? The subject is being carefully studied, and we can but point to the fact that some new stimulus might well have been responsible.[3]

We know that over a hundred vessels from Europe and America reached the Northwest Coast in the twenty years between 1774 and 1794.[4] They brought iron tools, and it is not until 1791 that we hear of the first totem pole.[5] All such poles we know were carved with iron tools and, in fact, would have been impossible without them. Were new designs and ideas imported along with the tools? That might have been the case, for ships trading along the coast in 1785–95 had among their crews Chinese, Hawaiians, and Filipinos, some of whom remained to live with the Indians.[6] It seems quite possible that craft from across the Pacific could have reached the coast even before this, bringing not only new tools but new ideas. There is nothing derogatory to American Indians in assuming that they may have shared in the flow of ideas which has always washed to and fro between various countries, producing a different sort of climax in each.

The question of possible importations applies only to some extravagant productions of the Maritime tribes in art and ceremony. In basic equipment the whole coastal strip was much the same. The costume was like that of the neighboring Plateau and Basin, which means short skirts or kilts for women and for men a breechcloth—when they wore anything at all. The material was the fibrous lining of cedar bark or of goat wool. They went barefoot, as people must who are constantly stepping in and out of water. Indeed, buckskin, which tears and hardens when wet, would be useless in most of the area. To shed rain, people wore fitted capes of bark matting and shaded their eyes from the water's glare with hats of twined basketry on which designs were painted. This was an everyday costume. Dressed for a feast, a Puget Sound man might be draped in a magnificent bearskin robe or a blanket of mountain-goat hair, traded in from the northern Chilkat. Californians wore more buckskin and sometimes moccasins, while their ceremonial dress utilized the brilliant bird feathers of the locality for capes, skirts, and long bands to hang down the back.

Houses, at least the permanent winter ones, were gathered in villages along the streams, with canoes pulled up on the bank before them. White pioneers who first saw these houses on Puget Sound could not believe that they were made by Indians without nails or saws, for they resembled the huge, unpainted barns of New England. To build them, huge trees had been felled by burning, floated down-

stream, and then set up as house frames, the builders using earthen
ramps, as the Egyptians did to raise their obelisks. For the walls, slabs
were split from tree trunks with wooden wedges, then stood up in the
ground between the corner posts or tied on horizontally with roots,
clapboard fashion.[7] Such slabs could be raised, like the slats of a Vene-
tian blind, and through them a corpse might be carried out, thus fool-
ing the ghost about the location of the door, or a maiden in seclusion

PLATE XLVII

 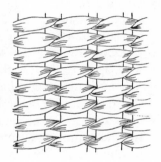

KAROK BASKET HAT

This hat was made to fit the woman's head closely so that the pressure
of the carrying-basket strap was lessened. Close-twined technique. The
foundation is of finely split hazel sticks, with California redwood roots as the
main sewing element. In this cap the decoration was made by laying an
extra weft of different material against and parallel to the main sewing
element. These materials are white grass (*Xerophyllum tenax*), maidenhair
fern (*Adiantum pedatum*), and yellow dyed porcupine quills. The hat is
about 4 inches deep. (From O'Neale, 1932.)

might flirt with her lover. Inside, the house was arranged like an Iroquois dwelling, with its raised cubicles for families along the sides.
From the rafters hung drying fish, and along the earthen floor blazed
fires, surrounded by cooking baskets.[8] Farther north, houses would be
even larger and perhaps fronted by a carved crest, while in California
they were reduced to a conical frame of logs over an excavation. The

equipment was mostly of wood, supplemented by reeds and grass. Men, helped by visions and ritual, worked the wood, which responded even to a stone adz and a beaver-tooth chisel, while sewing with roots or sinew took the place of nails. They made dugout canoes of a dozen types, for river travel, freighting, fishing, and sea travel. Those of the Nootka, traded down the coast, were thirty feet long and fit to chase a whale far out to sea. The Inland tribes of this chapter used baskets for stone boiling, and their wood-carving was in simple human and animal shapes, often beautifully polished but unpainted. Rarely did they steam, bend, and sew wood into cooking boxes like the Maritime tribes, and neither did they make huge feast dishes in the shape of an animal split down the back or belly.[9]

Puget Sound women, however, had one art which belonged particularly to the Salish and which has puzzled students because there is nothing like it for hundreds of miles around. They wove blankets on a loom.[10] True, the apparatus was a very simple one, with roller top and bottom, made and threaded differently from the looms of the Southwest (see Pl. LIII). The warp was goat wool and the weft a white fluff as thick as a finger. It was made of mountain-goat hair and milkweed fiber, but more often of dog wool. Herds of little white dogs were owned by women and kept separate from other dogs on islands in Puget Sound. When a group moved to its fishing grounds for the summer, a woman drove her dogs along like sheep.

These coast dwellers were a pompous people, more given to personal publicity than even the Indians of the Plains. Shall we consider that a result of wealth and opportunity? At any rate, even their family life cannot be described without some reference to the potlatch—the great give-away feast from which this chapter is named. We know the give-away of the Plains and have, perhaps, seen its germ in the Eat-It-All feast of the Algonkian. Neither could approach in extravagance the feasting and distribution of gifts of the Northwest. Or shall we say "gift investment," since the value of any gift must be returned, sometimes with interest? From the time when an infant was strapped to his cradleboard with a pad of cedar bark tied over his forehead to give it a pointed shape, his parents began saving toward the potlatches to be given on his behalf. There was one when the child cut his first tooth, when he first ate solid food, when his ears were pierced, and when a boy caught his first little fish or a tiny girl picked a few berries.

It was an excellent teaching practice for the old men or old women to sing the young worker's praises and so stimulate him to further ef-

PLATE XLVIII

RED
YELLOW
BROWN

STOLLER

KLIKITAT BASKET

Commonly called a "berry" basket, these pack or storage containers are made by coiling bundles of split white cedar roots (*Thuja plicata*) and by sewing the coils with the same material. The design is made by imbrication (small diagram), from the Latin word *imbrex*, "tile." It is accomplished by folding the material back and catching it under the structural stitch. Squaw grass (*Xerophyllum sp.*) is dyed red, yellow, brown, and black to form the designs. This one is 18 inches high. (From Mason, 1902.)

fort. Doubtless it was a fine object lesson to have goods given away in his name instead of presents being made to him as in the white man's culture. Still, one of the essential attitudes of the white man's culture was there. Even though the way to pre-eminence lay not through hoarding but through giving, the child was early imbued with the idea that pre-eminence was necessary. Like any modern businessman, he must get to the top.

Hereditary privileges would help, and the Coast people acknowledged many such, especially at the north. An elaborate society like theirs, where much of the routine work was done by slaves, could afford specialists who practiced only one craft and were well paid for it. Whaling and other sea hunting, carpentry, canoe-making, wood-carving—all were handed down in families. A youth who had some relative to teach him must spend years learning not only the craft itself but the rituals which insured its success. Even with such a start, he should not try to learn unless a vision had empowered him to do so. Coastal youths, therefore, went out for visions as strenuously as any of their neighbors, sleeping in weird places, jumping into cold streams, and scratching themselves with thorny branches. Even in visions the rich man's son had the advantage. He was usually helped to find the same spirit as some older relative or to join a select society of spirit protégés. A poor or visionless lad could be reduced to routine fishing. A slave was not expected to have visions at all, and, when such a thing happened, it made news—which is to say, a place in the mythology.

Girls rarely had visions, unless they were to become shamans, and this often did not happen until later life. The duty of the average girl was to be modest and home-keeping, so that she could make a good marriage. In this culture, where wealth, owned by men, was the important thing, the bride was expected to come to her husband well dowered and a virgin. Therefore, as she neared adolescence, she was constantly chaperoned. The daughter of a prominent man, being especially valuable, never left the house alone. Although she must show her industry by gathering clams and berries, she was always attended by female slaves. At maturity, she had a strenuous seclusion which might last a year. For part of the time she was confined in a cubicle of the big house, eating and drinking very little (which would insure plenty of food in her later life) and touching her head only with a scratching stick.[11] Sometimes old women came to sing to her about the joys of marriage.

Suitors, of course, knew about the girl's wealth, and they and their

PLATE XLIX

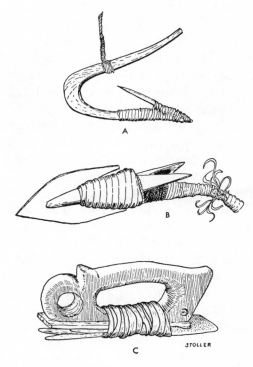

Halibut Hook, Whale Harpoon, and Nootka Adz

a) The fishhook of the Kwakiutl is made of fir driftwood and has a bone barb. The wood is steamed into shape, and chewed tallow is rubbed into the heated surface. It is cooled again, and the barb is affixed with twisted spruce-root fibers. Two such hooks are hung by cedar-bark cords to a cross-piece, and this is tied to a strong kelp rope. They are hung over the side of a boat in very deep water. A piece of bait is put on the barb, and the fish grabs the lower part of the hook with its mouth to take the bait and is caught on the barb. About 8½ inches long. (From Boas, 1909.)

b) The two large halves of antler or bone are joined over the blade of mussel-shell and bone barbs with wrappings of cherry bark and then coated with spruce gum. Several of these heads are taken along on a hunt and are kept in a cherry- or cedar-bark sheath. The 12–14-inch heads are fastened to a 14-foot shaft with nettle fiber string in such a manner that they will come off in the animal. A lanyard is fastened to the shaft and in turn to a bladder float. The lanyard is made of whale sinew rope wrapped spirally with nettle fiber string. (From Waterman, 1920.)

c) The flat blade is made of soft serpentine stone fastened to a handle of willow with cedar withes. A small cedar wedge is put between the handle and blade, at the back, to protect the blade and to tighten it during use. This blade is 7½ inches long. (From Boas, 1909.)

families considered the match as carefully as any crowned heads of Europe. When a suitor arrived with his gifts, he might sit at the house door for days, proving his worth and patience, while the whole household insulted him and sent him on errands. If he was admitted, he and the father bargained, and he might have to send home several times for more skins, canoes, and fish oil. The wedding involved a grand feast, with many goods given away in the girl's name. Then she went to her husband's canoe, sometimes walking all the way on skins or other wealth which were to be her dowry.

The husband might take several more wives, paying for each, even though they were sisters of the first. All would help him accumulate wealth by making baskets, weaving blankets if they were in the right area, or even drying clams to be used for trade with people farther inland. Divorce was unlikely, no matter what troubles came up, for too much wealth had been exchanged. The families of both husband and wives would try to smooth over any quarrels. Especially in a chief's family this meant loss of dignity, which could not be endured.

The northwesterners had that fear of the returning of the dead which we have heard of before, but here they took extreme measures against it. In some places the whole house was torn down, so the ghost could not return home. To avoid this expense, a dying person was often taken outside. Failing that, some of the wallboards might be lifted and the dead carried out that way. The ghost would turn away foiled. It was dangerous to touch a dead body, and those who performed funeral rites must be purified afterward. Around Puget Sound the apprehensive relatives turned the work over to special corpse handlers who went through a purification as strenuous as that of a southwestern warrior. We remember the practices something like this among the Navaho. Instead of a grave, the body was often laid in a canoe, raised on supports out of the reach of marauding animals. Northerners, who made handsome wooden boxes, used these for coffins and placed them in trees or caves. Gifts were laid beside them, and perhaps a slave was killed to do service in the next world. Then the name of the dead must not be uttered, perhaps for a year, perhaps until all his near kin had joined him. If the name were composed of common words, such as Black Bear, even these must be avoided. The animal would have to be spoken of as "the one of the color of night who walks on his hind legs."

It is plain from the above that, in the Northwest society, all men were neither free nor equal. Classes of rich and poor had developed,

PLATE L

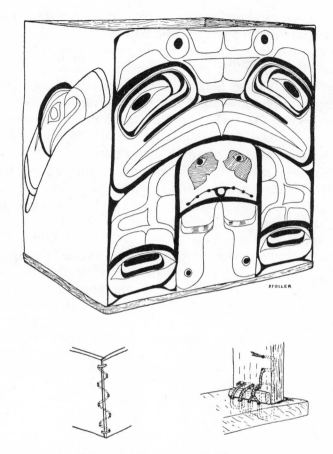

WOODEN BOX OF THE HAIDA

These storage boxes were made by shaping and thinning a board of suitable length to form the four sides. A V groove was cut at the corners. These grooved sections were then steamed until the boards could be bent to right angles. The two ends of the box were drawn together and the edges pegged or sewn with spruce root (small diagrams). A solid bottom was made, with a groove to receive the edges; this was also sewed or pegged into place. The box was then tied securely with cord until dry and "set." The Haida are known as the best carvers, and this totemic design in black and red is a fine example of their art. (From Inverarity, 1950.)

as they often do when there is surplus wealth for the ambitious to gather in. Rich men were those who had inherited wealth, made wise marriages, or had large families of industrious wives and children who had boosted them to the top. In the North there were even what might be called "noble" families whose ancestral myths went back to "the beginning of the world" and were symbolized on house posts and totem poles. On the other hand, a commoner sometimes managed to amass wealth and attain a fine name. To begin with, he was probably a poor relative of a rich man or an orphan with no family to help him. He might live in the rich man's house, doing the routine work and running errands, while the rich man in return would support him and purchase his bride. In the end, a fortunate vision and skill at craft or war might send him up the ladder.

Only slaves could not hope to improve their position. These were members of another tribe, or perhaps only another village, who had been taken in raids. The northwesterners indulged in no such wasteful practice as torturing captives to death. They had food to support a staff of servants and work for them to do, so they captured all the women and children they could (men were too difficult), or they bought them from other raiding tribes. Among the Yurok of Cali-

PLATE LI

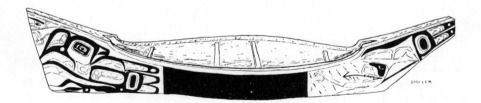

HAIDA CANOE

Although this model is only 16 inches long, it is an excellent copy of the Haida type of canoe. These seaworthy craft are usually more than 60 feet in length. The whole log is floated to the working place and then is charred with a torch and scraped with an adz again and again until it is the desired thickness and shape. At times the men will drill a hole through the sides to see if the thickness is right. They polish the outside with sharkskin to make it slip easily through the water. The two-dimensional totemic designs are carved and painted on the prow and stern. (From the Denver Art Museum Collections, on loan from Indian Arts and Crafts Board.)

fornia a man could even offer himself as a slave in payment for debt. Slaves were treated like members of the family, unless it was necessary to bury one under a house post or kill him at his master's grave. They could also be ransomed, but after this it was necessary to give a potlatch in order to remove the shame. Stories tell of one prominent chief who allowed his wife to remain a slave for life. He could have rescued her but could not afford the necessary potlatch.

A chief was a powerful man, yet he gained his eminence neither by heredity, war exploits, nor election. He was simply the richest man in the community, which was probably an aggregation of his relatives. He owned the big house in which the others lived and the fishing weirs and stations, the whaling or war canoes, by which they got their livelihood. People clustered around him like retainers around a lord in the Middle Ages, because that was their only way to livelihood and security. In some tribes he appointed one of them a speaker to take charge of potlatch etiquette, and another a war leader, unless he performed that function himself.[12] Or he might choose likely young men to perform at dances, always paid with gifts. Some villages had several rich men, with one pre-eminent, or a number of related villages might maintain a loose alliance. There was no head chief, and the village "boss" had no responsibility, except to remain popular with his retainers so as to get good service and with neighboring chiefs so as to further his financial plans. The chief, like a modern millionaire, could lose his position of influence if he lost his wealth. Therefore, he must be ambitious and thrifty. He must keep the goal of wealth before him so clearly that the whole system sometimes looks like a parody of our modern economic life or a diagram roughed out on simple lines so that the essentials stand out.

Wealth usually meant blankets, baskets, skins, shells, dried fish and fish oil, and certain peculiarly shaped copper plates which may or may not have been imported. In California the prized objects were obsidian blades, the skins of albino deer, and the bright feathers of small birds, like the woodpecker and yellow warbler. In addition, all the Northwest used a form of shell money which should not be called wampum. It was the conical dentalium, about two inches long, which was fished up by the Nootka of Vancouver Island and strung on strings of standard length. These "money beads" were traded up and down the coast and far inland. They were used in all ceremonial exchanges and often in trade, though blankets, furs, or slaves could be bartered direct. A string of the little white beads was as meaningful to an Indian as a bag of gold used to be to the whites. Yurok (California) boys were advised to think about dentalium all the time and to imagine that they saw the shells along the trail. At night they would weep and call out for the spirits to hear: "I want to be rich. I wish dentalia."[13]

Dentalia, and, in fact, all wealth, were thought to abhor women, and the man who was out to succeed must go through long periods of continence. Also he must not eat too much, and, above all, he must work. The virtues of industry and thrift, the wickedness of being

PLATE LII

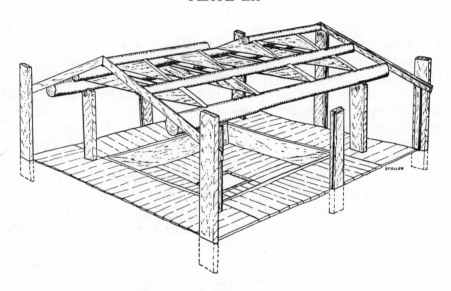

FRAMEWORK OF A CHILKAT DWELLING

In olden times these houses were erected entirely without nails, all the different parts being grooved and fitted so as to support one another. Spruce or other trees were felled and adzed to uniformity for the framework; these were grooved to receive the planks, which were laid horizontally on the sides and back and vertically in front of the house. Inside were two floor levels. The central part was earth-floored and had a fireplace with a smoke hole above; it was the general living area. A wooden platform around the house walls gave an upper level for sleeping and storage. Four pillars were spaced about the upper level and were carved with heraldic devices. Between the two rear pillars was the great carved screen of the chief. In the lower part of the screen was an opening leading to the chief's apartment. Some of the houses were more than 50 feet square. (From Shotridge, 1913.)

PLATE LIII

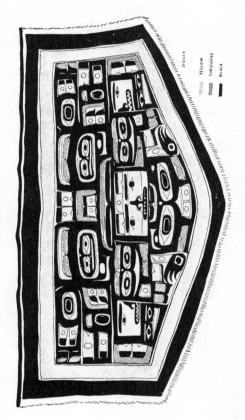

Chilkat Blanket

Twined wool from the mountain goat and cedar-bark warp were used in making this blanket. The loom, an enlarged version of a sawhorse (poles supported a cross-piece), had no bottom piece, and the warp hung free or was tied in bundles to keep the threads from tangling. Black, yellow, and green were dyed with fungus and minerals and were combined with natural white to make the two-dimensional, highly conventionalized, bird design. The weaving was done by the women, but the designs were copied from a pattern board painted by the men. These designs are now so symbolic of the actual body parts that they are no longer clearly recognizable. However, the human face in the center represents the body of the bird, the two double eyes near the top are the eyes of the bird (joints are represented by eyes in Northwest art); each set of figures represents some duplicating part of the bird, such as legs, feet, wings, etc. The blanket is 65 inches long and 47 inches wide. (From Emmons, 1913.)

dreamy and unambitious, were impressed upon the young northwest-
erner quite as much as upon the white American. If he were the son
or nephew of an expert in some particular craft, his career was assured.
All the skilled occupations, such as whaling, seal-hunting, elk-hunting,
wood-carving, and canoe-making, required ritual knowledge as well
as manual skill. The boy must first dream that he would be able to
do the work and then undergo years of training. Ultimately, he might
own a whaling canoe and act as harpooner, bringing back blubber and
oil for a distinguished feast. Or he could qualify as carpenter, boat-
builder, or wood-carver and be paid publicly at a potlatch. He might
follow his chief to war and bring back a captive or even venture out
with a few bold comrades in a small canoe. Failing all these, he could
work hard at routine fishing, with net, spear, or hook. If he could
not collect enough for a potlatch of his own, he could make a few
gifts at his chief's potlatch and begin to earn credit.

Every career was punctuated with gift-giving, on minor as well as
major occasions. The modern custom of tipping is a mild burden
compared to the constant small gifts which an ambitious man must
hand out when invited to a feast, when seated wrongly, when he
stumbled, when his name was mentioned, or when he danced. Chiefs
going to a feast usually wore three or four blankets which they could
hand out, as a modern takes money from his pocket. The potlatch
proper was the give-away at which a prominent man might beggar
himself in order to establish his position. He would in time get back
in return feasts the full value of what he had given.

A potlatch by an important chief required years of preparation,
with formal visits of invitation by the chief himself or his speaker. At
least this was so with the Quinault, who were close to the Maritime
people and had acquired some of their formality. The Quinault feast-
giver would appoint (and pay) members of his family to supervise the
cooking and to cut up meat, while a special tallyman kept a bundle
of sticks, each representing a particular guest and the gift he was to
receive. When the great day came, the guests arrived in canoes and
paddled up and down in front of the village singing. They were es-
corted to the house, where several days were spent in singing and
dancing by both parties, varied by athletic games. Guests and family
were feasted daily upon dried fish, clams, berries, and fish oil, with
cedar bark for napkins, and everything must be eaten before the guests
departed.

Finally, the gifts were distributed with as much protocol as at a modern diplomatic dinner, each guest being called up in the order of his rank and appropriately honored. If the gift was too small, he might drag it along the ground to show his scorn. When everything was gone, the host folded up his last blanket and asked the company, "Who wishes to take it?" This was a challenge for someone to give the next potlatch, and, to avoid the disgrace of seeming stingy, some visitor would be sure to accept it. He would try, if possible, to do better than his host in order to win greater credit.

A rich man might give only two or three feasts of this sort during a lifetime, though there were smaller ones after a birth, a death, a child's first achievements, or the coming of spirit power. If we should go farther north among the Maritime tribes, we should find greater and greater display with boasting of the host's greatness which sometimes amounted to an insult for his guests.[14] Among these northern tribes the Nootka and Bella Coola say that the return gift need be no greater than the gift received, but the Kwakiutl of Vancouver Island demanded double the value or 100 per cent interest. Such definite counting is unusual for Indians, and one questions whether even greater wealth would account for it. Perhaps, since this extravagant form of the potlatch is admittedly recent, we may suspect white influence and particularly that of the Hudson's Bay Company, which exacted double return for loans of guns and traps made to Indians.

Whatever may be said on that score, it is plain that wealth and the display of wealth characterized the whole coastal strip. However, as we go south from the Quinault, we find the potlatch less formal until, in Oregon and California, it includes no donations whatever. Here there was a yearly dance "to keep the world in order," in which the dancers carried valuable objects such as albino deerskins, obsidian blades, or feather headbands belonging to some prominent man. The whole object was to display this wealth, while religious aims seem to have fallen into the background.[15]

War was not of great importance to the tribes of this chapter. Their Maritime fringe, the Quinault, Quileute, and Makah, did go forth in canoes to raid an enemy village, wearing a sleeveless elkskin shirt as protection against arrows or sometimes a barrel-like arrangement of upright wooden slats. They even brought home heads to stick on poles outside their villages. (Heads are as easy to carry as scalps when there is canoe transportation.) They still tell tales of dragging their canoes at night up some hidden inlet, then throwing torches on the roof of a house so that the inmates would rush out the narrow door, where they clubbed them. Houses faced the water, but most had a back door facing the forest, and by that the women and children were trained to flee. Such attacks were infrequent and only a faint imitation of the more bloodthirsty northern tribes, who paddled their seagoing canoes far down the Pacific Coast to capture slaves for use or barter. Tribes of this chapter took captives less frequently but obtained them in trade.

For the tribes of Puget Sound and farther south, war took the shape of intervillage feuds, perhaps over a murder or suspected witchcraft. Often the fight was decided on beforehand to settle a dispute. The volunteer warriors, under their chosen "brave man," danced to work up their enthusiasm, then spent the night making magic against the enemy and taking omens to know who would be killed. One who received such a death notice left the war party and went home. The engagement was usually a brief one, ending in elaborate peace negotiations. Neutral envoys were sent out from each side, and, one by one, they totted up every killing, injury, or property loss perpetrated by either one. Each damage was paid for separately, in shell money, and, after the final dance and ceremony, it is obvious that the victor came out the loser. The killers, too, were losers, for here, as in the Southwest, there was profound fear of the enemy's ghost. Enemy slayers were treated very much like murderers,[16] dancing a purification dance, undergoing various taboos, and finally being purified by a man who had learned sacred rituals.

Much the same treatment was given a murderer. We have noted before that these River and Bay tribes seem particularly sensitive to supernatural danger, so the murderer, like the corpse handler, was secluded and took the purifying baths. Often, he had diet taboos, ate out of special dishes, and was not free until he had performed a purification dance and both he and his weapons had been cleansed by the recitation of ritual. Then, unless he wished to have a feud started, he must settle with the victim's family. About this there was more or less formality, but the Yurok of California, who seem to have been particularly money-conscious, had a fixed price in shell money for every injury, from murder down to an unintentional arrow wound. Even damage to property in Yurok territory was paid for, and property was not only arrows and fish traps but songs and ceremonial privileges. It was valued, not on a fixed scale, but according to the status of the owner, the rights of men and chiefs counting for more than those of women or poor people. So a man who had trespassed or allowed his women to trespass in any way must arrange payment or be outlawed from Yurok society.

People as conscious of property as the northwesterners, of course, engaged in commerce. There was much trade up and down the coast, especially in dentalium. Canoes also went up the Columbia to the yearly fair held on Wishram territory, where coast products were exchanged for inland ones. In this way many ideas and ceremonies also passed to and fro. These trading customs were a great convenience when the whites came and the Chinook at the mouth of the Columbia became middlemen, bringing furs from inland to the ships.

The religion of the Northwest is as dramatic as their secular customs and sometimes as much involved with rank and privilege. They believed in an original world which was out of shape and put in order by the Transformer, who was sometimes Raven, sometimes Robin, Blue Jay, or Mink, all noticeably clever creatures. Just as in the Plateau, the animals, earth's original inhabitants, were able to give visions. They lived in villages, like the northwesterners themselves, and, among the Salish tribes, after a man had bathed and lacerated himself, they might take him to the Wolf village in the forest or the Salmon village under the sea, where they gave songs, dances, and a magic token. Salish even had a wealth spirit, represented by people in a canoe who looked as though coming to a potlatch.

Some Salish had a most practical idea about spirit help. It would be promised a boy after his youthful fasting but would not show itself until he had worked hard to attain the skill or the wealth the vision had promised. If, then, he was not successful, he could simply decide he had seen a false spirit. Probably, however, the spirit arrived, and in some tribes it even came with no preliminary vision. The time was always winter, for the Salish had decided that in summer, when everyone was busy fishing, the spirits were on the other side of the earth. In winter, when there was leisure for their entertainment, they made themselves known by an illness which attacked each spirit protégé in turn. One who had received his spirit before knew the trouble and began to sing his spirit song, perhaps continuing for days. A new visionary fell ill, and the medicine man easily diagnosed the trouble. He gathered the sufferer's friends around him, and they all listened to the spirit song as it issued from his lips. Soon all had learned it and could help him sing at the feast which he must give. It has been mentioned that potlatches were given on the occasion of first spirit return, and, with the more northerly of the River and Bay people,

these were important occasions. The person undergoing this visita-
tion would have painted boards made according to the spirit's direction and would have his face painted. Then in the big shadowy house
he would dance wildly and sing his song, friends following to help
him and to see that, in his excitement, he did not jump into the fire
or rush against the house posts. Even today, at the Swinomish community house, dreamers dance once a year when their spirit protec-
tors arrive! No spectator can forget the low moans which they give as
they feel the power approaching or their tranced look as they dance
around the blazing fires.

Among the Maritime tribes to the north there were even more
impressive performances, with masks and mimetic drama. Such tribes
had societies of people who had seen the same spirit, such as the
Wolf or Cannibal Monster. There were vestiges of the same arrangement in the Maritime fringe. However, these societies were dying
out even fifteen years ago.

South of the state of Washington—and of the Salish-speaking
people—the belief in a guardian spirit for everyone died away. In this
area it was only the medicine man or, more often, medicine woman
who gained spirit help, but it came as just described, through a
mysterious illness.[17] In Oregon the aspirant for doctor power sweated
and trained before an older shaman finally shot into his or her body
the magic crystal or "pain" which would dwell there forever after and
give the ability to suck out illness. A dance among older shamans initiated the new doctor into his or her profession. Northwestern California preferred women doctors, who also had their visions unsought
but bathed, sweated, received instruction, and took part in a public
shaman's dance before becoming members of the curing profession.

In such a crossways of culture as the Northwest, we might expect
many different ideas as to the cause of disease, and that is the case.
That ancient idea of the foreign object which must be sucked out
was a common one. Then there was failure in ritual, a frequent
danger, considering the number of taboos to be observed in all kinds
of work. Finally, there was loss of the soul, a belief especially strong
in the Northwest and in near-by Asia. Shamans around Puget Sound
made a mock-voyage in a canoe to the land of the dead where people
walked with their legs crossed. They retrieved the strayed soul after
some difficulty and perhaps the souls of others who were not yet ill
enough to be aware of their loss. These were returned through the
crown of the head. Still other practitioners owned knowledge of heal-

ing herbs and the formulas for their use. Such formulas were bought or inherited and required no vision at all. The beginning of a modern medical practice!

We have mentioned the taboos of daily life. These brought all people constantly in touch with the spirit world, which allowed them their food and health. The northwesterners, like other Indians, had reconciled themselves to killing their benefactors, the animals, by the belief that these did not really die but left their clothing of flesh and went back to the village where they lived like human beings. If the flesh were properly treated (for instance, not cut with a white man's knife) and if the bones were collected and thrown into the water, the salmon would reclothe itself in its fish body and come again to serve mankind. If any bones were missing, so that it was crippled, or if dogs—or women who should be in seclusion—were allowed to touch it, the salmon run would stop. The same practice applied to other food animals. One is inclined to believe that this respect for the dead animal's "clothing" may be a very old hunter's custom.

Besides these duties of individual hunters and fishers, the Northwest had a series of ceremonies to sanctify the first eating of important foods. We have seen such ceremonies in the Southwest applied to corn, berries, and other wild foods. Here they were used for salmon and herring. Often a prayer and a ritual cooking were enough, but the prayer was offered by a regular officiant who had learned his formula. It meant a religious attitude different from that of the excited vision-seeker and probably with dissimilar tradition. Those who performed it possessed the germs of a priesthood, and so did those who owned inherited formulas for good luck and simple curing. These were passed down in families, mostly by the women, and were even sold.

This sketch does little justice to the wealth of ceremonial and the great range of practices regarding wealth and war which grew up in the vigorous little societies of the Northwest. They were as well developed, in their own way, as the Five Civilized Tribes of our Southeast, who withstood transplantation and are producing successful American citizens. However, there was no way to transplant fishermen when their territories were wanted. The Northwest culture had to give way, and a few of its members are now, one by one, climbing up again.

Vitus Bering, of Bering Strait fame, discovered the Aleut and some Alaska Indians in 1741. Thereupon followed years when the sea otter was being exterminated around the Aleutian Islands as ruthlessly as the buffalo on the Plains. A Russian fur-trading empire was managed from Sitka, even though the Tlingit, who lived near by, rebelled manfully. It endured from 1799 to 1867, when Alaska was bought by the United States.

The other coastal Indians did not come under Russian domination. During the late 1700's they were visited by ships, Russian and Spanish, and they learned to trade such furs as they had on hand for bits of iron and copper. Very likely also there were unrecorded wrecks or landings of craft from China, Japan, and the Pacific islands. None of these made much impression until George Vancouver came to explore the coast for England, and Robert Gray, the American sea captain, entered the mouth of the Columbia. The Chinook, who dominated that region, immediately took charge of trade with the foreigners, bringing in the furs of other tribes and demanding toil, such as the Huron and Iroquois had done in the East. (We pause to note here that Indians have been consistently accused of having no business sense. That statement applies only to business which they do not enjoy.) Then began what we have elsewhere named the "period of pleasant contact." It meant, as usual, an upsurge of artistic vigor, when the Indians used the new tools and materials to improve their own crafts while still their native lifeway went on as before. Ships continued to come from the Old World, bringing crews of all nations, but Yankee skippers, known as the "Bostons," were the chief traders. They sailed around the Horn with a cargo of nails, guns, kettles, cloth, and beads. On the Northwest Coast they exchanged this cargo for furs, sea otter if possible, otherwise beaver and smaller animals from inland. Thence they proceeded to Hawaii and China, where the furs were traded to good advantage for carved furniture, chinaware, and silks.

With the new tools, Indians could do larger and sharper carving, and it is from this period that we date the totem poles of the Maritime tribes. Brass kettles put an end to stone boiling; guns and traps, to laborious hunting with harpoon, bow, and ritual. Also they practically put an end to the fur animals. This was particularly true when the Hudson's Bay Company established its post at Fort Vancouver (outside present Seattle) and began to collect furs from hundreds of miles around. Their gray woolen "trade blankets" became the regular medium of exchange, and few Indians any longer appeared in bearskin or woven goat hair. The great company did not want dried salmon or fish oil, so many a man stopped producing these and took to hunting. As we have noticed in other areas, the hunters, when paid by whites, felt themselves under a new spirit power and gave up all ideas of conservation. They were ruining their own livelihood.

The new wealth, in some cases, became overpowering, for the Indians did not change their simple way of life. After a man had acquired enough blankets and utensils for his household, the company had nothing new to give him, and all he could buy was prestige at a potlatch. Potlatches became more frequent and extravagant, and it was perhaps at this period that the conspicuous waste made its appearance.[18]

The rank system, of course, felt the strain, for now any young commoner could join the crew of a schooner and come back with enough money to outdo the most famous potlatcher. The drop in population was extreme, owing to the new white man's diseases. Measles and scarlet fever, against which the Indians had no immunity, killed off thousands, especially since the only remedy known to the red man was to take a violent sweat, then plunge into cold water. Rich families died out, commoners came to the fore, and the whole system tottered.

It did not fall until Indians were actually forced to live under white dominance. This happened at various times in the different regions beginning with what is now Washington and Oregon. The covered wagons reached Oregon's fertile Willamette Valley in 1842. Then came the influx of settlers, bent, not on buying furs from the Indians, but on clearing the land and establishing towns, mills, and railroads. Oregon had a territorial government in 1848; Washington, in 1853. In 1854 the Indians of this region and near-by Canada were hustled into agreements which placed them on reservations. Often these did not include their old fishing and gathering grounds, and sections of them fought a hopeless war for the next fifteen years. Finally, a small number went to the reservations which had been set up, but many more lost themselves among the whites.

It was time for a consoling vision. The cult of Smohalla,[19] which was so influential in the Plateau, had, indeed, given rise to a whole succession of dreamers in the Columbia Valley. Still they preached a complete ignoring of the white man and all his ways, and this was growing less and less possible. In 1881 John Slocum, a Squaxon of Puget Sound, "died" and saw God, then revived to found the Shaker church, which is active today.[20] This time, there was no promise that the whites would disappear. Instead, the Indians were told that they must give up wickedness and become Christians, receiving miraculous rewards. Gradually there developed a ceremony which was a combination of the old Spirit Dance with a Christian church service. It involved shaking or perhaps dancing when overcome with holy power, and it even gave ability to cure. Also its members must believe in Christ and God and must not drink, smoke, or gamble. In a way, this combined trance and ceremony constituted a bridge between the Indian's old practices and the new religion which was so strange to him. However, the whites would allow no compromise. Forgetting that their own ancestors had once celebrated the birth of Christ with a heathen solstice fire, they had one of the leaders arrested and put in chains. However, since the Shakers are law-abiding and industrious, they have now been allowed to organize and to conduct their services in peace. The religion has spread into British Columbia, Oregon, and California.

Economically a number of Indians on reservations are doing well, farming, attending to the leasing of their allotted lands, and owning at least one community fish trap. They belong to various modern churches besides that of the Shakers, and some groups hold the old Spirit Dance once a year.

The Indians of northern California and southern Oregon were spared the white influx a little longer than their neighbors, since they were not in the country of the gold rush or of the first covered-wagon settlers. As settlement spread, however, they were pushed out with little perception that they had human rights. They received reservations in the 1860's and in the 1870's were swept by an early form of the Ghost Dance; thereafter there was a succession of dreamers and religious movements, At present they are on the reservations listed (Table 12), living much like whites, though some semblance of the ancient ceremonies exists. The Klamath, whose reservation included excellent timber, have grown rich from lumber leases, and their problem is how to use their affluence effectively in white life.

TABLE 12

Present Reservations and Numbers of Northwest Indians

Tribe	State and Agency	Population, 1945
	California: Hoopa Valley Agency	3,556
	Hoopa Valley Reservation	1,639
Hoopa.............		636
Karok.............		42
Yurok.............		957
	California: Quartz Valley Reservation	51
Karok.............		46
Shasta.............		5
	Oregon: Grand Ronde-Siletz Agency	1,785
	Grand Ronde Reservation	489
Clackamas.........		89
Rogue River.......		44
Umpqua...........		79
Other tribes.......		277
	Oregon: Siletz Reservation	561
Chastacosta........		20
Galice Creek.......		10
Joshua............		43
Klamath...........		64
Maguenodon.......		39
Rogue River.......		121
Tutuni............		17
Other tribes........		202
	Oregon: Fourth Section Allottees	708
	(public domain)	11
Klamath...........		119
Kusa..............		228
Rogue River.......		120
Tutuni............		28
Umpqua...........		70
Other tribes........		204
	Oregon: Klamath Agency and Reservation	1,547
Klamath...........		937
Modoc............		329
Paiute............		151
Pit River..........		123
	Washington: Taholam Agency	3,125
	Chehalis Reservation	27
	Makah Reservation	453
	Nisqually Reservation	60
	Ozette Reservation	1
	Quinaielt Reservation	1,822
Chehalis...........		105
Quileute...........		281
Quinaielt..........		1,293
Upper Chinook......		120
Other tribes........		22
	Washington: Skokomish Reservation	233
Clallam............		1
Skokomish.........		233
	Washington: Squaxin Island Reservation	529
Squaxin...........		29
Other tribes........		500
	Washington: Tulalip Agency	4,245
Lummi.............	Lummi Reservation	761
Muckleshoot.......	Muckleshoot Reservation	253
Suquamish.........	Port Madison Reservation	177
	Puyallup Reservation	470
Swinomish.........	*Washington:* Swinomish Reservation	336
Snohomish.........	Tulalip Reservation	736
Clallam............	Public domain	1,000
Nooksak...........	Public domain	269
Skagit.............	Public domain	243

RIVER AND BAY TRIBES OF WASHINGTON

FOOD

Vegetable.—Roots, wild greens, berries, seaweed, bulbs (especially camass), nuts.

Animal.—Fish, sea mammals (whales for Makah, Quileute, and Quinault), moose, shellfish, deer, birds, small game, mountain goat (for Skokomish).

HUNTING METHOD

Fish: traps, nets, harpoons, hooks, spears, weirs. Animal: calls, bow and arrow, traps, deadfalls, harpoons, snares. Bird: nets, traps, bow and arrow.

CLOTHING

Male.—Very little usually. Poncho-like fiber rain capes, robes of whole bearskin, fur, feather, and skin. Some imported buckskin from Inland tribes. Basket hats. Tattooing.

Female.—Basketry hats; shredded, fringed cedar-bark or goat-wool skirts; conical rain capes; sometimes sleeveless jackets of fiber or goat hair.

HOUSE TYPES

Gabled plank houses, walls pegged or tied together. Boards vertical or horizontal. Plank roof. Compartments for chief and families. Sweat houses for men and women. Some female segregation.

EQUIPMENT

Household.—Basketry: twilled, coiled, imbricated and overlay; for cooking, storage, gathering, burden. Cattail mats; some wooden dishes, boxes, and spoons. House posts and grave posts.

Transportation.—Canoes: wooden dugouts for travel, war, and hunting.

Hunting.—Simple and sinew-lined bows; arrows, clubs, and spears.

Other.—Cradle: hollowed-out wooden box, also coffin-shaped imbricated basket, cradleboards; head-flattening. Pipe: tubular wood, stone bowls with wood stem. Miscellaneous: many stone tools for woodworking, adz, and wedge. Drums, wooden box or skin head, plank in floor, long poles for hitting roof beams. Rattles, whistles, bull-roarers, shell money, masks, true weaving.

WAR

Not so aggressive as Maritime tribes. Some raiding; took heads. Slat armor.

GAMES

Shinny, hoop-and-pole, hand-and-stick games, hidden ball, wrestling, tug of war, ring-and-pin, races, tops, cat's cradle.

RIVER AND BAY TRIBES OF OREGON AND NORTHWEST CALIFORNIA

FOOD

Vegetable.—Acorns, the staple. Seeds, wild greens, berries, pine nuts, fungus, seaweed (especially for salt).

Animal.—Deer, rabbits, birds, rodents, shellfish, salmon, elk in Oregon, fish.

HUNTING METHOD

Fish: nets, weirs, pens, traps, hooks, scaffolds, harpoons. Animal: fences, run-down, deadfalls, bow and arrow, deer whistle, brush fires, bird snares and traps.

CLOTHING

Male.—Usually very little. Caps of fur. Deerhide robes, skin breechcloths and aprons, leggings in winter; two-piece moccasins (upper of deerskin, sole of elk). Headdresses of bird scalps and hoops of stuffed deerskin. Flowing headnets. Tule-mat rain capes. Arm and hand tattooing marks for measuring dentalium strings.

Female.—Twined basketry caps, fiber string aprons. Fore and aft aprons of skin, front decorated with seeds, back with shell below hips. Skin robes. Tattooing on chin.

HOUSE TYPES

Low, conical-roofed plank houses with side entrance. Camp shelters, dome-shaped, brush or grass thatch. Male sweat house. Some female segregation.

EQUIPMENT

Household.—Basketry: twined, with quill and grass overlay. For eating, serving, stone boiling, seed-beating, winnowing, storage, mortars. Spoons of horn, mussel shell, and wood. Some wood platters and hollowed-out chests.

Transportation.—Dugout canoes.

Hunting.—Self-bow, sinew-backed bow; arrows, spears.

Other.—Cradle: sitting type of basketry. Pipe: tubular wood, some with mortised stone bowl. Miscellaneous: wood foot drum; rectangular rawhide drum (Oregon). Stick-clappers, deer-hoof rattle, whistles, flutes. Horn and wooden wedge and adzes. Dentalium and clamshell disk money, decorated elkhorn purses.

WAR

Bow and arrows, clubs of wood and whale bone, elkhide armor, a few twined rod jackets. Surprise attacks; took heads and slaves. Tournaments.

GAMES

Shinny, archery, ring-and-pin in south, hand and many stick games, shell dice, tops, cat's cradle.

TRIBES OF THE POTLATCH-GIVERS

COAST OF WASHINGTON

Quinault: Salish stock, coast of Washington.
Quileute: Chemakum stock, possibly part of Algonkian-Wakasham.
Chehalis: Salish stock, coast of Washington.
Sanetch (East and West): Cowichan, with subdivision Nanaimo; Comox, with subdivisions Sechelt, Slaimum, Klahuse, and Holamco; Squamish: Small Salish groups living on the protected waters of the Gulf of Georgia, British Columbia, and Straits of Georgia and Juan de Fuca.

MAP IX

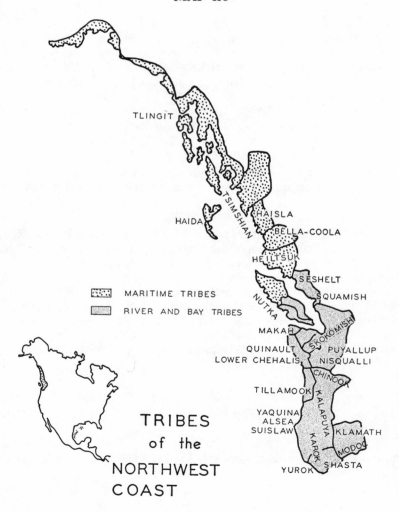

TLINGIT

TSIMSHIAN

HAIDA

HAISLA

BELLA-COOLA

HEILTSUK

SESHELT

SQUAMISH

NUTKA

▨▨▨ MARITIME TRIBES

▨▨▨ RIVER AND BAY TRIBES

MAKAH

SKOKOMISH

QUINAULT
LOWER CHEHALIS

PUYALLUP
NISQUALLI

CHINOOK

TILLAMOOK

KALAPUYA

YAQUINA
ALSEA
SUISLAW

KLAMATH

KAROK

MODOC

YUROK

SHASTA

TRIBES
of the
NORTHWEST
COAST

PUGET SOUND

Lummi, Samish, Swinomish, Skagit, Snohomish, Suquamish, Puyallup, Nis-qually, Twana: Small Salish groups, Puget Sound.

Klallam: Salish, Strait of Juan de Fuca.

Chemakum: Stock possibly related to Salish, Puget Sound.

OREGON

Chinook: Possibly related to Penutian, indefinite, mouth of Columbia River.

Chehalis, Tillamook: Salish, Lower Columbia River.

Yaquina, Alsea, Siuslaw: Possibly related to Chinook, Lower Columbia River.

Kalapuya: Possibly Penutian, Willamette Valley.

CALIFORNIA

Klamath: Possibly Penutian, northern California.

Yurok, Wiyot: Algonkian, northern California.

Hupa, Chilula, Tolowa: Athapascan, northern California.

Karok: Hokam, possibly related to Iroquoian-Siouan, northern California.

CHAPTER XIV.

Protective Uncle

A GROUP of European students were badgering their American professor with what they considered to be humiliating and, perhaps, unanswerable questions. The replies surprised not only the Europeans but also most of the Americans in the class.

What sort of passport must an Indian have to leave the reservation?
No passport. He comes and goes as he wishes.
Are any steps being taken toward making Indians citizens?
They have been citizens since 1924.
Why does not the government give them better houses and better food?
Except with some special treaties, the government has no obligation to house and feed Indians. They earn their livelihood like anyone else.
Aren't they given anything?
They receive social security benefits in the case of old age, blindness, and dependent children, just as all citizens do. A few tribes still have annual payments due them by treaty.
Well, when are you going to close the reservations and set them free?
As to closing the reservations, we should hope this will never happen, since this tax-free land was in the nature of payment to the Indians for other lands they ceded. As to freedom, social and economic, that depends considerably more on the attitude of their fellow-citizens than on any measures a government could take.

This discussion is typical of much that is being said and written about the Indian situation today, with its misinformation, misunderstanding, and careless distribution of blame. The Indian is not a prisoner, not forbidden citizenship, not deprived of rations due him. Nevertheless, a wrong has been done him—a wrong due to ignorance, to irresponsibility, and to a careless sort of kindness, unaccompanied by wisdom. It is in this failure to think, to plan, and patiently to carry out plans that the white man of the last few generations has been to blame. When one reads of thirty and forty millions spent in one year for the benefit of Indians, the accusation of cruelty is scarcely appropriate. But an accusation of unwisdom? That comes nearer the mark.

The fate of some individual tribes has been sketched in preceding chapters. Here we follow the history of government policy, from the first negotiations to the final assumption of intelligent responsibility for the betterment of one group of citizens. This slow growth could be divided into many periods, but in the interests of clarity these have been reduced to five, each connected with a stage in the nation's growth. Perhaps we may look forward to a sixth, when red men will merge on equal terms with their fellow-citizens.

I. COLONIAL PERIOD: WHITE DOMINANCE EXTENDS TO THE APPALACHIANS (ROUGHLY, 1607–1775)

In this period the seaboard tribes, treated as independent nations, were first conciliated by treaty, finally conquered. A few were placed on reservations by the provinces whose obligations were later taken over by states. The British government, in full command by the end of the period, established three Indian superintendents for the north, south, and middle of the area, their duties being to distribute promised gifts, supervise trade, and, in general, keep the peace.

In this and the next two periods the Indians were treated as sovereign nations, which could be handled only by treaty. The Dutch, a small nation, edging in among more powerful ones, set the example of paying for the land they occupied, and most of the English followed suit, even after receiving grants from the crown.[1] The Indians, whose activities were collective, who had plenty of land for roaming and no need for private ownership, considered that they were selling only the right to use the land, not its permanent possession, with all trespass forbidden. For this a small price, in goods rare and precious to them, was enough. They could not understand the land hunger of the whites, who had lived in something like a caste system, under landlords who could eject them at any time. Nor could they understand their demands for obedience to the white customs, which soon caused trouble. The two groups lived side by side, with frequent clashes, until the stronger ousted the weaker.

What should have been done for the weaker? A few centuries ago that question could not have been asked. The weaker would have been left to survive or perish, as the Saxons were under the Normans, or, in the eighteenth century, the Poles under Prussians, Austrians, and Russians. Indeed, for a time, the British colonists took this very attitude, making treaties with the conquered which demanded everything they could get and paying what they must in reserved land and rations. It was under this system that Maine, Virginia, and South Carolina set aside tax-free land for the tribes they could not elim-

inate and promised small yearly payments in food and goods, some
of which are continued to this day.[2]

II. WHITE DOMINATION EXTENDS TO THE MISSISSIPPI, AND INDIANS EAST OF THAT RIVER ARE REMOVED (1775–1845)

Eastern Indians, still treated as sovereign nations, were forced to sell more and
more land. Ultimately, most agreed to exchange lands east of the Mississippi
for others bought for them in the West. Meantime, western Indians, not yet
a menace to settlers, were conciliated, in an effort to win their trade from England, France, and Spain. At the beginning of the period the thirteen states retained the system of three superintendents, under a committee of Congress.
In 1786 these were changed to two. In 1789 a War Department was created,
with the supervision of the superintendents and other Indian affairs among its
duties. In 1824 a Bureau of Indian Affairs was organized within the War Department with a chief and two clerks. In 1832, when wholesale removal and
payment of Indians was going on, this small organization was enlarged to a Department of Indian Affairs, with a commissioner, clerks, agents, and subagents.
So originated today's Indian Office.

Indians were still treated as sovereign nations, but the cruelties
practiced on both sides in the French and Indian War and the sub-
sequent fighting with the Lakes and Prairie tribes (1794–1813)[3] and
the Creek[4] had swept away friendly attitudes on both sides. The Indians were now in a losing position. The list of their land cessions
beginning in 1784 presents a wearisome series of agreements by the
Iroquois and the tribes of the Southeast, the Lakes, and the Prairie,
each one reducing the holdings previously agreed to.[5] Voices were
raised against this injustice, George Washington's among them, but
the infant Congress was almost powerless. With little authority and
less funds, it was trying to weld a republic out of a growing number
of states, none of which felt permanently committed to union. Some
of those on the seaboard had land claims which theoretically extended to the Pacific and had ceded these to the federal government
on condition that Indians should be expelled from their accepted
boundaries. West of them, the flood of settlers, hacking their way
toward the Mississippi, were loud in their demands that the land
should be taken away from roving Indians and "given to those who
could use it." Hence the treaties put through by any device of force,
purchase, or chicanery.

The lands left to the Indians in each treaty were generally guaranteed them in perpetuity[6] or, in Indian terms, "as long as the grass
shall grow and the waters run." It seems a gesture of almost infantile
idealism on the part of a Congress which would be forgotten before
the grass had grown for many summers. Or did the lawmakers trust

that, even before that happened, the smallpox which was devastating the Indian tribes would kill them off? In any case, it was a promise fraught with trouble. Congress might have done better to adopt the uncompromising realism of British Canada, which, from the beginning, treated her Indians as subject people, obliged to take whatever was given them. As a result, Canadian Indians have been surprisingly peaceful and received more than they expected. On the other side of the continent, tyrannical Spain was starting church schools and reserved Indian land long before America got around to such a thing. Be it remembered, however, that Spain and Canada represented strong, centralized governments, not struggling for their lives, either economically or politically.

America's gesture of idealism cost millions of dollars. In addition to new lands given in exchange for old, the treaties generally contained a "solemn pledge" of payment in cash annuities, rations, tools, and domestic animals. From the origin of the government to 1840, over thirty-one million dollars were spent in this way,[7] besides the yearly allowances made for missionary schools and the civilization fund. True, the money did not all reach its destination. Some went into the pockets of dishonest contractors, and some, be it admitted, into the pouches of Indians. (Of $247,000 paid after one Creek treaty, $160,000 went to individual chiefs, two of whom were not even Creeks.)[8] War and disorganization were producing their usual quota of evil fruit. Some annuities, as well as the land, were promised "in perpetuity." A few such promises are still in force and, at present, are being amortized by the government. Others were superseded over and over again until a court of claims is needed to decide what is legally owing to a given tribe. Many payments, however, were faithfully made. A ten-thousand-dollar-a-year civilization fund was set up for Indians (1819). Church schools were subsidized out of treaty funds, and, by 1820, these had a thousand pupils.[9] While Indians east of the Mississippi were in the position of enemies and inferiors, those to the west of it were still free people, to be coaxed into friendship. Here hovered Spain and England, working to make alliances which might, perhaps, destroy the new republic or at least usurp the trade which helped support it. Indian trade, therefore, was carefully cultivated. At first, traders were licensed as they had been under France. Finally, the government itself set up a series of trading posts which lasted from 1796 to 1822. In spite of losses during the War of 1812, they were successful and were only given up because of private interests.[10] To compete with Spanish trade from the south, there were two posts among Creek and Cherokee, and it was from these and their neighbors that the government received a request to forbid all liquor sales to Indians. Such a law was passed in 1802 and is still in force.

Meantime, the country east of the Mississippi was being progressively organized into territories and then into states. (By 1820 only the land around the Great Lakes was still outside the United States.) A few Indian groups had already moved from their eastern homes, and the cry arose that all must go. The idea was not a new one. In 1783 Washington had planned that the United States should have a western boundary, with all Indians moved beyond it. In 1803 the great vaguely bounded Louisiana country beyond the Mississippi had been purchased from France. Jefferson had sent Lewis and Clark to explore it with the idea that it might serve as a permanent Indian country, forming a buffer between the United States and Spain. Some Choctaw and Chickasaw, who lived just east of the Mississippi, had already been making expeditions to the west. In 1820 these small groups chose to move permanently. The government bought lands for them on the Arkansas River and set up an agency. In 1826 some of the Creeks made the same arrangement.

In 1830 was passed the Removal Act, authorizing the President to "cause the lands west of the Mississippi to be surveyed and divided into districts and to offer these tracts to Indians living within the limits of any state or territory in exchange for the lands there held by them."[11]

In accordance with this act, treaties were gradually made, not only with the Five Civilized Tribes of the Southeast, but with most of the Prairie and Lakes people, granting them new lands in fee simple,[12] though these could not be sold and would revert to the United States should the Indians abandon them. Their old lands were to be paid for. (The Cherokee asked for twenty million dollars and received five.)[13] Moreover, a half-million dollars was allocated for expenses of migration and maintenance during the first years. In theory, the proposal was not too cruel; in practice, though, hurry and lack of planning produced tragedy for the Indians. During the next ten years, under the management of the newly created Indian Department, some seventy thousand tribesmen were paid off and settled across the Mississippi.

We may pause a moment over this plan of payment and removal

which set the pattern for future treatment of Indian groups, no matter what their history or occupation. The largest Indian population concerned was that of the Five Civilized Tribes, agriculturists, with a well-developed government and mixed-blood leaders who were already asking for resident instructors in weaving, dairying, and blacksmithing. There was a serious proposal that these tribes should consolidate, form a state of the Union, and be represented in Congress. Could this have been done?

If it had and if settlement and marriage had been freely allowed between the red men and their neighbors, we can picture a clash of customs which might have caused an earlier war between the states. Communal ownership! Providing for extra women by making several the wives of one man! Descent and property ownership reckoned through the mother! The cult of war and, above all, its method! These would have stood out so starkly from the white man's ethics of that day that we cannot imagine a state allowed to keep them. The Indians would have had to change the customs hallowed by age and familiarity, and no people makes that sudden shift except under force. Even in the new land, as a previous chapter has shown, the Indians gradually gave up their system of communal ownership and their simple and intimate form of government. Their culture succumbed, at most points, to that of a larger and more powerful population.

III. White Dominance Extends to the Pacific, and Western Tribes Accept Reservations (1845–68)

During this period the United States grew to almost its full size, acquiring its southwestern territory from Spain in 1848 and 1853; California in 1849, and the Pacific Northwest in 1851. The War between the States (1861–65) brought about the organizing of new states in territory which had once been considered permanently Indian (Kansas, 1861; Nebraska, 1867) and, later, set loose a flood of ex-soldiers, eager for land.

Indian tribes were still treated as sovereign nations, and the history of fighting, land cessions, and recessions was repeated here as in the East. It ended in the acceptance of reservations by most of the western tribes, though there were to be revolts and changes later. Some of the smaller groups in California and Nevada were ousted from their lands without provision.

Most of the negotiations were carried on by army officers, while they, as well as civilians, were used as agents for the new reservations. In 1849 an Interior Department was created, and the Indian Bureau transferred to it, though the War Department still continued to deal with "hostiles." Thereafter, there was constant friction between the civilian and military authorities as to which should function in a given case.

During this period, which ended with the War between the States, the United States grew into an established nation, with a sense of responsibility toward Indians and a consistent policy. Congress could now command funds and troops, though in limited quantity, and these were needed. The situation in the West was somewhat like that met by the first colonists, for powerful tribes were in possession of the soil, ready to fight or treat. Western Indians had not suffered the attrition of the French and Indian War, and, if they had been organized like the Iroquois, their resistance might have been a much more serious matter. However, as newcomers with no firm allegiance to leaders and no experience in planned campaigns, they were more or less subdued within twenty years.

The plan for an unbroken line of Indian settlements just west of the Mississippi had been given up. With Spain and her successor, Mexico, ousted from the West, no buffer state was needed. When the huge Kansas-Nebraska area was cut out from the middle of supposed Indian country and the resident Indians moved, only Indian Territory and the Dakotas were left as homes for the displaced tribes. The rest of the western country had been proved suitable for white men's use, and ranchers and miners were moving in. In 1862 the Homestead Act arranged for the taking-up of public domain by any who would work on it. In the same year the transcontinental railroads were started.

Many of the western tribes had now signed treaties which bound them to keep within certain limits. They were supplied with rations to make up for the lack of hunting facilities, but there was constant revolt and breaking of bounds. It was time to look into the whole Indian situation. In 1865 a congressional committee toured the West and reported deplorable conditions. The buffalo were practically exterminated and the Indians' livelihood gone; tribes were broken and helpless; schools were not functioning. In 1867 a peace commission was appointed to come to permanent terms with the "hostiles." They recommended better-planned reservations and more government authority, schools for the children, and farming instructors for adults. Within the next few years a rash of treaty-making broke out. Reservations were surveyed; rations, goods, and annuities were promised; and the Indian population was settled in about the area where it is today.

The reservations now "set apart . . . for occupancy" were not granted in fee simple.[14] Since the land had usually been won by conquest, it was considered government property but was reserved tax free for Indian use, as part payment for the ceded lands. Other payments were rations, tools, and equipment with which the Indians were expected to start a new life. An agent, generally a military man, was stationed on the reservation to distribute the goods and keep the peace as well as he could. Sometimes the Indians had, by treaty, reserved the right to hunt in off-reservation territory. However, since the departure of an armed group often resulted in a fight, either with whites or with other Indians, they were forbidden to make these expeditions without permission from the agent. This was the situation in the West when President Grant's administration ushered in a new era in Indian affairs.

IV. PERIOD OF STRICT RESERVATION SUPERVISION (1869–1921)

This period, from the end of the Civil War through World War I, brought the United States to adult industrial growth. Near its beginning (1871) the policy of treaty-making was ended and the Indians pronounced "domestic dependent nations." The nation for the first time assumed full responsibility for their education and rehabilitation. Western Indians resisted their subjection, and there were outbreaks (Southern Plains, 1874; Dakota, 1876; Bannock, 1878), while the Nez Percé (1877) and Cheyenne (1878) made their tragic attempts to live elsewhere than on the reservations assigned them. The general despair resulted in such religious movements as the Shaker religion of the Northwest (1881) and the Ghost Dance (1890).

President Grant made efforts to improve the management of reservations by appointing agents nominated by the churches (1869–79). It was no solution. The church nominees were often poor administrators and more interested in gaining converts for their sects than in studying the Indian question. Another expedient was an unpaid Board of Indian Commissioners, appointed in the same year. They did good work until 1935 in checking on contractors and inspecting reservations. Also some reservations courts were set up, handled by Indians and dealing with minor offenses. In 1870 the first annual appropriation for Indian education was made. Following the example of Carlisle, Pennsylvania (see below), boarding schools were instituted on most of the reservations. They were at first run by missionaries on contract; then government employees were gradually substituted, until contracts were abolished in 1897. Boarding schools reached their peak of popularity about 1885, after which some day schools were built and some Indians were paid for at public schools.

By 1887 it was obvious that the Indians were not changing their way of life, and many were still being subsisted by the government. As an incentive to farming and a means of using the land not farmed, the Allotment Act was passed, permitting allotment of land to individuals in severalty with full ownership when they proved able to handle money. Unallotted reservation land was opened for white settlement. Allotment proceeded slowly and never reached some tribes in the Southwest. It rarely inspired the Indians to farm, and in 1891 a law permitted them to lease allotted lands to whites. There were continued attempts to improve living conditions and the management of reservations. In 1891 the first field matron was appointed. Doctors and teaching staffs were put on civil service in 1892 and all Indian Service employees except the commissioner and assistant commissioner in 1902.

World War I temporarily reduced the funds and attention given to the Indians. The red men were not drafted in that war, though many volunteered, and the Comanche, with several other tribes, rendered unique service in the use of their unwritten language for telephone communication across German lines. When the war was over and depression looming, both Indian education and Indian livelihood were in a discouraging state. The period of strict supervision and education according to white man's ideas had not been successful.

Looking back on this period with today's knowledge, we are appalled at the lack of understanding shown the red man. Most of the planners were not even aware of the fact that some of the tribes were agriculturists who, with intelligent help, could be expected to settle peaceably, while some were hunters whose very roots were being destroyed. True, neither England, France, nor Holland was any wiser at this period. The tide of the white man's eminence was at the full, and all believed that the darker races were simply at lower points on the ladder of evolution, hoping only for a chance to mount higher. So no one considered how the Indian tradition of co-operation could be put to work; how the potlatch and give-away feast could be turned into mutual benefit societies; how some psychological satisfaction could be found for the warrior deprived of his function.

Here and there we see a tiny candle flame of light which might have showed the way, had there been any means of following it. Such were the achievements of Colonel Dodge with the Navaho, Agent Clum with the Apache, and a few missionaries and field matrons who treated the Indians as brothers. Reading the official accounts, one is amazed at the response which flamed up when a group of Indians had personal contact with a white man whom they trusted. To him it seemed that they were open to all suggestions and would follow anywhere. Rarely could such a friend remain with them long, for official necessity generally replaced him with some impersonal supervisor. Then suddenly the flame dies. Instead of reading, "These Indians are eager for education. They are always at my house, learning to build, plow and use our tools," one finds the statement, "These people grow more sullen and intractable every year. I doubt whether they can ever be civilized."

Whether agriculturists or hunters, the Indians were used to close personal relationships. Their chiefs were like fathers, always approachable, willing to spend hours in a slow envisagement of problems. The impersonal white man, glancing up from his desk to issue an order, even an order to their advantage, was to them a psychological horror. Perhaps it was this lack of kindness, even more than the bad beef and the flimsy tools which made reservation life so worthless. To add to the Indian's discouragement, his native ceremonies were forbidden, particularly the Sun Dance, whose temporary discomforts were set down as barbarous—an idea almost comic in view of the happenings of World War I! That the children might learn English more quickly, their native language was forbidden in the schools.

These schools, though often manned by kind and devoted people, made no attempt to reconcile the old life with the new. In early reservation years the log buildings, hastily rigged for school purposes, had little attendance and were frequently closed for lack of teachers. Better-planned schooling began when young Lieutenant Pratt, after the revolt of the southern Plains Indians in 1874, was told to pick up some Cheyenne and Kiowa captives for confinement at Fort Marion, Florida. Pratt decided to make the experience worth while to the young warriors, so he trained them industrially. Under this stimulating attention, the Indians blossomed and wanted more education. From this start grew the Indian school at Carlisle, Pennsylvania, a fort lent by the army and serving, in 1900, twelve hundred pupils from seventy-nine tribes.[15] "To civilize the Indian," was Pratt's formula, "put him in the midst of civilization. To keep him civilized, keep him there."[16] The formula worked perfectly, and Carlisle graduates employed in the Indian Service or living in towns seem practically indistinguishable from their white neighbors. True, they have given up the warm contact with kinsmen, bound to help and companion them under all circumstances. If the white man's culture satisfies them, they can be successful. If it does not, and they return to the reservation, they are likely to meet suspicion and a lack of the equipment they have learned to need. Taking the Indian away from his people makes a white man of him but provides few channels through which Indian attitudes and achievements can flow to the whites.

Nevertheless, taking the Indian away from his people was the education plan, once the government had settled to its responsibility. Settled, that is, as far as possible, for there were never funds or personnel to implement a complete, long-term program. The dirty, screaming youngsters were extracted, often by force, from what seemed to the white teachers impossible hovels. They were washed, clothed, and housed in dormitories of a prison-like cleanliness. There, white teachers of earnest middle-class ideals tried to make the children over in their own image. There was no thought of helping them to live intelligently on the reservation. Instead, they were urged not to "go back to the blanket," and those who did led a disturbed and unsatisfied existence. There are tales of cruelty in the boarding schools, but to this writer, who has seen scores of the institutions and their graduates, cruelty seems the exception, not the rule. It was the desperate reaction of a teacher who had slaved hard for his education and who saw privileges never offered to him being thrown away by "ignorant savages." Why not spank them when they would not study and lock them up when they persisted in running away! The officials who had innocently expected a complete change in one generation became hardened or resigned.

Compare the experience of three mission schools with the Santee Sioux! Eight hundred of this tribe were moved to Nebraska after an uprising (1862) and settled on empty land to begin farming. True, their women had always done a little planting, but now the men must take it up in lieu of war. Persuasion to the change needed patient, day-by-day contact, such as government workers never had time to give. Nor could they usually visit the families in their homes and know the whole community. We grant that many missionary schools achieved no more than did the transitory government workers. Still, this particular group, with their personal touch and long-term program, could finally show a community with large farms, well-built homes, and a native newspaper. If Indians had been better understood at that time, some of the money poured out on rations might have supported a number of such friendly helpers who would encourage the Indians to work for themselves. The kindly field matrons, who were later discontinued as untrained, often gave proof of how useful this informal contact could be.[17]

The Allotment Act of 1887 shows again how far the white man was at this time from any understanding of Indian needs. It was as hotly debated as the Removal Act had been and with friends of the Indian on both sides. Some of these, with traditions of tenantry and land hunger in their blood, felt sincerely that no man could have greater incentive to labor than land of his very own. Even though they could only bring him this boon by making common cause with those whose motive was to get holdings away from the "lazy savages," and even though the Dawes Act, when passed, fell far short of their ideal, it seemed a forward step. By this act, each head of a family was to receive 160 acres, or a quarter-section, in a locality of his selection. Each person over eighteen and each orphan received 80 acres, and children under eighteen born before the passage of the act, had 40 acres.

Since it was known that Indians placed no value on individual owner-ship and instantly sold land so given them, they did not receive full title to their allotments but a "trust patent" holding for twenty-five years and to be extended further at presidential discretion.

The failure of this benevolent scheme is now well known. Even the agricultural tribes did not think of choosing their quarter-sections for their worth as farms but for nearness to their old homes or to relatives. A few revolted at the iniquity of dividing tribal land, refused to accept allotments, and went to jail. The trust patent, which was supposed to educate the Indian in finance, under the tutelage of a white guardian, worked out to an iniquitous "racket." The guardian, appointed by the courts, was seldom disinterested. He took fat fees and left the Indian to struggle miserably with inadequate stock and tools or else leased his land for him to a white who paid the owner just enough for some food and whiskey. As soon as he could get the Indian judged "competent," the land was usually sold.

Between 1887 and 1935, when the process was stopped, most of the reservations in Oklahoma, the Lake States, the Plains, and the Pacific Coast were allotted.[18] At the beginning of that period the Indians had a total of 138 million acres. In 1934 they possessed 52 million acres, half of which was desert or semidesert. Some of this loss was due to sales by Indians. It also involved the sale by government of land left over after allotment. The wisest plan, it can now be seen, would have been to save this land for future allotments to future generations or to keep it as tribal property. The land-hungry settlers made this im-possible. True, they could make far more out of 160 acres than any Indian could, since they usually had tools and stock to begin with or could borrow and buy them. Their nearness to Indian farmers did not bring about the brotherly teaching which philanthropists had envisaged. Instead, they despised the "lazy" red men, took every advan-tage of their ignorance, and usually ended by leasing their land, while whole groups of dispossessed Indians gathered on some small acreage living on lease money and odd jobs. No one considered conserving the soil or planning for its most efficient use, and dust-bowl years approached.

V. RECONSTRUCTION OF INDIAN POLICY (1921–71)

The country was recovering from a world war, suffering a depression, and re-organizing its policies, both foreign and domestic. Indian conditions gradually received full consideration and drastic change. In 1924 an act of Congress pro-nounced all Indians citizens whether or not they were on tribal rolls or held lands in severalty. In 1928 a thoroughgoing report by the Brookings Institution of Washington published drastic criticisms of the whole acculturation policy and recommended far-reaching changes.[19] In the next years a financial depression gripped the country. President Roosevelt, taking office in 1933, acquired from Congress large sums for public works as a means of providing employment. A due proportion of this was spent on Indians, while there were also large appropriations for schools and general improvement of the Indian Service. In 1934 the Indian Reorganization Act was passed, a Magna Carta for the red man, allowing groups of them to incorporate and appoint a council to manage tribal affairs. They could also borrow and spend money as a group, thus maintaining some of their communal customs. Allotment was stopped, and sale of Indian lands to any but Indians was forbidden. Toward the end of the period there was undertaken a large-scale program of research into Indian needs—material, physical, and psychological. Meantime, the second World War had developed. Indians were drafted, and a discouraging number proved unfit for service, either physically or because of lack of English. Navaho and others, however, rendered unique service by the use of their language in the Signal Corps. Indians traveled; many achieved the rank of petty officers and became acquainted with the advantages of the white man's world.

The idea that the Indians should manage themselves was the right one, but its achievement needed more than a law and a little money. At first the tribal councils limped along in their unaccustomed role; but as more than a quarter century passed and a new generation arrived, the councils began to be more usefully operative. There was a retrogression after Collier's day, when the country was occupied with war and economics. Still, the country was aware of the general Indian problem as it had not been before, and several legal measures were taken to alleviate the situation. These can only be mentioned briefly and without extensive qualifying details.

The first was the establishment in 1946 of a court of claims to hear Indian complaints about unfulfilled treaties and land taken without payment. That court is still in session, and by 1970 it had heard 158 cases and paid out $341,000,000; 160 claims had been refused, and 290 are still pending.[20] The next landmark was the proposal to terminate government responsibility for any reservation which seemed to have reached a point where it could manage its own business and pay taxes as white citizens did. Under a law passed in 1954, three reservations were so terminated: that of the Klamath in Oregon; the Menomini in Wisconsin; and Paiute in Nevada.[21] In every case the move turned out a failure, and with the Menomini and Paiute, a tragedy. The Indians were not prepared, either in business experience or in finances, to manage their property. In 1958 the Secretary of Interior announced that no more terminations would be carried out without the Indians' full consent.[22] No tribe so far has consented.

Health

Meanwhile the wretched situation of Indians was in many respects coming to notice. A main element in this was their bad health. Millions of dollars were needed for hospitals, doctors, and nurses; but the Bureau had never had funds for such outlay. Indian health was taken over by the Public Health Service which, by 1970, had built 13 more hospitals as well as 13 health centers for outpatients and 50 health stations.[23] Training centers were established for Indian practical nurses and dental assistants, with the hope that they would go on to higher positions. Some Indian groups themselves hired visiting nurses and sanitary inspectors.

Alcoholism was a main problem, for due to Indian protest the law against serving alcohol to Indians had been repealed. Drunkenness spread, as it did with the whites, among returned soldiers and unemployed. Hospitals gave treatments, groups employed representatives to deal personally with drinkers, and sections of Alcoholics Anonymous were organized.

Inferior housing was one cause of bad health since the dwellings, old and new, usually had no running water and no disposal of waste. Infections were common. Diet was bad, now that the old foods were given up and new ones not yet understood. The Public Health Service, the Indian Bureau, and the Department of Housing and Urban Development combined to build new houses with correct water and sewage systems or to put such systems into old houses. Indians helped with the work, and their labor was counted as payment for the house which ultimately they could own.[24]

Education

Changes in education have been going on for a long time. War service and wartime jobs made Indians aware of the desirability of training. All at once, there was need for many more schools. One large army hospital was taken over. Vacant places in boarding schools were filled with children, even from distant tribes. In some places where children lived near a public school and spoke English, the government paid the school a subsidy for taking them. By 1970, 61 per cent of children were in public schools.[25] If they did not live within bus distance of the school, the government furnished a supervised dormitory where they lived during the week, going home for weekends. Kindergartens were established as fast as possible, and reports stated that by 1971 all children should have preschool opportunity.[26] The Indians' language difficulty became apparent, and some schools stressed the teaching of English as a second language. In some Bureau schools, the first grades were taught in the Indian tongue. Indian parents by now were taking an intelligent interest in the teaching of their children. They demanded more share in deciding what was taught. In the Navajo area, a school was established financed by the Bureau and the tribe and with a board of directors entirely Indian. A Navajo Community College is also being established under Indian direction. With financial assistance from the Bureau and from various private donations, Indians are also going in increasing numbers to the white men's colleges. There are now a number of Indian professors, writers, and doctors.

Employment

Indians who have learned no special skill are faced with unemployment due to automation. The Joint Economic Commission reported in 1969 that 50 per cent of the national Indian labor force 16 years or older is unemployed.[27] The Indians, like other minorities, have protested that there is discrimination against them. In response, the Indian Bureau hires Indians in preference to others whenever possible. The Indian Commissioner is now a Mohawk Indian who has a group of Indians as his advisors and proclaims that he plans radical changes for the Indians' benefit.

Projects have been funded by the Office of Economic Opportunity and other agencies. One hundred and fifty industrial plants were operating in or near the reservations in 1969. Indian employment in such plants increased in that year from 1,050 to 4,630.[28] Moreover, the Indians themselves are managing and financing some industries. Such are the Navajo Forest Industries; the Cherokee Nation Industries; the cattle enterprises of White Mountain Apache and Florida Seminole; the recreation area of the Paiute at Warm Springs, Oregon. Some tribes are managing their own tribal improvements with their own funds, often hiring experts for the purpose. The pueblo of Zuni has decided to do entirely without white supervision. School teachers or other officials, not Indian, are asked to stay only long enough to train Indians for their positions. Zuni makes its own business arrangements and handles its own funds, though not "terminated" under the law.

Organization

The National Congress of American Indians (NCAI) was organized in the early 1940's with representatives from almost all the tribes. It has held yearly meetings to educate the members and discuss activities. There also have been a number of local organizations, sometimes several in one city. A new organization, Native Americans United, is now working to get the tribes operating together and is receiving donations from government and private sources.

Changes

In a century or so since the large western reservations were established, Indians have certainly changed their outward habits. They wear the same dress as other citizens, whether cowboy costume or business suit. Their houses are in the white man's style and changing rapidly from makeshift to acceptable. In many Indian towns there are some modern, attractive dwellings such as can be seen in any well-to-do suburb. Running water, electric lights, and radios are not at all uncommon. There are tribes where everyone speaks English and others where the younger people do. Many of the tribes publish newspapers in English, such as the *Navajo Times*. Books by Vine Deloria (Sioux) and Scott Momaday (Kiowa) have had a wide reception, the latter winning a prize. Hundreds of young Indians are now in colleges, financed sometimes by their tribes and sometimes by other organizations. There is a movement to have Indian studies taught as a course in college, and several colleges have already taken up the proposal. Academic study has gained such a place in Indian life that in 1970 there was a convocation of Indian scholars. Scholars were representative of twenty-five universities and colleges in the United States and Canada.[29]

The Indian studies which they recommend perhaps do not stress the ideas of work and achievement which the white citizen has. Indians still see the virtue of intimate group life, the desirability of leisure to ruminate and enjoy nature. They suggest that perhaps the white man has gone too far in his cult of success in economic matters and that he could learn by closer contact with Indians. Such expressions indicate a group which is no longer living in hopelessness and uncertainty. In the words of former Commissioner Bennett, himself an Indian, "the Indian people have rediscovered themselves . . . and have begun to establish cultural and historic identity."[30]

Notes

NOTES TO CHAPTER I

1. *The Vinland Sagas: The Norse Discovery of America*, translated with an introduction by Magnus Magnusson and Hermann Pálsson (Baltimore: Penguin Books, 1965).

2. J. R. Arnold and W. F. Libby, *Radiocarbon Dates* (Chicago: University of Chicago Institute for Nuclear Studies, September, 1950), inferred from pp. 8–12.

3. *Ibid.*

4. Philip S. Smith, "Certain Relations between Northwestern America and Northeastern Asia," in *Early Man*, ed. George G. MacCurdy (Philadelphia: J. B. Lippincott, 1939), p. 85.

5. Ralph Solecki, "How Man Came to North America," *Scientific American*, CLXXXIV, No. 1 (January, 1951), 14.

6. Arnold and Libby, *op. cit.*, p. 9 (Lime Creek).

7. Henry F. Osborn, *The Age of Mammals in Europe, Asia and North America* (New York: Macmillan Co., 1910), p. 285 (Florissant, Colorado).

8. H. M. Wormington, *Ancient Man in North America* ("Denver Museum of Natural History, Popular Series," No. 4 [rev. ed.; Denver, 1949]), p. 75 (referring to Dr. Kirk Bryan).

9. John C. McGregor *Southwestern Archaeology* (New York: John Wiley & Sons, 1941), p. 112.

10. Solecki, *op. cit.*, p. 14.

11. Arnold and Libby, *op. cit.*, p. 10.

12. *Ibid.*

13. Wormington, *op. cit.*, pp. 87–88.

14. Arnold and Libby, *op. cit.*, p. 10.

15. *Ibid.*

16. Edwin H. Colbert, "The Pleistocene Mammals of North America and Their Relations to Eurasian Forms," in MacCurdy (ed.), *op. cit.*

17. W. C. Bennett and J. B. Bird, *Andean Culture History* ("American Museum of Natural History, Handbook Series," No. 15 [New York, 1949]), p. 21 (by Bennett).

18. Arnold and Libby, *op. cit.*, p. 13.

19. *Ibid.*, p. 11.

NOTES TO CHAPTER II

1. E. Gordon Childe, *Man Makes Himself* (New York: Oxford University Press, 1939), p. 74.

2. J. R. Arnold and W. F. Libby, *Radiocarbon Dates* (University of Chicago Institute for Nuclear Studies, September, 1950), p. 4 (Irak: Jarmo).

3. Barbara Pickersgill, "The Archaeological Record of Chili Peppers (*Capsicum Spp.*) and the Sequence of Plant Domestication in Peru," *American Antiquity*, Vol. XXXIV, No. 1 (1969), pp. 54–61.

4. Robert F. Spencer, Jesse D. Jennings, *et. al.*, *The Native Americans* (New York: Harper & Row, 1965), pp. 440–41.

5. Adapted from Carl Sauer, "Cultivated Plants of South and Central America," in *Handbook of South American Indians* (Bureau of American Ethnology

Bull. 143 [Washington, 1950]), and M. D. C. Crawford, *The Conquest of Culture* (New York: Greenberg, 1938), pp. 145–46.

6. P. C. Mangelsdorf and C. E. Smith, Jr., *New Archaeological Evidence on Evolution in Maize* ("Botanical Museum Leaflets, Harvard University," Vol. XIII, No. 8 [Cambridge, 1949]), pp. 213–14.

7. Herbert W. Dick directed excavations for the Early Man Division of the Upper Gila Researches by the Peabody Museum, Harvard University, 1948.

8. For details on South American craft see Wendell C. Bennett and Junius B. Bird, *Andean Culture History* ("American Museum of Natural History Handbook Series," No. 15 [New York, 1949]), pp. 245–95.

9. Sylvanus G. Morley, *The Ancient Maya* (Palo Alto: Stanford University Press, 1946), p. 321 (Tikal).

10. *Ibid.*, p. 45.

11. *Ibid.*, chap. xiii.

12. Alfred M. Tozzer, *Landa's Relación de las Cosas de Yucatán: A Translation* ("Papers of the Peabody Museum of American Archaeology and Ethnology," Vol. XVIII [Cambridge, 1941]), pp. 86–87.

13. A sign for zero was used in Mesopotamia about 500 B.C. However, it was used only between digits (104), not following them (140). Thus, as Dr. Kroeber says, it was only half-applied (A. L. Kroeber, *Anthropology* [rev. ed.; New York, 1948], p. 468). Moreover, the counting system was based on 60, evidently derived from the weighing of metals, while those of the Hindu and the Maya were based on 10 and 20, the numbers of fingers or fingers and toes.

14. Morley, *op. cit.*, p. 216.

15. Thor Heyerdahl, *The Kon-Tiki Expedition* (London: George Allen & Unwin, Ltd. [Ruskin House], 1950), p. 200.

16. Betty J. Meggers, Clifford Evans, and Emilio Estrada, *Early Formative Period of Coastal Ecuador: The Valdivia and Machalilla Phases,* Smithsonian Contributions to Anthropology, Vol. I (Washington, D.C.: Smithsonian Institution, 1965).

17. A. L. Kroeber, *Cultural and Natural Areas of Native North America* ("University of California Publications in American Archaeology and Ethnology," Vol. XXXVIII [Berkeley and Los Angeles: University of California Press, 1939]).

NOTES TO CHAPTER III

1. For a description of Middle Mississippi cultures see Paul S. Martin, George I. Quimby, and Donald Collier, *Indians before Columbus* (Chicago: University of Chicago Press, 1947), pp. 353–68, 399–419.

2. Irving Rouse, "The Arawak," in *Handbook of South American Indians,* ed. Julian Steward (Bureau of American Ethnology Bull. 143 [Washington, 1948]), IV, 507.

3. Frans Blom, *The Conquest of Yucatán* (Boston: Houghton Mifflin Co., 1936), p. 3.

4. J. R. Arnold and W. F. Libby, *Radiocarbon Dates* (University of Chicago Institute of Nuclear Studies, September, 1950), p. 7 (Annis Mound, Ky.).

5. *Ibid.*, p. 9 (Adena material from Cowan Creek Mound, Ohio).

6. Jack Cotter, *Region Three Interpretative Notes 120* (Santa Fe: National Park Service, November, 1950) (Emerald Mound).

7. John R. Swanton, *Indian Tribes of the Lower Mississippi Valley and Adjacent Coast of the Gulf of Mexico* (Bureau of American Ethnology Bull. 43 [Washington, 1911]), pp. 263, 174, 351, and 357.

8. See chap. ii.

9. Swanton, *op. cit.*, pp. 191 ff. (Iberville, Charlevoix, Du Pratz, etc.).

10. *Ibid.*, pp. 158–66.

11. *Ibid.*, p. 107.

12. The Creek have been described at length in Swanton's magnificent volumes: "Aboriginal Culture of the Southeast," *42d Annual Report of the Bureau of American Ethnology* (Washington, 1928); *Early History of the Creek Indians and Their Neighbors* (Bureau of American Ethnology Bull. 73 [Washington, 1922]); *Indian Tribes of the Lower Mississippi Valley and Adjacent Coast of the Gulf of Mexico* (Bureau of American Ethnology Bull. 43 [Washington, 1911]); "Religious Beliefs and Medical Practices of the Creek Indians," *42d Annual Report of the Bureau of American Ethnology* [Washington, 1928]); "Social Organization and Social Usages of the Indians of the Creek Confederacy," *ibid.*; and *The Indians of the Southeastern United States* (Bureau of American Ethnology Bull. 137 [Washington, 1946]).

13. A. L. Kroeber, *Cultural and Natural Areas of North America* ("University of California Publications in American Archaeology and Ethnology," Vol. XXXVIII [Berkeley: University of California Press, 1939]), p. 147.

14. Edward Gaylord Bourne, *Narratives of the Career of Hernando de Soto* (2 vols.; New York: Allerton Book Co., 1904), II, 88.

15. Lila M. O'Neale, "Weaving," in *Handbook of South American Indians,* ed. Julian Steward (Bureau of American Ethnology Bull. 143 [Washington, 1950]), V, 107.

16. For other elements of costume see material culture list on p. 44.

17. James Adair, *History of the American Indians* (London, 1775), p. 66.

18. Swanton, *The Indians of the Southeastern United States*, p. 690.

19. Swanton, "Religious Beliefs and Medical Practices of the Creek Indians," p. 643.

20. James Mooney and Frans M. Olbrechts, *The Swimmer Manuscript* (Bureau of American Ethnology Bull. 99 [Washington, 1932]), p. 171.

21. Swanton, *The Indians of the Southeastern United States*, pp. 284 (quoting Bartram, 1792) and 291.

NOTES TO CHAPTER IV

1. Edward Gaylord Bourne, *Narratives of the Career of Hernando de Soto* (2 vols.; New York: Allerton Book Co., 1904), II, 59.

2. John P. Brown, *Old Frontiers* (Kingsport, Tenn.: Southern Publishers, Inc., 1938), p. 26.

3. Angie Debo, *The Road to Disappearance* (Norman: University of Oklahoma Press, 1941), p. 75.

4. Flora Warren Seymore, *The Story of the Red Man* (New York: Tudor Press, 1934), p. 183.

5. Grant Foreman, *Indian Removal* (Norman: University of Oklahoma Press, 1932), p. 383.

6. Seymore, *op. cit.*, p. 184.

7. Debo, *op. cit.*, pp. 105–6.

NOTES TO CHAPTER V

1. Frederica de Laguna, *The Prehistory of Northern North America as Seen from the Yukon* ("Memoirs of the Society for American Archaeology," No. 3 [Menasha, Wis., 1947]), p. 277; and "The Importance of the Eskimo in Northeastern Archaeology," in *Man in Northeastern North America*, ed. Frederick Johnson ("Papers of the Robert S. Peabody Foundation for Archaeology," Vol. III [Andover, Mass., 1946]), pp. 106–42.

2. For details on Indians of Canada see Diamond Jenness, *Indians of Canada* (Canadian Department of Mines Bull. 65, "Anthropological Series," No. 15 [Ottawa, 1932]), and other publications of that department. See also Regina Flannery, *Analysis of Coastal Algonkian Cultures* ("Catholic University of America Anthropological Series," No. 8 [Washington, 1939]); L. W. Bailey, *The Conflict of European and Eastern Algonkian Cultures* (New Brunswick Museum Publication No. 3 [New Brunswick, N. J., 1937]); and Johnson (ed.), *op. cit.*

3. F. G. Speck, "Land Ownership among Hunting Peoples in Primitive America and the World's Marginal Areas," in *Proceedings of the XXIIth International Congress of Americanists* (Rome, Italy, 1926), II, 323–32; and John Cooper, "Is the Algonquian Family Hunting Ground System Pre-Columbian?" *American Anthropologist*, XLI (new ser., 1939), 83.

4. F. G. Speck, *Naskapi* (Norman: University of Oklahoma Press, 1935), p. 76.

5. A. B. Skinner, *Notes on the Eastern Cree and Northern Saulteaux* ("American Museum of Natural History Anthropological Papers," Vol. IX, Part I [New York, 1911]), p. 68.

6. F. G. Speck, *Penobscot Shamanism* ("Memoirs of the American Anthropological Association," Vol. VI, No. 4 [Lancaster, Pa., 1919]), p. 241.

7. J. D. Prince, *Notes on Passamaquoddy Literature* ("Annals of the New York Academy of Sciences," Vol. XIII, No. 4 [New York, 1901]), p. 385. Quoted by Speck, *Penobscot Shamanism*, p. 241 n. (We have taken the liberty of arranging the lines in verse form.)

8. J. R. Arnold and W. F. Libby, *Radiocarbon Dates* (University of Chicago Institute for Nuclear Studies, September, 1950), p. 7 (Lamoka Culture).

9. *Ibid.*, p. 6 (Boylston Street Fishweir).

10. Johnson, *op. cit.*, pp. 106–42.

11. Erik K. Reed, "A Theory of Southwestern Prehistory" ("Region Three Archaeological Interpretation Circular," No. 8 [Santa Fe, N.M.: National Park Service, 1951]). (Mimeographed.)

12. F. G. Speck, *Penobscot Man: The Life History of a Forest Tribe in Maine* (Norman: University of Oklahoma Press, 1940), p. 53.

13. See the Southeast.

14. F. G. Speck, *The Functions of Wampum among the Eastern Algonkian* ("Memoirs of the American Anthropological Association," Vol. VI, No. 1 [Lancaster, Pa., 1919]), p. 5.

15. *Ibid.*, p. 19.

16. Reuben G. Thwaites (ed.), *The Jesuit Relations and Allied Documents: Travels and Explorations of the Jesuit Missionaries in New France, 1610–1791* (Cleveland: Burrows Bros., 1896–1901), LXVII, 137 (Father Rasles of Norridgewock).

17. F. G. Speck and W. C. Orchard, *The Penn Wampum Belts* ("Indian Notes and Monographs, Heye Foundation," No. 4 [New York, 1925]).

18. Speck, *The Functions of Wampum among the Eastern Algonkian*, p. 39.

19. M. R. Harrington, *Religion and Ceremonies of the Lenapa* ("Indian Notes and Monographs, Heye Foundation," No. 19 [New York, 1921]).

20. Francis Parkman, *Pioneers of France in the New World* (Frontenac ed.; Boston: Little, Brown & Co., 1899), II, 10, 52.

21. Marc Lescarbot, *History of New France*, ed. William L. Grant and Henry P. Biggar ("Publications of the Champlain Society," Vol. III [Toronto, 1914]), p. 177.

22. William C. MacCleod, *The American Indian Frontier* (New York: Alfred A. Knopf, 1928), p. 223.

23. *Ibid.*, p. 225.

24. "A Relation or Journal of the Proceedings of the Plantation Settled at Plymouth in New England," quoted in Ernest Gebber, *Plymouth Adventure* (Garden City: Doubleday & Co., 1950), p. 369.

25. Captain John Underhill, *News from America* (London: Peter Cole [Underhill Society of America], 1902), pp. 24–25.

26. *Ibid.*, p. 24.

27. *Anecdotes of the American Indian* (New York: Alexander V. Blake, 1844), p. 70.

NOTES TO CHAPTER VI

1. W. M. Beauchamp, *A History of the New York Iroquois* (New York State Museum Bull. 78 [Albany, 1905]), p. 180.

2. Paul Martin, George Quimby, and Donald Collier, *Indians before Columbus* (Chicago: University of Chicago Press, 1947), pp. 255–58 ("The Old Iroquois Culture").

3. W. N. Fenton, *Problems Arising from the Historic Northeastern Position of the Iroquois* ("Smithsonian Miscellaneous Collections," Vol. C [Washington, 1940]), p. 174.

4. F. G. Speck, *The Iroquois* (Cranbrook Institute of Science Bull. 23 [Bloomfield Hills, Mich., 1945]), p. 39.

5. Fenton, *op. cit.*, p. 22.

6. J. N. B. Hewett, "The Requickening Address of the Iroquois Condolence Council," *Journal of the Washington Academy of Sciences*, XXXIV, No. 3 (1944), 80 n.

7. H. Hale, *The Iroquois Book of Rites* ("Brinton's Library of Aboriginal American Literature" [Philadelphia: D. G. Brinton, 1883]), p. 131.

8. Hewett, *op. cit.*, p. 68.

9. *Ibid.*

10. *Ibid.*

11. Reuben G. Thwaites (ed.), *The Jesuit Relations and Allied Documents: Travels and Explorations of the Jesuit Missionaries in New France, 1610–1791* (Cleveland: Burrows Bros., 1896–1901), XVIII, 223.

12. Beauchamp, *op. cit.*, p. 185.

13. Thwaites (ed.), *op. cit.*, X, 224–26.

14. W. N. Fenton, personal communication, 1942 (this and the quotation on the following page).

15. *Ibid.*

16. G. T. Hunt, *The Wars of the Iroquois* (Madison: University of Wisconsin Press, 1940), p. 134.

17. Beauchamp, *op. cit.*, p. 196.

18. *Ibid.*, p. 212.

19. *Journal of Tobias Fitch*, p. 21, quoted in Angie Debo, *The Road to Disappearance* (Norman: University of Oklahoma Press, 1941), p. 5.

20. Hale, *op. cit.*, p. 153.

21. *Annals of Tryon County* (New York: J. & J. Harper, 1831), p. 125.

NOTES TO CHAPTER VII

1. Henry W. Longfellow, *Song of Hiawatha* (Philadelphia: Henry Altemus Co., 1898), pp. 13, 14. (We have taken the liberty of selecting the lines.)

2. W. J. Hoffman, "The Midewiwin or 'Grand Medicine Society' of the Ojibway," *7th Annual Report of the Bureau of American Ethnology* (Washington, 1886), p. 153.

3. W. C. McKern, "An Hypothesis for the Asiatic Origin of the Woodland Culture Pattern," *American Antiquity*, III, No. 2 (1937), 138–43.

4. J. R. Arnold and W. F. Libby, *Radiocarbon Dates* (University of Chicago Institute of Nuclear Studies, September, 1950), p. 8. (The radiocarbon date given is about 400 B.C. for Hopewell II, Havana, Illinois. However, other evidence points to a later date, and Dr. Griffin would prefer A.D. 800).

5. Frances Densmore, *Chippewa Customs* (Bureau of American Ethnology Bull. 86 [Washington, 1929]), p. 8; and A. E. Jenks, "The Wild Rice Gatherers of the Upper Great Lakes," *19th Annual Report of the Bureau of American Ethnology* (Washington, 1898), Part II, p. 1039.

6. A. B. Skinner, *The Mascoutens or Prairie Potawatomi Indians* ("Bulletin of the Public Museum of the City of Milwaukee," Vol. VI, No. 2 [Milwaukee, 1926]), p. 268.

7. T. Michelson, "Preliminary Report on the Linguistic Classification of Algonkian Tribes," *28th Annual Report of the Bureau of American Ethnology* (Washington, 1912), pp. 280, 287–89.

8. *Ibid.*, p. 250.

9. Carrie A. Lyford, *The Crafts of the Ojibwa* ("Indian Handcrafts," No. 5 [Phoenix, 1943]), pp. 88–93.

10. W. V. Kinietz, *The Indians of the Western Great Lakes, 1615–1760* ("University of Micigan, Museum of Anthropology, Occasional Contributions," No. 10 [Ann Arbor, 1940]), p. 173.

11. G. F. Carter, *Plant Geography and Culture History in the American Southwest* ("Viking Fund Publications in Anthropology," No. 5 [New York, 1945]), p. 51.

12. Sieur Deliette (?), nephew of Tonti, *Memoir concerning the Illinois Country*, ed. De Gannes ("Collections of the Illinois State Historical Library," Vol. XXIII, "French Series," Vol. I [Springfield, 1934]), p. 309.

13. A. B. Skinner, *Observations on the Ethnology of the Sauk Indians* ("Bulletin of the Public Museum of the City of Milwaukee," Vol. V, No. 3 [Milwaukee, 1925]), p. 124.

14. G. T. Hunt, *The Wars of the Iroquois* (Madison: University of Wisconsin Press, 1940), p. 148 (quoting La Salle).

15. Paul Radin, *The Road of Life and Death* ("Bollingen Series," Vol. V [New York: Pantheon Books, Inc., 1945]), p. 52.

16. "Totem," or "dodem," is an Algonkian word used as well for an individual guardian spirit as for a clan animal.

17. Hoffman, *op. cit.*, p. 146 (quoting Hiram Calkins on an Ojibwa performance).

18. *Ibid.*, p. 139 (quoting Charlevoix), and Kinietz, *op. cit.*, pp. 304–7 (quoting Allouez).

19. Kinietz, *op. cit.*, pp. 194–95.

20. L. Bloomfield, *Menomini Texts* ("Publications of the American Ethnological Society," Vol. XII [New York, 1928]), p. 69; and Sister Macaria, Ashland, Wisconsin, personal communication.

21. G. A. West, *Tobacco, Pipes and Smoking Customs of the American Indians* ("Bulletin of the Public Museum of the City of Milwaukee," Vol. XVII, Nos. 1 and 2 [Milwaukee, 1934]), p. 235.

22. Densmore, *op. cit.*, p. 100.

23. Radin, *op. cit.*, p. 25 n.

24. T. Michelson, *Contributions to Fox Ethnology* (Bureau of American Ethnology Bull. 85 [Washington, 1927]), p. 113.

25. Densmore, *op. cit.*, p. 87.

26. Radin, *op. cit.*, pp. 25, 70.

27. *Ibid.*, p. 221.

28. Paul Radin, personal information.

29. Bloomfield, *op. cit.*, p. 79.

30. Francis Parkman, *The Old Regime in Canada: France and England in North America* (Boston, 1874), II, 100.

31. Paul Radin, "The Winnebago Tribe," *37th Annual Report of the American Bureau of Ethnology* (Washington, 1923), p. 68.

32. F. M. Keesing, *The Menomini Indians of Wisconsin: A Study of Three Centuries of Cultural Contact and Change* ("Memoirs of the American Philosophical Society," No. 10 [Philadelphia, 1939]) (quoting Sabrevois).

33. R. C. Downes, *Council Fires on the Upper Ohio* (Pittsburgh: University of Pittsburgh Press, 1940), p. 83.

34. W. C. MacCleod, *The American Indian Frontier* (New York: Alfred A. Knopf, 1928), pp. 400–401.

35. Downes, *op. cit.*, p. 156.

36. Reuben G. Thwaites and L. P. Kellogg (eds.), *Documentary History of Dunmore's War* (Madison, Wis., 1905), pp. 368–72.

37. Downes, *op. cit.*, p. 324.

38. *Ibid.*, pp. 75–76 (quoting Alvord).

39. *Ibid.*, p. 324.

40. S. G. Drake, *The Aboriginal Races of North America* (New York: John B. Alden, 1880; 15th ed. revised by H. L. Williams), p. 618.

41. J. M. Oskison, *Tecumseh and His Times* (New York: G. P. Putnam's Sons, 1938), p. 152.

42. *Ibid.*, p. 144.

43. F. W. Hodge (ed.), *Handbook of American Indians* (Bureau of American Ethnology Bull. 30 [2 vols.; Washington, 1910]), II, 714.

44. Drake, *op. cit.*, p. 621.

45. *Ibid.*, p. 657.

NOTES TO CHAPTER VIII

1. John Champe, Ash Hollow Cave ("University of Nebraska Studies, New Series," Vol. I [Lincoln, 1946]), and William D. Strong, An Introduction to Nebraska Archaeology ("Smithsonian Miscellaneous Collections," Vol. XCIII, No. 10 [Washington, 1936]).

2. A. T. Hill and Martin Kivett, Woodland-like Manifestations in Nebraska ("Nebraska History," Vol. XXI, No. 3 [Lincoln, 1940]); see also Champe, op. cit.; and W. R. Wedel, Archaeological Investigations in Platte and Clay Counties, Missouri (United States National Museum Bull. 183 [Washington, 1943]).

3. W. C. McKern, "An Hypothesis for the Asiatic Origin of the Woodland Culture Pattern," American Antiquity, III, No. 2 (1937).

4. Strong, op. cit., pp. 245–50 (Upper Republican Culture); p. 274 (Nebraska Culture). Cf. Wedel, op. cit., and Champe, op. cit.

5. H. E. Bolton, Coronado—Knight of the Pueblos and Plains (New York: Whittlesey House, 1949), p. 291.

6. George Will, Corn of the Northwest (St. Paul: Webb Publishing Co., 1930).

7. John R. Swanton, Source Material on the History and Ethnology of the Caddo Indians (Bureau of American Ethnology Bull. 132 [Washington, 1942]), pp. 33–35 (quoting Suceso and Castaneda).

8. Strong, op. cit., p. 274.

9. Robert M. Dendhardt, "Our Indians," Historian, winter, 1938.

10. Alice C. Fletcher and Francis La Flesche, "The Omaha Tribe," 27th Annual Report of the Bureau of American Ethnology (Washington, 1906), pp. 502–3.

11. Fred Eggan (ed.), Social Anthropology of North American Indian Tribes (Chicago: University of Chicago Press, 1937), pp. 75–81.

12. Clark Wissler, Societies and Dance Associations of the Blackfoot Indians ("American Museum of Natural History Publications in Anthropology," Vol. XI, No. 4 [New York, 1913]), p. 387.

13. Fletcher and La Flesche, op. cit., p. 427. Cf. G. E. Hyde, The Pawnee Indians (Denver Museum of Natural History, "Old West Series," Vol. IV [Denver, 1934]), pp. 108–11; Alfred W. Bowers, Mandan Social and Ceremonial Organization (Chicago: University of Chicago Press, 1950), p. 74.

14. Fletcher and La Flesche, op. cit., pp. 437 ff.

15. Wissler, op. cit.

16. Alice C. Fletcher, "The Hako: A Pawnee Ceremony," 22d Annual Report of the Bureau of American Ethnology, Part II (Washington, 1901).

17. Ibid., pp. 217–51.

18. Bowers, op. cit., pp. 111–56.

19. Francis La Flesche, "The Osage Tribe; Rite of the Chiefs; Sayings of Ancient Men," 36th Annual Report of the Bureau of American Ethnology (Washington, 1915), p. 159.

20. Fletcher, op. cit.

21. Ibid.

22. Bowers, op. cit.

23. La Flesche, op. cit., p. 71.

24. Fletcher, op. cit.

25. Margaret Mead, *The Changing Culture of an Indian Tribe* ("Columbia University Contributions to Anthropology," Vol. XV [New York: Columbia University Press, 1932]).

NOTES TO CHAPTER IX

1. J. R. Arnold and W. F. Libby, *Radiocarbon Dates* (University of Chicago Institute for Nuclear Studies, September, 1950), p. 6.

2. Herbert W. Dick directed excavations for the Early Man Division of the Upper Gila Reseaches by the Peabody Museum, Harvard University, 1948.

3. P. C. Mangelsdorf and C. E. Smith, Jr., *New Archaeological Evidence on Evolution in Maize* ("Botanical Museum Leaflets, Harvard University," Vol. XIII, No. 8 [Cambridge, 1949]), pp. 213–14.

4. Paul S. Martin and John B. Rinaldo, "The Southwestern Co-tradition," *Southwestern Journal of Anthropology* (Albuquerque), VII, No. 3 (1951), 219–21.

5. H. M. Wormington, *Prehistoric Indians of the Southwest* ("Denver Museum of Natural History, Popular Series," No. 7 [Denver, 1947]), p. 22, and Paul S. Martin, George I. Quimby, and Donald Collier, *Indians before Columbus* (Chicago: University of Chicago Press, 1947), p. 87.

6. See n. 2 above.

7. Martin and Rinaldo, *op. cit.*, pp. 219–21.

8. Mangelsdorf and Smith, *op. cit.*, pp. 213–14.

9. Martin and Rinaldo, *op. cit.*, p. 223.

10. Volney H. Jones, *A Summary of Data on Aboriginal Cotton: Symposium on Prehistoric Agriculture* (University of New Mexico Bull. 296 [Albuquerque, 1936]).

11. A. E. Douglass, "The Secret of the Southwest Solved by Talkative Tree Rings," *National Geographic Magazine*, LXV, No. 6 (1929), 737–70.

12. H. S. Gladwin, *Excavations at Snaketown: Reviews and Conclusions*, Vol. IV ("Gila Pueblo, Medallion Papers," No. 38 [Globe, Ariz., 1948]), pp. 234–35.

13. Emil W. Haury, *The Stratigraphy and Archaeology of Ventana Cave, Arizona* (Albuquerque: University of New Mexico Press, 1950), pp. 530–37.

14. E. F. Castetter and W. H. Bell, *Pima and Papago Indian Agriculture* (Albuquerque: University of New Mexico Press, 1942), p. 148.

15. Ruth M. Underhill, *Singing for Power* (Berkeley: University of California Press, 1938), **p. 70.**

16. Ruth M. Underhill, *Papago Indian Religion* (New York: Columbia University Press, 1946), p. 196.

17. Underhill, *Singing for Power*, p. 47

18. Martin and Rinaldo, *op. cit.*, p. 219.

19. Ruth Bunzell, "Zuni Ritual Poetry," *47th Annual Report of the Bureau of American Ethnology* (Washington, 1932), p. 540.

20. *Ibid.*, p. 679.

21. Elsie C. Parsons, *Pueblo Indian Religion* (2 vols.; Chicago: University of Chicago Press, 1939), p. 877.

22. Bunzell, *op. cit.*, pp. 782–83.

23. *Ibid.*

24. *Ibid.*, p. 799.

25. Erik K. Reed, "A Theory of Southwestern Prehistory" ("Region Three

Archeological Interpretation Circular," No. 8 [Santa Fe, N.M.: National Park Service, 1951]). (Mimeographed.)

26. Charles F. and Erminie W. Vogelin, *North American Indian Languages* (map) (American Ethnological Society Bull. 20 [New York, 1941]).

27. For details see Ruth M. Underhill, *Pueblo Crafts* ("Indian Hand Craft Pamphlet," No. 7 [Phoenix, 1946]), and John Adair, *The Navaho and Pueblo Silversmiths* (Norman: University of Oklahoma Press, 1944).

NOTES TO CHAPTER X

1. E. T. Hall, Jr., "Recent Clues to Athapascan Prehistory in the Southwest," *American Anthropologist*, XLVI, No. 1 (1944), 102.

2. H. P. Mera, *Ceramic Clues to the Prehistory of New Mexico* (Laboratory of Anthropology, Technology Series Bull. 8 [Santa Fe, N.M., 1935]); F. Hibben, "The Gallina Phase," *American Antiquity*, Vol. IV, No. 2 (1938).

3. O. T. Mason, "North American Bows, Arrows and Quivers," *Annual Report of the Smithsonian Institution for 1893* (Washington, 1894), pp. 631–79.

4. H. E. Bolton, *Coronado—Knight of the Pueblos and Plains* (New York: Whittlesey House, 1949), p. 245.

5. J. R. Harrington, personal information.

6. Dorothy Keur, "A Chapter in Navaho-Pueblo Relations," *American Antiquity*, X, No. 1 (1944), 75–85.

7. W. W. Hill, *Some Navaho Cultural Changes during Two Centuries* ("Smithsonian Institution Miscellaneous Collection," Vol. C [Washington, 1940]), p. 403.

8. Edward Sapir and Harry Hoijer, *Navaho Texts* (Iowa City: Linguistic Society of America, University of Iowa, 1942), p. 359.

9. John Adair, *The Navaho and Pueblo Silversmiths* (Norman: University of Oklahoma Press, 1945), pp. 3–5.

10. Ruth M. Underhill, *Ceremonial Patterns in the Greater Southwest* ("American Ethnological Society Memoirs," Vol. XIII [New York, 1948]), pp. 41–46.

11. F. W. Hodge (ed.), *Handbook of American Indians North of Mexico* (Bureau of American Ethnology Bull. 30 [2 vols.; Washington, 1910]), II, 63.

12. Harry Hoijer, "The Southern Athapascan Languages," *American Antiquity*, Vol. XL, No. 1 (new ser., 1938).

13. E. W. Gifford, *Culture Element Distribution: Apache-Pueblo* ("University of California Anthropological Records," No. 4, Part I [Berkeley: University of California Press, 1940]).

14. B. Davis, *The Truth about Geronimo* (New Haven: Yale University Press, 1929), pp. 68, 78, 83, 107.

15. F. C. Lockwood, *The Apache Indians* (New York: Macmillan Co., 1938).

16. Davis, *op. cit.*, p. 102.

17. *Ibid.*, p. 114.

18. Bolton, *op. cit.*, p. 245.

19. J. L. Champe, "White Cat Village," *American Antiquity*, XIV, No. 4 (1949), 290–91.

20. Gifford, *op. cit.*, p. 29.

21. M. E. Opler, *The Character and Derivation of the Jicarilla Holiness Rite*

("University of New Mexico Bulletin, Anthropological Series," Vol. IV, No. 3 [Albuquerque, 1943]).

22. *Statistical Supplement to the Annual Report of the Commissioner of Indian Affairs* (Washington: Department of the Interior, 1945), p. 7.

NOTES TO CHAPTER XI

1. L. S. Cressman, "Western Prehistory in the Light of Carbon 14 Dating," *Southwestern Journal of Anthropology* (Albuquerque), VII, No. 3 (1951), 308.

2. Charles F. and Erminie W. Vogelin, *North American Indian Languages* (map) (American Ethnological Society Bull. 20 [New York, 1941]).

3. A. L. Kroeber, *Cultural and Natural Areas of Native North America* ("University of California Publications in American Archaeology and Ethnology," Vol. XXXVIII [Berkeley: University of California Press, 1939]), p. 55.

4. For a detailed description of beliefs concerning guardian spirit and soul see Verne Ray, *Cultural Relations in the Plateau of Northwestern America* ("Publications of the Frederick W. Hodge Anniversary Publication Fund," Vol. III [Los Angeles, 1939]), pp. 68–102.

5. Francis Haines, "The Northward Spread of Horses among the Plains Indians," *American Anthropologist*, XL (new ser., 1938), 435–36.

6. *Washington Historical Quarterly*, Vol. II, No. 3 (1908).

7. C. Schaffer, "The First Jesuit Mission to the Flathead," *Pacific Northwest Quarterly* (Seattle), Vol. XXVIII (1937).

8. Gordon MacGregor, manuscripts on the Flathead Indians in the Indian Service files.

9. Cressman, *op. cit.*, p. 306.

10. J. R. Arnold and W. F. Libby, *Radiocarbon Dates* (University of Chicago Institute for Nuclear Studies, September 1950), p. 10.

11. Albert Mohr, "The Hunting Crook, Its Use and Distribution in the Southwest," *Masterkey*, XXV, No. 5 (1951), 145–53.

12. Julian H. Steward, *Basin-Plateau Aboriginal Sociopolitical Groups* (Bureau of American Ethnology Bull. 120 [Washington, 1938]), pp. 9–247.

13. Beatrice Blythe Whiting, *Paiute Sorcery* ("Viking Fund Publications in Anthropology," No. 15 [New York, 1950]), pp. 27–37; Isabel T. Kelley, *Surprise Valley Paiutes* ("University of California Publications in American Archaeology and Ethnology," Vol. XXXI, No. 3 [Berkeley: University of California Press, 1932]).

14. Carling A. and Aline Malouf, "The Effects of Spanish Slavery on the Indians of the Intermontane Region," *Southwestern Journal of Anthropology*, Vol. I, No. 3 (1935).

15. W. J. Ghent, *The Road to Oregon* (New York: Tudor Publishing Co., 1934), pp. 88–91.

16. Ruth M. Underhill, field notes.

NOTES TO CHAPTER XII

1. For details on California Indians see the various volumes in the "University of California Publications in Archaeology and Ethnology" and "Anthropological Records," Berkeley. Cf. A. L. Kroeber, *Handbook of Indians of California* (Bureau of American Ethnology Bull. 78 [Washington, 1925]), and Roland B. Dixon, *The Northern Maidu* (American Museum of Natural History Bull. 18 [New York, 1905]).

2. E. F. Castetter and W. H. Bell, *Yuman Indian Agriculture* (Albuquerque: University of New Mexico Press, 1951), pp. 100–108.

3. *Ibid.*, p. 111; cf. G. F. Carter, *Plant Geography and Culture History in the American Southwest* ("Viking Fund Publications in Anthropology," No. 5 [New York, 1945]), p. 36.

4. Ruth M. Underhill, unpublished manuscripts.

5. C. Daryll Forde, *Ethnography of the Yuma Indians* ("University of California Publications in American Archaeology and Ethnology," Vol. XXVIII, No. 4 [Berkeley, 1931]), pp. 214–19.

6. Kroeber, *op. cit.*, p. 745; and Underhill, unpublished manuscripts.

7. Forde, *op. cit.*, pp. 162, 164.

8. Kroeber, *op. cit.*, p. 754.

9. Underhill, unpublished manuscripts.

10. Frances Densmore, *Yuman and Yaqui Music* (Bureau of American Ethnology Bull. 110 [Washington, 1932]), pp. 13–14, and Underhill, unpublished manuscripts.

11. N. C. Nelson, *The Ellis Landing Shellmound* ("University of California Publications in Archaeology and Ethnology," Vol. VII [Berkeley, 1910]); Frederick Johnson (ed.), "Radiocarbon Dating," *American Antiquity, Supplement*, XVII, No. 1, Part II (Memoir No. 8 [July, 1951]), 25.

12. H. M. Wormington, *Ancient Man in North America* ("Denver Museum of Natural History, Popular Series," No. 4 [Denver, 1949]), pp. 78–87.

13. For details on southern California organization see W. D. Strong, *Aboriginal Society in Southern California* ("University of California Publications in American Archaeology and Ethnology," Vol. XXVI [Berkeley, 1929]); E. W. Gifford, *Clans and Moieties in Native California* ("University of California Publications in American Archaeology and Ethnology," Vol. XIV [Berkeley, 1918]); Kroeber, *op. cit.*, pp. 611–709.

14. Ruth M. Underhill, *Ceremonial Patterns in the Greater Southwest* ("American Ethnological Society Memoirs," Vol. XIII [New York, 1948]), pp. 41–46.

15. Though we see no historical connection, this practice is similar to the function of the "Paired Clans" of the Sauk and Fox (chap. vii).

16. A. E. Kroeber, *Cultural and Natural Areas of Native North America* ("University of California Publications in American Archaeology and Ethnology," Vol. XXXVIII [Berkeley, 1939]), p. 155.

17. See n. 1.

18. R. B. Dixon, *Maidu Myths* (American Museum of Natural History Bull. 17 [New York, 1902]).

19. Kroeber, *Handbook of Indians of California.*

20. Kuksu dances in series were held by Yuki, Wappo, Kato, Pomo, Wintun, Maidu, Miwok, Costanoan, Esselen, and Salinan.

21. Cora Dubois, *The 1870 Ghost Dance* ("University of California Anthropological Records," No. 3, Part I [Berkeley, 1939]).

NOTES TO CHAPTER XIII

1. Nootka, Makah, and Haida were the chief whalers; others might use stranded whales found on the beach. See John R. Jewitt, *A Narrative of the Adventures and Suffering of John P. Jewitt* (Middletown, Conn., 1815); James C. Swan, *The Indians of Cape Flattery* ("Smithsonian Contributions to

Knowledge," Vol. XVI [Washington, 1870]); and Ruth M. Underhill, *Indians of the Pacific Northwest* ("Indian Life and Customs," No. 5 [Phoenix, 1945]).

2. Philip Drucker, *Culture Element Distributions: Northwest Coast* ("University of California Anthropological Records," No. 9, Part III [Berkeley, 1950]).

3. A. L. Kroeber, *Cultural and Natural Areas of Native North America* ("University of California Publications in American Archaeology and Ethnology," Vol. XXXVIII [Berkeley, 1939]).

4. George I. Quimby, "Culture Contact on the Northwest Coast between 1785 and 1795," *American Anthropologist*, L, No 2 (new ser., 1948), p. 247.

5. *Ibid.*, p. 254.

6. *Ibid.*

7. Ronald L. Olson, *Adze, Canoe and House Types of the Northwest Coast* ("University of Washington Publications in Anthropology," Vol. II [Seattle, 1927]), pp. 1–38.

8. Lila M. O'Neale, *Yurok and Karok Basket Weavers* ("University of California Publications in American Archaeology and Ethnology," Vol. XXXII, No. 1 [Berkeley, 1932]); Underhill, *op. cit.*

9. Robert B. Inverarity, *Art of the Northwest Coast Indians* (Berkeley: University of California Press, 1950). See also Paul Wingert, *American Indian Sculpture* (New York: J. J. Augustin, 1949); Gladys Reichard, *Melanesian Design* (New York: Columbia University Press, 1933); and Viola Garfield and A. Forrest Linn, *The Wolf and the Raven* (Seattle: University of Washington Press, 1948).

10. F. W. Howay, "The Dog's Hair Blanket of the Coast Salish," *Washington Historical Quarterly*, IX (1918), 83–92.

11. Harold E. Driver, *Girls Puberty Rites in Western North America* ("University of California Anthropological Records," No. 6, Part II [Berkeley, 1941]).

12. A. L. Kroeber, *Handbook of the Indians of California* (Bureau of American Ethnology Bull. 78 [Washington, 1925]), chap. ii.

13. *Ibid.*, p. 41.

14. The variations of the potlatch among different groups cannot all be taken up here. Excellent descriptions will be found for the Tlingit in John R. Swanton, "The Tlingit Indians," *26th Annual Report of the Bureau of American Ethnology* (Washington, 1908); for the Kwakiutl in Franz Boas, "The Social Organization and the Secret Societies of the Kwakiutl," *Report of the United States National Museum, 1895* (Washington, 1897), and in Helen Codere, *Fighting with Property* ("Publications of the American Ethnological Society," Vol. XVIII [New York, 1950]); for the Haida in John R. Swanton, *Contributions to the Ethnology of the Haida* ("American Museum of Natural History Memoirs," No. 8 [New York, 1910]); and in G. P. Murdock, *Rank and Potlatch among the Haida* ("Yale University Publications in Anthropology," Vol. XIII [New Haven: Yale University Press, 1936]); for the Tsimshian in Viola Garfield, *Tsimshian Clan and Society* ("University of Washington Publications in Anthropology," Vol. VII, No. 3 [Seattle: University of Washington Press, 1939]); for the Bella Coola in Thomas McIlwrath, "Certain Beliefs of the Bella Coola Indians," *Annual Archaeological Report of the Minister of Education, Ontario, 1924–25* (Toronto, 1926); and for the Nootka in Philip Drucker, *The Northern and Central Nootkan Tribes* (Bureau of American Ethnology Bull. 144 [Washington, 1951]). Cf. Homer G. Barnett, "Nature of the Potlatch," *American Anthropologist*, Vol. XI, No. 3 (new ser., 1909).

15. Codere, op. cit.

16. Marion Smith, *The Puyallup-Nesqually* ("Columbia University Contribution to Anthropology," No. 32 [New York: Columbia University Press, 1940]), p. 150; Catherine Holt, *Shasta Ethnography* ("University of California Anthropological Records," No. 5, Part IV [Berkeley, 1946]), p. 314.

17. Leslie Spier, *Klamath Ethnology* ("University of California Publications in American Archaeology and Ethnology,"* Vol. XXX [Berkeley, 1930]), p. 27; Holt, op. cit.

18. Codere, op. cit.

19. James Mooney, "The Ghost Dance Religion," *14th Annual Report of the Bureau of American Ethnology* (Washington, 1896), pp. 116–745; Cora Dubois, *The Feather Cult of the Middle Columbia* ("General Series in Anthropology," No. 7 [Menasha, Wis., 1938]).

20. Erna Gunther, "The Shaker Religion of the Northwest," in *Indians of the Urban Northwest* (New York: Columbia University Press, 1949), pp. 37–76; June McCormack Collins, "The Indian Shaker Church," *Southwest Journal of Anthropology*, Vol. VI, No. 4 (1950).

NOTES TO CHAPTER XIV

1. W. C. MacCleod, *The American Frontier* (New York: Alfred A. Knopf, 1928), pp. 193–208.

2. See *Report of the Board of Indian Commissioners, 1924* (Washington, 1925), pp. 5–6. Care of New York Indians was transferred to the state in 1882.

3. See chap. vii.

4. See chap. iv.

5. Charles C. Royce, "Indian Land Cessions in the United States," *18th Annual Report of the Bureau of American Ethnology*, Part II (Washington, 1897), pp. 648–780.

6. *Ibid.*

7. George D. Harmon, *Sixty Years of Indian Affairs* (Chapel Hill: University of North Carolina Press, 1941), pp. 375–77.

8. Flora W. Seymore, *The Story of the Red Man* (New York: Tudor Publishing Co., 1934), p. 170.

9. Evelyn C. Adams, *American Indian Education* (New York: King's Crown Press, 1946), **p. 33.**

10. Harmon, op. cit., pp. 100–133.

11. 4 *U.S. Statutes at Large* 411. See also Grant Foreman, *Indian Removal* (Norman: University of Oklahoma Press, 1932).

12. Royce, op. cit.

13. Seymore, **op. cit., p. 182.**

14. Royce, op. cit., pp. 848 ff.

15. Loring B. Priest, *Uncle Sam's Step Children: The Reformation of United States Indian Policy, 1865–1887* (New Brunswick, N. J.: Rutgers University Press, 1942), p. 142.

16. Seymore, op. cit., p. 355.

17. See *Report of the Board of Indian Commissioners, 1924.*

18. The Menomini of Wisconsin and the Red Lake Ojibwa excepted.

19. Lewis Merriam and Associates, *The Problem of Indian Administration* (Baltimore, 1928).

20. *Indian Claims Commission Report for 1970.*

21. William A. Brophy and Sophie D. Aberle, *The Indian, America's Unfinished Business: Report of the Commission on the Rights, Liberties, and Responsibilities of the American Indian* (Norman, Okla.: University of Oklahoma Press, 1966), pp. 193–94, 196, 199.

22. *Ibid.,* p. 182.

23. Public Health Service, *The Fourth Report on the Indian Health Program of the U. S. Public Health Service To The First Americans,* P. H. S. Publication No. 1580 (Washington, D.C.: Government Printing Office, 1970), p. 16.

24. Mr. Nelson, H.U.D., personal communication, 1971.

25. United States Department of the Interior, Bureau of Indian Affairs, *Fiscal Year 1970: Statistics Concerning Indian Education* (Lawrence, Kansas: Publications Service, Haskell Indian Junior College, 1970), p. 1.

26. Lyndon B. Johnson, "The Forgotten American," The President's Message to the Congress on Goals and Programs for the American Indian, March 6, 1968, in *Indian Record,* March 1968, p. 6.

27. Joint Economic Committee, Congress of the United States, *Toward Economic Development for Native American Communities: A Compendium of Papers Submitted to the Subcommittee on Economy in Government of the Joint Economic Committee,* 2 Vols. (Washington, D. C.: Government Printing Office, 1969), p. 302.

28. *Ibid.,* p. 348.

29. *The Indian Historian,* Vol. III, No. 2 (Spring 1970), p. 37.

30. Robert L. Bennett, excerpts from a speech made at the national convention of the National Congress of American Indians at Omaha, Nebraska, September 26, 1968, in *Indian Record,* November 1968, p. 1.

Bibliography

ADAIR, JAMES. *History of the American Indians*. London, 1775.

ADAIR, JOHN. *The Navajo and Pueblo Silversmiths*. Norman: University of Oklahoma Press, 1944.

ADAMS, EVELYN C. *American Indian Education*. New York: King's Crown Press, 1946.

AMSDEN, CHARLES A. *Navaho Weaving: Its Technic and History*. Albuquerque: University of New Mexico Press, 1949.

ARNOLD, J. R. and LIBBY, W. F. *Radiocarbon Dates*. Chicago: University of Chicago Institute for Nuclear Studies, September, 1950.

BAILEY, L. W. *The Conflict of European and Eastern Algonkian Cultures*. ("New Brunswick Museum Publications," No. 3.) New Brunswick, N.J., 1937.

BARNETT, HOMER G. "Nature of the Potlatch," *American Anthropologist*, Vol. XL, No. 3 (new ser., 1938).

BEAUCHAMP, W. M. *Metallic Ornaments of the New York Indians*. (New York State Museum Bull. 305.) Albany, 1903.

————. *A History of the New York Iroquois*. (New York State Museum Bull. 78.) Albany, 1905.

BENNETT, ROBERT L. Excerpts from a speech made at the national convention of the National Congress of American Indians at Omaha, Nebraska, September 26, 1968. In *Indian Record*, November 1968, pp. 1–2, 4.

BENNETT, W. C., and BIRD, J. B. *Andean Culture History*. ("American Museum of Natural History Handbook Series," No. 15.) New York, 1949.

BLAKE, ALEXANDER V. (ed.). *Anecdotes of the American Indian*. New York, 1844.

BLOM, FRANS. *The Conquest of Yucatan*. Boston: Houghton Mifflin Co., 1936.

BLOOMFIELD, L. *Menomini Texts*. ("Publications of the American Ethnological Society," Vol. XII.) New York, 1928.

BOAS, FRANZ. "First General Report on the Indians of British Columbia," *Report of the 59th Meeting of the British Association for the Advancement of Science, 1889*. London, 1890.

————. "The Social Organization and the Secret Societies of the Kwakiutl," *Report of the United States National Museum, 1895*. Washington, D.C., 1897.

————. *The Kwakiutl of Vancouver Island*. ("American Museum of Natural History Memoirs," Vol. V, No. 2.) New York, 1909.

BOLTON, H. E. *Coronado—Knight of the Pueblos and Plains*. New York: Whittlesey House, 1949.

BOLTON, R. P. *Indian Life of Long Ago in the City of New York*. New York: Joseph Graham (Schoen Press), 1934.

BOURNE, EDWARD G. *Narratives of the Career of Hernando de Soto.* 2 vols. New York: Allerton Book Co., 1904.

BOWERS, ALFRED W. *Mandan Social and Ceremonial Organization.* Chicago: University of Chicago Press, 1950.

BROPHY, WILLIAM A. and ABERLE, SOPHIE D. *The Indian, America's Unfinished Business: Report of the Commission on the Rights, Liberties, and Responsibilities of the American Indian.* Norman, Okla.:University of Oklahoma Press, 1966.

BROWN, JOHN P. *Old Frontiers.* Kingsport, Tenn.: Southern Publishers, Inc., 1938.

BUNZELL, RUTH. "Zuni Ritual Poetry," *47th Annual Report of the Bureau of American Ethnology.* Washington, D.C., 1932.

CARTER, G. F. *Plant Geography and Culture History in the American Southwest.* ("Viking Fund Publications in Anthropology," No. 5.) New York, 1945.

CASTETTER, E. F., and BELL, W. H. *Pima and Papago Indian Agriculture.* Albuquerque: University of New Mexico Press, 1942.

————. *Yuman Indian Agriculture.* Albuquerque: University of New Mexico Press, 1951.

CASTETTER, E. F. and OPLER, M. E. *The Ethnobiology of the Chiricahua and Mescalero Apache.* ("University of New Mexico Bulletin, Biological Series," No. 4, Part V.) Albuquerque, 1936.

CASTETTER, E. F., and UNDERHILL, RUTH M. *The Ethnobiology of the Papago Indians.* ("University of New Mexico Bulletin, Biological Series." No. 4, Part III.) Albuquerque, 1935.

CATLIN, GEORGE. *Illustrations of Manners, Customs and Conditions of the North American Indians.* 2 vols. New York, 1841.

CHAMPE, JOHN L. *Ash Hollow Cave.* ("University of Nebraska Studies, New Series," Vol. I.) Lincoln, 1946.

————. "White Cat Village," *American Antiquity,* Vol. XIV, No. 4 (1949).

CHILDE, E. GORDON. *Man Makes Himself.* New York: Oxford University Press, 1939.

CODERE, HELEN. *Fighting with Property.* ("Publications of the American Ethnological Society," Vol. XVIII.) New York, 1950.

COLBERT, EDWIN H. "The Pleistocene Mammals of North America and Their Relations to Eurasian Forms," in *Early Man,* ed. GEORGE C. MacCURDY. Philadelphia: J. B. Lippincott Co., 1939.

COLLINS, JUNE McCORMACK. "The Indian Shaker Church," *Southwestern Journal of Anthropology* (Albuquerque), Vol. VI, No. 4 (1950).

COOPER, JOHN M. "Is the Algonquian Family Hunting Ground System Pre-Columbian?" *American Anthropologist,* Vol. XLI, No. 1 (1939).

————. "The Culture of the Northeastern Indian Hunters: A Reconstructive Interpretation," in *Man in Northeastern North America,* ed. FREDERICK JOHNSON. ("Papers of the Robert S. Peabody Foundation for Archaeology," Vol. III.) Andover, 1946.

COTTER, JACK. *Region Three Interpretive Notes 120.* Santa Fe: National Park Service, 1950.

CRAWFORD, M. D. C. *The Conquest of Culture.* New York: Greenberg, 1938.

CRESSMAN, L. S. "Western Prehistory in the Light of Carbon 14 Dating," *Southwestern Journal of Anthropology*, Vol. VII, No. 3 (1951).

CULIN, STEWART. "Games of the North American Indians," *24th Annual Report of the Bureau of American Ethnology*. Washington, D.C., 1907.

CUSHING, F. H. *Zuni Breadstuffs.* ("Indian Notes and Monographs," No. 8.) New York: Museum of the American Indian, Heye Foundation, 1920.

DAVIS, B. *The Truth about Geronimo.* New Haven: Yale University Press, 1929.

DEBO, ANGIE. *The Road to Disappearance.* Norman: University of Oklahoma Press, 1941.

DENDHARDT, ROBERT M. "Our Indians," *Historian*, winter, 1938.

DENSMORE, FRANCES. *Chippewa Customs.* (Bureau of American Ethnology Bull. 86.) Washington, D.C., 1929.

———. *Yuman and Yaqui Music.* (Bureau of American Ethnology Bull. 110.) Washington, D.C., 1932.

DIXON, ROLAND B. *Maidu Myths.* (American Museum of Natural History Bull. 17.) New York, 1902.

———. *The Northern Maidu.* (American Museum of Natural History Bull. 18.) New York, 1905.

DOUGLAS, F. H. *The Ute Indians.* (Denver Art Museum Leaflet 10.) Denver, 1930.

———. *The Iroquois Long House.* (Denver Art Museum Leaflet 12.) Denver, 1930.

———. *The Apache Indians.* (Denver Art Museum Leaflet 16.) Denver, 1930.

———. *Apache Indian Coiled Basketry.* (Denver Art Museum Leaflet 54.) Denver, 1934.

———. *Zuni Silverwork.* (Denver Art Museum Leaflet 104.) Denver, 1941.

DOUGLASS, E. A. "The Secret of the Southwest Solved by Talkative Tree Rings," *National Geographic Magazine*, LVI, No. 6 (December, 1929), 737–70.

DOWNES, R. C. *Council Fires on the Upper Ohio.* Pittsburgh: University of Pittsburgh Press, 1940.

DRAKE, S. G. *The Aboriginal Races of North America.* New York: John B. Alden, 1880. (15th ed. revised by H. L. WILLIAMS.)

DRIVER, HAROLD E. *Girls Puberty Rites in Western North America.* ("University of California Anthropological Records," No. 6, Part II.) Berkeley, 1941.

DRUCKER, PHILIP. *Culture Element Distribution: Northwest Coast.* ("University of California Anthropological Records," No. 9, Part III.) Berkeley, 1950.

———. *The Northern and Central Nootkan Tribes.* (Bureau of American Ethnology Bull. 144.) Washington, D.C., 1951.

DUBOIS, CORA A. *The Feather Cult of the Middle Columbia.* ("General Series in Anthropology," No. 7.) Menasha, Wis., 1938.

———. *The 1870 Ghost Dance.* ("University of California Anthropological Records," No. 3, Part I.) Berkeley, 1939.

EGGAN, FRED (ed.). *Social Anthropology of North American Indian Tribes.* Chicago: University of Chicago Press, 1937.

EMMONS, GEORGE T. *The Chilkat Blanket.* ("American Museum of Natural History Memoirs," Vol. III.) New York, 1907.

EWERS, JOHN C. *Plains Indian Painting*. Palo Alto: Stanford University Press, 1939.

FENTON, W. N. *Problems Arising from the Historic Northeastern Position of the Iroquois*. ("Smithsonian Institution Miscellaneous Collection," Vol. C.) Washington, D.C., 1940.

FLANNERY, REGINA. *Analysis of Coastal Algonkian Cultures*. ("Catholic University of America Anthropological Series," No. 8.) Washington, D.C., 1939.

————. "The Culture of the Northeastern Indian Hunters: A Descriptive Survey," in *Man in Northeastern North America*, ed. FREDERICK JOHNSON. ("Papers of the Robert S. Peabody Foundation for Archaeology," Vol. III.) Andover, 1946.

FLETCHER, ALICE C. "The Hako: A Pawnee Ceremony," *22d Annual Report of the Bureau of American Ethnology*. Washington, D.C., 1901.

FLETCHER, ALICE C., and LA FLESCHE, FRANCIS. "The Omaha Tribe," *27th Annual Report of the Bureau of American Ethnology*. Washington, D.C., 1906.

FORDE, C. DARYLL. *Ethnography of the Yuma Indians*. ("University of California Publications in American Archaeology and Ethnology," Vol. XXVIII, No. 4.) Berkeley, 1931.

FOREMAN, GRANT. *Indian Removal*. Norman: University of Oklahoma Press, 1932.

GARFIELD, VIOLA. *Tsimshian Clan and Society*. ("University of Washington Publications in Anthropology," Vol. VII, No. 3,) Seattle, 1939.

GARFIELD, VIOLA, and LINN, A. FOREST. *The Wolf and the Raven*. Seattle: University of Washington Press, 1948.

GEBBER, ERNEST. *Plymouth Adventure*. Garden City: Doubleday & Co., 1950.

GHENT, W. J. *The Road to Oregon*. New York: Tudor Publishing Co., 1934

GIFFORD, E. W. *Clans and Moieties in Native California*. ("University of California Publications in American Archaeology and Ethnology," Vol. XIV.) Berkeley, 1918.

————. *Culture Element Distribution: Apache-Pueblo*. ("University of California Anthropological Records," No. 4, Part I.) Berkeley, 1940.

GIFFORD, E. W., and KROEBER, A. L. *Culture Element Distributions: Pomo*. ("University of California Publications in American Archaeology and Ethnology," Vol. XXXVII, No. 4.) Berkeley, 1937.

GILPIN, LAURA. *Temples of Yucatan*. New York: Hastings House, 1948.

GLADWIN, HAROLD S. *Excavations at Snaketown: Reviews and Conclusions*, Vol. IV. ("Gila Pueblo, Medallion Papers," No. 38.) Globe, Ariz., 1948.

GUNTHER, ERNA. *Klallam Ethnography*. ("University of Washington Publications in Archaeology," No. 1.) Seattle, 1927.

————. "The Shaker Religion of the Northwest," in *Indians of the Urban Northwest*. New York: Columbia University Press, 1949.

HAINES, FRANCIS. "The Northward Spread of Horses among the Plains Indians," *American Anthropologist*, Vol. XL, No. 3 (new ser., 1938).

HALE, H. *The Iroquois Book of Rites*. ("Brinton's Library of Aboriginal American Literature.") Philadelphia: D. G. Brinton, 1883.

HALE, H., and HALL, E. T., JR. "Recent Clues to Athapascan Prehistory in the Southwest," *American Anthropologist*, Vol. XLVI, No. 1 (new ser., 1944).

HALL, H. V. "Some Shields of the Plains and Southwest," *Museum Journal* (Philadelphia), Vol. XVII, No. 1 (1926).

HARMON, GEORGE D. *Sixty Years of Indian Affairs.* Chapel Hill: University of North Carolina Press, 1941.

HARRINGTON, M. R. "The Devil Dance of the Apache," *Museum Journal* (Philadelphia), Vol. III (1912).

————. *Religion and Ceremonies of the Lenapa.* ("Indian Notes and Monographs," No. 19.) New York: Museum of the American Indian, Heye Foundation, 1921.

HAURY, EMIL W. *The Stratigraphy and Archaeology of Ventana Cave, Arizona.* Albuquerque: University of New Mexico Press, 1950.

HEWETT, J. N. B. "The Requickening Address of the Iroquois Condolence Council," *Journal of the Washington Academy of Science,* Vol. XXXIV, No. 3 (1944).

HEYERDAHL, THOR. *The Kon-Tiki Expedition.* London: George Allen & Unwin Ruskin House), 1950.

HIBBEN, FRANK, "The Gallina Phase," *American Antiquity,* Vol. IV, No. 2 (1938).

HILL, A. T., and KIVETT, MARTIN. "Woodland-like Manifestations in Nebraska," *Nebraska History,* Vol. XXI, No. 3 (1940).

HILL, W. W. *The Agricultural and Hunting Methods of the Navaho Indians.* ("Yale University Publications in Anthropology," Vol. XVIII.) New Haven, 1938.

————. *Some Navaho Cultural Changes during Two Centuries.* ("Smithsonian Institution Miscellaneous Collection," Vol. C.) Washington, D.C., 1940.

HODGE, F. W. "The Early Navajo and Apache," *American Anthropologist,* Vol. VIII, No. 3 (1895).

————. (ed.). *Handbook of American Indians.* 2 vols. (Bureau of American Ethnology Bull. 30.) Washington, D.C., 1907–10.

HOFFMAN, W. J. "The Midewiwin or 'Grand Medicine Society' of the Ojibway," *7th Annual Report of the Bureau of American Ethnology.* Washington, D.C., 1886.

HOIJER, HARRY. "The Southern Athapascan Languages," *American Anthropologist,* Vol. XL, No. 1 (new ser., 1938).

HOLT, CATHERINE. *Shasta Ethnography.* ("University of California Anthropological Records," No. 5, Part IV.) Berkeley, 1946.

HOWAY, F. W. "The Dog's Hair Blanket of the Coast Salish," *Washington Historical Quarterly,* Vol. IX 1918).

HUNT, G. T. *The Wars of the Iroquois.* Madison: University of Wisconsin Press, 1940.

HYDE, G. E. *The Pawnee Indians.* ("Denver Museum of Natural History, Old West Series," Vol. IV.) Denver, 1934.

Indian Claims Commission Report for 1970.

The Indian Historian, Vol. III, No. 2 (Spring 1970), pp. 37–38, 50.

INVERARITY, ROBERT B. *Art of the Northwest Coast Indians.* Berkeley: University of California Press, 1950.

JENNESS, DIAMOND. *Indians of Canada.* (Canadian Department of Mines Bull. 65, "Anthropological Series," No. 15.) Ottawa, 1932.

Jenks, A. E. "The Wild Rice Gatherers of the Upper Great Lakes," *19th Annual Report of the Bureau of American Ethnology*, Part II. Washington, D.C., 1898.

Jewitt, John R. *A Narrative of the Adventures and Sufferings of John P. Jewitt.* Middletown, Conn., 1815.

Johnson, Frederick. "Radiocarbon Dating," *American Antiquity, Supplement*, Vol. XVII, No. 1, Part II (Memoir No. 8 [July, 1951]).

Johnson, Lyndon B. "The Forgotten American," The President's Message to the Congress on Goals and Programs for the American Indian, March 6, 1968. In *Indian Record*, March 1968, pp. 1–14.

Joint Economic Committee, Congress of the United States. *Toward Economic Development for Native American Communities: A Compendium of Papers Submitted to the Subcommittee on Economy in Government of the Joint Economic Committee.* 2 Vols. Washington, D.C.: Government Printing Office, 1969.

Jones, Volney H. *A Summary of Data on Aboriginal Cotton: Symposium on Prehistoric Agriculture.* (University of New Mexico Bull. 296.) Albuquerque, 1936.

Keesing, F. M. *The Menomini Indians of Wisconsin: A Study of Three Centuries of Cultural Contact and Change.* ("Memoirs of the American Philosophical Society," No. 10.) Philadelphia, 1939.

Kelley, Isabel T. *Surprise Valley Paiutes.* ("University of California Publications in American Archaeology and Ethnology," Vol. XXXI, No. 3.) Berkeley, 1932.

Keur, Dorothy. "A Chapter in Navaho-Pueblo Relations," *American Antiquity*, Vol. X, No. 1 (1944).

Kidder, A. V. *Artifacts of the Pecos.* New Haven: Yale University Press (for the Phillips Academy, Andover, Mass.), 1932.

Kinietz, W. V. *The Indians of the Western Great Lakes, 1615–1760.* ("University of Michigan, Museum of Anthropology, Occasional Contributions," No. 10.) Ann Arbor, 1940.

Klimek, Stanislaus. *Culture Element Distribution: The Structure of California Culture.* ("University of California Publications in American Archaeology and Ethnology," Vol. XXXVII, No. 1.) Berkeley, 1935.

Kroeber, A. L. *Handbook of the Indians of California.* (Bureau of American Ethnology Bull. 78.) Washington, D.C., 1925.

———. *Native Cultures of the Southwest.* ("University of California Publications in American Archaeology and Ethnology," Vol. XXIII, No. 9.) Berkeley, 1928.

———. *Cultural and Natural Areas of Native North America.* ("University of California Publications in American Archaeology and Ethnology," Vol. XXXXVIII.) Berkeley, 1939.

La Flesche, Francis. "The Osage Tribe: Rite of the Chiefs; Sayings of Ancient Men," *36th Annual Report of the Bureau of American Ethnology.* Washington, D.C., 1915.

Laguna, Frederica de. "The Importance of the Eskimo in Northeastern Archaeology," in *Man in Northeastern North America*, ed. Frederick Johnson. ("Papers of the Robert S. Peabody Foundation for Archaeology," Vol. III.) Andover, 1946.

————. *The Prehistory of Northern North America as Seen from the Yukon.* ("Memoirs of the Society for American Archaeology," No. 3.) Menasha, 1947.

LESCARBOT, MARC. *History of New France,* ed. W. L. GRANT and H. P. BIGGAR. ("Publications of the Champlain Society," Vol. III.) Toronto, 1914.

LOCKWOOD, F. C. *The Apache Indians.* New York: Macmillan Co., 1938.

LONGFELLOW, HENRY W. *Song of Hiawatha.* Philadelphia: Henry Altemus Co., 1898.

LORANT, STEFAN. *The New World.* New York: Duell, Sloan & Pearce, 1946.

LOWIE, ROBERT H. "Some Problems in the Ethnology of the Crow and Village Indians," *American Anthropologist,* Vol. XIV, No. 1 (new ser., 1912).

————. *The Social Life of the Crow Indians.* ("Anthropological Papers of the American Museum of Natural History," Vol. IX, No. 2.) New York, 1912.

————. *Notes on Shoshonean Ethnography.* ("Anthropological Papers of the American Museum of Natural History," Vol. XX.) New York, 1924.

LYFORD, CARRIE A. *The Crafts of the Ojibwa.* ("Indian Handcraft Series," No. 5.) Phoenix: Office of Indian Affairs, 1943.

————. *Iroquois Crafts.* ("Indian Handcraft Pamphlet," No. 6.) Phoenix: Office of Indian Affairs, 1945.

McCAULEY, CLAY, "The Seminole Indians of Florida," *5th Annual Report of the Bureau of American Ethnology.* Washington, D.C., 1887.

MACCLEOD, WILLIAM C. *The American Indian Frontier.* New York: Alfred A. Knopf, 1928.

McCLINTOCK, W. *Painted Tipis and Picture Writing of the Blackfoot Indians* ("Southwestern Museum Leaflet Series," No. 6) Los Angeles, 1936.

MACGREGOR, GORDON. Manuscripts on the Flathead in the Indian Service files.

McGREGOR, JOHN C. *Southwestern Archaeology.* New York: John Wiley & Sons, 1941.

McILWRATH, THOMAS F. "Certain Beliefs of the Bella Coola Indians," *Annual Archaeological Report of the Minister of Education, Ontario, 1924–1925* Toronto, 1926.

McKERN, W. C. "An Hypothesis for the Asiatic Origin of the Woodland Culture Pattern," *American Antiquity,* Vol. III, No. 2 new ser., 1937).

MAGNUSSON, MAGNUS, and Pálsson, Hermann (translators). *The Vinland Sagas: The Norse Discovery of America.* Baltimore: Penguin Books, 1965.

MALOUF, CARLING A. *The Gosiute Indians.* ("University of Utah Museum Archaeological and Ethnological Papers," Vol. III.) Salt Lake City, 1940.

MALOUF, CARLING A. and ALINE. "The Effects of Spanish Slavery on the Indians of the Intermontane Region," *Southwestern Journal of Anthropology,* Vol. I, No. 3 (1945).

MANGELSDORF, P. C., and SMITH, C. E., JR. *New Archaeological Evidence on Evolution in Maize.* ("Harvard University, Botanical Museum Leaflets," Vol. XIII, No. 8.) Cambridge, 1949.

MARTIN, PAUL S. *The SU Site Excavations at a Mogollon Village, Western New Mexico, 1939.* ("Field Museum of Natural History Anthropological Series," Vol. XXXII, No. 1.) Chicago, 1940.

————. "Mummies, Sandals, Snares from Mogollons' Cave," Chicago: *Field Museum of Natural History Bulletin,* Vol. XXI, No. 11 (November, 1950).

———. "Expedition Finds Victim of Sacrifice in Cliff House," *ibid.*, Vol. XXII, No. 11 (November, 1951).

MARTIN, PAUL S.; QUIMBY, GEORGE I.; and COLLIER, DONALD. *Indians before Columbus*. Chicago: University of Chicago Press, 1947.

MARTIN, PAUL S., and RENALDO, JOHN B. "The Southwestern Co-Tradition," *Southwestern Journal of Anthropology*, Vol. VII, No. 3 (1951).

MASON, O. T. "North American Bows, Arrows and Quivers," *Annual Report of the Smithsonian Institution for 1893*. Washington, D.C., 1894.

MAXIMILLIAN, PRINCE OF WIED. *Travels in the Interior of North America*. London: Ackerman & Co., 1839.

MEAD, MARGARET. *The Changing Culture of an Indian Tribe*. ("Columbia University Contributions to Anthropology," Vol. XV.) New York, 1932.

MEGGERS, BETTY J., EVANS, CLIFFORD, and ESTRADA, EMILIO. *Early Formative Period of Coastal Ecuador: The Valdivia and Machalilla Phases*. Smithsonian Contributions to Anthropology, Vol. I. Washington, D.C.: Smithsonian Institution, 1965.

MERA, H. P. *Ceramic Clues to the Prehistory of New Mexico*. ("Laboratory of Anthropology, Technology Series," Bull. 8.) Santa Fe, N.M., 1935.

———. *Pueblo Indian Embroidery*. ("Laboratory of Anthropology Memoirs," No. 4.) Santa Fe, N.M., 1943.

MERRIAM, LEWIS, and ASSOCIATES. *The Problem of Indian Administration*. Baltimore, 1928.

MICHELSON, T. "Preliminary Report on the Linguistic Classification of Algonkian Tribes," *28th Annual Report of the Bureau of American Ethnology*. Washington, D.C., 1912.

———. *Contributions to Fox Ethnology*. (Bureau of American Ethnology Bull. 85.) Washington, D.C., 1927.

MINDELEFF, C. "Navaho Houses," *17th Annual Report of the Bureau of American Ethnology*, Part II. Washington, D.C., 1898.

MINDELEFF, V. "A Study of Pueblo Architecture," *8th Annual Report of the Bureau of American Ethnology*. Washington, D.C., 1887.

MOHR, ALBERT. "The Hunting Crook, Its Use and Distribution in the Southwest," *Masterkey* (Los Angeles), Vol. XXV, No. 5 (1951).

MOONEY, JAMES. "The Ghost Dance Religion," *14th Annual Report of the Bureau of American Ethnology*, Part II. Washington, D.C., 1896.

MOONEY, JAMES, and OLBRECHTS, FRANS M. *The Swimmer Manuscript*. (Bureau of American Ethnology Bull. 99.) Washington, D.C., 1932.

MORLEY, S. G. *The Ancient Maya*. Palo Alto: Stanford University Press, 1946.

MURDOCK, G. P. *Rank and Potlatch among the Haida*. ("Yale University Publications in Anthropology," Vol. XIII.) New Haven, 1936.

NELSON, N. C. *The Ellis Landing Shellmound*. ("University of California Publications in American Archaeology and Ethnology," Vol. VII.) Berkeley, 1910.

NORDENSKIÖLD, ERLAND. "Origin of the Indian Civilizations in South America," in *The American Aborigines*, ed. DIAMOND JENNESS. Toronto: University of Toronto Press, 1933.

OLSON, RONALD L. *Adze, Canoe and House Types of the Northwest Coast*. ("University of Washington Publications in Anthropology," Vol. II.) Seattle, 1927.

————. *Quinault of La Push, 1775–1945.* ("University of California Anthropological Records," No. 14, Part I.) Berkeley, 1950.

O'NEALE, LILA M. *Yurok and Karok Basket Weavers.* ("University of California Publications in American Archaeology and Ethnology," Vol. XXXII, No. 1.) Berkeley, 1932.

————. "Weaving," in *Handbook of South American Indians,* Vol. V, ed. JULIAN H. STEWARD. 6 vols. (Bureau of American Ethnology Bull. 143.) Washington, D.C., 1945–50.

OPLER, M. E. *The Character and Derivation of the Jicarilla Holiness Rite.* ("University of New Mexico Bulletin, Anthropological Series," Vol. IV, No. 3.) Albuquerque, 1943.

OSBORN, HENRY F. *The Age of Mammals in Europe, Asia and North America.* New York: Macmillan Co., 1910.

OSKISON, J. M. *Tecumseh and His Times.* New York: G. P. Putnam's Sons, 1938.

PARK, WILLARD Z. *Shamanism in Western North America.* ("Northwestern University Social Science Series," Vol. II.) Evanston, Ill., 1938.

PARKER, A. C. *Iroquois Uses of Maize and Other Food Plants.* (New York State Museum Bull. 144.) Albany, 1910.

————. *An Analytical History of the Seneca.* ("Researches and Transactions of the New York State Archaeological Association," Vol. VI, Nos. 1–4.) Rochester, N.Y., 1926.

PARKMAN, FRANCIS. *The Old Régime in Canada: France and England in North America.* Boston, 1874.

————. *Pioneers of France in the New World.* ("Frontenac ed.") Boston: Little, Brown & Co., 1899.

PARSONS, ELSIE C. *Pueblo Indian Religion.* 2 vols. Chicago: University of Chicago Press, 1939.

PETERSON, SHAILER. *How Well Are Indian Children Educated?* U.S. Indian Service Publication. Washington, D.C., 1948.

PICKERSGILL, BARBARA. "The Archaeological Record of Chili Peppers (*Capsicum* Spp.) and the Sequence of Plant Domestication in Peru." *American Antiquity,* Vol. XXXIV, No. 1 (1969), pp. 54–61.

PRIEST, LORING B. *Uncle Sam's Step Children: The Reformation of United States Indian Policy, 1865–1887.* New Brunswick: Rutgers University Press, 1942.

PRINCE, J. D. *Notes on Passamaquoddy Literature.* ("Annals of the New York Academy of Science," Vol. XIII, No. 4.) New York, 1901.

PUBLIC HEALTH SERVICE, *The Fourth Report on the Indian Health Program of the U. S. Public Health Service To The First Americans,* P. H. S. Publication No. 1580. Washington, D.C.: Government Printing Office, 1970.

QUIMBY, GEORGE I. "Culture Contact on the Northwest Coast between 1785 and 1795," *American Anthropologist,* Vol. L, No. 2 (new ser., 1948).

RADIN, PAUL. "The Winnebago Tribe," *37th Annual Report of the Bureau of American Ethnology.* Washington, D.C., 1923.

————. *The Road of Life and Death.* ("Bollingen Series," Vol. V.) New York: Pantheon Books, Inc., 1945.

RAY, VERNE F. "The Historical Position of the Lower Chinook in the Native

Culture of the Northwest," *Pacific Northwest Quarterly,* Vol. XXVIII (1937).

―――. *Cultural Relations in the Plateau of Northwestern America.* ("Publications of the Frederick W. Hodge Anniversary Fund," Vol. III.) Los Angeles: Southwestern Museum, 1939.

REED, ERIK K. "A Theory of Southwestern Prehistory." ("Region Three Archaeological Interpretation Circular," No. 8.) Santa Fe, N.M.: National Park Service, 1951. (Mimeographed.)

REICHARD, GLADYS. *Melanesian Design.* New York: Columbia University Press, 1933.

―――. *Navaho Medicine Man.* New York: J. J. Augustin, 1939.

RITCHIE, W. A. *The Pre-Iroquoian Occupation of New York State.* ("Rochester Museum of Arts and Sciences Memoirs," No. 1.) Rochester, N.Y., 1944.

ROUSE, IRVING. "The Arawak," in *Handbook of South American Indians,* Vol. IV, ed. JULIAN H. STEWARD. 6 vols. (Bureau of American Ethnology Bull. 143.) Washington, D.C., 1945–50.

ROYCE, CHARLES C. "Indian Land Cessions in the United States," *18th Annual Report of the Bureau of American Ethnology,* Part II. Washington, D.C., 1897.

SAPIR, EDWARD, and HOIJER, HARRY. *Navaho Texts.* Iowa City: Linguistic Society of America, University of Iowa, 1942.

SAUER, CARL O. "Cultivated Plants of South and Central America," in *Handbook of South American Indians,* Vol. V, ed. JULIAN H. STEWARD. 6 vols. (Bureau of American Ethnology Bull. 143.) Washington, D.C., 1945–50.

SCHAFFER, C. "The First Jesuit Mission to the Flathead," *Pacific Northwest Quarterly,* Vol. XXVIII (1937).

SCHELLBACH, L. *An Historic War Club.* ("Indian Notes and Monographs," No. 5.) New York: Museum of the American Indian, Heye Foundation, 1928.

SCHOOLCRAFT, H. R. *Notes on the Iroquois.* New York, 1846.

―――. *Information Respecting the History, Conditions and Prospects of the Indian Tribes of the United States.* 6 vols. Philadelphia: Lippincott, Granbo & Co., 1860.

SEYMORE, FLORA W. *The Story of the Red Man.* New York: Tudor Publishing Co., 1934.

SHOTRIDGE, L. and F. "Chilkat Dwelling Houses," *Museum Journal* (Philadelphia), Vol. IV, No. 3 (1913).

SKINNER, A. B. *Notes on the Eastern Cree and Northern Saulteau.* ("American Museum of Natural History Anthropological Papers," Vol. IX, Part I.) New York, 1911.

―――. *Observations on the Ethnology of the Sauk Indians.* ("Bulletin of the Public Museum of the City of Milwaukee," Vol. V, No. 3.) Milwaukee, 1925.

―――. *The Mascoutens or Prairie Potawatomi Indians.* ("Bulletin of the Public Museum of the City of Milwaukee," Vol. VI, No. 2.) Milwaukee, 1926.

SMITH, MARION. The Puyallup-Nesqually. ("Columbia University Contributions to Anthropology," No. 32.) New York, 1940.

SMITH, PHILLIP S. "Certain Relations between Northwestern America and Northeastern Asia," in *Early Man*, ed. GEORGE C. MacCURDY. Philadelphia: J. B. Lippincott Co., 1939.

SOLECKI, RALPH. "How Man Came to North America," *Scientific American*, Vol. CLXXXIV, No. 1 (January, 1951).

SPECK, FRANK G. *The Functions of Wampum among the Eastern Algonkian.* ("Memoirs of the American Anthropological Association," Vol. VI, No. 1.) Lancaster, Pa., 1919.

———. *Penobscot Shamanism.* ("Memoirs of the American Anthropological Association," Vol. VI, No. 4.) Lancaster, Pa., 1919.

———. "Land Ownership among Hunting Peoples in Primitive America and the World's Marginal Areas," in *Proceedings of the XXIIth International Congress of Americanists*, Vol. II. Rome, Italy, 1926.

———. *Naskapi.* Norman: University of Oklahoma Press, 1935.

———. *Penobscot Man: The Life History of a Forest Tribe in Maine.* Philadelphia: University of Pennsylvania Press, 1940.

———. *The Iroquois.* (Cranbrook Institute of Science Bull. 23.) Bloomfield Hills, Mich., 1945.

SPECK, F. G., and ORCHARD, W. C. *The Penn Wampum Belts.* ("Indian Notes and Monographs," No. 4.) New York: Museum of the American Indian, Heye Foundation, 1925.

SPENCER, ROBERT F., JENNINGS, JESSE D., *et. al. The Native Americans.* New York: Harper & Row, 1965.

SPIER, LESLIE. *Klamath Ethnology.* ("University of California Publications in American Archaeology and Ethnology," Vol. XXX.) Berkeley, 1930.

SPINDEN, H. J. *The Nez Percé Indians.* ("Memoirs of the American Anthropological Association," Vol. II.) Lancaster, Pa., 1908.

STEVENSON, M. C. "The Zuni Indians: Their Mythology, Esoteric Societies and Ceremonies," *23d Annual Report of the Bureau of American Ethnology.* Washington, D.C., 1904.

STEWARD, JULIAN H. *Basin-Plateau Aboriginal Sociopolitical Groups.* (Bureau of American Ethnology Bull. 120) Washington, D.C., 1930.

STRONG, W. D. *Aboriginal Society in Southern California.* ("University of California Publications in American Archaeology and Ethnology," Vol. XXVI.) Berkeley, 1929.

———. *An Introduction to Nebraska Archaeology.* ("Smithsonian Institution Miscellaneous Collection," Vol. XCIII, No. 10.) Washington, D.C., 1936.

SWAN, JAMES C. *The Indians of Cape Flattery.* ("Smithsonian Institution Contributions to Knowledge," Vol. XVI.) Washington, D.C., 1870.

SWANTON, JOHN R. "The Tlingit Indians," *26th Annual Report of the Bureau of American Ethnology.* Washington, D.C., 1908.

———. *Contributions to the Ethnology of the Haida.* ("American Museum of Natural History Memoirs," No. 8.) New York, 1910.

———. *Indian Tribes of the Lower Mississippi Valley and Adjacent Coast of the Gulf of Mexico.* (Bureau of American Ethnology Bull. 43.) Washington, D.C., 1911.

———. *Early History of the Creek Indians and Their Neighbors.* (Bureau of American Ethnology Bull. 73.) Washington, D.C., 1922.

————. "Aboriginal Culture of the Southeast," *42d Annual Report of the Bureau of American Ethnology*. Washington, D.C., 1928.

————. "Social Organization and Social Usages of the Creek Confederacy," *ibid.*

————. "Religious Beliefs and Medical Practices of the Creek Indians," *ibid.*

————. *Source Material on the History and Ethnology of the Caddo Indians.* (Bureau of American Ethnology Bull. 132.) Washington, D.C., 1942.

————. *The Indians of the Southeastern United States.* (Bureau of American Ethnology Bull. 137.) Washington, D.C., 1946.

TEIT, JAMES A. "The Salishan Tribes of the Western Plateaus," *45th Annual Report of the Bureau of American Ethnology*. Washington, D.C., 1930.

THWAITES, RUBEN G. (ed.). *The Jesuit Relations and Allied Documents: Travels and Explorations of the Jesuit Missionaries in New France, 1610–1791.* Cleveland: Burrows Bros., 1896–1901.

TOZZER, ALFRED M. *Landa's Relación de las Cosas de Yucatán: A Translation.* ("Papers of the Peabody Museum of American Archaeology and Ethnology," Vol. XVIII.) Cambridge, 1941.

TURNER, L. M. "Ethnology of the Ungava District," *11th Annual Report of the Bureau of American Ethnology*. Washington, D.C., 1894.

UNDERHILL, CAPTAIN JOHN. *News from America.* London: Peter Cole (Underhill Society of America), 1902.

UNDERHILL, RUTH M. *Singing for Power.* Berkeley: University of California Press, 1938.

————. *Indians of the Pacific Northwest.* ("Indian Life and Customs," No. 5.) Phoenix: United States Indian Service, 1945.

————. *Papago Indian Religion.* New York: Columbia University Press, 1946.

————. *Pueblo Crafts.* ("Indian Handcraft Pamphlets," No. 7.) Phoenix: United States Indian Service, 1946.

————. *Work-a-Day Life of the Pueblos.* ("Indian Life and Customs," No. 4.) Phoenix: United States Indian Service, 1946.

————. *Ceremonial Patterns in the Greater Southwest.* ("American Ethnological Society Memoirs," Vol. XIII.) New York, 1948.

UNITED STATES DEPARTMENT OF THE INTERIOR, BUREAU OF INDIAN AFFAIRS. *Fiscal Year 1970: Statistics Concerning Indian Education.* Lawrence, Kansas: Publications Service, Haskell Indian Junior College, 1970.

UNITED STATES DEPARTMENT OF THE INTERIOR. *Statistical Supplement to the Annual Report of the Commissioner of Indian Affairs.* Washington: Department of the Interior, 1945.

VOGELIN, CHARLES F. and ERMINE W. *North American Indian Languages* (map). (American Ethnological Society Bull. 20.) New York, 1941.

WATERMAN, T. T. *The Religious Practices of the Diegueño Indians.* Berkeley ("University of California Publications in American Archaeology and Ethnology," Vol. VIII, No. 6.) Berkeley, 1910.

————. *The Whaling Equipment of the Makah Indians.* ("University of Washington Publications in Anthropology," Vol. I, No. 1.) Seattle, 1920.

WAUGH, F. W. *Iroquois Food and Food Preparation.* ("Canadian Department of Mines, Geological Survey, Memoirs," No. 86.) Ottawa, 1916.

WEDEL, W. R. *Archaeological Investigations in Platte and Clay Counties, Missouri.* (United States National Museum Bull. 183.) Washington, D.C., 1943.

WEST, G. A. *Tobacco, Pipes and Smoking Customs of the American Indians.* ("Bulletin of the Public Museum of the City of Milwaukee," Vol. XVII, Nos. 1 and 2.) Milwaukee, 1934.

WHITING, BEATRICE. *Paiute Sorcery.* "Viking Fund Publications in Anthropology," No. 15.) New York, 1950.

WILL, GEORGE. *Corn of the Northwest.* St. Paul: Webb Publishing Co., 1930.

WILLOUGHBY, C. C. *Antiquities of the New England Indians.* Cambridge: Peabody Museum of American Archaeology and Ethnology, 1935.

WINGERT, PAUL. *American Indian Sculpture.* New York: J. J. Augustin, 1949.

WISSLER, CLARK. "Decorative Art of the Sioux Indians," *American Museum of Natural History Bulletin,* Vol. XVIII, No. 3 (1904).

――――. *Material Culture of the Blackfoot Indians.* ("American Museum of Natural History Publications in Anthropology," Vol. IV, No. 1.) New York, 1910.

――――. *Societies and Dance Associations of the Blackfoot Indians.* ("American Museum of Natural History Publications in Anthropology," Vol. XI, No. 4.) New York, 1913.

――――. "Material Cultures of the North American Indians," *American Anthropologist,* Vol. XVI, No. 3 (new ser., 1914).

――――. *North American Indians of the Plains.* ("American Museum of Natural History Handbooks," No. 1.) New York, 1934.

WOODWARD, ARTHUR. *Indian Houses of Southern California* ("Los Angeles County Museum, Leaflet Series, History," No. 6.) Los Angeles, 1949.

WORMINGTON, H. M. *Prehistoric Indians of the Southwest.* ("Denver Museum of Natural History, Popular Series," No. 7.) Denver, 1947.

――――. *Ancient Man in North America.* Rev. ed. ("Denver Museum of Natural History, Popular Series," No. 4.) Denver, 1949.

ZIMMERMAN, WILLIAM (acting commissioner of Indian affairs). Statement made before the annual meeting of the Home Missions Council of North America, Buckhill Falls, Pennsylvania, January, 1949.

Index

Abenaki, 78, 80; confederacy, 69
Acceptance of reservations, 325
Acculturation, Spanish, 202
Acoma, 203, 324; clans, 206; ceremonial leader, 206; embroidered shawl, 217; houses, 215; initiation required, 206; kiva, 206; priests, 206; society, 206
Acorn: as food, 287, 317; preparation of, 275; use of, 275
Acorn baskets, 275
Adiantum pedatum, 295
Adobe houses, 221
Adoption: Creek, 38; Fox, 119; Iroquois, 96, 104; Prairie People, 119; *see also* Captives; Slaves
Adz, 299
Agave, 243
Age group, 151, 152; Southeast, 31, 33
Agencies, government, 171, 328, 332, 333, 334
Agency rations, 173
Agriculture, 83, 86, 112, 145, 147, 190, 191, 205, 243; early, 187; Indian, 252; implements of, 192; lack of, 267
Agriculturists, 147
Aireskoi, 97, 98, 104
Alabama Indians, 36; parchesi, 44
Alaska, 4, 5, 6, 11, 13, 145
Albany (N.Y.), 104
Aleutian Islands, 311
Aleuts, 311
Algonkian, 71, 72, 78, 83, 84, 98, 112, 142, 143; animal beliefs, 63; animal ceremony, 63; beadwork, 75; Canadian, 60; cannibalism, 70; captives, 70; chiefs, 121; clans, 121; clan ceremonies, 121; clan totem, 121; clothing, 67; corn, 66; country, 57; creation myth, 64; culture hero, 64; descent, 66; design elements, 75, 102; Eastern, 82; eat-it-all feast, 296; family rites, 117; fasting, 119; father-clan, 121; feasts, 64, 296; female segregation, 63; government, 63; Great Lakes, 110; guardian animals, 121; hunting bands, 60; hunting territories, 63; immigrants, 114; land rights, 66; language, 183, 253, 270; legend of Mississippi Valley, 110; Manitou, 70; marriage, 119; medicine man, 70, 127; Menomini, 114; moiety, 121; murder, 121; names, 57; ornaments, 67; pottery, 65, 76; prisoner exchange, 114; segregation, 117; sha-
man, 64; spear points, 60; snowshoes, 60; taboos, 63; tobacco, 64; trade, 114; trance, 64; tribes, 80; trickster, 255; use of vegetable material, 67; visions, 119; war honors, 70; war methods, 70; white contact, 70, 71; Witigo, 65
Allegheny, 57, 108
Alliklik, 291
Allotment Act, 327, 330
Allotment lands, 179
Allotments, 274; cessation of, 332
Alpaca, 7
Altar River, 190
Ambush, 44
America: discovered, 1; Nuclear, 84
American colonies, 135
American Constitution, 83
American Revolution, 104
American Southwest, 7, 145
American Stone Age, 20
American trappers, 257
American Treaty, 135
Amole, 205
Anasazi, 189; cliff dwellings, 201; culture, 201; history of, 200; life-way, 200; Pueblo ancestors, 201
Ancestor, 201; spirit of, 125
Ancestral myths, 302
Andean irrigation, 20
Andean technology, 20
Angry Man, 194
Animal belief, 63, 98, 309, 311
Animal ceremony, 63
Animal clan, 33, 91
Animal deadfalls, 317
Animal deer whistles, 317
Animal domestication, 11, 13, 14, 18, 19
Animal fences, 317
Animal guardians, 121
Animal hair, braided, 44
Animal lord, 41
Animal illness, 41
Animal powers, 264
Animal spirits, 40, 41, 63, 70, 71
Animal stealing, 228
Animal taboo, 63
Animal totems, 123

Map X

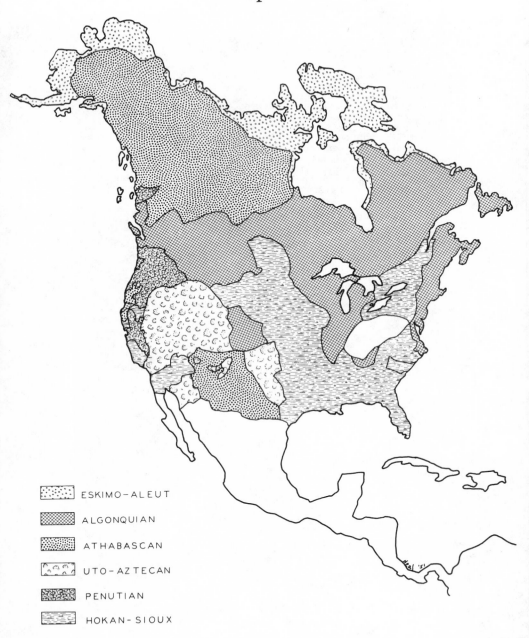

ESKIMO—ALEUT

ALGONQUIAN

ATHABASCAN

UTO—AZTECAN

PENUTIAN

HOKAN—SIOUX

NORTH AMERICAN
INDIAN LANGUAGES

Map XI

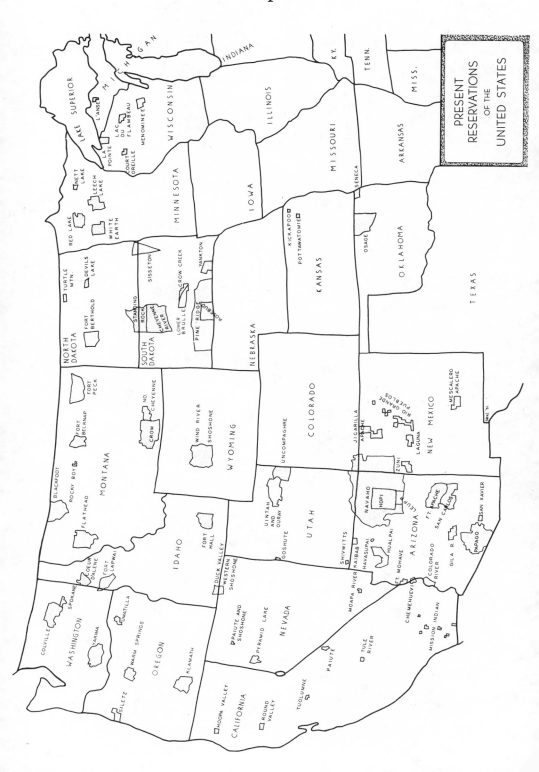